BOOKS BY ANNE MORROW LINDBERGH

Against
Wind and Tide

Against Wind and Tide

LETTERS AND JOURNALS,
1947–1986

Anne Morrow Lindbergh

Edited and with an introduction by
Reeve Lindbergh

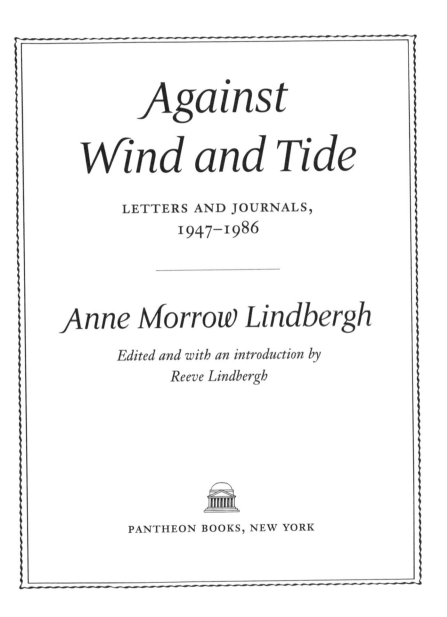

PANTHEON BOOKS, NEW YORK

Grateful acknowledgment is made to Houghton Mifflin Harcourt Publishing
Company and Faber and Faber Limited for permission to reprint excerpts
from "The Dry Salvages" and "Little Gidding" from *Four Quartets*, copyright
© 1941, 1942 by T. S. Eliot, copyright renewed 1969, 1970 by Esme Valerie
Eliot. Reprinted by permission of Houghton Mifflin Harcourt Publishing
Company and Faber and Faber Limited, London.

Unless otherwise indicated, all photographs are courtesy of the Sterling
Memorial Library at Yale University and the Lindbergh Literary LLC.

Library of Congress Cataloging-in-Publication Data
Lindbergh, Anne Morrow, 1906–2001.
Against wind and tide : letters and journals, 1947–1986 /
Anne Morrow Lindbergh.
p.   cm.
Includes index.
ISBN 978-0-307-37888-0
1. Lindbergh, Anne Morrow, 1906–2001.   I. Title.
PS3523.I516Z48 2012   818'.5209—dc23 [B]   2011037784

www.pantheonbooks.com

Jacket image: portrait of Anne Morrow Lindbergh at home, January 1, 1956,
by Leonard McCombe/Time & Life Pictures/Getty Images
Jacket design by Linda Huang
Book design by M. Kristen Bearse

Printed in the United States of America
First Edition
2 4 6 8 9 7 5 3 1

Against
Wind and Tide

Introduction

REEVE LINDBERGH

Anne Morrow Lindbergh was born in the year 1906 and died almost ninety-five years later in 2001. Not only did she live through most of the twentieth century, but her adventures, her personal history, and her written reflections made a significant mark upon her era. A pioneer aviator and an author, she was an explorer of the world outside herself as well as the world within. Her gift in both worlds was for communication, and her writings touch readers deeply to this day.

Represented here are four decades of her previously unpublished diaries and letters, written between 1947 and 1986. During her lifetime she published five earlier books of diaries and letters, covering the years 1922 through 1944.* These focus upon her meeting, marriage, and early life with my father, Charles Lindbergh. They begin with her school years and go on to the Christmas she spent in Mexico when her father was the ambassador there and the famous young aviator visited on a goodwill tour following his nonstop solo flight from New York to Paris in 1927. The account continues with the Lindberghs' courtship, wedding, and youthful flying days together, when my mother became a pilot, too, and they explored possible air routes for the fledgling aviation industry, all over the world. The story extends through the tragedy of the death of their first son, Charles, and then into the years before and during the Second World War.

My parents' flying trips together ended before the war, and my mother stopped flying entirely. With the pioneering days of aviation in the past, she turned to her writing and to raising her family.

Bring Me a Unicorn: Diaries and Letters of Anne Morrow Lindbergh, 1922–1928 (New York: Harcourt Brace Jovanovich, 1972); *Hour of Gold, Hour of Lead: Diaries and Letters, 1929–1932* (Harcourt, 1973); *Locked Rooms and Open Doors: Diaries and Letters, 1933–1935* (Harcourt, 1974); *The Flower and the Nettle: Diaries and Letters, 1936–1939* (Harcourt, 1976); *War Within and Without: Diaries and Letters, 1939–1944* (Harcourt, 1980). She also published eight other books during her lifetime, including both fictional and nonfiction accounts of her flying experiences, poetry, a novel, and personal essays.

During my lifetime, my parents did not even own an airplane, though my father continued to fly, serving as a consultant with the airline industry and the Air Force and traveling throughout the world for the rest of his life. My mother's path was very different. Outward explorations were replaced by an inward journey, one she described later in her life as a "journey toward insight."

The material collected in the following pages was written between my mother's fortieth birthday and her eightieth, and follows a period of substantial growth in her life and thought, as well as some marked changes in her relationship with her husband and in her sense of who she was as a woman and an artist. The book begins early in 1947, at a time when she was assessing her own physical and emotional turmoil at the end of her childbearing years, as well as the damage and devastation she witnessed on a trip to postwar France and Germany. It ends in the mid-1980s with a letter to me, her youngest daughter, a year after the death of my infant son. In between these selections is a treasury of vivid, poignant, perceptive, and often delightful pieces of communication, each in its own way directed toward a greater understanding of what it means to be a human being, a writer, and a woman.

To collect, read through, and edit anyone's diaries and letters is an unusual kind of journey. To work with material written by a parent is to travel inside one's own personal history as seen from a very different, yet very intimate perspective. For me there is a quality of double vision and some self-centered, unanswerable questions: Where was I when she was writing all this? Where is she now, as I read it?

Surely, I feel, she is not far away. The familiarity and directness of my mother's voice brings her close to me again, though she has been dead for more than ten years as I write this. And yet, going over these pages with my brother Land, our niece Kristina, and our close friend and colleague Carol Hyman, I begin to realize that the same thing is true for each of us: we feel, unavoidably, close to the writer. This is the effect she has always had upon her readers. She speaks to every one of us directly, personally, offering the whole of herself at every stage of her life.

In this book we see her first at the age of forty-one, unexpectedly pregnant for the seventh time and seriously considering abortion. The practice was not only dangerous and illegal, but also violated some of her strongest principles. We see her a few years later on Captiva Island in Florida, in the 1950s, writing home from a rented beach cottage where she was working on a book she referred to in her letters as "The Shells," later to become *Gift from the Sea*. We see her again at the end of 1963, writing to my sister, Anne, about Anne's upcoming wedding plans in France, while reeling from the recent shock of the assassination of President John F. Kennedy. We see her writing four years later to President and Mrs. Johnson to decline an invitation to the White House because she does not know, literally, where in the world her husband is, or when he will return. We see her exploring the first years of widowhood in the mid-1970s, after my father's death from lymphoma, with grief, exhaustion, and openness, and we see her reflecting a decade later upon her recent and long-ago losses, and the discoveries she is making as she enters old age.

As a writer she was honest, eloquent, and deeply reflective, always seeking to understand life as it unfolded before her, always wanting to share her understanding with others: her husband, her children, her family and friends, and ultimately her readers. It is her openness to life that has made her writing so popular with readers for more than half a century. She struggled with issues women and men have to face in every era: what to make of a complex, difficult marriage to a person one loves; how to reconcile the impulse toward creativity—and the need to work—with the practical demands of home and family; how to respond to the larger events and issues of the day; how to give and receive friendship and love throughout a lifetime; how to meet old age and the certainty of death: first the death of those we love and cannot bear to lose, family and friends, young and old, and then one's own old age and inevitable death, the end of life.

This was her journey, not mine, but the geographical context of these writings is familiar to me. I know the territory: the big house in Connecticut on the shore of Long Island Sound where she raised her five children from 1945 until 1963, when the children had grown and the house was sold to a younger family; the smaller house my parents built on a section of the same property and lived in for much of the rest of their lives. They also built a small chalet in Switzerland in 1963, in a field overlooking Lac Leman, and spent summers there, enjoying visits from my sister, Anne, also known as "Ansy," who then lived in France with her family, and from their other children, family members, and guests. Finally, I came to know the bare, windswept A-frame they later constructed on a tiny piece of property on the island of Maui, a place my father had visited toward the end of his life and immediately loved for its isolation and wild beauty.

They would visit Maui in the spring. This was the house where there were mongooses and bougainvillea, and the floods my mother described in her letters. Although he loved Maui, my father was often absent from this house, too, as he was from the other homes they shared. Even now, when I think of her all alone in the torrential Hawaiian rains and the accompanying mud, trying to bail the floodwater out of her kitchen with an omelet pan, I can only shake my head in amazement.

How did she do it? How could she possibly live in such conditions, again and again, without her husband? Another question comes to mind almost simultaneously. How could she possibly live in such conditions, or in any conditions, *with* him? Neither was easy.

Thinking back to the 1950s, I realize that the quality I associate with my father in that era is iron. Those were the iron years. The color of his hair was like iron, and the discipline he administered was like iron: unbending, with stern lectures and occasional spankings. To be fair, there were also moments of joy, when he'd break into an enormous grin at something one of us said, or at some antic of the German shepherd puppy we had then. There was laughter, too, perhaps during a conversation with our mother or during a bout of roughhousing with the boys. There were quiet times with him, sitting on the wide tiled porch overlooking Long Island Sound or walking with him in the woods, not talking at all. I remember how much I loved him, always, no matter how scary he sometimes seemed. I remember that I missed him intensely all the time he was gone, that our family felt only half complete without him. I also remember, though, the relief and relaxation that settled like a kind of warmth over the household when he went away and our mother was once again in gentle command.

All these many years later, missing him and puzzling about him, wondering how my mother could have stayed married to such a husband, I have concluded that it must be the very absences we minded so much, the absences she lamented in her letters to him, that made the marriage and our family life possible. I even wonder whether his absences were what she had in mind when she wrote, in *Gift from the Sea*, about the importance of "intermittency" in relationships.

He traveled so much, in fact, that the later letters in this book make it clear she had difficulty adjusting when he finally stopped traveling, in the last year or two of his life. She wrote to her sister Con, "The trips away (to the Philippines, Africa, etc.) that gave him so much freedom and stimulus and adventure, and which are so creative for him, will not be possible in the near future—if ever—(I don't know, of course). This virtually isolates me from the people I used to see when he went off."

I am convinced that no woman could have lived with my father full time, twenty-four hours a day, over a long period. And he lived his life in a way that meant no woman ever really did, except for my mother, and then only during their early years together. I was certainly amazed to learn, a few years after my mother's death, that my father had had several relationships with other women during his travels in the 1950s and 1960s, and that there were children from these relationships. However, it did not surprise me at all to learn from these children, when I met them, that the paternal pattern was the same for them: our lives were all marked by our father's perpetual comings and goings, by a brief intensity of presence followed by long absences, over and over again.

Despite my father's frequent disappearances, I have an unmistakable sense of the strong and interdependent partnership my parents shared, however strained their connection at certain periods and however deeply my father's absences impacted their union. They knew each other well and they helped each other immeasurably during the almost forty-five years they spent as husband and wife: first flying together, then writing together while raising their family.

In these letters I understand once again how much she relied upon him, as he relied upon her. I saw them working together, sitting side by side, pencils in hand and a manuscript before them, discussing, marking, editing, and proofreading, talking back and forth for hours on end. It might be his manuscript, it might be hers, it made no difference; the depth of concentration was the same. They depended upon each other to make a book complete, right down to the acknowledgments and the final galleys. In this work they were equals, professionals, as they had been a team when they were pilots charting early air routes: Charles and Anne Lindbergh, together.

I felt surprised, therefore, and almost queasy when I first read the letter in this collection that my mother wrote to my father on December 18, 1947. She wrote, to my astonishment, "I would rather have you think me 'a good girl' than be right myself, or to have anyone else think me a good girl. And I am afraid you will not. All the time I feel like a bad girl—that I am not living up to your idea of a good girl."

I was shocked. The writer of this letter sounded so weak, so clinging and self-deprecating, so cloyingly pathetic, not at all like the woman I knew. "Good girl"? "Bad girl"? What was this? And yet as I kept reading, letter after letter and diary entry upon diary entry through the following years, I found my mother again, the perceptive, quiet, resilient person so familiar to me. I also began to see how the relationship between my parents altered as my mother grew older. There was a time when she thought that he was usually right and that she, especially in opposing him, was usually wrong.

But this changed. Oh, how it changed! As I read into the 1950s and 1960s and beyond, I recognized the person who had learned to stand up to a man whose good opinion she had once craved above all else. I knew the wise, quiet woman who trusted her own feelings and convictions, and who taught her children to trust theirs.

Her growing freedom became ours as well. Our mother encouraged our development as individuals, and loved us unconditionally. Even when our views or actions became troubling to our formidable father, she defended us: Anne was entitled to consult a psychiatrist at a time of emotional trouble even if our father distrusted psychiatry; Scott had the right to follow his own beliefs about the war in Vietnam, even though our father believed one must fight for one's country in wartime despite what one believed. (He had flown in the Pacific during the Second World War, even though he'd opposed America's entry into that conflict.) She herself was perfectly justified in refusing the invitation of President and Mrs. Marcos to visit the Philippines in 1971 because Anne was expecting a baby. The upcoming birth of a grandchild, my mother explained to my father in a letter, took precedence over all other events and invitations.

Her refusal to budge on this issue delighted me. No more "good girl"! This was a woman who lived her own life and stated her case with spirit, unafraid to confront her husband on his own terms. "You don't tell me ahead of time what your plans are: where you are going and how long you'll be away, when you'll be back, etc. I don't mind, actually. I know that's the way you live, and must live. But I can't, on the other hand, sit around and wait for you, and make no plans."

She did make plans: to work, to see her family and her friends, to enjoy the outdoors, to nourish her inner self. From the earliest diary entries here, it is clear that her interior existence was as rich as her outward, active life. While not willing to withdraw from the world or from her family for too long—she had five children to raise and, even with the household help available to her, she was most often the person in charge—she sought to establish a measure of solitude within her daily routine. She would see friends in the afternoon and evening, but she tried to spend mornings alone at her desk, whether in the house itself, in the trailer that Henry Ford had given my parents after my father worked for Ford during the war, or eventually in the Little House, a cabin adapted from a prefabricated toolshed and set a hundred yards away from the main house on the property in Darien.

This one-room retreat contained a desk, a chair, a cot against a wall for resting, and a chemical toilet in a corner behind a curtain. There was also a sparse collection of books, and stones and feathers and seashells, too, lining the unfinished beams.

The Little House was built in the 1950s. Before it there was the Point House, another small structure my mother used as a writing retreat, on a rocky outcropping overlooking Scott's Cove. I barely remember the Point House, but I do recall that wherever she lived, there was always a separate, tiny writing house away from the main house. In Switzerland the little house was called the Cuckoo Clock, which was exactly what it looked like, perched up against a cliff above the meadow. In Maui there was a little house, too, though I don't think my mother used it for writing, perhaps because she was usually alone, with the entire main house at her disposal.

Toward the end of their lives together my parents decided to name their houses after seashells: the Darien house was called Tellina (after the bivalve mollusk my mother referred to as "Double Sunrise" in *Gift from the Sea*), the Swiss house Planorbe (French for snail), and the Maui house Argonauta (named for the Paper Nautilus, the last shell described in her book). In the 1960s they moved from one house to another over the course of each year, traveling from Connecticut to Maui in late winter, then back to Connecticut in spring, then to Switzerland for the summer, and back to Connecticut again in the fall.

I have never been able to decide whether my mother was just going along with my father's lifelong restlessness (certainly she did in the early years of their marriage, when they were flying together) or whether, in her own way, she shared it. My parents moved many times in their early married years, and even later, in my own time, there were all those houses: a house in one part of the world, then a house in another part to "get away" from the first one, and finally, with Maui, another house in a third location altogether. In addition to each house, moreover, there was a "little house." (To get away from the getaway house?)

Wherever she was, my mother would write to friends and family members about the difficulties of being there: how rushed and pressured life was in the environment surrounding New York City, how isolated she felt on Maui, how constrained and proper the Swiss were—they made her want to "go out and get drunk." I remember her telling me that she could never recall which house was stocked with what kitchen supplies, and that no matter where she was, she couldn't find any tarragon.

I loved all of the houses, and visited her whenever I could. Switzerland was my favorite of her places, and reading these letters I see how casually I settled into her Swiss life in my teenage summers, happily taking it for granted that she would welcome me and my friends, not thinking much about the extra work our presence demanded of her. I think I remember doing at least some of the laundry and the dishes and the shopping. I wish I could go back and do it all.

However flawed I may have been, she loved me thoroughly, as she did all of her children. She would respond to our lives and our needs at any given moment, whatever else she may have had on her mind, with long, thoughtful letters: to Jon in the Navy, to Land in college, to Anne in France, to Scott as he struggled with issues of military service and citizenship, and to me, when my first child was born and I thought I would never write again. She addressed our joys and our sorrows with the gifts of her openness and wisdom, her willingness always to listen, never to judge, never to insist upon one course of action or another. To be treated with this kind of loving respect is priceless. None of us will ever forget it.

In letters to other family members and to friends, there is that same openness and understanding, whether she is writing to her sister Con (Constance Morrow Morgan), her brother Dwight (Dwight W. Morrow Jr.), her former sister-in-law and lifelong friend Margot Wilkie, or her beloved doctor and dear friend Dana Atchley. There are so many people here whose presence in her life, and in ours, I remember with affection: Helen Wolff, Alan and Lucia Valentine, Mina Curtiss, Dana Atchley, and others. Yet it touches me to see that she also wrote with an unchecked outpouring of compassion to Ruth Goodkind, a woman she had never met, whose son was killed by lightning at a summer camp he and my brother Land both attended in 1948.

I am a little sorry that she felt compelled to respond at all to what must have been a very angry letter from another Ruth, my mother's sensitive and complicated friend Ruth Thomas Oliff (did she really tell my mother to "drop dead"?). It gives me a startled kind of satisfaction, though, to notice the tartness of tone in my mother's response. I am reminded here that my mother was brought up to be a lady, not a saint.

I believe that there are love affairs, among my mother's other experiences, revealed in some of her correspondence here, though "revealed" may not be the right word to use. She was remarkably discreet, so much so that one could argue (and some have) that these were not physical but emotional relationships, affairs more of words than of caresses.

Perhaps, but I can recall a conversation with her after my father's death, a discussion of marriage in general and of her own marriage in particular, in which she talked about the most difficult time in her life with my father. It was not, as I expected it to be, the period following the death of her first child, but instead the years following the Second World War. (Maybe my "iron years" were also hers.) She told me that she had promised herself, during that very difficult time in her marriage, that "if things did not get better" by the time I had reached my tenth birthday (in October 1955), she would leave her husband.

"What happened?" I asked. I knew she had not left my father, but that was all I knew.

"Things got better," she told me, enigmatically. She went through psychoanalysis with Dr. John Rosen in the early 1950s. She destroyed most of the written material related to that process, but she often said that the analysis made a tremendous difference in her life. I think, though, that certain intimate relationships also sustained her during those years. There are indications in the letters to both Dana Atchley and Alan Valentine that a loving friendship existed between my mother and each of these two men, something private, intimate, and exhilarating, yet able to fit into the context of the friendships among the married couples: Dana and Mary Atchley, Lucia and Alan Valentine, Anne and Charles Lindbergh.

Interestingly, most of my mother's letters to Dana Atchley and to Alan Valentine were not destroyed or hidden away. In fact, the Alan Valentine letters were saved all together in one folder, not as handwritten originals, but typed in the manner of a manuscript. For whose eyes, ultimately, were these letters intended? Did my mother think she might someday incorporate this material into a book? Perhaps a book about the complexities of love? I don't know. Some of the letters are here in this collection, for readers to wonder about. What I chiefly wonder myself, having read them, is whether there were others.

Did my mother really keep copies of absolutely everything she wrote? Or did she, as it seems likely my father did, destroy some of her most intimate correspondence entirely, while at the same time sending hundreds of carefully carbon-copied letters to the archives of Sterling Memorial Library at Yale?

My feeling, having known her for fifty-five years, is that my mother was more likely to employ subtlety than to engage in active conceal-ment. I suspect that she started making carbon copies of her diaries and letters in deference to my father's lifelong impulse to save all written materials "for the record," in order to avoid being misrepresented (or, one might speculate, in order to control his own archive). After a while, it must have been second nature to make carbon copies, just another aspect of the experience of writing.

As I remember, my parents had what seemed an endless supply of light blue "air mail" pads of stationery, each pad with several accom-panying sheets of carbon paper cut to size. Before writing a letter, my mother would tuck a piece or two of the carbon paper (shiny side down) between the top two or three sheets of paper on the pad. When she had finished the first page of her letter she would tear it off along with the two copies, and place the carbon paper neatly between the next two or three sheets. In that way, for every letter she sent she had a copy to keep and another to send to the archives at Yale.

I thought all this record keeping was odd, but no odder than any of the other things my parents did. As an adult I have been both grateful for the personal material my parents kept so carefully—how many peo-ple can see such meticulous and articulate evidence of the lives of their forebears?—and, at times, bewildered.

In one folder at Yale, along with the carbon copies (duplicates and triplicates) of letters to friends and relatives, Land and I found several charming postcards, one written to each of her children: Jon, Land, Anne, Scott, and Reeve. These were real postcards, decorated with Beatrix Potter–like scenes of little animals, with affectionate messages in my mother's handwriting for each child at summer camp. But they were so clean! Had they never been sent? Or had she retrieved them from us somehow at the end of the summer, none of them the least bit grubby, each one pristine enough for the Yale archives? How could that have happened? And why?

"They're copies," Land said suddenly. I stopped, thought about it, and agreed with him. We looked at each other, trying to imagine our mother first writing five postcards, one to each child, then copying each message, word by word, on five other postcards. (Were they identical, the postcards? Did they have the same Beatrix Potter scenes?) Postcards for the archives. I still don't know how to think about it.

Yet it is because of this remarkable and, yes, perhaps excessive saving of letters and diaries and postcards and telegrams, this extraordinary preservation of her own written output, that we can experience something of the life of a twentieth century woman with an acknowledged public presence and a remarkable interior life.

When she traveled to Europe after the war and observed devastation in Germany, she wrote; when she felt a deep conflict between her life as an artist and her life as a wife and mother, she wrote; when she spent an evening at the Kennedy White House, she wrote; when she learned of the death of a child or the death of a president, she wrote. She often wrote three or four long letters in one day, and yet in many of them she apologized for not writing soon enough, or often enough, or well enough. In her diaries, too, she often despaired of her inability to get "enough writing done." One of the paradoxes of my mother's life was that she wrote constantly, always chastising herself, in writing, for "not writing."

She left us a bountiful record of conscious and compassionate thought, brought to life in words: not only in her published books of autobiographical fiction, her essays, and her poetry, but, equally importantly, in her diaries and letters. Her reflections upon her individual journey have brought meaning and inspiration to the lives of readers since she first put pen to paper. Her best-known book, *Gift from the Sea*, was first published in 1955; it has never been out of print.

These letters and diaries shed light upon some of the conditions that caused her to write that book, and follow the path of her life before and after its publication, from midlife through the beginning of old age. Her journey, though very personal, became a universal one. In speaking for herself, she spoke for us all.

LETTERS AND JOURNALS,
1947–1986

Trailer,* Contentment Island [Darien, Connecticut]
January 5th, 1947 [DIARY]

This is the beginning of a New Year. I am back at the trailer again after a two-month absence. Such a difficult two months—so much learned from it—so much affecting this New Year that has been given to me that some of it must go down here, even if it is just a mental summing up.

As with all real conflicts, when one examines the particulars, they seem negligible. The particulars, in fact, *are* negligible. But when they have been pared away, one finds the basic conflict which is not negligible—but the basic conflict coming up again in one's life. The same old conflict that one can never solve once and for all—the same patterns of behavior ready to catch you, the same pitfalls waiting for you. The trouble lies in believing one can settle these things once and for all. Why does one believe in the fairy tale pattern, the dragons killed at a single stroke and the Princess living happily ever after?

One wrestles with one's dragons until the end of one's life—it is a constant and eternal process. The crises in one's life only show up in intensity what is going on every day. The crises are there, perhaps in order to illuminate the everyday struggle, so that one may recognize the adversary more quickly, so that one may learn the weaknesses in one's own armor or tactics, so that one may be better prepared to fight, not "next time" but all the time—tomorrow and the day after.

With me it was again the basic conflict between the woman and the artist. Perhaps there are other ways of stating it. Perhaps one could say the ego of the artist. I found I was pregnant for the seventh time and felt, with an intensity and wildness of rebellion, that I could not go through it again.† I felt it was terribly *wrong*—a mistake and *wrong* and not meant to

---

*The trailer had been given to CAL by Henry Ford in 1942 for use as an office or writing studio, as well as for several road trips. AML used it as her studio until a more permanent structure was built.

†Charles and Anne Morrow Lindbergh had six children: Charles Jr., born in 1930, died in

be. I rebelled against it with every fiber of my being, physically, mentally, emotionally. I was frightened of it—terrified—both physically and mentally. Afraid of the months of illness at the beginning that I always have, afraid of the abdication of the artist, the ego afraid of the depression that follows, afraid of the actual delivery, afraid of the long convalescence afterwards.

It was not the unreasonable fear of a woman who had never been through this.

I had been through it six times willingly, although after the fifth I felt afraid. It was a difficult ordeal but I had gotten through it saying, "This is the last. This is for a sister for Anne, but this is the end. You will never have to do this again."

And after climbing up that long hill—the mountain of last winter—feeling exhausted, ill, depressed all winter, finally—finally—climbing up at the end of the summer to free mornings at the trailer. Pushing the details back, sitting still, alone (how long since I'd been alone), quiet, passive. To find—yes!—the first tender shoots of thoughts, of perceptions, of poems coming back. I could still write. I could write again! It wasn't dead, as I had feared. My life opened up. I felt again, for the first time in years, young, alive, full of love and hope.

And then suddenly to be told, *You must go through it all again!* I felt unreasonably, irrationally despairing. This is the end. It will never come back again after this. This will kill me—probably not physically (though I dreaded it physically), but it will kill the person in me who writes. It will kill the real me.

At the same time I felt, perhaps equally strongly (and this grew as time went on), that I could not take it into my hands to interrupt the act already done. Would I spend my life then trying to justify it? Could I take what seemed to me the destructive, noncreative, negative way out? And if I did, would I bear incurable guilt over it—and what would that do to my life, my writing, my marriage? Could I say no to a child, to that act of God which had been the greatest experience in my life, from which I had learned the most? That experience—almost the only one—which I felt in other terms and had to put into writing the lesson life had taught me. "The word made flesh."

How could I say no to that? And still write it? Would it not nullify

---

1932; Jon, born in 1932; Land, born in 1937; Anne, born in 1940, died in 1993; Scott, born in 1942; and Reeve, born in 1945.

all I had learned or believed? How could I justify it to myself, to my conscience? And yet instinctively, deeply, I felt it was wrong. I cried out against it. I would try to accept it and then fall back in a deep inner resentment and feeling of wrongness. I felt, in fact, exactly balanced between two wrongs. My body, my instincts and my ego said one course was wrong. My conscience, my patterns of behavior, and the patterns of outsiders said another course was wrong.

And yet one must take actions—to play the part of a rational being. And so I did. I went to my obstetrician (who had said after the last child that I shouldn't have any more, that the uterus was getting thin, that after forty was when one got into trouble and he had also offered to perform an operation on me so I shouldn't have any more—which I had refused).

He said there was nothing that he could do for me, that I was a "fine healthy woman" and to go ahead and have the child. "Give it away if you don't want it!" (As if *that* were the point.) When I asked him about danger, he said there was no danger, that there was more danger in an abortion. When I said I was afraid, he said, "What are you afraid of? You've been through *much* harder things than this."

I went away feeling bitter. I know that a friend of mine had been told by this same doctor that if she "got into trouble" to come to him and he would fix her up. But *she* had had a nervous breakdown and I had not. As far as the doctors and the legal end went, you could just go on and have babies until you die or go crazy—before anyone will help you. He was just scared to death to touch my case because I was famous. Also he embodies the world's conservatism in these matters. "It's taking life." Well—I felt that too.

I found out that legally, before interruption could be legal, you would have to prove permanent physical or mental disability would follow having the child. This let me out unless I was willing to get an old family doctor and a psychiatrist and convince them that I would go crazy if I went through with it. I felt I could make out quite a good case, but I couldn't stomach it, probably because I didn't really believe it true.

I went to Dr. A.* at the Medical Center. At the first interview he said

---

*Dana W. Atchley (1893–1982), a physician from Englewood, New Jersey, who practiced in New York City. He was recommended by AML's friends Adelaide Marquand and Ellen Barry as a physician with a warm bedside manner and excellent diagnostic skills. Among his other patients were Katharine Hepburn, Greta Garbo, and Nancy ("Slim") Hayworth. See also Introduction.

he would put me through a complete checkup but that probably Dr. H.'s* second estimate ("You're just a fine healthy woman") was more correct than his first warnings. He then swept the physical aside and said, "Why are you afraid of it?" When I finished talking to him he said, "You have told me enough to convince me that an abortion is completely justified."

I then told him how strongly I felt against abortion and that I could not accept a merely mental reason to interrupt this, that it would have to rest on the physical side of it. If I could go through it safely physically, that was my choice. If I *couldn't* go through it safely, then I would accept, with difficulty, the other course. This was C.'s† feeling too.

He went ahead with the tests. Everything looked all right. I found I could, after talking to Dr. A., adjust much better to the ordeal ahead. I felt sure that if he checked me as all right physically, I would be. But more important, he accepted as valid all the other side of the conflict, the non-physical side, the non-physical fears and revulsions. He did not laugh at them, like Dr. H., nor find them un-understandable and untenable, like C. They were valid facts but not frozen facts. Something could be done about them. (I suppose this is basically C.'s thesis too—only it is easier to accept from a more dispassionate source like a doctor.) I felt, with this man's help, I could go through this ordeal with more wisdom and ease than ever before.

The first tests showed everything all right. Then, on two small clues ("Probably nothing at all, but it is the kind of thing a doctor must run down"), I had more X-rays taken and it was discovered that I had a gall bladder full of small stones and that the "appendix attacks" I had had—especially that terrible one at the Ford Hospital after Scott's birth, so much more painful than the delivery itself . . . after which I felt deeply and instinctively, "I *cannot* have another child" . . . which lay back of my dread of having my sixth child, Reeve—these were gall bladder attacks, not appendix.

Dr. A. explained that gall bladder conditions are irritated and increased by child-bearing. This had evidently been going on a long time. (An early report of an X-ray taken before Anne's birth showed the same clue that Dr. A. had followed.) Dr. A. then felt that I should

*Dr. Everett M. Hawks, AML's obstetrician.
†Mrs. Lindbergh often refers to her husband as "C." or "CAL" (Charles Augustus Lindbergh). She is referred to in these notes as AML. Her mother, Elizabeth Cutter Morrow, is referred to as ECM.

probably *not* go through with it. It is easy enough apparently to take a gall bladder out but if a stone gets out and lodges in the intestinal tract somewhere (which possibly happened in the attack in the Ford Hospital, though if it did, it passed through safely), then you have a very difficult operation under *any* circumstances, and really a dangerous one in the middle of a pregnancy.

Dr. A. consulted with a surgeon and an obstetrician and the result was to advise me to interrupt the pregnancy and have the gall bladder out three months later. Here was my legal out. Even a moral one. I began to prepare to take it, somewhat reluctantly in one sense, but relieved. When C. brought up the possibility of my having the gall bladder out first and then going ahead with the pregnancy ("If it's such a simple operation"), Dr. A.'s surgeon advised against this. C. then called two surgeons he knew and they said it was perfectly possible and could be done, etc., and weren't worried about the situation at all.

On being presented with this, the doctors at the Medical Center then said they *could* do it. And the proposition put before me was: the safest course we still advise is to have an abortion and the gall bladder out in three months. However if you insist, the next safest course is to have the gall bladder out at three months and then go on with the pregnancy (in a semi-convalescent state). We do *not* advise, and consider dangerous, your going through the pregnancy with the gall bladder left in.

Again it was put up to me. I, who thought I had made the decision once and for all. I felt the trap had closed down again. For though the *legal* out was still there, the moral one seemed to me to have been taken away with the possibility of that mid-pregnancy operation. An operation which made the ordeal far more difficult than it was originally (when I had felt it was unbearable) but which made it safer. (Ironically.)

Feeling desperately trapped and low, I again made the only decision that it seemed possible for me to take, the second and hardest course. I then went home and let down—or rather started to adjust to the long ordeal.

Two days later, apparently for no reason at all, I had a miscarriage. After the first shock, I was incredibly relieved. That is too mild a word. I took it as a pure act of mercy from God. An act of mercy to be accepted without a shred of guilt but with a heart full of humility and gratitude. A sign from heaven, a rainbow, a promise of presence. A deliverance which exacted not guilt from me, but a challenge—a sense of responsibility about what I was delivered *for.*

The whole incident was perhaps a warning to me—before it is too late—that "I must be about my Father's business." This is now the task, to find out what it is—for me—my special task.

January 29th [1947] [DIARY]

The afternoons, especially the late afternoons, belong to the children. (Anne coming to me at my desk, "I'm glad you say 'yes, yes,' Mother, but I wish you'd *come*.") And Reeve. I suppose this is my greatest joy of the moment, to sit in a room with Reeve, on the floor with her, and let her give me bits of thread or broken toys. What wonderful wordless and completely satisfying communication it is!

The first communication—how pure it is—and yet how it holds the essence of all communication in it. What words of a lover could be more miraculous than the gesture of a child giving you a half-chewed crust of bread or a piece of raveled thread she picked off the floor? It is sheer communication, that is all—it is the first lip of land rising up out of the flood of the unknown, the unshared, the vast depths of the unknowable. It is the olive branch that the dove brings back.

Communication is wordless at both ends of the arc. When one has said all one can possibly say and when one is just beginning to speak. The lover and the child are one.

February 4th [1947] [DIARY]

Yesterday I drove into town for a long dentist's appointment. I shopped and ate cold coconut pie at the Cos Club* by myself. A rather brisk clubwoman was just getting up as I sat down. She said something about the club being crowded. I answered without thinking much what was in my mind, "Yes, when I saw that great pile of coats downstairs, I was quite frightened."

"Yes," she said, with assurance, "but usually, if you come late, you can still get something to eat." She had interpreted my being frightened as a fear of not getting anything to eat! I had to remind myself that there are some people to whom a pile of coats means nothing to be afraid of! It maybe even induces a pleasurable and anticipatory sentiment in them: How wonderful! A *crowd* of people upstairs!† They lick their lips.

---

*Founded in 1909, the Cosmopolitan Club is a private club for women on the Upper East Side of New York City.
†Here AML draws a wide-eyed smiley face.

February 5th [1947] [DIARY]

Scott looked up solemnly from his lunch yesterday and said: "Does anyone want to be turned into an ugly little worm?" He looked at each of us in turn, around the table, and then let his gaze fall finally and rest mightily on his father.

February 13th [1947] [DIARY]

I am sitting up in the hospital bed the night before an operation.* I know it is a simple "routine" operation. I know intellectually that I should not be afraid, but I have this panicky feeling that things are unfinished—untied-up—if anything should happen to me. One always has this before a baby, a voyage, an operation. So much is unfinished—in relationships, that is. One longs to explain, to be sure they understand, the people one loves.

C. first—does he understand, does he know how much I love him, value him? Will he always believe it in spite of all the contradictory things he might think or find, all the contradictions in me? They do not contradict my deep love for him. Will he forgive me for all mistakes, errors in judgment and actions, all stupid blind stumblings after truth and right? Believe that the main current in me is true and loving? Yes, I think he will. I am grateful for that.

One would always die with things unfinished. Always. You must live so that people understand, and trust in their forgiveness.

Forgiveness—mercy seems to me the most beautiful thing on earth, perhaps because it is unearthly, and the touch of God in us: the miracle of mercy, the unexpected, the arms of the prodigal son's father, the ravens bringing food in the night, the cup running over.

Dr. A. told me that when coming out of ether after an operation was "*not* the time to practice being a girl scout." I laughed. "If it hurts, *say* so," etc.! How very perceptive he is! How well he knows me.

A week later [DIARY]

After two days of really incredible pain and weakness, one slowly finds one's way back. I feel so unable to concentrate, to think, to read, to dwell on anything for long. And the world seems enormous and chartless. Only the tiny world of the hospital is safe, like a boarding school with its routine and its rules and its hero-worship and jealousies. The very

---

*Gall bladder operation mentioned previously.

charming, witty surgeon—yes, I understand his warmth and charm, but it is not what Dr. A. has—that steady quality of dry compassion.

This is one of my landmarks now in this chartless sea. I seem adrift for the moment.

Home again
March 6th [1947] [DIARY]

I got home three days ago. The day you come home is difficult, of course. You have "elevator stomach" all day, just from emotion, but you get through it. How beautiful the children looked, unbelievable, each one ripened and whole, like a fruit. One sees them more clearly when one has been away. But in spite of one's joy in them—and what a joy it is—one gets quickly exhausted. Reading a story, watching five people at once, and the noise: one finds oneself homesick for the hospital.

March 10th [1947] [DIARY]

When one is tired or weak, one is unable to be other than one's most real and honest self. Only the bottom of the well is still there—nothing flowing on top. And so, one can only be with the people with whom one can be completely honest, completely oneself. It takes too much effort to put on a mask. My intellect does not function well when I am weak. My heart functions always, whether I am weak or not. It is the deepest part of me.

I was reading the story of Esau and Jacob last night to Scott and Anne. I explained about the birthright and how in that country the younger brother had to listen to the older brother.

"You understand that," I went on, "because you have older brothers and you listen to them. You listen to Land and Jon."

"I listen to Jon," said Anne quickly, not willing to admit she listened to Land.

"I listen to *myself*," said Scott squarely.

I threw my arms around him and said, "That's right, Scott. Never do anything else!"

Scott was pleased by this show of emotion and then turned and, looking at me with his straight blue eyes, he said gravely, almost accusingly, "*You* listen to Father." I laughed. Oh my children. . . .

I am convinced that Jon has whooping cough. That means they'll all get it and it takes weeks to get over it. I wonder when we'll all be through! C. might get it too—poor C., with a house full of invalids when he should be free to work on his own work. . . .

I have been reading a very good novel and also an article by Jung, "The Fight with the Shadow." Very exciting—the price of unconsciousness in the world and in individuals. Perhaps the mind is not dead but working in new channels!

April 4th [1947] [DIARY]

We have had three appalling weeks, the kind one hardly believes while one is going through it. And afterwards, as now, it seems quite unbelievable—except for the inexplicable weariness. Written down it sounds merely funny.

Jon came down with whooping cough. When Land started his cough a few days later, we assumed it was the early stages of whooping cough. He sleeps in the same room and we did not bother to change him. We watched him go through the same stages of fever, cough, etc.—waiting for him to whoop.

At the end of a week, I realized to my horror one evening looking at him that [Land] was coming down with *measles*! Dr. S. came down the next morning and confirmed it. But he said not to worry about Jon as it was very rare to have two contagious diseases at once. Then, after saying this, he crossed over and looked into Jon's throat and said, "Well, he already has it!" And from the coughing paroxysms, he guessed Land had whooping cough too.

Then followed a week of trays, making beds, taking temperatures, alcohol rubs, reading, carrying drinks, emptying basins, washing, etc. I felt excruciatingly tired from running up and down stairs. After a week of this, when Land's spots had melted (he also had an earache one night), and his temperature was down, we let him get up one day. The next day he came down with *mumps*! Well, at least Jon couldn't get that—he'd had it. Land was discouraged and Dr. S. incredulous.

In the meantime, the little ones were starting. Scott and Anne both coughing. Reeve with a fever (four in bed by now). Scott was clearly whooping, Anne coughing and feverish. There was *always* a child calling for you. You left one to run to the other. After a few days, Reeve came down with measles—and then Anne—and then Scott. (Five cases of measles, four cases of whooping cough, and one mumps!) And Land got some kind of intestinal flu, and another earache. Scott was throwing up and Anne whooping and Jon still whooping badly. And oh, how they *sneezed*—Scott tearing through box after box of Kleenex.

"But Scott, you use them up so *fast*!" I protested.

"But my nose runs so fast," he answered quite justly.

I read *Mary Poppins* and distributed presents and rubbed backs with witch hazel and washed out slop buckets and gave medicine and ran up and down stairs and dropped into bed at night too tired to think.

Outside Lexington, Virginia
May 26th [1947] [DIARY]

I am sitting in the trailer parked under a cliff by the side of the road in Virginia. The clutch has given out in the car and C. has taken it to town to fix, so I have a "lost day" to use before going on with our journey home.

I have been five weeks in the trailer with C. touring the West—Arizona, Utah, California, Oregon, Washington, Nevada, Colorado, New Mexico, Texas—then across the South, motoring all day. Every night in a new place, almost.

It has been a strange life, very lovely for a while, life in a vacuum. Pure, so to speak, with no distractions, no outside people or demands—or outside pleasures. A very simple day-to-day life. No intellectual problems and very few physical ones. Housekeeping in this tidy compact little room, following the road, making the day's run, watching the map, counting the mileage, shopping for food, deciding where we'll stop for the night, cooking a hot meal, washing up and to bed—usually very late and tired. . . .

A single thread, a single simple life. Not really (curiously enough) so very different from the big trips (the flights) we used to take. The same simplicity of living in a world in which there were only he and I, of a life that looked (for me) ahead only as far as the night's stop—a set job to be done and no complications once I learned my job. It was not as arduous as the flights, of course, nor so dangerous. This was playing at something, not a life-and-death contest. And yet there was that same quality of adventure that C. puts into anything he does.

This business of taking an overloaded trailer lurching over rocky cattle tracks, or slithering down gullies, over mountain passes (Cloud-Croft, La Lux, N.M.). We pay, of course, for this adventurousness—in tires, leaking radiator, broken clutch, etc., and general wear and tear. How many times has C. jacked us out of a position his adventurousness got us into (mud, sand, a ditch we got stuck in)? And our tires are gone with rock bruises. How many times, too, have I climbed out, jammed rocks or blocks under the car or trailer to get out of a tough place? Going over the pass at Cloud-Croft, we unpacked five hundred pounds of equipment; I sat on it while C. took the trailer over the hump and then came back for me and the load. At Pagosa Springs we were stopped by hills too slippery with mud and rain—and we just put up and waited until they dried.

But these adventures have not meant danger. They have, at worst, meant discomfort, delay, a lot of hot work for C. (he always manages to get himself *out* of the fixes he gets into), long dusty waits for me, irregular hours of sleeping and eating. And if we paid for them, we gained by them too. Campsites unusually beautiful, remote, silent—like the High Sierras or Silver Bell Mountain or our last campsite in the Blue Ridge Mountains. (The clutch finally gave out here and we had to be pulled back up the hill by tractor.)

Actually these were not—did not seem like—ordeals to me, but more like adventures. The difficulties lie for me, curiously enough, in what is most ordinary for all the other women in the world—in keeping house, in shopping, in cooking, in ordinary living. I am very stupid at it because I have really never done it. I have never shopped and cooked and cleaned for my husband like an ordinary woman.

When most women learn this—when they are first married—I was learning to fly and to operate a radio and to navigate and fly a glider. So I do not know a good cut of meat from a poor one or what things cost by the pound (I know about how much thirteen people eat in a month) or how to cook a good steak or omelet or how to light a lantern or a stove (a gasoline one). But I am learning and I am glad to learn such simple things—it seems ridiculous what confidence it gives me: how to tell stringy meat from tender, how to fry chicken and cook vegetables, how to time one's meals so one doesn't burn everything. I feel sometimes just like the funny paper jokes about Miss Newly-Wed!

[France, August 1947]*
Dearest C.,

I am sitting, quite cold. The smoky waiting room is jammed with people, baggage, etc.: paper parcels, wicker trunks, string bags, a bicycle, sailors in red pompom caps, two old Bretons in black with their white horned caps, a baby wrapped in blankets—wide-eyed, placed on the wooden bench. I arrived at six a.m., the stars still out, cold and still on the platform, no porters. I can just manage to carry my three bags a few steps at a time. Finally made the station.

---

*At Charles Lindbergh's suggestion, *Reader's Digest* contracted with AML for a series of articles on postwar Europe. She left on August 1, 1947, traveling across France, Germany, and England; Charles remained in Connecticut with the children. On her return nine weeks later, she wrote five pieces, which were published in *Life*, *Harper's*, and *Reader's Digest*.

Last night was really an experience! I arrived in the sleeper car with my three bags (carried by a porter this time, for it was Paris) to find it a small compartment with two bunks made up (one above the other), and a stranger's portfolio in the top bed! "What? I'm not alone?!" I protested to the porter. "But no, madame. One is never alone in a sleeping car, there are two berths. You thought . . . ?" I said, "In America . . ." I sat down on my lower berth—and waited.

Pretty soon a little Frenchman came along—young Breton. "You permit, madame?" he said politely sticking his head in the door. "Ah, it's yours?" I asked, nodding to the portfolio.

"If that does not disturb you." The berth was his but if I really minded he could get his sister-in-law in the same car to change with him. Only he admitted, discreetly sympathetic, that his brother and sister-in-law were newly married; it would be a shame to separate them. It turned out my room-mate was also newly married (that makes *him* pretty safe, I jotted down mentally).

We then embarked on a discussion of American trains, French trains, American customs, French customs, etc. He was in the Resistance under De Gaulle, "a great man. The people will have him back in six months." Also was a translator for the Americans when they came into Brest. He learned English at school. He likes Americans—likes American women better than Englishwomen—finds them less reserved! I prod him a little on the American soldiers in France. He was polite and didn't want to hurt my feelings, but it is always the same story: they destroyed too easily. "*C'est la guerre américaine.* You are quick. You go fast. You save men. But you destroy the country—it was an Allied country."

While he goes out of the room for a moment, I decide to get into bed fully dressed; I only have a few hours anyway and it isn't worth dressing and undressing, especially in front of a strange man. I take off my skirt and coat and wrap myself in my raincoat and get into bed.

My friend returns. Realizing that I am new at a sleeper car, he starts to explain it to me. "*Voilà,*" he says, opening up the wash-basin with gallant posture. "Now, I will go out and let you get ready for the night."

"But I *am* ready for the night," I protest. "I shall sleep just like this."

"But madame!" His face is a mixture of dismay and hurt feelings. "You cannot sleep like that. You will not be comfortable. It is for that I suggested my sister-in-law coming in here—only she is newly married. I am confused," he says, pulling at his tie.

Not nearly as confused as I, my dear young man, I think, drawing my raincoat closer about me. Is he going to *insist* that I undress?! "Oh, no," I say, wanting to put him at ease again, "I'm not afraid. I have five children and I'm not very young."

"All the more reason," he says, with real concern, "for your having a comfortable night!" (Goodness. Do I look as old and as unattractive as that? I suppose I do. Maybe the raincoat wasn't such a good idea.)

"Ah well, excuse me, madame," and he holds out his hand to say good night as he starts up the ladder for the upper berth. Before he puts out the light, he calls down "*Bonsoir, madame*. I have enjoyed our little talk. It is so interesting to get a view of another country."

"*Bien sûr, Monsieur, bonsoir.*"

Paris
Sunday, September 7th, 1947
Dearest C.,

I am back in Paris. I got back yesterday evening, rather tired after getting up at 5:30 in Berlin, driving in a jeep to Templehof, taking off in an Army plane (European Air Transport—bucket seats—parachutes etc.—no woman allowed on without slacks—I had none so they lent me some!) for Frankfort. Then an hour's wait for Air France's plane to Paris.

I went out alone to supper, with that familiar sunk feeling of coming "home" and finding no one to tell my adventures to. My *enormous* pile of mail comforted me a great deal (five letters from you!). I took your letters to the restaurant with me—not to read, just to hold in my hand. "Madame is alone?" "Yes, all alone." It takes a lot of self-restraint, when you feel like that, not to fall into the arms of the first Frenchman who eyes you. Restraint—& also discrimination!

I guess I really just want you to talk it over with. I have the whole English adventure to go through before I can get home to that understanding. I need to talk to you *so badly*! Poor C., how are you surviving there in the way of household troubles?

How right you were about Germany! That is really why I am so exhausted, emotionally and mentally—from the impact of Germany and no one I can talk frankly to about it. The impact of Germany is terrific. Truman* suggested that I get a "human story"—it is impossible. There are too many and it is too universal: the suffering and the tragedy, the need, the hunger, the hopelessness, the fear. The personal is dwarfed by

*Major Truman Smith (1893–1977) was a military attaché in Berlin from 1935 to 1939, later a German specialist in the U.S. Military Intelligence Division and personal adviser to General George C. Marshall.

the immensity of the tragedy. Everyone in Germany has a tragic story to tell. You hear too many. Everyone is in desperate need, everyone is near starvation, everyone is worn out with the struggle to survive, everyone is hopeless, everyone is afraid of war—afraid of Russia, afraid of the winter. Everyone looks to America as the last hope, and even here there is great disillusionment and bitterness. "Is it too late?" everyone is asking. There is apathy—hopelessness and a kind of fatalism. "The Allies don't *wish* Germany to get on her feet; they *could* help us but they don't *want* to." "It is the Russian century." "What is Germany but one big concentration camp today?" "Why don't the Americans just drop the atom bomb on us and be done with it?" etc., etc.

What is horrible to see, and what dawns on you before you are long in Germany, is that *even without Russian pressure* the whole of Europe is sinking down to a level of existence that heretofore one had considered possible only in the East (India, China, etc.). And this is true in every field: physically, mentally, and morally.

As I said to you in my first letter from Frankfurt—one of the most terrible things about Germany is the glass wall that separates you from the Germans. Germany is no longer a country—it is a colony. The press is equally insulated from Germany. They get superb treatment: press clubs with tons of food, hot water, swimming pools, drinks, transportation, etc., all over Germany. The press clubs are generally run by Army, or retired Army officials—very efficient. The press go off *in a body*, in cars to the Nuremberg Trials, to Hamburg to see the *Exodus* shipload of Jews come in to the Leipzig Fair, etc. They sit around when they come back from these mass jaunts and drink and argue far into the night and no one even gets up in the mornings until noon.

Of course there are exceptions, the quiet hardworking ones you don't notice so much. The person I liked the best was Gault McGowan, a crusty Scotch Irishman. He was so nice, so honest and independent. He is head of the European staff of the *New York Sun*, and though rather a rough diamond, a lot more perceptive and less sheep-minded than the rest of them. He won't live at the press clubs and has a house in Heidelberg, on the river, where he insisted I come on my way back from Baden-Baden. I was so grateful to him for that quiet evening and good talk. We went up the hill to the observatory and looked at the moon through the big Bruce telescope there. Such a relief to be in a city untouched (relatively) by the war and to feel some continuity of intellectual thought—of the old culture of Germany. "This is the only thing that keeps me sane—living out here," said McGowan (I'm going to read the *N.Y. Sun* after this!).

I have rather broken the rules by seeing the Germans and by *not* asking to meet important people and by *not* going to all the big news shots. Also by having Germans to the press club.

It was such a relief to walk the streets of Paris yesterday—to see cigarette butts lying on the street (not quickly snatched up by barefoot children; a cigarette butt is worth money in Germany), to see people with shoes, stockings; to see fat children, fruit in the stands, streets intact, houses standing, roofs on, buses running, people walking arm in arm casually—not hurrying like animals, haunted & hunted.

France is a country. It has been very ill—it is drawn—it is tired—but it is whole: breathing, living, functioning (and how beautiful life is when it functions!). Germany is no longer a country. It is ill—dying perhaps—struggling to breathe under an iron lung. I feel as if I had just gotten out of that iron lung myself. That weight of fear, panic, misery, hopelessness. Do you remember how we felt when we reached Romania after flying out of Russia? The sense of breathing again—of relief, ease, normal life? Well, I felt like that yesterday afternoon after flying from Berlin. I felt also the French don't know how beautiful their life is, how easily it can be lost, how near the danger is. (Perhaps they *do* know how beautiful life is, since they were once "occupied," but they do not see the new danger; they are thinking in terms of the old one.)

Everyone should see Berlin—everyone. It is like a city of the dead. It is like some coral colony from which the living organisms have gone. It can only be seen in terms of the sacking of Rome by the barbarians. There is grass growing in the streets of Berlin, grass and pink fireweed on the piles of rubble from collapsed buildings not yet cleared away. The hammer and sickle float over the bronze horses of the Brandenburg Gate and the trees of the Tiergarten have disappeared long ago for firewood. In their place is a wide expanse—like the flats of Flushing: little truck gardens, dumps, shacks of corrugated tin, fences, tin cans, patches of beans, tomatoes. Dominating this vast slum of truck gardens, on the Charlottenburger Chaussee, is an *enormous* marble-columned semi-circular monument on top of which strides a colossal statue of a Russian Soldier, cloak behind him in the wind of conquest, hand outstretched over the vast ruin of the truck gardens—over destroyed Berlin. A real Russian soldier (human size & living) stands at attention below this great statue day and night—symbolizing the Russian victory.

That great black-cloaked figure—like a storm—like a tornado towering over European civilization.

I hope the Congressmen saw this! But what does it take to *see*? I don't know. There are people with eyes to see who don't see.

Paris
Tuesday, September 30th [1947]
Dearest C.,

The poems are wonderful (the children's). They give me such a marvelous *inside* feeling about them. How different they are. Land's are vivid—*visually*—and in action (the Horizon one is best, with the horses coming over the horizon) but *not* musical. Scott's are spare, strong, secretive—with a secret and surprising force in them. But Anne's are the stuff of poetry—musical always, dream-like, a wellspring gushing up: images, music, color, and magic. Magic—she has—so important for poetry. She can spin a spell. I am excited about it.

I shall try to rest and write on the boat. I am, of course, tired. I am also doubtful of what I can write. I see so well the lacks. But, on the other hand, I know I was right to come. I know what it has done for me. I know it was right and that I can give back some of it.

Dear Charles—I have been lonely. It has been difficult. I have made mistakes and yet it has been one of the big things in my life. Of all the things you have given me in life, and you have given me so much, perhaps this is one of the biggest: your sending me out on this mission alone (for I should not have done it if you had not pushed me a little and told me I *could* do it!).

I am grateful to you for it. You are always giving me life, life itself. May I make something of it! Bless you.

Scott's Cove, Darien
December 18th, 1947
Dearest C.,

You have been gone just over a week and it feels like a month. I realize I have been delaying to write you until I should have something to report—on the writing end. Because I really have nothing very tangible, this fills me with a kind of panic, a negligent pupil, a bad-girl guilt. I want so much for you to think me "a good girl." It is my great weakness: I would rather have you think me "a good girl" than be right myself, or than to have anyone else think me a good girl. And I am afraid you will not. All the time I feel like a bad girl—that I am not living up to your idea of a good girl.

I felt this very strongly when I got your letter from Chicago. In fact it really upset me, though I don't believe in the least you meant to. It struck me with the pressure of a fire-hose, though you did not mean it that way. I cannot work well under pressure—and I feel as if I have been under pressure for about six months.

I feel like explaining to you quite honestly (as if you were here—oh, if only you were here) the metamorphosis I am going through and what I have been thinking out. After you left—and I got back the pieces from Wallace*—I felt an extreme nausea about writing, especially that kind of writing. It seemed to me that I had been writing with blinders on, or trying to run with shackles on my ankles, ever since I got back. And that even during the trip I had had those blinders on: of "Writing for the *Digest*." Now they don't want any more, but it is a little hard to throw the blinders away. It is hard to start all over again and this is what I must do. I must look at all my material again—with no blinders *at all*. And no magazine *at all* and no circulation *at all* in mind. Just look at it. And see what there is and let something spring from it.

I feel a hunger now—a real hunger—for letting the pool still itself and seeing the reflections. I feel a hunger for the kind of writing that I feel is truly mine: observation *plus* reflection. I believe this hunger is good and must be followed regardless of time, circulation, crisis, etc., because it is not just the luxury of an artist, it is the law of the date tree: you must not try to give coconuts if you are a date tree. You must not give in order to do good, or to benefit mankind, or to reap praise or reward, but only because it is your nature to give forth dates. As a matter of fact, I don't know of anyone who follows this law with as much integrity as you do. It is incredible how you cleave to it, even when I often sneakingly wish you wouldn't—when I can see you in other roles. But you *always* know—unnervingly.

I am not like this. I get pulled off—by people generally, by wanting to excel in *all* fields! By wanting to live up to other people's standards, to be thought "a good girl" when I do sit still and listen to my own law. I also have power—not the same kind as you—but a power and rightness and clarity of my own which you are the first to recognize.

Did I have *anything* more to say on Europe? I wasn't sure. I felt my

*DeWitt Wallace, founding editor of *Reader's Digest* magazine.

ideas had been crippled by trying too hard to write for the *Digest* and that it was now a dead experience. Only one clear idea came to me and that was a conviction that what I wanted to say was on a scale above the struggle between Communism–Democracy.

The next day I got your letter and I felt chiefly upset by it. (You didn't mean to do this—I have reread the letter now I am steadier and feel sure I took it wrong.) The still pool was ruffled by a fifty-mile-an-hour gale. *I must do something fast. I must have something to show C. I must hurry. Time is short. The hound was at me again. Hurry—Hurry—Hurry!*

No, I began to realize, I mustn't hurry. If I try to force something this month, it will be soulless. In a sense, I feel—rereading my notes, diaries, etc.—the time for timid articles is past. (Perhaps Wallace knows this.) All those facts and notes are not what is important now to say. They are ephemeral. One must start on the timeless. And from the whirlwind of your letter I remembered one still place. And it had struck a chord in me, because I had come to the same conclusion. And I felt—*this* is the important part of the letter.

I think I can make an informal piece which still has a kind of pattern and says something too, in the reflections—something critical and questioning—but which *doesn't* preach. I think this is the thing I do best.

I realize, after my week of reflection, certain things about my writing:

I. That I do the indirect thing best and that this is my sort of writing. I like to suggest, to say "Here it is," not "I love," or "I hate," or even "This is true," "This is false," or "This is good," "This is bad." I don't think the *Digest* people particularly like or understand this sort of thing. And I don't think you completely approve. It is not trivial but it is not *direct*. Perhaps you will say: there isn't *time* to be indirect.

The only answer to this is that you must always take time to be yourself; otherwise the time is completely wasted. You can say, and I frequently do, I am not right for my time. I am not the kind of voice or the kind of writing that is needed. Then you must be quiet. You cannot speak with any voice except your own. If you can't do that, be quiet.

II. I also realize again that my constructive or creative periods come in waves and that there are definitive troughs, depending on the energy spent, etc. I don't think the work done in the trough, or against the tide, is any good—or you wear yourself out, like swimming against an undertow. I think I made that mistake on the boat. I should have just gone to sleep in a deck chair instead of sitting at my desk in the cabin producing nothing. If I had sat in a deck chair, letting the ideas turn over in the deep well—*but not forcing them*—and resting, relaxing, then I think I should have been much fresher to work that two weeks at home. And what is more, I believe the seeds would have been further along left to themselves for that ten days. So much of creation (how much?!) is in the dark. I believe I am in some such period now. And I allowed myself, stupidly, to be panicked by your letter (as I let myself be panicked on the boat by the thought of a *Reader's Digest* deadline) when I was still in the deep-well period.

I think the deep-well period needs some studying. It needs diversion and getting out—refreshment but not distraction, not dispersal of forces. There is no use freeing yourself from the pressure of deadlines and submitting yourself to the pressure of Christmas shopping or late nights.

It is possible, of course, to do another thing about Christmas and sometime I would love to do it. This is to get *out* of the stream. All of us as a family go off alone—to a log cabin in the snow and make our own Christmas there. It would be simple. It would be quiet and no one would contribute to it or enter it but ourselves. But it can't, I believe, be done in Darien.

I have spent the whole day writing you and lots of other hours thinking it out. But it has helped me. How I wish you were here and we could have talked. As I reread your letter now, now I am stronger about my own convictions, I find it gives me an entirely different impression. I really believe everything you say in it and it is very beautiful. It has also great power. This I felt and interpreted wrongly as pressure. You have so much power. When you concentrate it like that in strong writing, the result really is a fire-hose.

I am going to take this to the post office. I am very doubtful of its reaching San Francisco in time to catch you with the moved-up schedule but I was not clear enough to write it ahead of this.

The children have mild colds. Land has had earaches but no temperature, which Dr. S.* with his usual facility has diagnosed as a strep infection and prescribed sulfa for. Land is in bed, gay as a lark and very un-sick-looking and -sounding. Radio on. Also practicing on his guitar and making Christmas cards. He should be up Sat. or Sun.

Reeve still asks for you. "When is Father coming back?" And "Where is all the family?" she asked one day at lunch. Scott was an angel in the

---

*Dr. Shoup, the family pediatrician, who made house calls.

Christmas play, in a white robe and pink wings. His star got broken. "How?" I asked him. "I was walking vewy quietly and John was walking vewy fast." Anne was a German Frau in the Christmas play. (They did Christmas in many lands!) She looked charming in a black velvet bodice and full skirt, her two gold braids hanging down. They sang "O Tannenbaum." Another girl wore her Swedish costume. I wondered why Anne was made German instead of Swedish?! But I think it was accidental.

Jon is busy making presents for the children in the toolshed. I don't know *what*, but it pleases me. He can make anything—and this is a real Christmas thing to do, to give gifts you make with joy. Mrs. Hepner* made us a lovely wreath for the door. Same kind of gift. One should give from one's own gift. That would be the truest kind of Christmas. In that sense, perhaps I should write. But not, I mean, articles—write my warm thoughts to people, not conventionally, but what I feel. I should touch them that way, not by giving bought presents. I have not done much buying and shopping this year. The shops are horrible—nauseating.

It is the compromise with the world that is so hard. The other day I was thinking of all the conflicts one lives in the midst of every day—real conflicts below superficial issues. I want a quiet and peaceful and serene living room—and I have five children with no very good place to play and no desire to starch them in discipline. I want to be pure in heart—but I like to wear my purple dress. I want to live so quietly that the flight of live swans over my head is an occasion for a hymn and yet I want to go out in the world and meet people. One cannot be *half*-monk. But perhaps one can be a monk for half the year—or even just one month out of the year.

I cannot let this get any longer! What a letter. There is still so much to say.

Forgive my not getting an article all out and ready. I think you will understand. We miss you terribly. And I shall think of you.

My love,

A.

Do you disapprove of this day wasted writing to you?!

[Winter 1948]
Dear C.,

Just a scratch—I realize sitting down to my desk it has been weeks since I have written or tried to write you, but I was still hoping you might turn up for Christmas.

---

*A housekeeper for the Lindberghs.

Christmas, despite Scott in bed, was quite nice—quiet and peaceful. Anne was an Angel (*The* Angel) in the school play, with long golden hair and folded arms on a white nightgown, and pink and gold wings—and a clear voice that announced, "Fear not for behold I bring you good tidings of great joy." Jon and I dug out the garage and Jon got the Mercury out, with chains. (Jon is a *very good* snow-driver, slow and steady—drives like you—never loses his head.)

We had our little Christmas Eve service: candles and singing and Bible verses. Reeve sang "Silent Night," and the crèche looked magical as ever. Reeve stops by it each night and says, "Look at the baby Jesus!"

Jon has been a real help to me—what a steady boy he is. He is out at a dance tonight in Fairfield looking very handsome in his dark blue suit.

Slightly bogged-down letter, but these everybody-sick times always seem longer and thicker than they are. But we are coming out of it now and it wasn't really very long. But how long you've been away!

The sun is shining free of charge—everyone feels better this morning. Scott's temperature is normal!

Jon made me a bird-feeding station for Christmas—very nice—and an aquarium for Land, with (O Heavenly Day!) guppies in it. Mother guppy had eleven babies Christmas Night and then leapt out of the aquarium ("I understand it perfectly!" I told Land and Jon from my position prone on the hearth rug that night).

A *very* nice letter from Gault McGowan (head of *N.Y. Sun* in Germany) to whom we sent your book. I *knew* he was unusual. I shall hope you don't get this letter and I will see you first!

*Captiva, Florida,**
March 1st [1948] [DIARY]

. . . I have had Sinus almost steadily for two months. Not enough to go to bed—but never able to shake it & at times to a dizzying degree. At best—dulling me slightly all the time. I fall into bed at 8:30 unable to write a letter—or even read. Why? It is ridiculous. I must find out what it is—why am I so apathetic & exhausted all the time. Is it a deep physical depletion after last winter—the pregnancy—the emotional turmoil, the miscarriage—the major operation—the children's illnesses during convalescence—& then last summer's challenge—certainly not

---

*An island off Florida's southwest coast, where the Lindberghs vacationed.

a rest—& the pressure of the fall & early winter writing? Is it some-thing wrong with the technical set-up of our life in the East? The sense that one is going against the grain all the time—trying to lead a simple life near N.Y.? Is it the sense of the distractions of N.Y.? (But I have done so little this year I haven't felt up to it.) Is it the imperfections of household life—the small daily drains on energy? I have discovered certain things. The less people there are in the house the less tired I am. (Not the work—the people tire me.) My children tire me—all together—vying for my attention. (One at a time, not at all.) When C. is home, I am more tired. (But when we are off together alone—it is restful.)

How complicated it is. The Father & the Mother, the Husband & Wife—do not meet as individuals—separate—single—simple. It is like some sort of equation: A does not meet C. It is A + children + world + background + career + ambitions + children + friends meeting C + back-ground + business + plans + children—etc.—A^6. A to the sixth power meeting C to the sixth power—which is not at all the same thing as a simple A × C. Every couple should get away from each other alone & should get away alone *together* part of each year. The first is necessary for the finding & strengthening of the individual, which tends to merge into the dual relationship (esp. if a woman). The second is necessary to keep the relationship a living one. Get back to the essential—pure—basic A × C. Men—just normally—because of business—tend in their lives to get more of the going away alone—so they don't feel the need for this for themselves—or recognize the need for it for women. Women, on the other hand, get so absorbed in the $A^6 × C^6$ relationship that they forget there ever was an A × C relationship. They neglect this & don't even feel the need for it (they have it with a child)—or for renewing it. The search for the pure relationship is what tempts people into love affairs. That is the easy way to get it. But we shouldn't have to go there to get it. Every relationship should be pure. We should work consciously at keeping it pure.

Have I really too little strength for my program? Have I too many children?! *That* is not the answer. But what is it? Extreme simplification of life? And a hardening of the heart against the distracting & draining contacts & activities? No—all these are helpful but peripheral. They are helpful techniques—they are roads to grace—like the rules for a monas-tery. The answer is inside—it is *always* inside. The outside can only *help* you to find the inside answer.

I suppose that is why I am here. Here in a cottage as shabby & bare as a deserted seashell—swept with wind & sand & the sound of the casuarina trees & the waves on the beach. Here with Evie,* so gentle, so sensitive, so aware—so good we can be honest—really honest with each other—and with ourselves. I feel the skins peeling off from me.

Captiva
Friday, March 5th, 1948 [DIARY]

Florida is *not* the place to work. I should have remembered that from other times. It *is* the place to relax—rest. Sleep—sun. Get nervously ironed out. It is the place for the body to soak up strength—not for the mind to give forth energy. It is completely unstimulating—even debilitating. Too warm—too soft—too damp—for any real mental discipline—or sharp flights of spirit. But it is rather a good place—speaking of the mind, now—to dream—to ruminate—to let the mind also relax—play—turn over in gentle careless rolls—like these lazy waves on the flat beach. Who knows what these great easy unconscious rollers may turn up on the white sand of the conscious mind—a "Rose Murex" or a "Lion's Paw." But it must not be sought for—or—heaven forbid!—dug for. No—no dredging of the sea-bottom here. That would be *trop voulu*†—& defeat one's purpose. No, one should lie bare, open, flat as an empty white beach—waiting—without greed & without anxiety—for a gift from the sea.

Perhaps one should always do this? No—there are times for dredging the sea-bottom & times for waiting with the patience & choicelessness of a beach. "My times I do not know." I am always dredging when I should be waiting & waiting when I should be dredging. If one fights against the currents in oneself—one gets very exhausted—besides not getting where one wants to. On the boat coming back from Europe—for instance—that was definitely a time for waiting—for relaxing after the efforts of the summer—the terrific impacts & stimuli. I should have given in to the damp deck chair atmosphere of an ocean liner. I should have let the rollers of the subconscious wash over me. Something would have emerged after those ten days of rest—besides greater physical recuperation & strength for the problems at home.

---

*Evelyn (Evie) Ames, wife of Amyas Ames, author, poet, conservationist, and close friend from New York City.
†Too intentional.

But I did not have the wisdom or the courage. I was afraid of being caught by a deadline—of failing in my mission—my first professional mission. It was my cautious penurious Puritan soul that bound me to a card table in my cabin, with all my notes around me. Dredging the bottom of the sea, I was—a fruitless & exhausting effort.

And so I miss the fertilization that might come from a contact. And for me—yes, I think I might as well admit it—fertilization does come a great deal from contacts. Why then do I avoid them—in a sort of false pride—shyness—timorous modesty? I used to be afraid of falling in love with people—or having them *think* I was—that I was chasing them (how ridiculous—I am actually always running away!) but now surely—I should be mature enough to be over that. I am no longer afraid of falling in love, and the other false modesties should vanish. I cannot bear to think *"Par delicatesse j'ai perdu ma vie."** Anyway, here, at least, let me not try to dredge—it is the place & time to relax—to be as choiceless as a beach. That too can be an act of faith. That is what is wrong with dredging the bottom—it is not only greedy—it shows a fundamental lack of faith.

Dear God—how little faith I seem to have—sometimes, it seems to me it all comes down to that.

Thursday, March 11th, 1948 [DIARY]

I have had one full day & two nights alone. There is a special quality to being alone—that is precious beyond words to me. It is curious that though I dreaded Evie's going (and I always dread people leaving me—as if I were being drained of my life's blood—as if an amputation were taking place—a limb torn off—I should be unable to get on without it) nevertheless this day without her has been very rich. Very vivid. Extraordinarily so. It is as if one did actually lose an arm—when someone leaves—and then like the starfish one grows a new one. One is whole again—one is complete—round—full—more complete—fuller than before (when the person one loved had a piece of one).

I lay under the stars—alone. I made my breakfast—alone. Alone I watched the gulls at the end of the pier dip & wheel & soar & dive for the broken bread I threw them. A morning's work. And then a late lunch—alone—on the beach. And it seemed to me that, no longer united to my own species, I was nearer to others in their aloneness. The

*Because of discretion I have lost my life.

sky willet, nesting in the ragged tide wash in front of me. The sandpiper, running in little unfrightened steps down the shining beach rim ahead of my footsteps. The slowly flapping pelicans over my head, drifting downwind. The old gull, hunched up, grouchy, surveying the sea. Even the twisted gray arms of driftwood filled me with a kind of ecstasy.

I walked way down the beach drugged by the rhythm of the waves—the sun on my bare back & legs. The wind & mist from the spray in my hair—until I felt really quite drunk with it. I went into the waves with nothing on & then came home—drenched—drugged—reeling—full to the brim with my day alone.

Curiously whole for my aloneness, I feel like the full moon—before the night has taken a single nibble of it—ripe with a mysterious poem—fecund—full. The springs of creativity are filling up in me (was it just physical, then, their depletion? And depletion by people. I am depleted by all the people around me).

Filling up to the brim—May no one come—not even C.—or I might spill it all away!

Is it this then that happens to women—especially feminine ones? Physically, they are so made that they want to spill it all away. And all their natural ties as a woman demand that they spill it (the nourishing instinct—the eternal feeding woman does & must do). Her energy—her fertility seeps away into these channels if there is any chance—any leak—at least, if the artist & the woman are equally balanced. If the artist is stronger—as in Georgia O'Keeffe—then there are no children—there is no marriage—or a poor one. With me—damn it—the woman always wins! And yet not without terrible conflict—which is exhausting in itself. I work against myself all the time. I try to give as a woman over & over again. I want to. I prefer to. It is the primitive urge. Besides, it satisfies my conscience—my Puritan morality: what you do for another is good—unselfish—what you do for yourself is evil—selfish, wrong. The ethical, as well as the physical, pull against the aesthetic creative force in me. What hope then for the aesthetic in such an uneven tug-of-war? Perhaps very little—but at least it helps to know it—to see how difficult it is. Someone must tie me to a mast & stop up my ears to the siren voices of my own instincts (perhaps this is what poor C. has to do). Or like that poor girl in the fairy tale, to produce I must be locked into a room full of straw—with the command—under pain of death—to turn it into gold.

But not, I think in Florida. Not even at Captiva—liberating a place as it is. (Perhaps earlier in the winter—less hot & humid.) It is a curious island—not a bit like the rest of Florida. I feel it has a spell on it—& not even the tea-room atmosphere of the Tween Waters dining room (nasturtiums in the orange pottery on each table, fruit salads made of a single limp canned pear with whipped cream & a marshmallow on top!) can compete with it. It even has some influence on those middle-aged respectable marrieds in print dresses & bald heads who sit in front of the orange pottery & the marshmallow pears. It is curiously—almost humorously, possibly even dangerously—uninhibiting. One drops—as I felt the first week—the world—one's own cares—vanities—guilts, etc. One drops one's clothes—one's habits. One sinks into natural rhythms. One is even *forced* into them—willy-nilly. The pounding of the sea—the wind through the casuarina trees—the slow flapping of pelicans. One must—one cannot resist—giving in to it. One drops the clothes—chains—habits of civilization & one discovers one's own physical rhythms. They are in fact awakened in one. The body—so dead in the modern city—here wakes. Is first taken back into primeval rest—unconsciousness—drowsiness & then awakened—to all kinds of new tactile delights that it forgets & almost forbids the thought of—in civilization—wind on the body—firm sand under the feet—sun on skin. The springs of physical energy are filled up—as in me. It could, I suppose, be sinister & dangerous to live so completely sensuously. But one feels at Captiva a kind of purity about it. One sinks into childhood—not into sex. One can hardly think of anything *im*pure happening at Captiva. It would be washed clean as a shell—clean as a piece of driftwood—and left on the beach.

This is what happens to one—one becomes bare—empty—open as a shell—echoing the sea. The shell is certainly the symbol for Captiva. One lives in a cottage—bare, empty—deserted as a shell. One becomes like a shell—filled with salt & sand & sun & the rhythm of the sea. The only form of materialism here—the wealth—so to speak—is counted in seashells—a childlike wealth after all. One becomes childlike—one plays at house—plays at collecting treasures. And one becomes—almost against one's will—a child. Even the pompous bishop in his brown shorts—striding down the beach. He cannot quite maintain his worldly pose—not in those shorts—not with sand between his toes! Even if he does hold his head in the air, talk in sepulchral tones & use a piece of driftwood as a walking stick.

And all this childlikeness enters into people's manners, too. They are open—frank—smiling. Strangers smile at you on the beach &

come up & offer you a shell—for no reason—lightly—like a child & then go on by & leave you alone again—free. Nothing is demanded of you in payment—no social rite—no tie established. It was a gift—freely taken—freely given—in mutual trust—like a child's. People smile at you like that—like a child—sure that you will not rebuff them—sure that you will smile back. And you do—because you know that it will involve nothing. The smile, the act, the relationship in the immediacy of the present free of past & future—is living in space, balanced there on a shaft of air—like a seagull.

It is this, I suppose—the living in the present—that gives it its quality of extreme vividness & extreme purity—living like a child—or a saint—in the immediacy of time and space. Every day—every act—is an island, washed by time and space, and has an island's self-containment—wholeness—serenity. And one becomes oneself like an island—self-contained—whole—mysterious & fecund. "No man is an island," said John Donne. I feel we are all islands in a common sea.

But is there not a terrible lack of responsibility in living in the present? Should we not think of the past—of the future—of the lessons of the past? Of the consequences of the future?

I suppose the saint's answer is that if you live purely enough ("those in the gale of the Holy Spirit") one need not think of—nor fear—the consequences of one's acts. The fruit will be good because the tree is good.

But for us who are not saints—what is the answer? What the Guru said to Jali? "To live in the present one must be very simple—or very saintly—and you are neither!"

But for short periods it is permitted—even vital.

May 21st, 1948 [DIARY, ON PLANE TO PHILADELPHIA FROM CHICAGO]
. . . Perhaps it is not strange that I have not written more. And yet this is the normal condition of my life. It must be adapted to. I must find the time in this life—or never find it. I must cut to the bone the unnecessary things, the vanities, the wastes of time. It is not that I waste more time than other women—but that I can *less afford to waste.* I pay so heavily for my mistakes—not only in time but in energy—emotional waste—in frustration—in conflicts. There is so little leeway—I must budget time—space (being alone) & energy. And that isn't all either. One must replenish the spring.

I came to Chicago with C. partly just to get away from the crowd at home & partly—more—just to go off alone with him. I used to do it so much & now almost never do. I wanted to see him in his new setting—his new associates—I wanted to be a little a part of that life.* He has wanted me to come. ("The journey is always toward the other soul—never away from it.")† I came also for myself—to see (in terms of writing) the men who are important in the world today—the scientists—Fermi—Urey—dear Bartley.‡ (This, too, was C.'s idea.) This too has been rewarding. But the most rewarding thing of all was in the A × C relationship. A kind of proving & implementing of what I thought out at Captiva. The conscious attempt to recapture the pure relationship—the pure A × C that gets so obscured & encumbered in daily life. And it was marvelously rewarding. It was worth it for the breakfasts alone. Having breakfast together alone—how wonderful it was—I had forgotten. The slight formality of it—the sitting across the table—across the muffins & marmalade & coffee cups—the honeymoon strangeness of it (who is that good-looking man sitting across the table from me—my husband!). How my table has grown & how difficult to get the pure relationship through children—secretary—nurse—cook & man. Pressure of getting off to school—to work. Just the pressure of daily life & its duties. Here we are clear of all that—alone. Together—yes, it was right to come. . . .

Now—before I forget—bits from Chicago: Meeting the scientists. On the whole how ordinary these people are when they come out of the tunnel of their specialty! What children they seem in the field of living & feeling & being aware. How impractical, too, some of them. Like artists— but inarticulate ones. Like musicians, childlike—simple—wrapped in the cocoon of their own world. And since I only see them from the outside—when they come blinking out of their tunnel I cannot imagine what they are really like. Yes I can *just* imagine—because I can remember that feeling myself—when I have been drunk, drenched in something I was writing. Then coming out into the sunshine & activity of ordinary

---

*In 1946, in the aftermath of the bombing of Hiroshima and Nagasaki, Charles Lindbergh was asked to serve as a consultant to a secret committee called CHORE (Chicago Ordnance Research), which was based at the University of Chicago and included Enrico Fermi and other preeminent scientists. Its purpose was to assess the morality and practicality of using nuclear and other advanced weaponry in the future. Lindbergh gathered information, tested equipment, and spent a great deal of time analyzing it for several years thereafter, "often bringing the most humanistic perspective into the room" (A. Scott Berg, *Lindbergh* [New York: Putnam, 1998]).
†D. H. Lawrence.
‡Enrico Fermi, Harold C. Urey, Charles E. Bartley.

life—dazzled—dizzy—blinking—like a mole. I remember Yeats: "I was still under the influence of my three months' concentration on my work & was like those people in a religious meditation who if you lay a finger on an arm show a bruise where you touched them."

Fermi—who has perhaps the most to do with the Atomic Bomb development—is the most interesting & appealing to me.

This quiet little unassuming man—with kind, observant eyes—not wise exactly but *observant*—& a kind of humility—like a monk—gentle & quiet & unassuming. Is humility an attribute of all greatness? (Huxley's "Stand before fact as a little child.") I should like to think so.

Is the scientist—the true scientist—akin to the artist & the saint? In his humility before something greater than himself—in his looking on himself as a tool—a vessel—a road? In his childlikeness—in his simplicity? I had not thought so before, but Fermi makes me think of it. Perhaps—I must explore the idea.

Scott's Cove, Darien, Conn.
July 8th, 1948
Dear Jon,

How are you?! We have gotten some nice weather. Fine over the Fourth. (The first weekend it didn't rain for five weeks!) We all went swimming. Anne, like a fish, Scott, hunting and playing, and Reeve on your father's back: "Go Boat! Stop Boat!" We are still eating your fish and have had some delicious clam chowders. There are still too many horseshoe crabs on our beach.

Your father's book* is coming out (condensed) in the September *Reader's Digest*.

A word to the wise, Jon, send a postcard now and then! Your father is looking for one. I think I prefer the camp where they don't feed you Sunday dinner until you write your parent. (I think Land gave this one away!) Anyway, your director wrote us, so we know you arrived. Not a letter—just send a postcard now and then.†

Breakfast
"What kind of eggs, Scott?"
"Scrambled egg."

---

*Of Flight and Life, which was published in hardcover in August 1948 by Scribner.
†Here AML draws a smiley face.

Anne: "I want a poached egg."
Reeve: "I want a chicken egg."

Your corn is coming up, believe it or not, and the children's lettuce—smothered in weeds.

Scott's Cove
July 29th, 1948
Dear Mrs. Goodkind,

My husband and I have just come back from a trip away to find Mr. Wilson's letter on the desk telling us of the tragedy which struck your son at the camp he shared this summer with our son, Land.* Since the news came we have been unable to think of anything else, unable to accept such a thing happening, unable not to think of you and share with you the shock of that tragedy.

I feel I must write you, though I know that letters cannot help one to accept an arbitrary, unbelievable, unwarned accident. Nothing helps perhaps but another time-sense, another spiritual point of vision, which those in the midst of sorrow seem to have better than those of us on the outside.

I remember someone writing me—with our loss—sudden, unpredictable, unbelievable also—a little verse which gave me some of this vision.†

> *It is not growing like a tree.*
> *In bulk, doth make man better be;*
> *Or standing long an oak, three hundred year,*
> *To fall a log at last, dry, bald and sere:*
> *A lily of a day*
> *Is fairer far in May.*
> *Although it fall and die that night—*
> *It was the plant and flower of light.*
> *In small proportions we just beauties see,*
> *And in short measures life may perfect be.*‡

*Kenny Goodkind, a cabin mate of Land's at the Teton Valley Ranch in Wyoming, was killed when struck by lightning.
†Referring to the kidnapping and murder of the Lindberghs' first child, Charles A. Lindbergh Jr., in March 1932.
‡From "Ode to the Immortal Memory and Friendship of That Noble Pair, Sir Lucius Cary and Sir H. Morison," attributed to Ben Jonson (1572–1637).

I write from my heart. We could not help but let you know how our thoughts and our sympathy are with you.

*Point House**
Labor Day, September 6th, 1948 [DIARY]

Then followed a month of quiet work in this house. A month of learning a new technique of work—trying out a new system. Getting my business (household, head of family) done before ten. Then coming over here & working through lunch in solitude—a picnic lunch—rest & an hour or two of work in the p.m. Back about four or five—for tea etc. with the children. It worked really *very* well and technically was great gain. The work accomplished was perhaps not equal to the technical gain—I started out trying to pull my "of women's lives" bits into shape for an article suggested by *Harper's Bazaar*—realized I couldn't do it that way. Wrote Mary Louise Aswell[†] (in despair) that I couldn't but she would come out & discuss it with me sometime. And then—in the relief of having given up—got an idea—a form for my material—started writing v. intoxicated—wrote for three weeks. The material now growing to three times its planned length & not finished yet. And had it not outgrown its form? At this point I had to start recalculating—Land's imminent homecoming—the end of summer—& my own weariness made me face the fact that I had not finished the task I had set myself to do—the summer, with its wonderful quiet ease & freedom for me (two boys & C. away) was over. In the winter I should never be able to get such an opportunity again. If I couldn't do it now—I should *never* be able to. This was the *best* my life offered—I must face it & adjust to it. To come to the end of summer—exactly as I had come to the end of the winter—with only improvements in *techniques*—with only more experimentations in *form*—with nothing concrete to show—I felt very low about it.

Point House
October 6th, 1948 [DIARY]

Three weeks passed—one week of hard & good work on "The Shells."[‡] (It looked *good* to me—when I got to it again after my vacation!

---

*A small structure built on the point of Contentment Island, across the cove from the Lindbergh home in Darien, where AML went to write.
†An editor at *Harper's Bazaar*.
‡For many years the working title for what became *Gift from the Sea*.

What is more, once it was copied & Charles saw it—he was surprised & *delighted* with it. Thinks it is *very* good! A justification of my summer's work! Such a relief.)

Moving Scott in with Land (two boys together) giving Jon a room of his own. Giving Anne a room of her own (those two need solitude). Reeve into the nursery. A new school for Reeve—etc. etc. All this takes time & is necessary and rewarding for a mother—it is creative in relationships—but takes energy.

C. has been home for about six weeks (during a change of command in Washington). He is very happy about the success of his book—letters piling in—moving in their sincerity. . . . I feel at last that C. has given of his real self—& what people have guessed (sometimes) was there—they now *know* is there. He has opened himself in a way that he never has before to anyone except me—& perhaps a few others. It is a great triumph, too, to win in the world of intellectuals as well as in the world of popular appeal—which he has always had. No one has doubted his sincerity or failed to be moved by it—and all have been startled by the depth of what he had to say & the power & skill with which he said it.

If he should now die—he would at least have given to the world some of that unexpressed & most important side of him. I have always wanted him to do so—always worked with him for such an end—always prayed it would happen. And yet now that it has—I find myself in a curiously anticlimax state of feeling. (Of course, one feels thus after a book of one's own is published—a "well—that's that—*now what?*" feeling.) I cannot analyze it away. Is it a kind of envy of his entering my field & with such colossal success & at a moment when I am not very creative? And yet I am so pleased when perceptive people speak or write of it. Perhaps it is only that my shock of surprise—satisfaction at his writing of it—lies months—years, even—back. After all he has been writing it for years—parts of it. And so I cannot be newly excited about it. I had my surprise & pleasure back there.

Or perhaps it is only part of this cocoon period in me—when new things are growing in me—& I am somehow shut off from my old feelings, my old forms, my old relationships & I cannot *feel* as I should. A queer uncomfortable period—I feel locked out of the rooms I used to frequent—not by anyone else—by something of my own doing. I have lost the key. . . .

Darien, Conn.
October 27th, 1948
Dear Mrs. Goodkind,

I meant to write you after your first letter. I was so moved by it that I could not read it without tears—not only by the sorrow but by your courage and awareness and openness.

As for myself, I feel there is so little I can tell you that would be helpful. My first grief I feel I survived only through nature, through the fact that nature numbed me. I was carrying another child and I survived for that child. The self-protective instinct of nature pulled me through: a numb, blind, unconscious way through. (Perhaps the psychiatrists would say I never faced it and it is still there to be accepted. I do believe that there are times in one's life when one must accept—swallow whole, as it were—the "locked boxes" in one's life, unopened, unsolved. This is the hardest thing of all, I think—that undigested lump in one's heart.)

The second sorrow—a very close sister*—was in a way more difficult, and I wrestled, like you, with the problem of immortality. For myself it did not matter, as you say, but for *her* it was unbearable. As near as I could come to a solution was a strong instinctive belief in the immortality of the spirit and that growth of the spirit is the point of all life. But I feel unable to be convinced in the pilgrim's progress beautiful literal faith of joining one's fellows in the same identical form across the river. I finally accepted the "locked box" of not understanding in what form the spirit would survive—even if it were only in the great stream of compassion that feeds the world. (Though I tend to feel it is more individual than this—the individual candles swallowed in the great light and yet not extinguished by it.)

The third grief† brought only an intensification of this belief in spirit, and somehow an added feeling of the omnipresence of it here, now, everywhere. As if, in a way, people who have lost those close to them

*Elisabeth Reeve Morrow Morgan (1904–1934), AML's elder sister, was an educator and founder of the school now known as the Elisabeth Morrow School in Englewood, New Jersey. She died of complications following surgery.
†Family members believe AML is referring to the death of Antoine de Saint-Exupéry, the French pilot and author of *The Little Prince* (he wrote the preface to the French edition of her second book, *Listen! the Wind*). A brief but intense friendship grew between them after their first meeting in 1939. She learned in 1944 that Saint-Exupéry's P-38 had gone down in a reconnaissance mission over southern France and wrote in her diary that her grief was "this way with the baby and with Elisabeth. . . . I felt incredibly alone" (from *War Within and Without*, pp. 446–447).

have stepped across an invisible boundary line into the realm of spirit, are already in the real world of spiritual values which co-exists with the other period. I feel quite strongly this sense of interpenetration.

I gradually grew to feel this about my sister. It is a terrific responsibility too, to let them shine through you!

What I feel most like saying is *Do not try too hard.* You have done such a heroic job as it is, a superhuman one to fit a superhuman tragedy. You have met it with a vision that is superhuman too, at times. But we are human, too. And vision does not last, it only comes fitfully in lightning flashes to show us the way. Do not be ashamed or afraid of the dark patches of night in between the flashes. You cannot have the vision all the time. You would have to be dead to have that. And believe in the moments of illumination—they are the true ones. The black hours are when your very human, and overburdened with blows, body seeks the earth. It is natural and I think perhaps one should give in to it if one can. I once heard a very wise man say: "Live the four seasons every day of your life: plow, and sow, and reap—yes—and winter too. Every day one must die. One must die part of every day."

I think I, and perhaps you, tried to sow and reap every hour of the day.

Do not try to be too brave. For us of Puritan background it is hard to do otherwise. I *know* it was for my mother,* who bore in quick succession the death of husband, grandson, and daughter. As we went through the last together, each trying to be brave in front of the other—it seems to me now that this being brave in front of each other was a false Puritan reticence and perhaps even pride. The times when we really helped each other were when we broke down and cried together. I know it was a help to me to admit, and see admitted, my mother's grief. I could lay down for a moment the burden of being courageous. (Though I do not think it was weakness to do that, but humility.)

Do not ask too much of yourself too quickly. I wish there were some kind of earth-person there, on whose shoulder you could cry. But so often there is not.

Who takes you up and bears you on his breast is your own courage—and it may come late.

Please forgive me if I have said the wrong things. I feel really you have your vision already, only you are not strong enough to believe it day and night.

---

*Elizabeth Cutter Morrow (1873–1955).

[NOVEMBER 16, 1948, DIARY]

At last I have got the Moon Shell copied . . . repetitious, contradictory, unbeautiful, unwhole . . . just a first draft—is it too much for me?

Scott's Cove, Darien
Monday after New Year, 1949
Dear C.,

Another letter from you today! From Guam—written on Christmas Day. I wonder if you are in Europe by now. I have seen nothing in the papers. I read your letter to the boys tonight. Jon's eye glinted at the aerial gunnery accomplishments. I also gave Jon your letter from Japan to read, a very good one on our (U.S.A.) insulation from the worlds we speed over and conquer. You are right: it is *insulation* not isolation. I sent this letter to your mother, though I know you write her too. The children have sent pictures and I send their things (a theme of Jon's, a picture of Anne).

New Year's Day we all were together and alone as a family and we played a game and all guessed where you were. Anne said China (I think), Jon said Japan, Land, India, Reeve, "Elastic!" (Alaska). I said, "In the air!" And the children all said that wasn't fair, so then I guessed *Germany*. Scott refused to guess!

New Year's Day we *all* went out for the first time in days. It was clear and bright after four days steady rain (causing floods all through New England, after the heavy snow), ending with sleet and snow New Year's Eve. The world looked quite beautiful again and we looked for animal tracks in the snow. Then we came in, had lunch, naps, and then I put on *Swan Lake* and a Mexican skirt and we all danced wildly and gaily!*

I went out New Year's Eve for "music" after supper. Very nice, respectable party with Bach on the organ until twelve, when we all joined hands and the lights went off. "And everyone kissed everyone else," as I told the children the next day. Jon was amused, Anne and Scott wide-eyed. But Land was frankly startled and shocked.

"What! Did anyone kiss *you*?"

"Yes—two people!"

"What—someone you didn't even *know*? Hasn't a woman *any* protection? I wouldn't like *my* wife . . . I bet you don't tell Father!"

"Yes, I will, Land. I'll write him and he won't mind (very much)! You see, I didn't kiss anyone myself. I didn't want to; I just *got* kissed. And your father knows I'd rather have *him* kiss me than anyone else in the world!"

*Here AML draws a smiley face.

This silenced them all for a moment. It seemed solemn and impressive and they were quite pleased. Even Land seemed appeased. But Ansy* objected. "You'd rather have *him* kiss you than *me*—or *Reeve*??" What a conversation!!!!

It is 10:30 and I must go to bed. I'll add a line in the morning before I go to the Point House—for the day! Come home soon!

Eastern Airlines—D.C. 4—Jacksonville—Richmond
Saturday Eve., April 23rd, 1949
Dearest C.,

I have been thinking about you all day, sitting on the bus and watching the coast flick by: markers and harbors, bridges. I saw with *Aldebaran* eyes:† boat-conscious, sea-conscious—as I used to be plane-conscious, air-conscious. Following you with my thoughts all day—now they are pulling out of the dock—now C. is stacking up the icebox—now perhaps they are swimming—now . . . with a pang of longing to be there . . . putt-putting back to the big boat in the sunset. (My sunset was very beautiful on the deltas north of Jacksonville—wide ribbons of river like ribbons of smoke curling off in the distance.) And now, how homesick I feel for it! (They are sitting around that table in the hot smoky cabin: Jon, taciturn and contented; Land, sleepy and contented; Jim, gay; and you—what are you doing? Wondering if I made the plane, if I got a coat, shoes—if I was recognized, etc.)

Flying always makes me think of you and our life together. What worlds you have opened up to me: the world of the air, the world of practical life, even the underwater world! And I am always timid about new worlds. I must learn to go into new worlds on my own. And you must forgive my awkwardness in your worlds.

I have thought, too, of you and me down on Pelican Beach—turning over lazily and covering up for planes, me, even if they were miles high, and your saying: "Think of that world up there. People in city clothes, stewards and stewardesses passing trays" (all cooped up in civilization!). And here I am cooped up in one of those worlds!

I am so happy I had that week on the boat with the boys. You were right. It was a very special experience. Laughter waters the ground like tears.

We are approaching Washington. I have written on and off all

---

*Nickname for AML's daughter Anne.
†The name of the boat on which the Lindberghs had been exploring the Florida coastline, named for one of the brightest stars in the night sky, part of the constellation Taurus.

evening. It is a beautiful night. The great circle of Capella-Castor-Pollux-Procyon-Sirius—has kept pace with me outside my porthole.

Someone *did* recognize me at the Miami terminal. A rather fat lady in trousers kept smiling at me and finally came up and said: "Has anyone ever told you, you look like Mrs. Lindbergh?"

"Really? I thought (shrinking) she was a great big woman!"

"No, just your size. Not your coloring though; she's darker than you, dark eyes, complexion. You know who I mean, don't you? Anne Morrow, who married Lindbergh?"

"I know (attempt at levity!). I guess I must have a very ordinary face. People are always saying I remind them of somebody!"

"Well—I guess we all come from the same family tree—ha-ha."

(Danger past!)

Crowds of people on at Washington. Tempo up, everyone smoking. Someone next to me has *just* caught the plane, etc. Sense of tension.

I feel our month is very precious now. The newspapers seem to me rather ominous: tide of Communist armies sweep over Yangtze, British sloop trapped, fired on, etc. And people saying we are headed toward war with Russia. Is it just that I haven't seen any news for a month, or are things really tenser? I feel they are, yet there are signs that Russia is making feelers to break the blockade in Germany.

Over Baltimore—I can't write any more. Will mail this in N.Y. It has been an easy trip, but how far away I feel.

Tomorrow will be a peaceful day with the children. I will call your mother in the evening and get to bed early. I shall be thinking of you coming north in the trailer. I wish I could have had that too, but I have had much.

xo,
A.

12:15 a.m. La Guardia—intact with raincoat and bulging string bag—still holding. Daylight Saving starts tomorrow a.m. "The Sun rises in the East"!

[1949]

For Better or for Worse

On the occasion of my twentieth wedding anniversary* I read over my marriage vows. They are still beautiful and simple and moving. After

*AML and CAL were married on May 27, 1929.

twenty years of marriage I would probably say them over again in exactly the same words today. And yet a strange aroma arises from those familiar phrases, like the pinched scent of dead rose leaves. What false and fairy-tale notions I, and almost everyone of my generation, had of marriage. How much we expected of it, and how little we knew of its real riches. We looked for roses where there were thorns and thorns where there were roses, and we could not see that the measure of marriage was neither in the thorns nor in the roses, but in the growth of the rosebush.

What would I say—what would I promise—if I were starting over again today? If I, a middle-aged ghost, could project myself back in time and stand behind myself at age twenty at the altar? If I could whisper over the shoulder of my younger self, how would I annotate my marriage vows? Or, looking into the future, what can I put down for my three sons and my two daughters when they come to marry? (And I hope they all do.) What can I tell them of marriage? What kind of a pledge can I expect them to make?

Marriage, we are told, is a relationship in the process of change. Is it marriage that has changed, or is it we ourselves who have become more honest in looking at the relationship, at ourselves, and at one another? The good marriages of the past—and those of the future—will, I believe, follow certain basic if not too rigid rules of human relationships, however much their participants may differ in the way they express themselves on these rules. Certainly I would express myself very differently today than I did twenty years ago. *How then?* cry my husband and my five children, challenging me. I start to write.

Marriage Vows Annotated After Twenty Years

I, a most imperfect person, take you, also imperfect, to be my husband, in that most imperfect but also most challenging and rewarding of all relationships—marriage.

Since I know you are not perfect, I do not worship you. I have learned that worship of another human being is only a form of shirking one's responsibility, a shifting of the burden to another's shoulders. (*I* cannot accomplish this difficult task but *you*, O Superior Being, can do all!) Worship, I believe, is a burden too great for the human frame to bear and in the end is degrading to both the worshipper and the worshipped. On this earth one is permitted only to worship God.

I do not promise to obey you. Not that I do not long, with all of a woman's traditional desire to submit, to serve you hand and foot. But I know that this very natural desire to find myself a master is actually a selfish one and will not really serve you. I would not debase you by assuming that you want a slave.

I do not promise to love you. Of course, I *do* love you, deeply, sincerely, humbly. But to promise to feel exactly this way always would be like promising never to grow a gray hair. (I have many already.) It would be like the rose promising never to put forth a new bud. I cannot make a promise against time, against growth, against life. It would be perjury. These are my marriage vows, and I will not lie to you.

I do not look on marriage as a solution to any of my problems. On the contrary, I know that marriage will be a mirror for them, and that my imperfections will show up with merciless clarity under that naked light. But I will try not to be ashamed to have you see them. I will try not to hide them but, rather, to work on them in the advantage of that added illumination. In fact, I consider the sharing and working at problems together to be the challenge—perhaps even one of the deepest functions—of marriage: the perpetually unavoidable and, in fact, desirable friction which keeps the marriage and its partners alive and growing.

On the other hand, I do not promise to live up to any idealized image you may have of me. Please do not put me on a pedestal. Being adored is very close to being despised. It is the reverse side of the same coin, and one is apt to follow the other.

Neither will I ask you to live up to an idealized image I may have of you. I do not consider myself wise enough to be your judge or your mentor, to know what path of growth you will take. Nor do I expect to be your only nourishment in that growth, to provide you with everything: sun, rain, soil, and air. I will try to stand back and let your growth take whatever nourishment it needs, wherever it may find it. I trust in your growth.

I do not expect marriage to fill my essential loneliness, nor do I hope to fill yours, having learned that everyone is, in the last analysis, alone, and believing this is not something to grieve about but to rejoice in. Rather, I promise to respect and protect your aloneness, knowing that everything created must have its period of darkness: child and bulb, poem and personality. I promise not to pry into your loneliness, never to tear at the bud with frightened fingers to make sure there is a flower inside. I believe in the flower.

I have faith, too, in the direction of the flower, in the orientation of your growth. I feel this orientation, this basic intent toward life, to be similar to mine. And it is this basic sense of values, this orientation, that we share, that I feel justifies our marriage, our entry into this difficult and imperfect state together, and our bringing into the world children to whom we can give as a heritage—perhaps the only heritage—this common orientation. But I do not expect our common orientation to be carried out in both of our lives in exactly the same way. I would hope it might rather take parallel lines, for I believe that the infinite richness of marriage comes more from the exchange of differences than from complete identification of interests.

To cherish? Yes, I promise to cherish you. For to cherish is to feel compassion. I hope and pray that I may feel this always, not only for you but, because of you and through you as a lens, more and more compassion for all.

I promise then to respect you, to honor you as one of God's representatives on earth. I honor the spark of the divine in you. I will believe in this spark, even when I cannot see it, even when it is obscured, in sickness and in health, in poverty and in riches. I believe in it now and until—and after—Death us do part.

Amen.

Tuesday, November 29th, 1949 [DIARY]

Raining—as usual when I go to town. Take the train, which is restful & write Mrs. L.* on the way in. Long dentist's apptmt. Pick up my glasses. Get money from bank for C. & me. Stop at Guild Bookshop for two angels for Christmas (this is the right part of Christmas). Meet Stewart Preston—art critic of *Times* who had supper with us Sat. eve. (I am still feeling warm from that eve.—& not yet self-critical.) And it is nice to see him—I liked him immediately. Intelligent—charming—with a kind of American directness—an attractive American—sensitive & aware & rather healthy I should judge. Profound? No. To Cos. Club after trying to catch Evie. . . . Back to Margot's† for tea with Rajagopal‡ (Krishnamurti's great friend). He is v. perceptive—honest & practical. We talk England—Germany, etc. He thinks England is much better in morale

---

*AML's mother-in-law, Evangeline Lodge Land Lindbergh (1875–1954).
†Margot Loines Morrow (1912–), a former actress and longtime student of Buddhism, married AML's brother, Dwight Morrow Jr., in 1937.
‡D. Rajagopal, who with his wife, Rosalind Rajagopal, was a close associate of Jiddu Krishnamurti, through the Theosophical Society.

than two years ago. C. comes in at end & they talk briefly & rather well & I am pleased—since both are basically shy. Then C. & I walk to the Plaza to dine with the Frank Lloyd Wrights. They are alone—up in their room. And she is pouring out drinks. There is no sherry—which I prefer. So rather than ask for what they haven't got, I ask for a "very weak old-fashioned." It is so weak that it gives me no lift at all but only irritates C. who disapproves of "hard liquor." Mrs. W. takes me into the bedroom & talks to me about her early life with Gurdyev.* "I had beauty—brains—talent—youth—I gave him all—all!" I am completely bewitched listening to her & watching her gestures. "For I was a *vairry* beautiful woman. *Ayvairy*one wanted me—ayvairyone!" Then she went through the most realistic gestures of plucking these leech-like admirers off her knees & legs & hurling them from her! "For I wanted *more!*" Then she also described how G. felt that people were all machines running hither & thither (her beautiful fingers scurrying over the table like mice to illustrate), slaves to their habits, emotions, passions, etc. And how one must train the will to fight against these slave-driving emotions "to pull against ten thousand bulls—it would be easy (Mrs. W. is now standing up, one foot braced in front of her, pulling back hard—the reins in her hands) compared to fighting against one's emotions," etc., etc. We talk about grief too (here she is realest I feel) & how one must "consume one's grief," not forget it—as most people do. I say I think one's grief must ripen in one—like a child—until it becomes flesh & blood. And quote that line of C. Day Lewis: "He bore transplanting into a common ground." And tell her a little of how I felt at E.'s death.

She is still very beautiful, bone-beautiful . . . and dramatically exciting—old as the moon—with some of the moon's magic & some of the moon's sinister quality. I can't help feeling that G. was black magic & that the whole sect is prodigiously arrogant. Anything that exalts man's *will* to that extent seems to me arrogant. It is "super-man" stuff all over again—in an intellectualized & precious field. And then she married a super-man—in Frank Lloyd Wright. He, of course, is not black magic—& despite the Welsh background—seems to me terribly American—energy—genius—showmanship—independence—humor—arrogance—and a kind of "social mysticism."

The evening does not go very well. We sit in an *ornate* plushy Ger-

*George Ivanovitch Gurdyev, or Gurdjieff (1872–1949), philosopher who founded the Institute for the Harmonious Development of Man in 1919. His followers believed that most humans exist in an almost "sleeping" state, but that by adhering to Gurdjieff's principles one could achieve heightened states of being.

man nineteenth century dining room & eat $2.75 apiece chops. I can't really continue on the "ten thousand wild bulls" level of conversation with her—& general conversation breaks down. C. & FLW disagree on "War-as-a-means-of-settling-anything." So I take him on on reconstruction in Germany & it goes better.

Still it is an uncomfortable evening. C. is disturbed & I don't know why until I can talk to him walking back to the car & get things straightened out. I am too tired at night & sleep badly.

[DECEMBER 12TH, 1949, DIARY]

C. says he thinks marriage is "the most perfect relationship on earth." I think the relationship of mother & child is the most perfect.

On train, Washington to New York
Sunday evening, December 18th, 1949
Dear Farmor,*

Charles and I are on the train coming back from Washington. Last night C. received the Orville and Wilbur Wright Award at a big dinner at the Statler Hotel. It was packed with people—very dignified and moving evening. It was a big occasion with all the trappings—many uncomfortable ones like Movietones† and glaring lights, however it was all handled with the dignity of the occasion.

I don't suppose C. felt very happy up there making his speech and facing the lights and the cameras, but he spoke well—the best of the evening—a serious and impressive speech, and got tremendous applause. The citation read of his long record of service to aviation and his country, was very impressive and covered completely his war record and pre-war record. For me it was a most dignified and overwhelming testament to his life of contribution. A kind of justification and righting of the record for all to see.

The children are well and very busy over Christmas. Scott has made me a table I have stumbled over a hundred times (he keeps hiding it in different places!). I missed Reeve as an angel in her Christmas play. This is a rather tired train-note, but I wanted you to know what a real triumph it was last night.

*Swedish for "father's mother," this was the Lindbergh children's nickname for CAL's mother.
†Newsreels produced by Fox Movietone News between 1928 and 1963. The filming of CAL's takeoff from Roosevelt Field in 1927 was the initial motivation for the establishment of the company.

Captiva
March 13th [1950]
Dear Jon,

Evie Ames and I have just chased an ENORMOUS spider out of the house. Big and furry, about the circumference of a grapefruit. Also the woman next door found 4 "Palmetto rats" in four bureau drawers. Palmetto rats are the largest rodents in existence and live up in the palmetto trees and "drop down" occasionally! I wish you were here! Do you remember the spider that made Father jump on the boat? This was his grandfather!

Love,
Mother

Captiva
March 13th [1950]
Dear Land,

Some seahorses for you! I have never seen one—aren't they beautiful? The pelicans are still diving for fish in the bay and the sandpipers running on the sand. I haven't been swimming yet. But today our rented bicycles came on the mail-boat. We found them leaning against a Banyan tree by the post office and we rode them home and collected our groceries on the way. I wish you were here to cook for me.

Love,
Mother
xo

Captiva
March 13th [1950]
Dear Ansy,

All the little wading sandpipers on the beach running in a row after the waves make me think of dancing school or a ballet. I wish you could see them.

Very soon now it will be your vacation. I wish you would send me a poem. I am riding a bicycle about as big as yours. Is Father back? Give him my love, and love to you.

Mother

Captiva
March 13th, 1950
Dear Scott,

This made me think of you and Dana White putting two horns into your mouth at once and trying to blow them.

I have the picture of you and Reeve setting out on your "adventure" in my bag.*

I hope you are all well now and can go to school and have some fun on vacation. We have a big turtle in our back yard. He lives in a sand hole behind the house.

Love xo
Mother

Captiva
March 13th [1950]
Dear Reeve,

How are you? Is Father home? Have you shown him how you can skate—and skip? Give him a kiss and a hug for me.

There are lots of butterflies here.

And woodpeckers on the trees.

And a pussy-cat comes to eat what we haven't finished of our cereal bowls.

Love,
Mother

Miami Airport
March 23rd, 1950
Dearest C.,

I have just tried to call you in Connecticut—person to person, reversing the charges. But you were reported off on a trip not back for a week or two. I feel let down and had expected to hear your voice and have a few words with you.

And to ask your advice! Yes—Friday I got a wire (in the mail!) from Adelaide† asking me to fly over to Nassau! And—on the spur of the

---

*Eight-year-old Scott and five-year-old Reeve decided to run away to Alaska. A neighbor gave them a ride to a big open field and said, "This is Alaska." They were satisfied and walked home.

†Adelaide Ferry Hooker Marquand, former member of America First and wife of John Marquand (1893–1960), Pulitzer Prize–winning American novelist best known for his "Mr. Moto" spy novels.

moment I decided to go for a few days. It is something like $34.00 round trip from Miami and fifty-five minutes! I don't want to be there for more than a weekend—because I really want the solitude of Captiva. But I would love to see them and I have been yearning to *smell* Nassau again after twenty years—I haven't been there since the winter before we were married, with Elisabeth. And I kept remembering your saying "you ought to go off and take trips more." So I hope you approve. I feel very daring and very gay, suddenly picking up from Captiva this a.m. (after a normal breakfast) and landing in Nassau this p.m. The air age still staggers me.

But the silence has gone out of aviation, as you said—the solitude and the silence and the connection with reality. I can hardly believe it is the same medium you and I used to travel in. These stupendous plushy air terminals, with every comfort except silence and solitude and air. A "Musak" Victrola is playing syrupy tunes endlessly. It *never* stops. Yes, sometimes, for an instant—but it is not a real silence but only pauses between sounds.

Now in Captiva, silence is a phenomenon, like love. It has been beautiful, now I feel well. Early morning swims, nights under a cupful of stars. And less people every day. By the end of March, or the end of the first week in April, there will be scarcely anyone except the islanders who are so very nice and simple and real and kind.

I love having just a bicycle. It limits your circle. (And think of the money I've saved! Feminine like—I feel I have *earned* the trip to Nassau by having a bicycle and not a car!)

Maybe you could come down around April 7th or 8th (Con* comes from the 2nd → 8th) I must go now—I never take off without thinking of you and our take-off!

Love,
Anne
P.S. Oh, I forgot to say—I also wanted to ask you—for the Marquands— why not fly down and meet me for the weekend in Nassau?! Foolish. Well—we will all miss you.

[Captiva, March 1950]
Dearest Con,

How wonderful to find your letter in the mailbox when I bicycled down at four! (I work now, between ten and one—and sun for a half

---

*Constance Morrow Morgan (1913–1995), AML's younger sister.

hour—and then work till four when I meet Ellie* to walk and eat supper.) It is very good and the unconscious (I hope!) is beginning now to work on "The Shells"—the *third* shell (a double rainbow shell!) of relationships. Hah! No writing, but outlines and ideas sprouting untidily. This is about all I ever take back from Captiva, but it is the creative seeds. I never can manage to *weld into form* in Captiva. However, this is enough.

Ellie has just left, very considerately since I said I must write postcards, and now I cannot resist writing you. She is sweet and good and loving and lovely and I love her—but perhaps it is the contrast with you, or some subtle form of snobbery or the devil in me, but when she leaves in the evening I want to get drunk or have a cigarette.

It is partly that since I talk to Jim† and her as *one*—and I *can*, which is wonderful. Then I get her reactions back, and they are often good and true and right, but they are cloaked in symbolism that leaves me feeling cold, or embarrassed, or even slightly guilty. (The "put-out-your-hand-to-Jesus" school of language.) The other night she prayed out loud for me and C. on the beach and I prayed too—inwardly: Dear God, forgive me for my snobbery and my resentment. Help me to see that this expression is as natural to her as reading poetry is to me—and that her love is real and good, etc.

Why have I such a resistance to *Jesus*? God is all right, but Jesus comes right out of those Sunday school pictures with the too-sweet glue on the back one pasted into notebooks. It makes me understand Dana's aversion to religion.

Also, I suppose, I am allergic to immolation at the moment. I just *can't* "give all to Christ." I might to God, though. I feel he would understand and accept one's unruly emotions. Jesus wouldn't. Why, I wonder? I feel Jesus is Ellie's brother and somehow too personal and intimate for me. It's all a question of semantics, I suppose. And we really are talking about the same thing. But I feel it is not as simple—not as simple as all that. God has a plan. Jesus will save you. Do not resist evil. Throw your arms about him (Jesus *and* Charles!).

I begin to hanker for a nice dry agnostic like Dana—who will say, "Well now, Anne, to be *practical*—"

---

*Eleanor Forde Newton, a longtime friend of AML's from Florida. Along with her husband, Jim, she was an early activist with the Oxford Group, an evangelistic Christian movement later known as Moral Re-Armament.
†James Draper Newton (husband of Eleanor Forde Newton), real-estate developer, conservationist, labor negotiator, and lifelong friend of CAL's, Thomas Edison's, Harvey Firestone's, and Henry Ford's.

Jim is now with C. and the boys in the Keys somewhere. That is nice. He wrote Ellie he didn't think C. would get back here Friday. Maybe not—one more day on "The Shells." "Captiva weather" has returned, all the inhabitants say. The water is soft and milky. I sit and eat breakfast alone on the back porch; your little yellow table and chair sit simply in the sun. I have *much* too much food to eat up: the cat won't come for the saucer of sour milk and I make so little headway in the second carton of cottage cheese, and I have that unopened bottle of Dubonnet to drink up alone. Ah well, the guava jelly jar is at last empty and washed and will replace a breakage. And the large wolf spider behind my bed didn't even move when I made it this morning. He trusts me—it's nice. I miss you terribly.

Love,

A.

May 31st [1950]

Dear Ruth,*

You see, I also am inarticulate and there are many unwritten letters in me, not only because of my own inner state but because of the compulsion not to put that inner state on paper where it will someday be discovered and misinterpreted and hurt people I cannot bear to hurt.

I cannot write honestly and deeply to you because I am in some kind of turmoil myself, terrible turmoil which I must hide and cannot really understand or dissolve.

When I think of you I think it is better for me not to touch her because her own turmoil is great and my own must seem—even if she could see it—impossible and unreal.

Look, she will say—Anne has everything: happy home life, husband, good children, financial security, love, friendship, beauty, etc. What has she to struggle with? What right has she to be unhappy? If I were only in her shoes, I would be content, serene, constructive, etc.

I also feel that I have, in the past, in trying to help people, only hurt them—that it is a great error to try to help people when you are unsure yourself.

I have become a great deal more honest with myself in the past three years. I can no longer "play God" to people. I do not feel wiser or better or surer than they. I feel I cannot be dishonest with myself or with

---

*Ruth Thomas Oliff helped the Lindberghs with child care and secretarial work in the 1940s, then moved west and raised her own family, which included a daughter named for AML.

them. It is unfair. I feel I have so little to give. I feel chiefly terrifically inadequate, and so I withdraw into the only things I feel adequate for—rubbing Scott's back, soothing Land's temper, washing Reeve's face, trying to keep Anne's heart open, putting a hand occasionally on Jon's shoulder. And chiefly trying to be, with them, terrifically but *deeply* honest.

Of course, Land, I say. You hate people at times. Of course you get mad and want to throw everything up. We all do. Everyone has these feelings in them. We hate and we love at the same moment, the same person. Adults are just like children. They have bad days too. When I have a bad day, I hate myself. But one must go on and not inflict too much of one's feelings on other people.

To Anne I must say—who do you cheat, Anne? When you cheat us about not drinking your milk, when you pour it back into the milk pitcher and pretend you have had it? You only cheat yourself. Your teeth will become soft and full of holes, like mine (I didn't brush my teeth either, Anne. I pretended I did, but I didn't)—and that means time at the dentist and pain . . . fillings, etc.

To Scott I say—Dear Scott, I was afraid of the dark, too. I know. I know what it is to have bad dreams. Grown people are afraid, too, Scott. I am afraid of many things—but you learn. You learn, Scott, that if you look squarely at the thing you are afraid of, it gets less frightening. You even learn what to do about it sometimes.

But if you turn your back on it, it always gets worse—always.

I suppose what I am trying to teach them is to accept themselves, and others, as imperfect—to accept the validity of what they feel, even if it cannot and must not be implemented in outward action where it may be horribly destructive.

But real destructiveness, I feel, comes so much of the time from dishonesty—dishonesty with oneself about what one feels and thinks. We are afraid to admit, even to ourselves, what dreadful and stormy and black depths are in ourselves. We turn the other way. We pretend we are all sweetness and light. And so the ugly things just get bigger and blacker the more they are hidden.

I am glad when the children explode in front of me—when they tell me their fears, their irritations, their hates. I admit to them that I have them too (though I don't tell them what they are). We all have them. We must learn to deal with them, that is all. We must try to understand, through understanding our own black depths, other people's black depths, and forgive them for the strange actions that sometimes proceed from them.

I write you about the children because, at the moment, it is the only sphere that I feel adequate to and sure in. It is the lifeline of my life. It is my reason for existence. Of course I live for C. too. But here I am not so sure of what I am doing or whether I am doing right. With the children I feel I am doing as right as I know how at this moment, and this is all anyone can do at any given moment.

To write about you is very difficult. I feel appalled by what you are going through and have been through. I know, though for very different reasons, so much of the same despair, the same wild rebelliousness, the same numbness, the same sense that there is no place for one in this civilization—that one exists in a vacuum, that one can touch no one, that one speaks another language, etc.

And yet, Ruth, I do feel that this rebelliousness and even the despair is not entirely negative. It is in C. (and was in his book). It is in me. It is in many, many people—all of whom feel lonely and lost and that the times—or they—must be wrong. We do not fit.

. . . Communication is a great help. To know other people feel the same way and are struggling too. So do write me—when you can, Ruth. Your letters are honest and they echo in me. If I cannot write back it is because I cannot from my life—but not that I don't feel with you and for you and believe in the life-force in you, even if it is or seems hidden—and always send my love,

Anne

P.S. Dear Ruth—I break this open to say to you what perhaps I should say to myself: *letters always help.* Your letters help me and your understanding helps me. (Yes, you are right about Ansy. It is adults who make children hide and be devious. Adults and the fears they produce. I try so hard now to keep my children free of fear—of me, anyway—by letting them see I am very imperfect, too.) If I can't write back exactly in the same way to you it is because so much of what I feel now is underground and must be till it gets clearer and purer. What I feel with the children is *not* underground and that is why this letter is full of them. They teach me so much, so much, and I feel very close to them, though often very far away from everyone else. (Some of this is just emotional exhaustion. It produces numbness and it is what you are suffering from now, too.)

I must tell you a lovely story about Scott. The other night I was rubbing his back and saying good night and when I finished, Scott started to wriggle down under the bedclothes but he couldn't get down because I was sitting on the bed. He complained, "I can't get down!"

"Oh, Scott," I said, jumping up very quickly. "I'm sorry." (Overemphatically, as I always do.) "It's because I'm sitting on your bed, Scott. I'm *so* sorry!"

Scott looked up at me, smiling, and said, in such an adult way, as if I should know better, "Oh Mother, you don't have to say 'I'm sorry.' I love you so much, Mother, that you don't have to say 'I'm sorry' to me."

I felt it was the most beautiful thing anyone had ever said to me in my life. And that all the meaning of love was in it. And if he could have learned that from me, perhaps I was not so inadequate.

Scott's Cove, Darien, Conn.
July 9th, 1950
Dearest C.,

I have just sent off a cable to you saying I would like to postpone my flight two weeks. How I longed to talk to you. Cables are terribly unsatisfactory and I wonder now—in a panic—if you will get it?!! Will you be off in Brittany or Scandinavia or Austria—out of touch for a week?? I figure that probably with the tension in the world—the Korean situation, etc.—you will in all probability be busy in Germany and in touch with the Air Force. I have therefore acted on that and sent you two cables—one to the Air-Attaché Paris and one to Wiesbaden.

Now, to my plans and state here, that made me cable:

I have had a *wonderful* week. This is perhaps dreadful at first blush to say, in the face of the cloud that hangs over the world—a smoke cloud about to burst into flames. We always knew it was there: the situation does not seem to me appreciably changed. Only it is out in the open—more people see it and are excited about it (the excitement in itself is dangerous, of course). One must plan in the light of it. But actually my wonderful week of quiet, of no people, of writing, of sleeping, of hitting my rhythm again, of writing another long poem (on the *Birth of a Moth*—tell Jon all the moths are coming out—one a day!), has taken on greater importance—or maybe not importance but *validity* against the pall of smoke—because I feel I may not have wonderful weeks or months very often in the future, and because against world conflict, inner harmony seems more important than ever. And I believe they are actually more related than we think. Which, actually, is what you are so often saying to me.

This ten days of peace I wish to prolong for another ten days. I realize that I am sacrificing something—seeing you and perhaps Jon—for two weeks. Your plans may be such that you will only have those two weeks free. You may be absorbed in the Air Force, sent to Washington, to Korea etc. *But I do not know.* I have no inkling of how this crisis has affected you or what it means. And I have to go ahead on my own judgments of the crisis. The Korean situation, I gather, was a well-considered move—no accident. I mean we saw it coming and avoided it as long as possible because militarily it was so difficult, etc. Here we are again—political realities forcing us into military unrealities. Or no—forcing military realities on us which we had not really faced and do not wish to.

What I would *like* to do is to take another ten days here quietly. Of course I want to *finish* "The Shells"—or the poem—and then to join you and follow you on your contacts in Europe—if this would be possible. I tried to suggest this in the cable but I left out "if possible" trying to get it all in twenty-five words for $2.50!

I am outlining what I would *like.* It just would be wonderful, if it were possible, to go over Europe with you—talking to people, gathering information, as we did last summer—talking it over each night and in the car as we went. This summer of all summers, when everything is on the boil, I will be hungry for it.

Of course, I realize I may have missed the chance by delaying it or that it may not be possible. But dear Charles, one must act on one's moments of grace and this is what I have done. It took great courage, great faith in your understanding, in your backing of me—even in a mistake! Perhaps your letter to me—the only one I have had—has given me the courage and the faith to change my plans. But how I long for word from you, for confirmation, and how I worry lest the cable misses you altogether and you should be waiting at the airport! Nightmares!

And yet—you do understand and like to practice yourself—keep fluid in movement. You also sometimes postpone trips and don't let me know when you're appearing. It means, I know, that one must then accept the responsibility of finding the other person unprepared—unable to break his plans, etc. In other words—you may not be able to meet me or be with me, etc.—in two weeks' time. I must be grown-up and take that chance.

So much love—and to Jon if he is with you. Will write again soon. I am sleeping, now, and swimming in evening.

xo,

A.

Tegernsee, Germany
Monday, August 18th, 1950
Dear Mother,

We arrived here Wednesday night, the chalet farmhouse of an old Norwegian artist, Olaf Gulbransson,* whom we met last year. It is a beautiful spot, halfway up a mountain overlooking the valley and the lake. Mrs. G., a lovely soft-voiced, golden-braided Norwegian, met us at the door in Bavarian skirt and apron, with the word that Jon had been here and we had missed him by two days! He was here a week and G. did two sketches of him—good, but not as good as the one he did of C. last year.

Anyway, it warmed my heart the way both of them spoke of him. "A *wunderbar* young boy!" he said. And she, "Oh, he is such a charming boy, a charming boy!" I am sure he was well fed and cared for here, stuffed with good Norwegian pancakes and jule-cake.

Germany looks much better than a year ago, so far. Shops full (though expensive). People well fed—better dressed. (New baby carriages & new shopping bags the most obvious—and young people on bicycle camping expeditions everywhere.) But underneath, the despair at the growing cloud of war is very black. They know they have no arms, army, etc. with which to stop Russia and that she can sweep over Europe when she wants to. The French know this too, but it is not quite so close, and every German has immediate knowledge of Russia—relatives in the East Zones or a son or a father or a brother, a prisoner. They know that for them to be occupied by Russia is the end of the world. Many unbelligerent people soberly plan suicide when the Russians come. We cannot really conceive of it. You have to hear Frau G., a calm Norwegian, say quite quietly, "Today when I hear of someone dying I think: it is good, it is perhaps good."

She tells me of Churchill's speech at the Council of Europe yesterday suggesting a European army in which Germany should participate. And

*Olaf Leonhard Gulbransson (1873–1958), artist, illustrator, painter, and educator, was best known for his satirical cartoons and illustrations.

that the Germans are not very enthusiastic. They do not want to be the infantry thrown against the Russians. They know Germany will be the battleground and they fear our atomic bombs will drop on them. All the young are anti-war. I suppose we all are. Even the Russians. And us. C. has just arrived with mail from Wiesbaden—good letter from you. I am all for the portrait going to Smith.* It *should*. How about another portrait for us—in Chinese coat—white hair—very good—a small one? Time for no more.

Love,

A.

Scott's Cove
Monday, September 25th [1950]
Dearest C. (oh the damp paper—I forgot),

T.† has just driven over to see me and talk Europe and European Rearmament, etc.—was very anxious to get hold of you on what he feels is a most crucial development which might be turned constructively, or might turn destructively if not guided. He feels you are the person over there whom he trusts—your judgment, knowledge, ability, etc.

The children are back in school, except for Land who has his first cold and is in bed. Jim says (over the phone) that he looked pretty thin and wan when he arrived from camp. "You could have pulled him through a key-hole." But he is fattening up. Reeve volunteered, "I don't want anything for my birthday except to have Father come home!" Scott has learned to ride Land's old bicycle and went with me to the Point Saturday—does very well. Anne is going to play the flute in school (if we can rent one through the school). The gas stove has been repaired sufficiently for the new cook to bake in it and roast as well, so I am doing nothing on the electric stove till you come home and something should be done!

This morning we found in the trap that Land had put out to catch a chipmunk in (to tame!) a small skunk. Since Land was incapacitated and I didn't want him running down in the cold, I picked up the trap, holding the rear end of the skunk away from me, and carried it down onto the grass—opened it up and pointed it downhill to the bushes. The skunk just snuck out as quietly as could be, no fuss and no ammunition! And I

*Smith College was the alma mater of AML, her mother, and her sisters.
†Major Truman Smith (see note on p. 29).

am a heroine in everyone's eyes! But I am not sure the children will let the next one go. They all want a dog—"at least something alive." Scott has some caterpillars—rather harmless wildlife. Land is determined to catch a chipmunk or a coon. I say, "Wait till Father comes home!"

I am going into town to have a thorough examination of those disagreeable parts that bothered me this summer. It is unpleasant but probably wise. I must take two ounces of castor oil tomorrow morning. "Pewy!" as Reeve says.

No word from you!

It is beautiful but cold today. The leaves are beginning to turn. Scott and Anne and Reeve are collecting chestnuts!

New Boston Inn, New Boston, Mass.
February 9th, 1951
Dearest C.,

Your wonderful long letter has just reached me, much delayed by the train strike and my being away this week to work—Hah! I have read it over four times already. In fact I devoured it. It has given me such a sense of elation and I do not really know why—I guess just to feel in touch with you again, chiefly. I have been feeling so out of touch—so out of touch. I went home happier that night because I knew you must have gotten my letter and just to have that touch from you.

I hasten to answer although this letter may never get to you and it would take me all afternoon to say all the things I want to say and I don't want to spend all the afternoon on it because I want to go skiing! Write all morning, ski all afternoon. Ahh!

It was wonderful to get your letter here. I had been thinking of you so vividly. At home I haven't really time to miss you much. Sometimes at night. Sometimes outside, piling wood with Scott, or Sunday suppers. But I am so busy, trying so hard to live up to something—what? Your idea of me, perhaps. For I am conscious of you all the time. All the time I am thinking anxiously, "Charles would approve of this" or—quite often!—"Charles would *dis*approve of this."* You would have done quite a lot of *dis*approving last week, but I'll go into that later!

But here I just think about you—pure, so to speak. Spontaneously or with joy. The first day I felt not down to earth enough to write. It was a beautiful warm sunny day with still quite a crust of snow on the ground.

*Here AML draws a smiley face.

And I went out on skis and did gentle curves *on the hill* and took long strides over untouched snow through the woods. It was so beautiful, so still—the real stillness that Picard* speaks of, "Silence—which is not something negative—a mere absence of speech: it is an original phenomenon like love, faithfulness, death and life."

I could see the beauty of the world again. The dried seed pods with their fists full of snow. The bare branches black and beautiful against a soft evening sky. The rough pine-bearded hills, the soft blue-breath birch trees here and there, the strong hillside and strong fences capped with snow. Blue jays flashing through the trees, tracks of rabbits and squirrels like notes of music on a white page. Everything had significance again in the silence, in the winter space—in the bleakness of a New England winter. And I, coasting downhill, finding myself racing a stream—the stream that runs through this tiny village—felt alive and young and part of the world around me—and full of joy and suddenly very close to you. If only he were here, I thought. He would love you too.

Each morning before I start to work, I go out and climb the *incredibly* strong hillside behind the inn. (You know those hillsides in New England that are so strewn with boulders and rocks that you don't see how even *God* could have done it?) It is quite a climb, especially in snow, now crusty so you fall through up to the knee and now thin and wind-swept, just powdered over the stubbly grass stalks. And I sit in a special spot—on a stone, backed against a wood of white pines, with white pines around me, sheltering me—quite a circle of them, holding me in their arms—and marching a little in front of me, guarding me and my rock on either side and framing the view in front, to the side, across the narrow valley to the gentle pine-covered rounded hills of New England.

It is not a spectacular view. Round stubby hills, pine-bristled and stony—softened here and there with the blue breath of birch trees. But there is a gap in the hills where they come down and meet in the valley and you can see through to other hills, other valleys. I love this view and it makes me think of flying with you, and of Tegernsee, too. I know it is not Tegernsee. There are no Alps—there is no lake.

It doesn't pretend to be beautiful, but I feel nested in these New England hills. I suppose I am not really very adventurous and my roots

---

*Max Picard (1888–1965), a Swiss writer and philosopher whose book *The World of Silence* was published in 1948.

are in New England very deeply. I longed for you to be there too, sitting on the rock with me. I have sat there so many times. In midsummer when the cool dark of the pines felt good. And in autumn—bare November weather when the hills were still grape-colored. But now—only white and black—and the blue shadows of trees on snow. I thought: I must bring him here, I must sit with him here, where I have so often seen my life more clearly. Even if he doesn't feel about New England as I do, even if we could never live here.

It would not be the peaceful retreat it is now to me if I should move all my family here. And you would never be happy here. (You—Charles.) But perhaps we could have a weekend together here. You would see what it means to me. It would speak to you also. It recaptures something of Tegernsee for me. The Tegernsee person comes to life here. I thought, dreaming to myself, that I would like to build a chalet up on that hill, backing to the pines, and come here—even if we do move to the West. Not for the children. For me, and you, if you wanted to come. It would be a kind of Point House and we could lock it up and leave it and it could be my base in the East forever, so I would always have something of New England. And I would be three to four hours from New York, so I could see friends from here. Well, it is dreaming and impractical.

I realized that you perhaps were at that very moment also sitting on a hillside—finding *your* Tegernsee—somewhere else. I felt sad, a little, that you could never never find your identity in New England. It would always cramp you—those narrow valleys, those stubby hills, those strong, grim, eke-out-a-living-if-you-can pastures. Those prim clapboard houses and stiff little red barns. But I understand this: you could not fit here. Just as I, perhaps, am always going to feel deracinated in the sandy soil of California—in the dry sunshine—among the brittle ever-leafy trees who never dare to stretch their arms out bare, bone bare, against a steely sky.

But I do not mind really. I would like to travel, to buy, to taste, perhaps to base where land is good—there is space and opportunity for the children. But I shall *have* to come back regularly to this sparse, cold, stony, and yet warm and cradling New England landscape because it is in me. My fruit won't ripen without the frost—the winter—the surcease from sun.

Later—Evening

I have just come in from a ski-walk (from 4:30–5:45) just at sunset. I love this hour: no sun in your eyes, a clear golden sky tinged with pink behind the blue hills, and all the bare branches as black against the sky as the dry weeds are against the snow. It is very cold. I love winter—real bare-trees-and-snow winter—as you may love the desert. It is the season of the spirit, just as the desert is the landscape of the spirit. I would like always to have some of it. And I feel so good when I come in from that kind of a walk. It is as good as sleep, as food, as water to the thirsty. It is like a sun-bolt or like swimming, in that you feel united to nature again—part of the element you are bathed in.

I have had a very constructive week here: sleeping, overeating, skiing, thinking out my life—our life!—writing. I pulled the conclusion into shape. And drinking in the beauty of earth and air and solitude, and feeling very close to everyone I love in the process—you especially.

Why am I afraid of isolation, I think? Because it is only in solitude that I ever find my own core—out of which I can write, out of which I can love, out of which or through which I can feel related to people. We are so wrong about solitude, about relatedness. One must get related to one's own core first. Only through one's own core can one be really related to others. It is not by living next to them or by seeing them every day that you get related to people—sometimes this only succeeds in separating you. No, you must get related to your own core first and then you are not separated from anyone you love, no matter where they are in the world.

Certain places, certain modes of living, allow you to get related to your core. The place that may do it for you may not do it for me. The place that does it for me may not do it for you. But we must allow ourselves those differences. We must live where it is best for group life—for together family life—but we must always allow each other to be free to go back to the tap-root place or work that connects us to ourselves again for a renewal period. Then we shall never be separated, in the deepest and truest sense.

Dear Charles—what a long, long letter. I have spend half an afternoon and a whole morning on it. But it was good and I feel so close to you and sure that you will understand, somehow, all I am trying to say. I do not begrudge the last morning spent on this. I have done some good work here. I have rested. I have touched my tap-root again. And you with your delicate perceptions will feel this through my hastily written letter. You will understand. And if I came away only to be able to write all this to you, it would have been worth it.

But I go back full—happy—and at ease—and no sense of pressure. There is Captiva ahead!

Ah, but I do wish—despite not feeling separated from you—that you were here and we could go out after lunch or this evening just after the sun has set and ski gently down a slope, not speaking a word, just bathed in the same crystalline air—and in joy.

My love—my love to Jon, too.

A.

[Early 1951]

Dearest Jon,

My first reaction to the *Herald Tribune* announcement that a school-mate of yours had written an article about you was: *What a dirty trick.* I still feel that way now after having read the article. Even though the article is what is called "favorable," and seems to have been written with the best of intentions, reasonable accuracy and some degree of taste, not to speak of obvious admiration.

Very few people realize that *any* publicity is bad. It makes one's life more difficult, more artificial, less natural. It insulates one from normal natural life and relations with other people. I once told your father that to be famous was like having Medusa's head—life was arrested, turned to stone around one. People ceased to be themselves, to talk and act naturally in your presence. He said it was like having the Midas touch.

Of course, it isn't as bad as that for you and one or two articles aren't going to do it, but they make life more difficult. I'm sorry it has hit you but it's just as well to know about it—be on guard and see how best to handle it.

Now—there are two extremes here. One is to be *so* much on guard that you never talk naturally to friends at all for fear they may sell it to the papers: withdrawing into a shell, distrusting people, looking on everyone as a possible reporter. I don't myself think it's worthwhile living this way. It's better to act normally—make friends and trust them. If once in a while one gets caught—well, so what? It is better to get caught occasionally than to live perpetually in fear of it.

On the other hand, there is no use being naïve about it. One should be aware of the problem—that it exists—that people are apt to make capital out of you and that you have got to keep your wits about you and outsmart them.

Actually, I think the most destructive element in that article will be its effect on the readers—not on you. Young men who will read this article glorifying dangerous exploits and think that is the way to be a hero and gain fame. This article glorifies danger per se, which I think *and hope* you don't do! Since you have now been pointed out and put in the limelight as an example, it puts a responsibility on you to show that flirting with danger is not a sign of courage or greatness, but just being a damn fool or an exhibitionist. I don't think you *are* an exhibitionist or a "damn fool" but young people with poor judgment reading that article may become both those things and lose their lives in rash exploits trying to be that kind of a hero. It is too bad, but your actions will have to answer articles like this. You will have to show extra care, extra judgment, extra balance, to offset the adolescent attitude that risking one's life is inevitably noble. Sometimes one *has* to risk one's life but the bravest and best-balanced people don't take unnecessary risks. Courage is *not* rashness. Your father doesn't take unnecessary risks.

Actually, Jon, it was exactly this kind of courage that I felt you showed the last time you were back here—speaking your own mind, and standing on your own opinions, honestly and simply and fearlessly. And it impressed me more than all the mountain climbing or deep-sea diving in the world!

The courage to be oneself is so difficult to achieve. This is one of my grudges against publicity, now I come to analyze it. Publicity makes it *so* difficult to be oneself. It puts up a false picture and you find yourself acting up to it or reacting against it. It's like suddenly being surrounded with mirrors—it's almost impossible not to pose.

In fact it's worse than mirrors, because mirrors reflect truthfully, and publicity distorts. It reflects back an image distorted by the sense of values of the person writing. I suppose that's why I was irritated by that girl. She thinks I'm the kind of mother who doesn't care whether her son falls into a crevasse or drowns under a boat. "She's used to it"!! Hah!

You *don't* "get used to" worrying about the people you love!

Hence this long letter. Well, I assume you did not give an interview to this girl, or else gave it to her for the college paper, not expecting her to sell it to the world. I can remember the first time it happened to me—in Mexico—when your father and I were engaged and we went out to dinner and one of the guests asked me questions which I answered freely not suspecting she was a reporter—and then she made an article about it the next day in the paper! It came out that I preferred motoring to flying, etc., etc. And I felt humiliated and betrayed. I had just been naïve and a sucker. And she was definitely unethical. But there are quite a proportion of people like that around and one has to learn to look out for them.

Now (I've got that off my chest!).

We are going back to Stowe tomorrow for the weekend, I hope. All of us in the ranch wagon, how we will miss you!

Captiva Island
Friday, March 9th, 1951
Dear Dr. A.,*

I have been here a week and I am just beginning to let the mind work—a *little*! I think one should spend the first week of a Florida vacation all alone, or with very dull people, or with people one knows so well it doesn't matter. The effect of so much sun, warmth, leisure and the general softness of Florida atmosphere is soporific. I suppose it is good, this letting down. (I hope you can manage to get some of it—although it is hard to imagine you soporific!)

Or maybe it is just me. I do nothing but sleep and eat and lie in the sun and occasionally bicycle to the store for groceries. I can't manage to do anything the least bit useful. I can't even worry. I say to myself: *I have only a week or ten days more. I have done no work—I may never come back again. I have plans, decisions, to think about.* But I *can't* think ahead or back. A lotus-eater lethargy has enveloped me. Nothing seems to matter and the past and the future have melted away. Only the soft, soft nest I am sinking into. Perhaps it is necessary, this temporary amnesia. Perhaps it is weariness and the body taking its due again (it is nice to establish the habit of sleep anyway). I am sure C. would approve. Back to nature, the physical etc. There is something in me always that resents the body taking over completely. It seems so far away from the spirit.

But perhaps that is a false puritan conflict. I am not sure that the relationship between spirit and body isn't closer than that between mind and body. Spirit seems to leap up after bodily rest and ease, at the touch of physical beauty often: quick, flame-like, joyous and pure. The mind follows more slowly—and not spontaneously at all—harnessed and bridled and pulling a cart!

Anyway, I haven't recovered my mind yet. Con has been typing away at Henry James since the first morning. Margot has written out the outline of a skit for a club play. But I just sit and let myself sink down into the deep well of quietness in myself. I feel instinctively it is good to do. But it is rather blind and numb. Sinking down through the upper layers of articulateness—leaving them behind—through thoughts—through emotions—down to where everything is dark and still and formless. I

*Dr. Dana W. Atchley. See note on page 19.

feel I must sink to the bottom of the well before I can be renewed or be creative again.

You are probably in your last few days and much too busy to read drowsy philosophical discussions. The last days before one goes off are always—for me—so crowded that you feel it is hardly worth going away. It is, though, it is.

I have heard nothing from Charles, so I don't know what the Marquands said in reply to him and whether we are all going to see each other on Treasure Island or not. All the transportation decisions etc. are left in his hands—which at this point just seems blissful to me (don't have to think about *that* either!).

I think it would be rather sad to be there without you—like that last day last year when it seemed hardly worthwhile saying anything at all because you weren't there to catch it! However, at this point I don't feel I'll ever have anything to say to anyone again. I'm only halfway down the well.

I'm still walking around in a daze (light-struck, I think one is at first in Florida. I feel more at home under the stars at night). The other day I stepped backwards on a rickety pier *through* a hole in the planks. But with the traditional immunity of drunks and somnambulists (I was the latter), I escaped with only a skinned leg.

Con and I will now pedal up to the post office and collect groceries (Margot has just left). We look like a French bicycle race in our shorts and shirts and jockey caps, pumping down the road against the wind. I have the new Koestler book but I feel it's too intense to read here. Did you see Faulkner's Nobel Prize acceptance speech? Very beautiful and positive ("I believe that man will not merely endure: he will prevail"). I thought of you and Bill.*

July 14th, 1951 [DIARY]

I have been for six weeks to Dr. Rosen†—the beginning of analysis. I cannot go back to the weeks of despair beforehand—my inability & sense of hopelessness of working it out with Dana. Margot's urging me to R. and my final decision—to go tentatively.

What has happened since is just indescribable. The first week or two can only be described as a kind of "shock treatment"—though not in the

*Dr. William A. Atchley, Dana Atchley's son.
†Dr. John Nathaniel Rosen (1902–1983), a pioneering psychiatrist based in Pennsylvania, was initially engaged to treat Dwight Morrow Jr. when he was diagnosed with schizophrenia. Rosen would go on to treat AML and her daughter Anne for depression; Reeve was also treated by him for depression during her son Jonathan's illness and after his death.

usual sense—only through the deep & penetrating & therefore shocking probing. I felt violently shaken & couldn't sleep or eat. Everything & everyone got dim and far away except C. & the children.

I continue to have a personal relationship with Dana but of course he is not The Doctor any more. So it is very different. Every relationship is different. D. has been magnificent about it and the greatest possible help to me & to C. His faith, his steadiness, the warmth of his affection, his understanding—without explanations—without words. His simply being there—a shoulder.

I feel quite sad that I should have broken through to him at last in a personal relationship at a moment when I am so unsteady. So unsure and so empty—with so little to give. Will I ever feel creative again? With hands full?

It is very hard on C. in every way. I can see it & feel it & it is another burden to bear. I feel so convinced that it *is for* C. Also for *us*—for the children and that we will all gain from it. But even so—.

Outside of that basic sureness I have nothing—no steadiness—no sense of who I am or where I am going. I am adrift & rather blind & frightened to be so disconnected.

The experience can only be described in terms of myths or fairy stories—or a symbolic phrase such as "The bird fights its way out of the egg which is its world. Whoever would be born again must just destroy a world."

I feel like the little mermaid who has sacrificed her tongue to the Sea-Witch—& lost her tail for human stumps of legs. Every step was as if she were treading on sharp knives.

I feel like Psyche who had to light the candle & then was banished from her love, from her kingdom, only to come back after trudging around the world barefoot.

I feel like the moth, just fighting its way out of the cocoon, crawling out—a blind grub, dragging its useless atrophied wings after it—unable to fly—or see—or do anything but cling helplessly to a twig.

Who I am or who I will be I do not know. I feel completely disconnected from myself—the plug pulled out. And yet faith that there is only one way out—to go ahead. I cannot go back. Yet it takes so much courage to go ahead—esp. with C. feeling as he does about it. (He has backed me up magnificently but he does not understand & it troubles him so terribly.)

At the moment (R. is away) I can only return to the bed-rock of being a woman—my body—to keep well—exercise—sun—swim—sleep (I am gaining back the weight I lost & sleeping again)—my husband—my children (but the children are away & C. is away half the time or more)—my house—housework & gardening—cleaning—arranging the flowers (this is the only creative thing I can do)—for I have no job (I cannot write at the moment. There is no base—no personality—no *me* to write *from*). With all relationships removed from me (partly because it's summer & they're away & partly because I have told no one about the analysis—but C. & D.) & all work removed. I feel adrift—what justifies my existence? Who needs me? I write the children—fill the bird bath—let C. talk to me of all that is on his mind. Write D.

The other day—lying down on the couch in the trailer—feeling I had no justification for living ("The Shells" seem superficial & outgrown—I cannot work at them)—I looked out of the door & found the birds feeding on the crumbs from my lunch & it gave me a spurt of joy. I felt connected again to life—through the birds eating my crumbs. And I felt like that talking to Betsey* one afternoon—putting my finger on her pain—a point she hadn't analyzed—& it seemed a relief to her. ("Yes, that's why it's so terrible—I hadn't put it that way—yes you're right.") And when I get those joyous overflowing letters from Ansy from camp—I feel if I can be here for Anne's joy—for Anne's expression—the recipient—even the encouraging audience for her expression—that is enough.

If I can be the responsive & understanding friend to Betsey at this moment of trial—it is enough.

If I can send a joke or a note or a poem or my love to Dana—& it gives some light to his day.

If I can feed crumbs to the birds—then perhaps there is reason for my existence through this desert.

T. S. Eliot:

> *We shall not cease from exploration*
> *And the end of all our exploring*
> *Will be to arrive where we started*
> *And know the place for the first time.*[†]

---

*A friend of AML's who was going through a difficult period in her life.
[†]From "Little Gidding" (the last of the *Four Quartets*).

[From a letter to Alan Valentine]*

Saturday night, June 13th, 1953†

This has been a long rainy day full of small duties: children's camp trunks, lists, name tapes, interruptions, telephone calls, plans, all the children in the house, plus children's guests, children's quarrels, and contracts to read and sign for C. And through all of it, the sense that I must get alone to communicate anything, even though they must be "mental letters, torn up mentally."

The sense of loss is terrific and yet *not*, curiously, at the same time. I felt this, driving from the station to my appointment—terrific void and silence and then, with the incredible deviltry-humor of life, a large truck bearing your name made us stop as it crossed our path. And I laughed secretly. And then I began to feel better.

Perhaps "better" is not the word. It is something quite new and different from what I would imagine: a sense not of flurry and distraction, of pressure, but of calmness and quiet and strength. It seems to last. I am astonished. I am even efficient, more pulled together than usual! Do you know the George Eliot quotation: "Those children of God to whom it has been granted to see each other face to face and to feel the same spirit working in both can never more be sundered, though the hills may lie between. For their souls are enlarged for evermore by that union, and they bear one another about in their thoughts continually, as it were a new strength."

Life seems to me suddenly to have quieted, as if I had come to rest, as if I believed "we have years." I am in a new country. I do not know my way but I am not pressed. I am not even worried. I am sustained. I had the immense and unexpected joy of finding your ink marks on the things I had given you to read. Such communication.

Now I must sleep.

Sun. p.m., sitting on a rock

After a morning of driving Land to La Guardia and having a long educational talk on marriage with Judy‡ (Heavens, she knows *nothing*. Do they still bring up people this way?), I slipped away and came out

---

*Alan Chester Valentine (1901–1980), president of the University of Rochester, also served in the Truman administration. See Introduction, p. 11.

†A large number of diary entries and letters from the preceding two-year period were destroyed by AML after her analysis (see p.33).

‡Judy Guild, AML's secretary.

here "to sunbathe." It is raining now, intermittently and delicately, but it is so wonderful to sit alone and think. I *did* sunbathe too, in what sun there was.

I feel something else new. I want suddenly and very positively to be strong, to stay well, to stay young and alive and rested. I want so much to live those years we have. This is new. The nearest thing to it I have ever felt was when I was carrying and nursing Reeve. I must tell you about this. I learned with the last child how marvelous this process of living for another, with joy in the thought of another. (The rain is increasing. The spots will look like tears but they are not. I felt ashamed afterwards of my tears. At the time I could not feel shame, for it was only that I could not act unnaturally, or be other than what I was feeling.)

When you are carrying or nursing a child and really drenched in the act, everything you do in life is transfused with the thought of this other life: the sun on one's hand, the honey on one's toast, the milk one drinks, the sleep, the air one breathes. One is grateful for it all. One says to oneself, "How wonderful! This is for my child. This sunshine—this air—this sleep—this milk—this honey!" Every act has meaning, is transformed. One has a sense of direction, of dedication all day long, all night.

I tried once to describe this to Ned Sheldon,* whom I saw a lot of in the last year of his life, and the first year of Reeve's life. He listened from his bed (he was blind and paralyzed) and then said, in his beautiful voice, "But that is *love*, you are describing. That is love; it is what the poets have been trying to describe for thousands of years." I was startled, but I thought of it again today as I lay in the sun.

It is 5:30. I must go back to the house. Dwight† is coming for supper. The routine starts tomorrow again. How refreshed I feel for this hour and a half!

Thursday—sitting up in bed—early morning
I slept and woke early, my thoughts going on in all that I want to say to you, in answer to the letter and more. You told me just what I wanted and needed most to know: of the happy tenor of your family life. This was a help and strength to me. What you said about the facets—so *beautifully* said. Yes, it is true. I had almost realized it too (and this has been

*Edward Brewster Sheldon (1886–1946), American dramatist.
†Dwight Whitney Morrow, Jr. (1908–1976), AML's brother.

troubling me underneath as deeply as anything). It comes to me again as confirmation.

How beautifully you write. I did not realize this, but then, so much I did not realize. I really do not know you very well, and I want to so much, although so much of it seems, on discovery, not to be surprise but confirmation. There will be some time tonight to be quiet. I will walk through the day toward it.

Yesterday was long, tiring and picayune. But I swam when I came back, alone. Wednesday's swim was so wonderful *after* your letter (curiously mingled in my mind). I swam in this new element: a slight shock, surprising, releasing, restoring, freeing. And then lay on the sunny stones of the wall in utter peace and content. (Yes, I can repose on this. Yes, this is solid earth.)

There is so much to say about your letter. So much feeling the same in it: the *un*troubledness, the lack of regret. (But there is impatience in me.) Also I *do* get troubled at certain aspects, but you assured and helped me here (the facets).

Of "The Shells." Yes, you are right. I long to talk to you about it. Some of this can go in a real letter. On the weekend there will be time, I hope.

I feel "at ease" tonight—I do not know why exactly. Is this faith, this kind of repose? A kind of faith in life itself: that I will let it develop, that it has something in it for me—for us. That I do not ask "what" or "how" or "when."

Monday morning—before breakfast

My Birthday.* Yesterday I wrote you and Lucia.† But so much unsaid. I could have gone on and on. Both letters were sincere. Perhaps the one to you was the less sincere, because so much was left out. So much I could have written about Macmurray,‡ which I shall take on the train. You have marked: "The real problem of the development of emotional reason is to shift the center of feeling from the self to the world outside. We can only begin to grow up in rationality when we begin to see our

---

*AML was born on June 22, 1906.
†Lucia Norton Valentine (1902–1992), Alan Valentine's wife, was an architect and writer, a trustee of Smith College, and a trustee of the Morgan Library in New York City.
‡John Macmurray (1881–1976) was a Scottish philosopher and professor whose ideas on the nature of emotion as a motivational force were seen by some as contradictory to traditional Western philosophy.

own emotional life not as the center of things but as part of the development of humanity."

I am still so desperately personal. And yet, I had to get straightened out inside first—a *little* anyway. But now—now, I must start the other process.

Last week the children were wild. (It is better this week.) I kept taking it to heart and wondering what I was doing or *had* done wrong. I know rebellion in adolescence is natural and healthy, but how much to take, and *how* to handle it?

Evening. Now it is late. They are all in bed. I have just been out to look at the moonlight on the water. Not brilliant—milky and soft tonight—melting. I wish I could communicate some of this to you immediately, more fully. My real letter went off today but it says so little and goes so slowly. But you will know. (So you say and I believe you.) Now it is good night. "Happy Birthnight," as Reeve said to me sleepily tonight. "It isn't day any longer."

Thursday evening, June 25th, 1953

This was my first free day. Tuesday and Wednesday I was rushed in town and obsessively neat at home! A frenzy of picking up and tidying, cleaning out, and washing up, no doubt compensating for the disorder inside at the thought of ending the analysis. The end of *anything* is difficult. ("What have I done?" "What have I *not* done?")

But today, now it is ended, I felt free. I put fresh flowers in the living room. I lay on the rock in the sun. "The Shells" came back with a wonderful bit of lobster wisdom on the envelope. (I was horror struck at the messy state of "The Shells" when I gave them to you. I should have reread it: it looked like a clean copy, but evidently wasn't.)

I was also very busy with the children since the secretary is off. Scott stepped on his hunting knife. Reeve had a rowdy friend for lunch. Anne had her art teacher and children for tea. I was busy carrying, making beds, bandaging feet, delivering children, washing out things, etc. And yet, I felt, this is going to be all right: I will get time. I will get back to the trailer. I will manage better tomorrow. I will get back to the core in the center of me, soon. Soon.

It is hard not to press, not to want to share and talk and communicate, with the new ease—comparative ease. I find this new pressure more insistent. Is it wrong, I wonder, to want to share? Is sharing an impossibility, ever? Should one give up such a dream: sharing all the little things? Is it a falsity even to try because one never can? Only a certain number of the facets turn right! One shouldn't pretend that they *all* do. (Oh, but so many do!) Or twist oneself trying to make them all turn one way. But I find this longing in me to lean all one way, like a flower to the sun. I distrust the leaning, as if one might get off balance.

[JULY 27TH, 1953, DIARY]

[CAL] has had a wonderful trip abroad—Pan American*—all over—France—Italy—Switzerland—Sweden—England. Pan Am work & talking to interesting people on his own. He is alive—open—gay—warm & very interesting on everything. On the top of the wave. The book† is going into every conceivable language—& we have a first copy—a beautiful thing—perfect in every detail—cover—end-papers—maps—pictures—set-up. Reviewers' comments are beginning to come in— (Epic—*Seven Pillars of Wisdom—Arabia Deserta*—etc., etc.).

I am happy to see him so alive, so open—so active & growing—but it is hard to start clear on this level (—as we must—as we will). There is so much pain heaped up from the past. Old pain, banked up, makes for bitterness. One must try to understand it. For him, the two years of my analysis is pain & bitterness—which it is difficult for him to understand—to accept—to forgive even. Though now it is over, it is better.

For me—it is difficult to analyze, but the fact that he has not been with me (in understanding or sympathy or support) these two years of analysis is hard to bridge. Also I still find in myself when—as now—I hear paeans of praise for his book—bitterness—jealousy—sense of unfairness. I am ashamed of these emotions & when I can be quiet & think out why they are there, they vanish. But sometimes they catch me unaware as when someone called up & went off into ecstasies about the greatness of the book—an epic—smoothness of style—marvelous images—perfection of detail—etc., etc., compared it to *The Seven Pillars of Wisdom* and *Arabia Deserta*. Had no idea he had it in him—must go back & read *We*‡—which was just a simple story of a simple man, etc.

I am too much of a writer not to recognize this book as an epic. It is

---

*CAL was for many years a consultant to Pan American World Airways; in 1965 he was named to its board of directors.

†*The Spirit of St. Louis* (New York: Scribner, 1953), CAL's memoir of his solo transatlantic flight, was awarded the Pulitzer Prize for nonfiction in 1954.

‡CAL's first book about his transatlantic flight, published in 1927 by Putnam.

a great moment in history—greatly told—by a man of greatness. I also know that he would not have told it—could not have told it that way if he had not married me. Twenty years of living with me have gone into that book—before the man who said to me when we were engaged: "You like to *write* books?" (astonished and curiously condescending) "I like to *live* them"—before that man absorbed my values about the written word—from my books, both those I wrote & those I read, my education, my way of talking, my way of writing, my admiration of writers—to such a degree that he has put it all back in this epic of a book.

The difference between *We* & *The Spirit of St. Louis* is my impact on Charles—and life's—but life *with me*, as observer, as critic, as commentator at his side.

Actually—what I *did* on the book concretely—in cutting—transposing—criticizing—telling him where to end—where to point up—where to synchronize—weighing & analyzing paragraphs—sentences—words—commas—also *tone*—*tone* of this or that bit—changing the tone and a few good images—going over & over it with a fine-toothed comb for details—checking & rechecking everyone else's corrections—were they valid or not? And at least ten people did an overhaul job on it.

All this—though it added to the *perfection* of the book—was not as important as those twenty years of living with me—slowly changing & opening, sharpening his perceptions, his articulateness, his aesthetic & spiritual sensitivities.

As his reality-action-sense of life pervaded—shaped—formed me—& my life and my early books.

But then—why the pain? Why do I mind that he has blossomed so wonderfully—that I have been the soil—the sun—the rain, a little (*much!*)—for his blossoming? It was all *there*, before—the plant, the buds—the potentialities—I only perhaps freed them a little—why do I flinch at the extravagant praises coming for this very magnificent achievement? It is *his* very real achievement—whether or not I helped him to it. I should be proud, happy—overjoyed—that he *has* achieved it & that I could help him to it.

In a way I am—and I really enjoyed the *work* on the book. I enjoyed making it as perfect as it could be. I forgot myself in doing it.

Then why the pain? There is so much pain. It is not simply jealousy—or simply that I want the praise. That would not be fair. He deserves it & he has worked for it. It is *his* epic.

But there is too much pain in connection with this book. Too much pain has gone into it for me, to face its flowering at its face value—surfacely. Too much of our life—our pain—our marriage—has gone into the maw of that book. Four books of my own have been swallowed up in it—and my adoration of St.-Ex.* & his books. And years of life—& quarrels & misunderstandings. The book means pain to me. The cost has been high. It was written—most of it—in this last painful period of lack of understanding & support & sympathy for what I was going through. Lack of understanding is a mild way of putting it. He fought tooth & nail every inch of the way. To try to give *him* support for what *he* was doing (when it was an invasion into my own field—the only field I had of my own that he had not entered & absorbed)—when he was undermining—consciously & unconsciously—what I was attempting to do in the analysis—(which I felt—rightly or wrongly—was necessary for my survival). It was a knife-edge I walked for those two years. Trying to hold my own—to carry out what I had undertaken—under active opposition. To do this at great sacrifice in time, money—energy—(those trips to NY every day—those agonies of mind & emotions & spirit—which must be masked completely from an un-understanding & hostile companion). But chiefly the time—the creative years—the *years* that might have made a book—poems—going to a process of self-discovery & self-acceptance I found imperative if I was to go on living as wife & mother. To keep steady as wife & mother—through all this. To protect & *nourish* the children—through all storms—to be quiet—to be steady.

It was a long pull & I had no help from the person I hoped to have help from. (Dana gave me this, though. Dana pulled me through these two terrible years—kept me alive.) And no help from my usual sources of help—solitude & creative writing. There was no time for either. The only time I had left over went to the children or to C. in various ways. The book—or talking over plans or struggling to make him understand a little. *He* was being creative in these years; *I* was not—at least not in a way I could show. There was no flower for me to show. But I think there will be sometime.

At least, I have gained a steadiness & an ability to walk my tightropes & even gaily! This is much & reflects itself in the children—in the even tenor of our life now—this is enough.

But the banked bitterness remains. What to do with the bitterness?

*Antoine de Saint-Exupéry. See note on p. 49.

God—will you take it? Or must I always carry it—this bitter burden? I can perhaps dissect it—& understand it—then it evaporates a little. Bitterness & jealousy are allied & they, too, are voices to be listened to & to learn from. They are not to be dismissed or trampled down. Listen, listen. Listen deeply & courageously!

"Jealousy"—I once wrote—"is the unlived life in you crying out to be spent." This I believe to be deeply true & deeply true in this situation. C. has written HIS book. And this *is His* book no matter how much of me is in it—it is his book. He has put all of himself into it. Personality—emotions—thought—hours of work. He has written HIS book & I have never written *mine*. I know this. And I also know that it is chiefly my own traits of character—my cowardice—*my* inhibitions—*my* laziness—*my* lack of centeredness & sureness—*my* unhappiness & gropings—that have kept me from writing it. (I do not know that it will ever be written now.) But also the ground has not been propitious for its growing. The struggles to keep life—marriage—children afloat have not left enough extra for me to write with. And C., though he has often *tried to* (& sincerely), has not—consciously or unconsciously—made it easier.

Here are some of the roots of bitterness—It is really no one's fault. Now that I am freer—a little—how much I wish I had years of life ahead of me—how I wish I were Judy—just starting out—with my eyes open & my heart open!

[From a letter to Alan Valentine]

Plane, Portland to New York
Thursday evening, [September?] 1953

Already it is all so far away, and yet it is there too: a great, banked-up fire warming one hiddenly.

When we got to the thoroughfare, I saw the gray beach wagon ahead of us. Were you buying cat food? Were you in the door of Waterman's? Were you in the "Herreschaft" (spelling?) we passed beyond the Sugar Loaves? I could not tell. I watched the white sail out of sight, a very bright spark of light against the dark shores. And I found myself praying for you chiefly and deeply. (Surprisingly, I haven't prayed so literally for a long time), and it wasn't a selfish prayer either, for you in your life—all parts of your life: your marriage, your children, your work, for you alone in the midst of them, like the man alone in the sailboat out there in the bay. I felt you very alone at that moment. And I too.

I sat looking backwards the whole way—at the extravagant fling of the White Islands disappearing behind me where we were yesterday. Then Rockland Harbor, and I had to look forward. One must. I go into my life much strengthened. It will be very absorbing, very busy and occupying at first: distracting, uncontemplative, children's problems, schedules, and the restlessness of the last few days before C. goes off on a trip. I will be immersed in it all in a few minutes. So I want, while I am still attached to Maine, to the White Islands and Cabot's Cove, to say a little of all I thought last night.

Many of my thoughts were of your moving explanation—your understanding of the need for creativity in Lucia's life. You are right, and I was very moved by your perception of this and your expression of it: the generosity and fairness in this, as well as perception. You convinced me of much in that moment: that you were doing right, and that you would be able to do it, and the kind of person you were, and many other things.

I know myself how one fills creative hungers often with the next-best things (lame ducks* or flower arranging) when one can't get the time or energy or peace for the poem or the book. We land—goodbye!

Friday p.m., Scott's Cove

As for the more long-term advice, I find it difficult to say anything, except to be deeply touched and also strengthened. It seems, at times like this, so completely unreal as to be fantastic, and I am always able, in the good times, *not* to see what I do not *want* to see. Blindly. It is a characteristic that irritates me when I see it in my mother, and I know on many occasions it has irritated C. Perhaps it is a feminine characteristic, this ostrich gesture that we instinctively feel is self-preserving.

I have thought of something else, too, you said at Cabot's Cove. If I were in trouble. And I remember you at Hopewell.† And that is a great fire at my back—no, something that is more than warmth, sustaining the earth at one's back.

Saturday morning, sitting in the trailer

I feel now that C. and I pull much more together, most of the time, for the children. I think what children resent is not so much discipline, or

---

*"Lame ducks" was a family term for time-and-energy consuming friends.
†The Lindberghs moved to a house near Hopewell, New Jersey, following the birth of Charles Jr. in 1930. When he was kidnapped from that house in 1932 and it became the headquarters for the ensuing investigation, Valentine—an old family friend—was a source of great comfort for AML.

even temper, as the sense that they are not being looked at as *individuals* (with love and understanding, that is), but that they are being treated as battlefields for two opposing ways of life: as posts to hang principles on, as symbols of suffering ("I cannot bear to have my children go through what I went through," etc.), as projections of either side's pet belief or unfulfilled dream, as compensations for parents' failures, etc. We are always trying to make a Custer's Last Stand out of our children. At least, I have done all of those things. Perhaps still do. But I am a little more aware of what I do, which takes the inflammable quality out of it somehow, for it lessens the inflammable quality of C.'s reaction.

In other words (I am thinking out loud to you), every time you use a person as a thing—treat them without love, use them for your own ends—they perceive and resent it. Though the same thing may be done with another motive and be accepted. The essence is not in the act but in the motive. Am I oversimplifying? I used my children just as much as C., but for different ends. But the using of them was wrong—is always wrong.

It takes so long to learn how to love, to treat one's children with love, from love. And this doesn't rule out anger, indignation, etc., as long as this is an expression of love. And children know the difference. Rilke says it takes a whole lifetime to learn to love, and he is right, I think—a lot righter than Kinsey!

Evening, sitting up in bed
I did not mail this, remembering it would have a Darien postmark on it. I shall get it to New York by some means, or Stamford. I have just reread your last two letters, so that everything seems close and vivid again. (It seems so unbelievable and unreal at times.) Now I must go to sleep.

Sunday morning, trailer
I did *not*, alas. Perhaps it was a mistake to read the letters. But this morning it is, thank God, cool and cloudy with a promise of rain in the air. I have watered my few sprigs of mint and the lone bunch of chives (for vichyssoise!), and the rosebush and the two patches of chrysanthemums, and a small Japanese maple and one dogwood. I weigh carefully the relative value and need of the applicants for my largess, like the head of the World Bank!

I must write to the children and then take this to the post office. It is so good to be alone and quiet, even in the heat. I pray that C. will not come home until I have had a little time to be quiet and digest all this. I cannot work yet; I cannot get to "The Shells," or to poems. Tomorrow? Next week? How about you? Are you building walls? How much peace and companionship there is, in this kind of work. I think of you as I water the dogwoods, as I swim, as—as—as——Oh my dear . . .

[January/February 1954]
Dear Barbara,*

This has been a beautiful weekend—sunny and blowy, March-like. Lying in bed this morning, I heard for the first time the turtledove and found the first snowdrops pushing through the dead oak leaves on my way to the little house on the hill. I have wished so much that you and Janey† and your father could have been here *this* weekend instead of last for I feel so much more like myself and we could have sat in the sun and talked. However, it was a blessing to have you last week and I have thought about it a lot. I have had time to think because I have been quieter than usual.

I was much moved and pleased by what you told me of Jon reading the clouds ("for being sensitive to the clouds") on your face, in your mind. You must encourage him in this, teach him to be a good weatherman, for not only will he understand you better, but through you all people, and feel closer to them and know better how to help them and contribute to them. I was also terribly pleased to hear about his bad ski day and how you weathered it and that Jon had the perception to recognize and the openness *to say* what you had done for him.

I liked your admitting—though gaily enough—that you were sometimes quite scared, or astonished and wondering, of what you were doing in getting married. I don't think anyone with any imagination or sensitivity ever got married without feeling that: a kind of tremendousness and awe before this new and utterly unpredictable stage in life. Is one prepared for it, one thinks, one wonders? Of course not, how *could* one be prepared for it! Completely, that is.

It is like standing on the top of a new ski trail, waiting to take off, wondering what you'll meet on the way down, wondering if you'll make

*Barbara Helen Robbins (1932–) was a classmate of Jon's at Stanford University and his first wife. They would be married on March 20, 1954.
†Jane O. Robbins (1916–2004), Barbara Robbins's paternal aunt, who flew as a Women's Air Force service pilot during the Second World War and later became a Christian Science practitioner.

it all right and feeling a bit trembly in the knees! No one can really tell you what it's like, because no one knows—certainly not the person at your side. Not even the ones who have gone before, because it's different for each person. It is one of those moments when you have to make the best decision you can from that particular point (always a blind one) in time. No one can do more than this (maybe a bounce or two on the knees and start humming the "Blue Danube"!*)

Perhaps Jon is scared too, scared that he won't be able to make you happy, or scared he can't live up to the wonderful person you are, or scared *he* won't live up to the wonderful person he hopes *you* think *he* is! Well, he doesn't sound scared. I don't know. He just seems eager for March 20th.

I have been rereading Thornton Wilder's wonderful play *Our Town*, the Love and Marriage Act, which made me laugh and cry. He describes so well the universal feeling of parents thinking their children aren't old enough to get married and the children themselves rushing to get married and at the last minute feeling this inevitable hesitation before such a new step in growth and life, which seems to catapult you down the ski-slide ("You know how it is: you're twenty-one or twenty-two and you make some decisions; then *whisssh*! You're seventy—you've been a lawyer for fifty years, and that white-haired lady at your side has eaten over fifty thousand meals with you!")

And I loved the description of the old doctor on his wedding morning (I felt rather like this myself!): "I was the scaredest young fella in the state of New Hampshire. I thought I'd made a mistake for sure. And when I saw you comin' down that aisle I thought you were the prettiest girl I'd ever seen, but the only trouble was that I'd never seen you before. There I was in the Congregational church marryin' a total stranger!"

Well, Barbara, this is long enough. Don't bother to answer. You are going to be pretty busy these next weeks. I only wanted to send you my thoughts and my love, which go to you many times a day silently.

We were all so happy to have you here and all send their love. You will be interested to know what Anne announced at breakfast the other day. "Scott has changed his mind about not getting married. He is going to marry a female turtle!"

Love,
AML

---

*Here AML draws music notes.

[From a letter to Alan Valentine]

*Little House**

Tuesday morning, January 26th, 1954

When C. and I got back last night from his enormous dinner (Institute of Aeronautical Sciences, Guggenheim Medal: reception speech, thousands of people), I have rarely felt so prostrated. Perhaps I can't take those dinners any more. Perhaps the role I have to play, and the confusion and conflict *inside* contrasted to the Rosy Glow *outside*, is too much for me. I am exhausted. However, it was all a colossal success.

Wednesday morning

Con said, quoting someone once: "Each was the other's natural habitat." I thought about it coming home in the train. The sudden feeling of loss, of emptiness: not tragedy or despair, simply loss of what should be there, lack of continuity, as if one had been dropped off into space. As if one had been walking down a familiar road and it had stopped suddenly. Where is it? The path was so plain, so simple, so familiar, leading home. Why did it stop?

The children flung their arms about me—or Reeve did—as I came in the door. I stopped Land prodding Scott upstairs to bed with a bamboo pole, talked to Anne about her Halloween costume, tucked three children in bed, made myself some tomato soup, two pieces of toast, another glass of sherry and the rest of the canned grapefruit Anne had left. Then sat on my bed and ate it.

As I got ready for bed, I looked at myself in the mirror and was surprised at the face that looked back at me, so much prettier than that usual everyday face! Like a girl! Goodness, how strange!

Wednesday night, sitting up in bed

. . . and what is this strange world I am walking in? (Can you realize how strange, how young, how like a child I feel it in?) It is the new world of adult relationship with a subtle and beautiful and mature mind. Yes, I mean *mind*, or perhaps spirit. The whole living, growing, aware, questing, struggling with problems, thinking, weighing, enjoying, appreciating person. Sitting here tonight, I can realize how rare an experience

*After the Point House was damaged in a hurricane in November 1950, AML had a small writing house built in the woods near the large family home.

that is, to share thought, feeling, experience with someone like that, at one's own level of growth. I am shy sometimes at it, and new at it, and lack faith, and wonder if I have been greedy or grasping, bold or crude, or too frightened.

Tuesday morning

I meant to write you about Saturday evening, the day of the storm, high tides, floods, etc. We were cut off all day but in the late afternoon the mail man got through. And I had a goodly batch, and felt very gay, and put on a wide skirt and had sherry for supper (alone with the children). I put on *Les Trois Cloches* during the meal, and afterwards the children (they catching my mood) laid a fire, rolled up the rugs and danced wildly all evening, stopping only for occasional orange juice and roasted chestnuts. . . .

Little House
March 29th, 1954 [DIARY]

These last two months I have had two—really three—big experiences. My illness and all that it illuminated for me. And Jon and B.'s wedding, followed by the days in Detroit with the frail, emaciated, hardly living Mrs. L.* All of it unwritten. I should have written the illness after I came back from the hospital instead of trying to finish up "The Shells" (always behind!) while I was convalescing. Now it seems too far away and even the joy & beauty of the wedding is now somewhat blurred by the dark veil of the sadness of Detroit. Aging people & fading strength—everything darkening, dying, decaying in that old house!

But now—even at the expense of "The Shells"—I feel I must stop & write something about these weeks—in order that I may learn from them, in order that they not be wasted.

The first two weeks of February were spent on "The Shells"—working hard & talking to Mina† about them. Very exciting & good criticism & so encouraging. Somewhat interrupted by diarrhea & no appetite & some faint signs of nausea. I was already ill—with another pregnancy‡—and

---

*CAL's mother, Evangeline Lodge Land Lindbergh, suffered from Parkinson's disease for many years. She died on September 7, 1954.

†Mina Kirstein Curtiss (1896–1985) was AML's creative writing teacher at Smith College and a lifelong friend. She was also a noted translator and editor, and wrote books on Proust and Bizet. In later life she founded the Chapelbrook Foundation, which provided support for writers over forty in need of funds to finish works in progress. She was the sister of Lincoln Kirstein, cofounder of the School of American Ballet and the New York City Ballet.

‡Family members other than CAL were not aware of this pregnancy.

did not know it. We set off for the Laurentians & our weekend—our week of skiing with the Robbinses & children—on February 13th, C. & I. Although I was wretched I was sure it was just nervous indigestion & would disappear once we were off. (*That* should teach me!)

It didn't disappear but grew increasingly worse. At the end of our ten hours' drive to Montreal we turned up at the Cygne Motel & I fell into bed with my heat pad, taking only tea made with tap-water. We went on in the a.m. to Mont Tremblant—four hours or so & found eventually a little cabin. It would have been perfect if I had been well. Four double decker cots in the downstairs room—opening into a little kitchen & two rooms up a ladder-like staircase—under the eaves.

As it was, I fell into one of the cots downstairs, without even making it up. Heat pad & Luminol—clear tea with sugar. I decided to stay in bed for twenty-four hours & see if I could clear it up—still thinking it was a "bug." It became, however, increasingly worse—nausea—vomiting—unable to digest anything. And I became very weak (simply from lack of nourishment & dehydration). I still didn't know *why*.

C. in the meantime was marvelous. Kept the house warm, kept the stove (an old-fashioned wood stove) going—washed pots & pans—cleaned the kitchen from top to bottom—went shopping to try to find something that I could digest. In fact, worked like a dog all day long trying to save the situation and help me. His devotion touched me & I felt the strange irony of our relationship being so good when I felt so ill & helpless. And I looked at him from my cot—through the open window to the kitchen—across a chasm that lay between us. I felt so surprisingly enfeebled—he was working with all of his energy. I looked at his—and also my *own* usual—strength and health across an unbridgeable chasm of weakness. Usually, I thought, I can work like that—all day long driving like a horse—& my body never saying "no" to me. What an insight it gave me into health & illness—How I waste my strength. How precious it is! Also the understanding illness gives you. How can C. understand what it is to be ill, to be weak, to have the body say "no"? His body has never said "no" to him—Nothing and no one has ever said "no" to him. (Except me, sometimes, now.) *Il n'a jamais eu sa descente de la montagne,** I thought, remembering M.H.† *"C'est tout ce qu'il lui manque."*‡

After two days of this I begged C. to put me on the sleeper in Mon-

---

*He has never had his descent from the mountain.
†Maurice Herzog (1919–), was one of the first two people to ascend the Himalayan peak Annapurna in 1950. His book recounting the expedition, *Annapurna*, was published in 1952.
‡It's all that he lacks.

treal to N.Y. & proceed with the weekend without me. But this he would not do. We finally decided to turn around & start back & cancel the whole thing. It was too late to stop Barbara—she was already on the train from Chicago. But he telephoned home & stopped the children (from San Jovite). Then we started our long trek back. We had arrived in a thaw—which was why we went as far north as Mt. Tremblant—but we left in a blizzard—fighting it for ninety miles into Montreal—*through* Montreal—I with my basin—retching & spitting. C. wanted to get me to the Cygne Motel early p.m. & then go to meet B. in Montreal but the driving was so bad we barely got to the motel by dark. (I felt we had made a harbor out of the storm when we got into that driveway out of the mad swirling, blinding, wind-driven snow.) C. did not try to get back but telephoned & finally reached her & she telephoned Janey (in Boston!) & her father (in N.Y.!) & rerouted everyone to Scott's Cove!

The next a.m. we went on, I dying to get to the Medical Center before everyone had left for the four-day holiday weekend. However, we only got as far as Rutland & made home Friday p.m. Anyway, when we got to Bennington I called Dana from a drugstore. Never have I been so glad to hear anyone's voice. "Why Anne! Are you *ill?*" And then "*I* am taking over, Anne. Do you hear me? *This* time *I* am taking over!" However we didn't go straight to the hospital as he urged. I felt it was too much to ask of C., who was not too happy about my firm decision. On the basis of three doctors (Dana, Dr. Damon & R.) saying it would be madness to go ahead with it—which C. simply did not believe. However, he took my decision as my right & accepted it. (The responsibility, however, was mine—fully mine—& not the doctors'—in his opinion. All right, I could carry it. This time.)

Also, he would be left with B. & Janey for the weekend. So we went home & I went to bed—and felt a good deal more comfortable after the week of being sick in strange cabins & traveling. I sat in bed & sipped warm milk every two hours & felt better & saw Janey & B. each a.m. after breakfast for a little talk. They left Sunday & Monday I went into the hospital & Dana & Damon were both there the first evening & gave their decision & then I saw Dana alone for a little. He sat on the edge of my bed and—in between my *constant* spitting—we laughed & talked. My relief was very great & the joy of laughing—of suddenly seeing the humor of so much of it. I had almost five days in the hospital (Dana was anxious to build me up again after two weeks' malnutrition, etc.) and they had a rather wonderful quality—despite the disagreeableness of some of it. The peace, the quiet, the rest, the time to think (I didn't even play the radio. I wanted quiet—no distraction) & the healing quality of an undemanding but wholly loving relationship was quite marvelous. It was not something exciting or stimulating or romantic, heaven knows, but the continuity of a rather steady and serene relationship—warm, understanding, undemanding. D. would drop in four–five times a day. Sometimes we hardly spoke, but it was nevertheless nourishing, almost—I felt—like a transfusion. I felt life pouring back into me & with it a realization of how blessed I was to have this friendship—whatever it was—wherever I had found it. Some of it, of course is his great gift of healing, of devotion, of concentration on the patient, that he gives all his patients as a doctor. Some of it was simply our long & now taken-for-granted friendship. (But should one *ever* take it for granted?)

I said to him one day when he was sitting beside me, "Is this just the doctor-patient relationship again? Dependence? Transference?" ("O ye of little faith!") And he said quite simply: "I don't know, Anne. When I'm sitting in the sunshine I no longer pull out a prism and analyze the rays—I just accept it as sunshine."

My old fear of dependence! But this time I took the sunshine & grew strong with it & knew that it also fed him—to come in & share the little events of his day with me—or big events—to read me his radio speech & to work over the right word together. To talk over V. Woolf's diary I was reading—or his troubles with his children.

Saturday a.m. I left. C. came back from a trip to Washington & drove me home. The first week at home was—in spite of half-days in bed & all C.'s care & help—rather exhausting & depressing. I felt astonishingly frail still, & easily collapsible & unsteady. (Like the little mermaid in a new element—learning to walk—on knives!) I missed D's nourishing companionship & resented the demands that every mother-wife householder inevitably has. I felt unequal to them & felt them pulling on me—Judy—the children—C. Also too sensitive & vulnerable to people—Sue*—for twenty-four hours—Mr. Miller (B.'s uncle) & the next week—Alan—Yvonne—Mary Knollenberg.† When one is on the low side one feels suddenly surrounded by too many people—they impinge on one. And oversensitivity. I was too sensitive to Sue's criticism—& complete lack of response to "The Shells." Oh dear—how one minds!

*Susanna (Sue) Beck Vaillant Hatt was the daughter of old Morrow family friends in Mexico and a close confidante of AML
†Mary Tarleton Knollenberg (1905–1993) was an artist known for her bronze and stone sculptures.

However, I slowly got back to work & to strength & suddenly it was time to get ready for the wedding!

. . . Anne comes in & sits on the edge of my bed & says mournfully: "He doesn't belong to you any more; he belongs to Barbara now!" I realize *she* feels *she's* losing her older brother & I say she is *gaining* another sister & we'll see *more* of Jon—not less—etc. & that it's *fine!**

Alone, I realize that this queer jitteriness, this sense of pressure, is due to my feeling that I am being pushed through the door to another stage in life—and I don't feel quite ready for it. I, a mother-in-law?—like Mrs. Lindbergh? (One immediately projects oneself back into the way *they* looked to *you* as a bride!)

I a grandmother? (Like Grandma Cutter?!)† One feels, in a painfully vivid way, the ticking of the clock, the tolling of the bell—as if one were being pushed into old age—and the grave! Once I analyze this, I feel less pressed by it. We are always being pushed into a new stage, of course, by life itself, and one is *never* prepared for it. No one ever is. And one doesn't have to take the form that was taken by the one before you. One isn't doomed or forced to live up to their pattern. One will make one's own.

Perhaps B. & Jon feel this pressure also? Poor children. But they are readier than I was—& readier than they know.

I wake the next a.m. to a beautiful spring day. I feel rested & happy—ready for anything. Lying in bed I have an inspiration about A.'s hat—and suit. She can wear my old gray suit—and my pinky-red felt hat! We try them on before school & they fit perfectly & she looks charming & quite grown up. She is pleased. Land has left his bag packed & ready by the door.

Judy goes to town for my coat. I shop for Land's shirt & pants—pick up my dresses—old & new—from Mrs. Bannon, repack A. & my bags & still have time & peace enough to go to my little house & write Lucia & Alan.

Judy comes back with the gray coat, which looks beautiful & I put it right on & my new red hat & scarf & we set off for the schools with bags—extra coats, etc. Land & A. are right on time, running with arms full of books & off we go to La Guardia where we arrive one hour ahead of plane time! Hah!

*Here AML draws a smiley face.
†Annie Spencer Cutter, AML's maternal grandmother.

We get three seats in a row & settle down & relax. I write letters the first hour or so—we are due in at 6:35 Chicago time, but run into bad weather. All the old symptoms of suspicion & then fear & then doom come slowly back to me. From the first snatches of overheard conversation of the stewardess & a passenger—weather's supposed to change tonight. "Snow & sleet in Chicago"—the first "Fasten Your Seat Belts" and the first delays & a passenger saying "Thick—can't see the end of the wing." And then the long delays & the first announcements—circling Chicago—waiting for clearances—can't get "limits"—"four or five hundred feet" "may land at Indianapolis." (By this time I would have been glad to land *anywhere!*) I know *intellectually* that flying has completely changed since my early days. That they land by instrument every day in weather we would have turned back in—still, I can't help the old reactions. Tense—stiff—all ears. (There go the flaps & wheels whining down again!)

It was rough too—rough *and* thick. I wondered if they could navigate by instrument accurately through such *rough* air. Anne was also tense but Land (who has flown a lot in airlines today) went right on reading *The African Queen!* "How *can* he go on reading that!" Anne said to me & also, tentatively, "Do these planes ever go into a spin?"

"No," I said firmly and flatly. "No, Anne, flying is very different today. They fly through all sorts of weather on instrument—why, they do this every day!" (cheerfully)

"That's just it," growled Land from his book. "It happens every time I get on a plane. We're held up by weather & have to land somewhere else!"

I kept thinking—well, it's not so bad for me to be killed (though I minded most for I feel I haven't yet written *my book*—for *writing* I seemed to mind most!), but the children have their lives to live—they're too young to be snapped off like this.

Also it bothered me that we were all listed under the name *Scott*. If we crashed—who would know? How long would it take to straighten it out? (C. had the flight number, though.)

Finally, after two hours of circling over Chicago we went down again—I heard the whine of the wheels & the flaps going out. It was very bumpy—this time—thank God!—we landed. Down the ramp into cold rain & into the terminal & there was Janey & I threw my arms around her in relief. And then "At last" said a twinkling-eyed, kind-faced man—with a slight resemblance to Jane. Barbara's father. (He looked younger & definitely more open than I had expected.) A nice out-of-doors but perceptive & sympathetic man. I practically fell into his arms too—my relief at getting down safely & being met with warm friendliness was quite heady. His son Dick was there too. The same quality in his face—sensitivity, intelligence, understanding, warmth. They had been waiting for two hours, too!

Then at last we were there—in suburban Evanston—a house like our old Palisade Ave. home—Reeve runs out from the lighted door—Scott on the sidewalk. C. smiling & once in the door there is a roomful of family—Wendy, B.'s sister—flashing dark eyes & an open smile (quite a beauty). Another sister of Jim Robbins (I wasn't prepared for her—Ruth. She is unmarried too, I gather. Does she keep house for Jim? Older & not as attractive as Jane but a nice open, sympathetic face). Barbara, who threw her arms around me. Jon—whom I threw *my* arms around—beaming & at home. Kent Garland, a friend of B.'s—(girl she stayed with in Darien)—a French girl who is living with Barbara & her father. I feel quite dazed with the gaiety & warmth & relief of our all being there safely—& somewhat giddy!

A table is covered with supper: an enormous lobster Jon had caught (diving on the West Coast) & brought for the occasion—in a gunny-sack ("*with* the new suit?!" his father asked). Barbara looked rather tired & a bit tentative (I had never seen her like this before. I wished so much I could talk to her quietly but there was no chance & no time, one could only joke—about my letter to her on *Our Town*). (The man you're going to marry seeming suddenly like a total stranger!) She said she felt just that way when Jon arrived ("But it didn't last too long!"). About Ansy saying to me mournfully the night before: "He doesn't belong to you any more—he belongs to *Barbara*." About the last days being so full of *little* things ("Oh *yes*," breathed Barbara with a sigh of understanding, "that's it") that they obscured the *big* feelings. About her staying too late talking to Kent the night before. "It's a funny thing, you know, Barbara, I find you can *still* talk *after* you're married!" Yes, I was giddy, a little. My day of little things was over. But I felt for Barbara.

The young people—Dick, Land, Wendy & Kent—sat around the fire & sang, Dick stroking the guitar in true Latin languorousness: "*Borra chita me voy!*" (I thought of Mexico—C. & I in love & the smell of tuberoses at night.) Scott & Reeve sat on either side of me—& finally Reeve in my lap (it was midnight by now!). Then we sang the goodnight song—singing to Barbara too. I was so conscious of Barbara & my new awareness of her father—quietly watching, on the side.

We wake the next morning to the smell of bacon. Janey already in the kitchen getting breakfast. I talk to her as she makes a "cake" as a joke for Jon—covering a pemmican* can (given to Jane by Jon for Christmas!) with fudge frosting. On living one's own life—not being social, etc.

Then Mother & Aunt Annie† arrive—& the children come back—full of enthusiasm. They decorated the cake. One of the baby ducklings (raised by the naturalist boy of the Millers) went up Reeve's sweater! They addressed place-cards. Barbara's card was "Mrs. Barbie Lindbergh"! They are v. excited. We eat at card tables, which Jane has somehow set up while I was out walking in the wind. B.'s father appears—or was that in the morning?—and I give him the tiny joke-present (a double-sunrise shell in a little purse) for Barbara's pocket. (But no time to write her the note I want to.) Jon appears—carrying his new suit on a hanger—dresses in the bathroom. He & B. went to get the license in the a.m. & the clerk didn't catch on to the name at all! Jon seems perfectly natural, calm & happy. I put an old heart-shaped lucky bean found in Florida in his pocket. He takes it out—looks at it, "Where did *that* come from?"

Then we are all scurrying to dress, the girls & I in the bedroom Mother & Aunt A. have been lying down in. Everyone looks very well. Reeve in her lacey pink cotton party dress, Anne in the new full plaid cotton skirt & my old velveteen jacket on top—with a red carnation pinned to the collar (I pinned A. too, in my haste!), I, in my flowered silk—of all colors—red shoes & garnets.

Everyone is a little hushed & tremulous & Janey flutters in & out. Children peek & whisper at doors & on the stairs. Olga‡ starts playing the piano to fill in the pause. I envy the older generation—Mrs. Robbins, her serenity & Mother & Aunt A. their education in self-control. This is one of those times, one feels, when one would barter anything for self-control. C. of course is poised & controlled. Janey feels like me (can I keep my tears from showing—from rolling down my cheeks?). And Jim Robbins? I don't dare look at him but I feel for him—*with* him, really—all this day—he seems calm & poised—and natural too.

Then there is a flurry & they come. Jon is there—how did he get there? He seems calm & serene—if a little uncomfortable in his good clothes! He looks very handsome & I am proud of him—also sure he

*Emergency rations made up of dried meat, fat, and berries and pressed into small cakes. Originally used by Native Americans and later adapted by arctic explorers and the military.
†Annie Spencer Cutter, Elizabeth Cutter Morrow's younger sister.
‡Olga Sandor, an accomplished pianist, accompanist, and composer, and close friend of Janey.

will get through the day all right. It is Barbara I worry about. . . . The wedding march & B. & her father come down the steps. B. looks a little shy & tentative and very beautiful in a simple yellow gold dress (full skirt—belted—& a band of green-velvet leaves in her hair—she has a Botticelli look that makes me think of E.*). I don't look at her father—I *feel* him from the protective lean of his shoulders. I don't look at either of them long. This is the moment when all the emotion is fused—look straight ahead & barter for self-control. I am relieved when they are passed & standing at the fireplace & the minister takes over.

Now the uncontrollable moment is over for me—why is it and what is it that one feels at this moment? It is one of those crossroads of life when the past & the future meet. They rush together—they fuse—they melt in one fiery moment of the present that is too much for the human crucible to bear. That is why it must be held in a frame of formality— iron-clad & firm.

These pinnacles of life we cannot stand for long. One sees too much (like the moment looking at a newborn baby). All the ecstasy and tragedy of human life. One cannot bear it. Shut the door & don't look. Climb down & start on your way—keep your eyes on the path at your feet. Is this what the men were doing? C.? and Jim? I felt for Jim. He was losing more than his daughter. But he was calm & natural—even (B. said afterwards—when she slipped & started to say "I will" too early) leaning over to her & whispering during the music, "You don't have to be so eager!"

The service was very beautiful—arranged & rewritten by Janey & B. and broken in the middle by Dick singing—a wonderful full warm deep voice—golden in quality & steady & clear. I could—by now—let myself listen to it.

Jon's responses sounded strong & clear and with delicacy but no nervousness at all. At the end he lifted her tiny veil from her face & kissed her. (C. would not have done that! It must be B.'s influence.)

Reeve held Barbara's bouquet of yellow roses at this point, beaming with pride.

And then it was over. B. turned to her father & kissed him—others came up—& then went across to her brother by the piano—to thank him.

Then it all merged into a kind of reception. One had to shake

*AML's sister Elisabeth.

hands—say the right thing, hold a teacup, etc. Only moments stand out. Standing next to Jon & telling him how beautiful B. was (he nodded silently—beaming) & how well he did taking Mother & Aunt A. up to B. A few words to B. trying to tell her what I said badly or not at all the night before: that we all feel we are being pushed through the door to a new stage in life but it isn't so very different on the other side of the door—not as different as we think—and we don't have to be pushed any faster than we want, really. And we can be ourselves there as well as here—we don't have to be anyone else. She said, "I know"—& I think she does—a little. And she thanked me for the double-sunrise shell—"Ah—it's just a joke!" "Oh no—it *isn't* a joke!" "No—it *isn't* a joke."

And then supper which was gay. A children's table. A bride & groom table. Relatives & Friends table. A cake decorated by the oldest Miller boy (made by his mother) with lobsters, fish & seahorses around the bottom of it! Also, Jon's chocolate frosted pemmican cake. A wonderful sense of relief—joking—family ease & joy. I looked around at Mrs. R.'s serenity, Mother's happiness, Reeve's shining face at the other table—imagining what it meant to all of them—how they would remember it.

And then it was over—& very quickly it seemed to me. B. & Jon were upstairs. Then an expectant hush & down they came ducking under a rain of rice from all the children—& out the door. Jim R., the children & Reeve last (oh I wish I had gone!) ran out after them—we watched lights out of the window silently. And then Reeve came back & threw her arms around my neck & burst into tears: "I don't want them to go." "I know. I know—but you'll see them again."

What comfort is there to give? I felt the same way myself. And Jim relaxed on the sofa & said a few minutes later with complete honesty, "How dead the house seems now Barbara & Jon have gone!"

I blessed him for saying what we were all feeling—as if a light had gone out of the room. But the young people grouped around the fire & sang—Kent Garland talked to me about religion in the colleges—Scott & Jimmy were in a corner together & a pile of books fell on Jimmy's head while he was reaching for a porcelain duck! Duck was smashed but Jimmy survived. Scott helped to put up the books.

And then gradually the goodbyes. Mother & Aunt A. were taken back to the hotel—we went off with Janey.

Exhausted—speechless—but somehow still full of the warmth & joy of—what? Not exactly of a wedding but of the strength & solidarity of family—the sense of life, perhaps it is, the continuity of life—going on through a family (*two* families, but we both had the same kind of family spirit).

Is that what one feels about a wedding? Is that the strongest thing? The real sense of joy—just life going on—its richness & variety & renewal & its eternity & *continuity*. Was it *that* I caught at supper—Barbara & Jon—Reeve & Tommy—Mrs. Robbins and Mother? Was that the flame that warmed us—that we carried away?

Little House
May 7th, 1954 [DIARY]

I wrote the last entry almost a month ago. "One must withdraw!" Yes, but there are times when one *cannot*—if one is a conscientious wife & mother—not to speak of daughter—sister—friend, etc.!

Ten days of the children's Easter vacation followed my excited ten days of writing on the new idea. I have not been able to do anything at that since. C.'s return, the children's vacation—which means all of them are around all the time. More noise, more planning, more interruptions, more quarrels, accidents, mess, picking up, a disrupted schedule—less peace, and practically *no* solitude. The time has not been wasted—& I foresaw—somewhat—what the vacation would be, so planned to do necessary things away from home—like seeing publishers, etc. (Mina—Kurt Wolff—Denver Lindley)* & also doing the things *at home* that could be done there. C. & I going over & over "The Shells" for small picayune details, rough places—etc. This is *hideous* work—so uncreative, so myopic. You go through with blinders on looking only for the faults (how often you say "merely" or "inevitably"!) & missing the meaning completely. But we have cleared it up a great deal.

I have also been through a long period of indecision as to whether or not to change publishers—to go to Kurt Wolff whom I think I can work with more creatively & helpfully than anyone in Harbrace. But it is always so difficult to change—especially when C., at least at first, made it seem to be an act of infidelity to change—almost promiscuous!

---

*Kurt Wolff (1887–1963) was a German-born publisher, editor, writer, and journalist. He and his wife, Helen, fled Europe for America in 1941 and founded Pantheon Books in New York in 1942. Among the authors they published were Günter Grass, Boris Pasternak, and C. G. Jung. Wolff was Franz Kafka's first publisher in Germany.

Denver Lindley (1906–1982), a magazine and book editor and translator, was at the time an editor at Harcourt Brace.

I have finally made the decision & have told Kurt that I am giving him the book. I feel sorry in many ways to leave Harcourt Brace & it may be unwise in certain respects. But the overwhelming need for me at this moment is to work with someone who sees, feels & makes *me* feel the validity of my writing & my kind of vision. Kurt Wolff *always* does this for me. Denver Lindley *might* do it & I hope rather to go back to him if he is still at Harcourt in the future. But just now I need something firmer & stronger (an older person—who is *way* over on my side—as a counter-balance to the other forces in my life).

I also spent one night away from home (I ought to do this more often, it is such a help). Margot, Dana, Jack* & I motored, D. driving, to Princeton to hear Rosen give a seminar on Transference.

Scott's Cove
June 18th, 1954
Dear Kitty,[†]

I am certainly a hopeless correspondent, and especially in June, when the season of reconversion from winter routine to summer is going on: children's last recitals, plays, camp trips, dentist's appointments, doctors, etc., to be dealt with.

However CAL and two children go off tomorrow, another next week. By July 6th I shall be all alone and feel first desperately lonely and then, after a day or two, wonderfully released!

... We saw the Kennans,[‡] who stopped by on their way to Radcliffe. I was terribly pleased that they called and stopped. Charles had some good talks with him and was very much impressed by his mind—as I have always been. She was very easy and understanding. I enjoyed the conversation which I fed but did not enter between the men, but somehow did not feel it was nearly as good as the times I met him before, with you. (Evidently we need your ambiance.) Or maybe I was so anxious to have it go well and worked too hard. They arrived on a sizzling afternoon and the water had been turned off—a break in the main! And I worked too hard at getting supper—flowers, etc.—ready (Martha[§] was

---

*Jack Huber was a writer, actor, teacher, and close family friend.
[†]Kitty Taquey, wife of Charles Henri Taquey (1912–1999), foreign service officer, diplomat, political adviser, and writer.
[‡]George F. Kennan (1904–2005), American diplomat, political analyst, Pulitzer Prize–winning author, and historian who played a key role as a government adviser during the cold war; and his wife, Annelise.
[§]Martha Knecht, cook and housekeeper for the Lindberghs during the 1950s and 1960s.

off, and Judy out). Because I do this badly I always over-estimate its importance and feel it has to be *perfect*.

I realized listening to the conversation why it was I found G.K.'s mind so sympathetic. It is not the brilliance or the enormous wealth of information or even the quickness and delicacy of perception, but basically the intensity of his dedication to the search for the truth. Not, of course, a black and white truth but truth in all its shifting subtle gradations of gray. It is an elusive, painstaking, tortuous search and exhausts one in that process, and demands—besides always honesty—agility, a kind of humility, an *un*-preconceived openness to the truth, whatever it may be and wherever it may turn up.

I realized that CAL also is a determined seeker after the truth but he is looking for a black and white truth—which means that he has a preconceived notion of truth, an axe to grind somewhere (though often it is hidden). I think Dana with his patients—not in his social conversations, where he is always grinding axes—has this open dedication to the truth. This alert, open watchfulness keeps you on the jump, never lets you rest or stop at a half truth or an oversimplification or pat answer. It is applying to the search for truth the precision and objectivity of a scientist and the delicacy of discrimination of an artist—also of course, the dedication of a monk.

I use it only inwardly and sometimes in my writing.

Well, I hope they come again. How difficult communication is! (I remembered, though, that you had said it was difficult to talk to both of them at once and also that perceptive people say the same of us. How difficult communication and how impossible human relations!)

[THURSDAY] *July 9th, 1954* [DIARY]

Yesterday—a beautiful day—I went to town. I lost the early train & had already left the car to be serviced. So I had to kill over an hour in Darien! I did odd jobs but wasted precious time. Then off on the 11:10 & straight to the Brussels to meet Kurt Wolff. We had lunch at the King of the Sea—& talked. He was very helpful & enthusiastic about the new idea. He said I must "see the polarities," by which he meant maintain the balance between the abstract & the concrete. He gave me marvelous suggestions & the idea took fire with him—and with me—as we talked. He also said—as we sat down—that I had the same problem in writing as St.-Ex. The problem of finding a vehicle for contemplative prose that was not fiction. Possibly being afraid of betraying one's own life—possibly being unable to create fiction for real. . . .

Kurt said that it seemed to him today that the novel was outmoded but people went on using it in order to have a vehicle for their ideas and so often he wanted to say to them, *"Just say your ideas*—don't try to make a frame for them."

However, the end of the lunch went to discussing my wedding idea—which he said was a brilliant one (whether I can execute it or not is another matter). He was afraid I might not be vulgar enough in it. I should be vulgar too! Also said the religious point of view on marriage should be stated. "Marriage as a sacrament." The Catholic position is that marriage is a *sacramentum natural*. Once two people have come together with the sincere desire & intention of being one—their marriage is consummated. It really needs no priest, civil service, etc.—*and cannot be dissolved.*

I felt stimulated—clarified—encouraged. The change to a good editor is paying off!

September 10th, 1954 [DIARY]
. . . Over the past month . . . C. back—the galleys* to be corrected & sent off . . . also negotiations with *Harper's Bazaar* to take the *Gift.* . . . Quite a bit of work & many lessons about working.

Little House
September 18th, 1954 [DIARY]
This diary really starts with C.'s mother's death, which we heard of as we landed on the dock at Rockland on Tuesday morning September 7th. The message came, telephoned by Martha to North Haven after we had left. We drove C. to the Portland airport but he had such difficulty getting through (weather) that he did not reach Detroit until late that night. I drove the children home—or rather Land drove me and Ansy and Scott; Jon drove Barbara and Reeve. Through storms and traffic.

The sense of death was very real to me all that day. But its full impact did not strike me until I flew to Detroit the next Sunday and found C. and his old uncle† struggling with the ghastly details of funeral parlors and caskets. The whole week, now I am back, seems like a kind of nightmare (though there were some very positive things in it) due to various elements that I perhaps cannot fully evaluate now. The house

---

*For the book now formally titled *Gift from the Sea.*
†Charles Land Jr., brother of CAL's mother, was known in the family simply as "Uncle."

itself was old, gloomy, dark and dusty and they never would allow C. to change it in any way, though he wished to. Mrs. L. was buried Thursday, after a simple service in the old country church on Orchard Lake where her grandfather used to preach and where she and her brother went to church as children, in Pine Lake cemetery—a simple country graveyard nearby—on a hill with an orchard behind—old stones, old trees in the graveyard. We were able to do it quietly—no press—a few relatives—and it went well. Both C. and his uncle were pleased, and this I must remember. The other horrible steps—a modern funeral parlor and its techniques, the casket factory, the florist's ideas, etc. I must forget. I was made really rather ill by them, although they meant to be kind.

One has only to look at a dead person to realize this has *nothing* to do with the real person—with the spirit. It bears no resemblance. The spirit has left. And all this attention to the body is somehow wrong. The wrong emphasis.

I felt better after the service. No one could wish her poor suffering body to live on and now one can remember her spirit—her frightened and gallant spirit that endured so much. I feel I was able—by being there, choosing her dress, some psalms for the service, talking to the minister—to do something for her and for Uncle that I was never able to do in life—or only rarely. I felt really so guilty that I had not done more but the situation had always baffled me: I had from the beginning been so afraid of doing something to offend her. This pall (created in the beginning, I suppose, by C.'s overanxiousness not to offend her and for us to get on, etc.—and *her* extreme sensitivity and unpredictableness) lay on our relationship, although whenever I had the courage to break through it, it was better.

I could have done more—one can always do more. But the exigencies of life are such that it is sometimes difficult. And in the last years I was struggling with so much inner conflict myself that it was hard to make any kind of sincere gesture to her.

Looking back now, one can see her life in more proportion. The dimension death gives is not a phrase. One suddenly sees people's lives in better proportion, not as a flower growing upward toward the final bloom of those last days; more like the length and breadth of a tree that has been felled. One sees it all of a piece: the continuous grain of the wood. The last days, the final illness (whether of days, months, or years, as it was with her) is seen in undue proportion until death gives life its perspective.

October 31st, 1954 [DIARY]

. . . The nicest thing this week was lunch with Alice Morris who is the fiction editor of *Harper's Bazaar*, who is taking *Gift from the Sea*—& who likes it!

November 1st, 1954 [DIARY]

I took C. to the station last night, after getting the children to bed—washing up supper dishes—and doing themes with Land (following me about from kitchen to pantry with his definition of "Lady") and Scott. The usual gloom descending on me as I leave him and see the lighted train go off with the big tall figure in the passage.

Why this sunk feeling always? Not just parting, I don't think. It is more a sense of responsibility left with me—left *on* me by him as he leaves. Will I do it right without him? Can I deal with *Harper's Bazaar* and the publicity? (C. warns me about their not doing it right, etc.) Can I deal with children? Uncle? Martha? Responsibility plus a sense of sadness that somehow the week *could* have gone better—why did it not go better?

C. also, I think, feels some of this regret and says he is sorry that the week has been so full of pressure and that he had to use "the fire-hose" technique, as I called it. But a great deal has been accomplished in a short time. That is true and I understand, though I am tired. I go back to bed and sleep well—except for a *bad* dream—and wake to a sunny crisp day and feel *much* better.

November 3rd, 1954 [DIARY]

Back at the Little House after a long day in town. Land and Scott also came in by train and we all came out together by car. It poured all day, sheets of rain. The parkway was flooded and traffic blocked—an exhausting drive back in the dark and rain—with that needle pain in the shoulders from tenseness (three hours in dentist's chair as usual). I will never *drive* back after that session again. One is too tired, teeth ache; I was cross at the boys who squabbled, etc.

Usually I see Dana after my three hours. I am too tired to talk much, but it is pleasant and restful. Today I stopped on the way in after voting in Darien. It was very pleasant to see him when I was fresh—and he also. We ate our sandwiches together like children and compared notes on the week. We talked of Bill and Con and Christmas and of some of his problems. I told him of my bad dream (of learning I had cancer and trying to get to him). He said: "I would cure you. I wouldn't let you die. I would take care of you and I would cure you!" It was so sweet and so human and pathetic. That is what we all want: someone we can go to in any emergency, who will straighten it all out.

I said: "But I didn't expect you to *cure* me. I just wanted you to hold my hand when I died."

"But I wouldn't let you die," he protested. "I would cure you. I would make you well." And one is strangely comforted and warmed by this.

Little House
December 12th [1954] [DIARY]

The wheel has turned again—one of those complete turns one knew was coming but somehow did not anticipate so soon. Mother has had a stroke and is probably dying. I have been there since it happened and am back here only in the static interim—where she is hardly conscious of anyone and we are waiting—simply waiting for some sign of a trend. It was terribly hard to leave her after being with her constantly for two weeks, but she has now withdrawn so much from us that it is more possible to leave than I thought it could be a week or ten days ago. I have lived through so much in these two weeks and the stages have melted into each other so swiftly and so irrevocably that it is hard to recall each one as it went.

There was Thanksgiving—a warm gay family gathering. A big table piled with fruit, Mother at one end, gay in red, and Dwight at the other. It was a beautiful lunch. Mother asked Scott to collect the guesses on the weight of the turkey and Stephen won the prize. After lunch the children played basketball; we took walks; Mother rested. In the evening, between children's supper and adults', Reeve put on her ballet skirt and danced for Grandma Bee.* Anne played the flute—rather briefly and reluctantly—and the children talked of a play—which did not come off.

Friday I had breakfast with Mother and started to organize the day—I took crowds of children to town for dentist's and other appointments. Only Scott was left out. I asked him if he wanted to go with us and go to the movies. But he preferred to stay in the country with Grandma Bee and Sigee!† Such a blessing, for they took a walk together—Mother, Scott, and Sigee—up to the garden to cut the last roses. There had been

*The pet name Elizabeth Cutter Morrow's grandchildren gave to her.
†The Lindberghs' German shepherd.

a heavy frost, and were still a few. Mother spoke of it later to me with such joy. ("You must tell that dear boy what it meant to me.") We discussed Christmas presents. Mother had them all planned. We went to bed early.

Saturday morning I went in a little later than usual to Mother's sitting room for breakfast. She was still in the bathroom, her breakfast waiting on her table. (She had—which I did not know—been out once, tried to drink her coffee, spilled it, gone back and changed her dress.) When she came out she said she felt queer, putting her hand to her head. I asked whether she felt dizzy and she said, "No—*queer.*" And I urged her to go back to bed. But she said no, and sat down to breakfast. She started again to take coffee and choked on it. Then I went to her, and Gertrude* somehow was there, and we got her back through her bathroom into her bed, undressing her.

I did not realize that her speech had now left her, though I suspected a stroke. I asked her if she were in pain and she shook her head, and then if she wanted me to call Dana and she nodded. We got him fairly quickly, and while we were waiting I was in and out and realized she couldn't speak. She motioned for pencil and paper and we brought it and she wrote something—words not in logical sequence—which terrified me because I thought her mind had gone—which it had not. (The stroke which deprives you of speech often deprives you of the power to find words—although you understand what is said to you.)

Then Dana came and she put out both arms to him—in a moving gesture. He made some tests, asked her questions she could answer with nod or shake of head, spoke calmly and reassuringly to her, and called the neurologist who had seen her before. While we were talking in her little room and before the neurologist came, Gertrude came running in and said that Mother was recovering her speech and had said she was hungry! Dana said it was an extremely good sign that she had recovered so quickly. Then the neurologist came and made tests. She seemed completely recovered—took some soup. Dana prescribed "your favorite medicine, Betty, rest in bed." And she shook her fist at him gaily. We then left her to rest. I was in and out of Mother's room all Saturday when she was not resting—and a good part of the evening. I do not remember *when* we talked but we said *everything*. The blessed miracle of that, I shall never get over.

*ECM's personal maid.

She said of course she thought she was dying as she lay there wait-ing. She wasn't afraid of death but she didn't want to frighten us. She thought, "How frightened they will be when they come in and find me." She said how much communication meant to her—she never real-ized. She wanted to say "I love you" and she couldn't. And I said, "Oh, Mother. But I *know* that. I knew you were thinking that, I felt it. I wanted to say it too. I wanted to sit right there and hold your hand all the time but I didn't want to tire you."

She spoke about her not wanting to be a burden to us. That was the only thing she feared. And I answered, "A burden? Heavens. I wasn't thinking of that. Suppose you *were* a burden—haven't you given enough to others all your life so that you could be a burden a little now?"

I tried to get a concert on the radio for her, but we managed to get the college quiz bowl, with Smith girls answering questions. "You don't want *this*, do you Mother?" "Oh yes I do!" And she listened to it all eagerly. When I came in to say good night to her, she was still reading. She turned and first gave an inarticulate sound—which chilled me with fear again. Then spoke naturally.

I went back to the New Wing. I was waked at 2:30 by the bell (just like with Elisabeth's death so many years ago) by Gertrude to say Mother had lost her voice again. I came right over and put my arms around her and said, "Oh Mother, remember the man Dana told us about who lost his voice for twenty minutes every day?" I called Dana (got Mary—alas). He said it was bad. Of course, but there was really nothing that could be done immediately. Sleep would be the best thing.

That long half night—four long hours—I stayed in the room watch-ing every movement, listening to her breathing, helping her to turn, helping her to the bathroom. (She had to put her bedroom slippers on each time! What a sense of form!) I lay on the sofa (not on the bed) where, propped up, I could see her.

I thought, of course, she was dying. I felt completely fused with a sense of knowing what to do or what not to do. I moved completely instinctively with Mother, feeling—for once—that I knew better than anyone what she wanted, what she was feeling. I could interpret every gesture, every look. I felt, too, that I was in the room with death, or with dying, but it did not frighten me nor did I feel inadequate. Nor was it strange. It was familiar, like childbirth. It had a rhythm of its own. I could go with it. This is not strange—this is not new—this is not fright-ening. Perhaps she feels this way too?

One moved to help her instinctively, without hesitation. Action and feeling were one: no thought, no hesitation (to wash her face, to get her cracked ice, to move her, to say something comforting). Fused to certainty by a new emotion—or a new intensity of emotion. Love, I suppose. I had thought birth had taught me all there was to know about love, but death teaches more still.

With this I entered into a long pilgrimage that it is hard to go back over now, as if I had traveled through many different countries. Each day a different country, sometimes several to a day. All strange, all new, all different, and once you have left the borders of one and gone into the next it is hard to remember the last one. The landscape, the events, the customs, even the language has left you. And the time—each country has its own clocks—its own time.

The next day was a nightmare of doctors—consultations—new techniques—routine established. This was Sunday. It began early—Dana at eight (I was still in my nightgown & wrapper). Then Dr. Viccar, the neurologist—Dr. Roberts, who was to be Mother's physician—the nurses—the hospital bed—the nasal tube for feeding, etc. Mother was perfectly aware & I felt I couldn't leave her side for a moment. I felt no one could interpret her but me. And, in fact, that was true. Whenever I was out of the room Gertrude came for me & said she wanted me. Again, it was like the night, in the sense of being so fused that actions came instantaneously & rightly—without hesitation—even the right words came—when I came up after lunch to find the men setting up a hospital bed & Mother *sitting* on Daddy's bed with the nurse & Gertrude holding her up, I ran & put my arms around her & said, "Oh poor Mother—the hospital bed—but it's better than going to the hospital." And she managed a smile & a nod. And the nurses and the feeding tube—which horrified me—& I pleaded with Dana about it & he agreed that if it bothered her we would not go ahead "but let nature take its course." But Dr. R. was so skillful & so slow & the tube so fine that it didn't bother her. Dana & I were there & Dana kept asking her & she shook her head when he said, "Does this bother you, Betty?"

In between these terrible technical things I would sit with her & hold her hand & sometimes she would put her arm up to wrap around me & draw me down to her—her face distorted with emotion & I would say, "I know. I know, Darling—we said it all yesterday—we said it all. All the important things can't be said anyway—they just get across."

And sometimes—"Yes—I know *you* are thinking about your *body*—but we who are trying to help you don't *see* your body—we just see *you*."

I told her I would call Con & tell her what the doctors had told me, "that complete recovery was entirely possible."

But sometimes when we helped her up she would shake her head wearily—& I felt sure she was saying, "Don't bother with me—I am dying—Don't bother—I don't want to live halfway."

A long harrowing day—I got Con. Dana had said, "If she goes quickly there won't be time for her to get here & if it stabilizes there is no hurry."

Telling Con was hard—*thinking* about telling her even broke me down. It is seeing it with *new* eyes that is so difficult. I had already been through that the first night & the first day. I couldn't go back to the country where it wasn't so.

Con decided to come—Margot—Charles—got to work & got her a seat on the worst night of the year—Thanksgiving Sunday night. The last time he did this was for Mother catching a plane to get to Elisabeth, dying in Pasadena.

I told Mother that Dana had advised Con it wasn't necessary to come but that she was coming anyway. Her face puckered with anguish & joy—& mine too.

I did not try to hide anything this day—my tears & my words came freely—in front of Mother. I think it was right. It gave her a sense of closeness—of communication—of love.

Monday morning Con came—Margot went to meet her at the airport ("Tell her to look at her *hands*, Margot, *they* speak—they are like faces"). Her face is a little distorted with the adhesive tape holding the tube. But actually one sees none of this when one is with her constantly. One sees *her.* It is like caring for a tiny newborn baby—all gestures—all moments are illumined with love—all service is illumined with love—no matter how insignificant or menial. There is no menial task—there is no ugliness—no *dégoût.** All is illumined by love—as with the newborn baby, so also with the dying.

When Con came in & came to the bed—Mother put both arms around her & they rocked in each other's arms—Mother moaning with joy & anguish. Con saying, "I know—I know, Darling—I'm here." All of us crying.

I am so glad—so glad she could express that.

Even the nurse said—"But it's wonderful to hear a response like that."

And then we were in another country again. She has become increasingly withdrawn—with restless periods. How I have tried to inter-

*Distaste.

pret these. Was it merely—as Dana said—physical reactions—half automatic—or as I felt—a last unhappiness & concern lest we stop our lives for her? Were her waving gestures trying to tell us to go on with our lives? At any rate, I knew she deeply *wished this* & feared to burden us. So I kept saying to her, "Con is going to be with Saran* this weekend—tomorrow I am going home to Darien—I'll be back."

A last effort to ease her mind. She has been easier since then, so perhaps some of it got through. And in this new country I realize the nurses can interpret her gestures better than I. They are sensitive & loving—& now they know her they are aware & sensitive to every breath & movement.

It makes it easier to go on with my life, which was unthinkable ten days ago. The most difficult decisions drop like fruit when they are ripe.

. . . The devotion of all the household—moving still to her breath & her rhythm—a great procession of loving people moving with her. C.'s touching desire to help (the difficulty of *any* man in this atmosphere—like a maternity ward—in which only doctors can help really). His *very real* help in talking to J.P.M.† on what I call (& dread) "the Empire." Everyone has brought their gift—their special gift to show their love.

January 2nd, 1955
Dearest Barbara and Jon,

We thought of you so much at Christmas and I meant to write you about it—not that you need or expect a letter but only that it is a joy to share it with you.

We had a really happy Christmas, though we missed you very much after last year. I came back from Englewood rather late Christmas Eve afternoon and we set to on decorating: tree, window, crèche, etc. We had made the wreaths on Wednesday. I had picked out a deformed Christmas tree in the rain one day (wasp-waisted!). But by cutting off the bottom and adding artificial limbs to the middle, we managed to make a perfect shape! Land and Anne lighted and decorated the tree. Scott made a fire. Reeve lit the red candles everywhere. I unwrapped and set up the old crèche on the windowsill. I also put the rest of the Christmas tree's lopped-off branches in the picture window, interspersed with red berry branches and some whitened birch twigs and the Mexican tin angel in

---

*Saran Morgan, Constance Morgan's eldest daughter.
† J.P. Morgan & Co.

front. (I *suspended* all this from the window sill to make sure it didn't topple over!) Uncle Dwight watched while the messy room took shape. Ole Man River* hung wreaths and suspended the gilded angel exactly where it should float on the manger.

Then we got out Janey's books of carols and had Bible verses and singing and poems in front of the fire. And Reeve played "Silent Night" on the piano (treble, to sound like bells!) and Anne played an old carol. The crèche looked very magical this year and we all thought of *our* (*your*) baby to come! And Reeve remarked pensively: "I wish Jesus had never grown up!"

The children all had presents from Grandma Bee—she had thought ahead so far. And I saw one for the baby she had planned *months* ahead, for you, the last time I was in Englewood. I felt very close to her, closer perhaps in these vivid thoughts of hers for our happiness than from where one sits in the room with her now in Englewood.

I am going back tomorrow. They do not believe she can live much longer. I really think we will feel closer to her when she has died. Now she seems so far away and separated by sick-room details, but after death I think we will have a vivid sense again of her spirit, her quality, and the whole perspective of her life.

Waiting for death is so much like waiting for birth. Perhaps it is another kind of birth. I keep thinking of you—each day. I envy CAL the possibility of seeing you perhaps this week. He will give you what news there is. (Scott has learned to drive the Crosley and *backs* it round and round the circle.) I gave Land a moo-oo horn for the Crosley. I felt it was appropriate. Sigee got balls with bells in them. Land and Anne made a flying trip to Florida to visit Uncle. Just back, very rosy. We have had our regular Sunday supper together, Reeve making blueberry cake. It ended in a water fight, I fear. Now all are in bed, I also. Much love to you *three* and to Janey if she is there.

—Mother

January 20th, 1955
Dearest Barbara and Jon,

I wanted to say over the telephone last night: Has she fingernails? What color hair? If any? Just exactly *when* was she born? Who does she look like? What do her hands look like? Long fingers? Big feet? Eyes

*Family name for CAL.

wide apart? Etc. But all I could say was "It's wonderful" and "Is she all right?" and "Is Barbara all right?" over and over again.

However it was wonderful to hear your voices very reassuringly and very real. What a girl Barbara is! Don't overdo it. There should be no one in your world but the baby and her father (her father!!!) and Janey. That is enough. It is a universe—a whole new universe.

How wonderful to have it come over the horizon at just the moment when another universe is departing. I keep repeating the prayer of St. Augustine: "I behold how some things pass away that others may replace them, but Thou dost never depart, O God, my Father, supremely good. Beauty of all things beautiful, to Thee will I entrust whatsoever I have received from Thee, and so I shall lose nothing."

I wrote your father immediately. I *wanted* to telephone or cable but I had no idea where he was. The only way I could have got a message to him immediately was to telephone Juan Trippe's office at Pan American and have it sent over the ticker-tape to *every* station in the world! I had discussed this with CAL before he left and he thought that would be (for publicity reasons, I think) a bad idea. But he may get the news sooner than we think.

I feel sad not to share this great joy with Grandma Bee. I went right in to her bedside after the children telephoned me. I said: "Darling, you have a great-grandchild. Jon and Barbara have a baby girl!" There is no response now but I shall say it to her again. Anyway, I feel she knows in some way—is a part of our joy—even though we can't see it. Her first child was a girl, too, so she knew the joy and comfort of the oldest being a girl.

I am now in Englewood and plan to go back to Darien tomorrow. I do not expect Grandma Bee to live much longer than this week. She is however very peaceful—not in pain. I will feel grief when she goes, but not regret. She has had—has *lived*—a magnificent life, fully and richly and courageously. And I cannot but feel triumphant about it. She has had almost no old age—no illness until now—or infirmities.

I am so grateful that you came to Maine for that weekend. It made her very happy. And you were a part of her life. And we can all remember it all our lives.

I think of you all the time. Love to Janey.
Mother
P.S. I have just been in to Grandma Bee again. She was more alert and I told her about your wonderful news. There was certainly a response.

So I am hoping that she heard and understood me. It made me happy and perhaps brought happiness to her.*

Next Day Hill[†]
February 15th, 1955
Dear Barbara,

I find it appalling that I have not written you and yet I have thought of you so much every day. It is only that—in very different ways—we are both going through periods in which there is not one extra instant to oneself—and for you not an extra ounce of strength, sleep, energy, etc. It must all go to the baby.

I lay awake in bed early this morning remembering what it was like having a tiny baby and wondering if I could do something or say something to help the weariness of that period. You are an extraordinarily strong person, physically and spiritually. You have already been through, gallantly and triumphantly, the hardest and greatest experience of a woman's life. But now, these first weeks and months, one does have a let-down. Or rather, one has to struggle against the long pull of *perpetual* weariness and sleepiness. You say the baby is very hungry. This I interpret as meaning that she wakes you often for scheduled and *un*scheduled meals! This means that you *never* get quite enough sleep, that you seem to have no time at all between feedings, that there isn't time or strength for anything else but feeding that baby! (Not even time to brush one's teeth.)

I used to feel so strange—very oversensitive (to joy as well as difficulty), as if one layer of skin has been peeled off. Also curiously *dull*—couldn't read (even if there *had* been time!) or listen to people's conversation. It all seemed unreal and I was too sleepy and only felt alive and myself and real when I was nursing the baby. (And this was a kind of reality and aliveness that linked me to the whole world better than letters or speech.) I feel sure this is the way it is meant to be, and one should give in to it and live in a very small circle for a while.

Do take all the help you can get. Remember you're climbing back to normal. You won't always feel tired. This is a special period for special help if you need it.

---

*ECM died on January 24, 1955.
[†]The name given to the large Georgian house built by AML's parents in 1928 in Englewood, New Jersey. After Elizabeth Cutter Morrow's death in 1955, the building was converted to house the Elisabeth Morrow School (see note on p. 49). Like the Morrows' "Casa Mañana" in Mexico, "Next Day Hill" was meant to be a pun on "Morrow."

I am writing before breakfast in the bathroom. Con has just waked and I must go to breakfast. We have worked hard these weeks starting to dissolve and distribute possessions. (Oh dear!) I find it hard work and very unreal and very removed from mother and my feelings about her. But I am hoping I will get these back when it is over.

Don't Write. Your communication now is feeding the baby. I will write Jon from Montreal.

Love—Love to all of you,

Grannymouse*

Train to Northampton
February 15th, 1955
Dearest Jon,

I addressed this envelope weeks ago, when I meant to send you and Barbara a copy of the service for Mother. In the middle of the St. Augustine Prayer, I thought of you and your child. "We behold how some things pass away that others may replace them . . ." And also in the middle of the reading from *Pilgrim's Progress* (Christiana! Of course—Christ) I thought you would like to read it. It was not a gloomy service but quite triumphant, as it should have been for Grandma Bee.

Since then Con and I have been absorbed in the terrible process of dissolving the "empire" Mother left behind. We have done a lot of it and I will have to go on alone in March when Con goes back home. I have not taken too many things—most of them seem to me too elegant and delicate for my life or any of you children's lives! But I have taken some things—with simple lines and *strong*! A little silver and china. (We haven't got to the linen yet. Do you need any? There are *masses*. Sheets—pillowcases—towels—bureau scarves? Let me know if you want me to save you some. I could keep it till you want it.) Also on the furniture and silver, I will keep a certain amount in my house and if and when you want some you can have it. But if there is something you *especially* think of or want (desk—bureau—dining room table? chairs?), you might let me know.

Janey's letter made me very happy because she told me how wonderful you had been with Barbara at the time of the baby's birth, how you had read to her and entered into *whatever would help her*. The ability to express love through service and action is a great gift. It is a privilege to the giver as well as to the recipient but it is the mark of a truly mature person *to be able* to express it! And to be *free* enough to express it.

*The pet name AML and Barbara chose for use by AML's grandchildren.

I dreamed about the baby the other night. She looked like you! Are her eyes *really* blue? *All* babies' eyes are blue for the first few months. I *loved* your letter about her—and talking to you. It is a breath of fresh spring air.

Love love,
Mother

Scott's Cove, Darien
[March 1955?]
Dear Mrs. Vining,*

I would like to thank you for the beautiful review of my book in the *New York Times* book review section. But I have another debt to thank you for first. This November a friend sent me your little anthology with comments: *The World in Tune*. It came as I was going to my mother's for Thanksgiving with the children. I tucked it in my bag for that lovely moment of reading before going to sleep. On the Saturday after Thanksgiving my mother had a stroke, which led to her last illness ending in her death in January.

Your little book during these two suspended months was so much more to me than reading. It was meat and drink, or a hand in the dark, or the thread that led Ariadne (was it?) out of the Minotaur's maze. Not that I think death—or the experience of watching another die—is a dark cave. It was for me quite a magnificent experience. But a map is such a help in a territory where there are few maps. That is what your book did for me, gave me the feeling that someone else had been there before and had seen it from the same angle—in the same light—a confirmation of one's own vision, of one's own discovery of an old truth. I was very grateful to you and was able to give the book to my sister and my aunt who were waiting with me and who were equally helped by it.

And I have said nothing about your beautiful review. But I feel you will understand how much it meant to me coming as it did from you who had led the way during the winter. It was a kind of bridge for me between the real world of death to the rather unreal one just now of book publication. I could cross it—thanks to you.

Anne Lindbergh

---

*Elizabeth Vining (1902–1999), a librarian, former teacher of Emperor Akihito of Japan, and Newbery Medal–winning children's book author, had reviewed *Gift from the Sea* on the front page of the *New York Times Book Review* on March 20, 1955.

Little House
Friday a.m. [1955]
D.D.*

I am sitting in the Little House. I have finished the draft of the Psychologist† (absolutely solid thoughts on love, sex, marriage, etc. all through twenty-six pages! *Undiluted* and rather wild. How Rosen will disapprove! I am rather anxious—though timid about it—to read it to you).

The object of this letter is to copy out for you something I found in my "Notebook File" as I was going through it this morning for new-old material to use in my next character, Frances. It seemed to me very pertinent to your piece on faith. I will copy part of it for you:

Dana and Spontaneity

I say: You do not know how to help him *now*, but when you are there it will spring out of the moment. You *will* know. That is your great gift, that spontaneous creative understanding that springs out of the moment itself, the problem itself, when you focus on it.

He said: Yes, that he knew this *was* his gift. It was hard sometimes to trust it. The young interns would say, "What will you say to her?" and he would say, "But I don't know. How can I know until I listen to her? How can I know—*it must unfold*."

And I went on thinking about it and realizing that this is what life is, or should be: this spontaneous activity springing from the moment creatively. This is faith. This is the God in Homer (which one?), saying to Ulysses' son when he hesitates, "But how will I speak to Nestor, I have not the gift of words?" And the God replied: "Somewhat thou wilt look in thy own heart and somewhat the God will give thee what to say."

It is the Quaker saying, "We must move as the way opens"—based on faith, on the premise that "the way" *would* open. This is Gideon at the walls of Jericho. And David with his stone.

I go on, into Zen philosophy (going with life, etc.), Krishnamurti, and Macmurray, and then go on to "It is in all the great moments of art or creativeness, and in the great moments of love also."

*D.D. is AML's usual greeting in letters to Dr. Dana Atchley from this point forward.
†The character "Don," who is a disillusioned psychiatrist and uncle-by-marriage to the bride in AML's book-in-progress, *Dearly Beloved*, which would be published under the newly established Helen and Kurt Wolff imprint at Harcourt, Brace & World, in 1962.

Then I end up, "But one must have passed through a great deal of discipline before one can reach this point. (See Rilke's letter on the creation of a poem. He says one must have had a lifetime of experiences and have thought and felt deeply upon them. One must have understood, worked, digested, etc. Then when all that experience, discipline, work, etc. has "become flesh and blood in you"—"nameless and no longer distinguishable," *then* comes the first word of a poem.)

Then comes the spontaneous action. But it comes out of that long background of experience, thought, feeling, work, reasoning, etc. This is the ground for one's faith. This is the "trimming of the branches" which must precede any flowering of the tree (in St.-Ex.'s image). Trimming the branches is an act of faith in the spring and the power of the sap of life. Yes?

Well, I have wandered on. But there is something here. I wish I could talk it all out with you. The essence of your faith seems to me in your saying, "it must unfold."

I forgot to tell you about Rosen saying, "Well, you know, I'm prejudiced about you. I see you through Rosen-colored glasses!"

Writing this down I think, I *hope* you don't see me Atchley as I am?

Darien, Conn. [1955]
Dear Ruth,*

Oh dear, oh dear! Well, anyway, your little Anne was made happy by the dress for a few minutes, at least. I am sorry for all the bitterness. Oh dear. But I didn't put that bitterness into you or Harold. It is there. It has been there since you were children, just as there is bitterness in me, ready to be touched off by an accidental blunder of a stranger here, there, anywhere. One never knows just when it is coming and what touches it off.

I felt unable to answer your other letter; it was so full of bitterness and bad feeling, a total misunderstanding of what I had meant in my letter of last spring (I still haven't read all that mail that came while I was in Englewood from unknown people but I do try to pick out the letters from friends, though often these are buried and lost) and total misunderstanding of my life. I just felt hopeless about it: sad and sorry and hopeless. But I thought I could send a present to Anne, a gay extravagant foolish present but a beautiful one. I enjoyed finding it and remember the color of her hair and imagining her in it.

*Ruth Thomas Oliff. See note on p. 63.

But it was a mistake. I am sorry. I think I *had* better "Drop Dead" or drop out of your life if it makes you both so bitter and unhappy. You see, I cannot write long letters any more, to anyone. Call it time, call it old age, call it weariness and dwindling energy: I haven't got it any more to give in such profusion! What I have, I give to the children. What is left, I give to writing. And there isn't anything else left over, a crumb here and there. Of course, crumbs are awful. I can understand your despising them. I am sorry, but the loaf has gone. I wish it hadn't. I mind too. But there it is.

I think probably it is just as well that you are disillusioned about me. It is a terrible burden you put on people, to dream them up into something they never were or could be and then throw them out for not living up to your dream!

You see me surrounded by people crowding to give me love! I am glutted with it! Heavens! Do you really believe all the people who crowd my life want to *give* me something? They all—or almost all—*want* something (even as you and I!). They want money or an autograph or a book, or for me to address their club or church society or meeting, or they want a letter. They want help on their problems, they want understanding, attention, solutions (just as you and I do).

Last year I felt overwhelmed (I was exhausted by the long illness, the split life, the grief of death, and the months of work after). There was the crowd after Mother's death. It seemed to me everyone wanted something: money or clothes or furniture or possessions. And then that enormous mail on the book—all *those* people wanting things. And I felt inadequate and squeezed dry, and wondered why they should think I was the fountain of goods or wealth or wisdom or understanding?

But really, now I understand better. I see they don't really want bureaus and chairs or clothes or books or autographs—or even letters. They all are hungry for love—just like you and me. We all want that little postcard sent to us alone out of free will. Yes, that I understand, and forgive. But I still can't supply it, except in my own limited world. And I am unwilling to cheat and give false coin to pretend I have love or money or answers for all!

I am most anxious to give to my own children enough love and understanding so that they won't grow up with an aching void in them—like you and I and Harold and Martha. That can never be filled, and one goes around all one's life trying, trying to make up for what one didn't get that was one's birthright, asking the wrong people for it.

As for your pictures of me sitting here glutted by an excess of love! Dear me, there are other things to envy me. My children first of all: five children and a daughter-in-law and a grandchild. Yes, they *are* enviable. Or you can envy my money, possessions, fame, and what these things can do for one. These are fair causes of envy.

But surely you don't equate the Midas touch of money—or the Medusa's head of fame—with *love*? Oh no, Ruth.

And as for that crowd of "interesting exciting friends" I live in! Dear me, where are they? Where were they ever? They are not here. You are thinking of Cranbrook*—six weeks that were different from the rest of my life—that you think of as a permanent state.

Yes, one *is* lonely, and loneliness is the natural state of man. But here and there one touches occasionally people one can communicate with and it is wonderful. It is a great deal. It is worth living for, I think.

In the meantime, there is your Anne and my Reeve, and your Harold and my Charles. This is worth living for too. This *is* life, in fact. I am glad you are finding a new, free life out west. Your letters before you left sounded so dreading of the break that I was worried for you. But, as I said before, your courage has always been rewarded. And Harold's courage . . . perhaps it was more *his* courage this time? I feel so. And I am glad he has a world equal to his courage and energy.

Now—the morning has gone and mornings should go to work. I am almost fifty and there are still some things I want to write in this life—a few. I can't say them all.

Little House
Sun., April 24th [1955]
D.D.,

I feel so much better about you, having talked to you this morning. Yesterday, though I did not let myself write, or get to a desk, I thought about you all day and wrote in my mind very emphatic letters to you! All the time: while cleaning house, throwing out old flowers, arranging new, driving Anne to flute lesson and Reeve to buy a paint brush (she and a friend are building a shack in the woods!), I was outside most of the day in shorts and it was warm and lovely, but I was obsessed with pleas and sermons to you. I guess it is just as well I didn't write them.

---

*Cranbrook Academy of Art in Bloomfield Hills, Michigan, where AML took classes in the early 1940s.

This morning—what is left of it—I have cooled down. (My Little House is cold and damp. The stove won't light and the electric heater is burned out. I have just traipsed back to the house for another.) I am also relieved. I feel you are still *there.* Yesterday I wasn't sure. And I also felt frustrated because there seemed to be nothing I could do now—or ever—for you. If I could only give you back some of the strength and hope and faith in life that you always have given me.

I can hear you saying many times: "But Anne, you are *ill.* If you could get some rest, get by yourself, you would look at it all differently." I could say it to you, but it would not help you because the cure seems worse than the disease and so you feel trapped and hopeless. I am sure this is partly if not wholly the *pain.* Pain simply blots out past and future. There is no future and only a very unpleasant *now.* This is of the nature of pain. I should have remembered that Thursday for you seemed to *want* no future.

At this point, someone from the outside (a "Dana" for Dana!) should come along and say, "This is *my* department. You are to do as I say. You are to cut your hours in half. You are to rest. You are to go on a long vacation with a whole new set of friends." If I were your wife I would be such a tyrant. I would snatch you away, complaining, to some island like St. Croix, where you could do nothing but lie in the sand, drink gin and tonics and occasionally walk by moonlight. You are overtired from years of overwork. Now there is no tragic or terrific emergency to keep you going (all of us whom you were worried about made our various ports or halfway stations), you are having a let-down.

The let-down is natural enough, but the *cure* is a nightmare. The nightmare has to do with none of us: it is the threatened desertion of *work.* I can see this and I understand it. I know what your work has been to you, a little. It is meat and drink and sleep and love and home and human relationships and base and creativity and escape and peace. It is, and more so, what my first little house on the point was to me, before the hurricane took it away. It is as if someone said to me: "Your eyes are failing and to prevent total blindness you must stop writing." The cure is almost worse than the disease. Should I then write *the* novel and use up all the light that was left? It is hard to work *differently.* Not to write at high speed, strike the iron while it is hot, etc. But surely *you* would be advising me to restrain myself: to work *a little* each day, to make new patterns of work, instead of throwing it all away in one desperate gesture. To *preserve* the light *longer.*

You are now at a point in your career—wise enough and experienced enough and adored enough, and yet young enough—to let all that experience and wisdom and creativeness blossom in some of the new philosophies of teaching that you have envisaged and practiced for years. It is a crime if you don't conserve yourself for this. The people who use you as a crutch will find *other* crutches. Crutches are replaceable. Originality and creativeness are *not*. They are very rare!

You have this. Now is your time to use it. Run away. Retire. Stop up your ears. Say you're going to St. Croix to study tropical diseases. Say *you're* under doctor's orders. *Anything*. But don't go on living *half*-alive. You don't want to drop *that* way, do you?

I have said nothing personal. How can I? Let me say only that I am one of those who will not "adjust" to your dropping dead from over-work. My life would be cut in half by the absence of this wonderful communication which has so upheld and enriched and guided and warmed and lit my life (only part of it, alas). No one can, could, or would take your place. Is this nothing, Dana? *Please* stay alive. We will have some sharing yet. Perhaps the best, if you will only leave your slave-bench for an hour or two a day!

My love always,

A.

Darien
Saturday, May 7th, 1955
Dearest Con,

I am now at home. I never got to the important things I had to say to you—that I thought out Thursday night lying awake after going into the hospital to see Dana, now flat on his back in the hospital taking tests. He must stay another two weeks. They took a "lumbar test" (testing spinal fluid looking for a possible tumor to explain his constant headaches) which was not entirely satisfactory, though not necessarily negative. So he must lie there another two weeks and then take another test of the same kind. If it is no worse, or better, he can and will, I believe now, go on a six-week vacation—alone. *Where* is still undecided. If the tests are worse—well, one can't face that.

Dana himself felt rather better: less headache and more resigned to a vacation and taking it easy, etc. But he is of course in suspense and I felt a kind of desperate heart-ache seeing him there—his life-quality so subdued and myself so raw with the sense of mortality we have been living in. (Of course, he must grow old and die—a fact one never faces about those one loves who are older than oneself.)

Lying in bed at night (sleeplessness for me is due not so much to too much activity as to too *little* time to think things out alone—too *little* contemplative life. It takes its toll at night). I realized something very simple and obvious but that I had not faced before: we are now living in the time in our lives when we *must* lose our parents—all of them, not only our Father and Mother. And to face these years—year after year of goodbyes—is, or seems, unbearable. But it is natural and must be borne and there must be another way of looking at it. We must not be rooted in the past or in our parents—or even in our own loves and fortunes which are so transitory, but in our children. And I mean by this *all* our children, as I said *all* our parents. Whoever one can pass on one's joy and insight and wisdom to, whether it be Smith College, as it was for Mother, or the young who sit at one's feet hungry for insight, or the people who read what one writes (we are daughters for Mina in this sense), as well as one's own children. This was the truly rooting quality of my week with Barbara and Jon and their baby, and of your weekends with Saran. It is not just "life carrying on." It has a more precise and personal and *functional* meaning: this is how I must function from now on—not looking for shade and windbreak for oneself, but providing it for the young trees growing up at one's feet. The image is not perfect because it is a function that is both active and passive. While nourishing others you are nourished yourself. I have not really thought it out very well—but now I think I have something to work *at.*

Last night Rosen called me. He was so warmly and genuinely worried about Dana that I wanted to throw my arms about him. He was also rather comforting and thinks, as I did originally, that it is emotional and extreme overtiredness—and says the spinal fluid test means nothing as long as everything else is normal (which it is, Dana says).

It is not really that I think Dana is going to die—next week or next year—but that night I faced the fact that he *would* die *sometime* and that I would have to live a long time without that understanding and communication that has become so precious to me. I suppose all one can do is to pass on that gift of understanding and communication to another generation.

This must go—love

A.

Decoration Day, May 30th, 1955
D.D.

Today has been warm and nostalgic. Saran, Faith* and Uncle departed in different directions. The rest of us picked up the pieces and ourselves a little. Con wrote a speech for Reunion; I cleared my study a little. Then—oh bliss!—I lay down for an hour and thought out letters to you.

It was good to see you looking better—looking very nice indeed, in the dark CAL shirt and the unicorn tie! But it was hard to talk and I felt I said only irrelevancies. But still it *was* nice to see you. I only felt you should not have to struggle with conversations like that. When one has not much strength, one should not have to make conversation. The touch of a hand or a smile is enough.

I felt today, during my nap, thinking with nostalgia of old Memorial Days, that next to the kind of lightning communication I have had, that kind of communication (the kind we have had lately) is like "shouting through a mattress with words of one syllable."† In fact, I feel it has been shouting through *two* mattresses: the mattress of the exigencies of your illness, pain, hospitalization, anxiety, weariness, phenobarbital, routine; and also the equally thick mattress of my routine: pressure, weariness, and unreality.

It is sad, but it is of the nature of the two situations and it will not, I believe or hope, be forever—in either case.

You are better—not under such a hideous threat. This is all we must think of now, our gratitude at that. (Yes, I did pray too. Not beforehand really—I have not so much faith in the effectiveness of my petitions! But afterwards—in gratitude—the morning I knew you were all right.)

I must go to bed. C. is off until Saturday. Con and I will go to Englewood tomorrow. Friday I return to pick up the scraps.

Many thoughts—good night

Little House
July 4th, 1955 [DIARY]

"The way to resume is to resume. It is the only way. To resume."‡ I find it hard. Here it is July 4th. The children are off to Camp. C. is off on a trip. I must begin to find myself again—and then the way forward—to work.

---

*Faith Morrow, daughter of Dwight Morrow Jr. and Margot Loines Morrow.
†Attributed to Clarence Day.
‡Gertrude Stein.

This long winter and spring after Mother's death has been arid, though not entirely so. There has been no time to digest and assimilate what has happened to me: Mother's death, the birth of Jon's daughter, Dana's illness (though he has recovered, he is somehow lost to me, almost like Mother's loss). There has been no time to think out these things. The steam-roller of time, the *business* of life has pushed me on. The machine part of life has to go on—or rather, it has to be managed while in process of being turned off. Someone has to sit in the locomotive and pull the levers as it eases to a stop!

Darien
July 6th, 1955
Dearest Land,

I was so glad to get your first letter from Chilco.* (Your father is away.) But oh, the pace I sense in your letter: the backbreaking work, the newness of it, and the lack of being in training, which makes it even harder work than it is anyway.

I think back to the stories your father has told me of his first day's work on a farm—or Jim, taking over a new job (and not able to *ride!*) on a ranch. And Jon, on that rolling tub on the Atlantic trip, in the storm with the explosives rolling around.† I suppose it is a kind of man's coming of age. And one feels one should be able to take it if the others do. (Why, one thinks, is one so much tireder than the others? Because it is *new* and you are not yet used to it, or in training for it, like an athlete, trying to run a mile with no build-up. In two or three weeks it will not seem as hard.) I don't know what the woman's equivalent for it is. Perhaps, bringing home a new baby—with all the cooking, washing, diapers, housework, etc. and feeding the baby too.

In a way, also, I felt like this this winter, thrown into a job at Next Day Hill that was completely new to me, a job that seemed endless, like Hercules cleaning the giant's stables. One goes to bed each night thinking, *I am not equal to it. I shall never be able to get it done.* But one learns—adapts—and becomes skilled.

---

*Land spent the summer of 1955 working on the 850,000-acre Chilco Ranch, one of the original large ranches along the Cariboo Road in British Columbia.
†In 1952, between his sophomore and junior years, Jon worked as junior technical crew aboard an oceangoing tug, with researchers who were making seismic profiles of the Atlantic Ocean floor. In rough seas off the Grand Banks, several heavy depth charges broke free on the deck. While not armed with detonators, the charges, which weighed several hundred pounds each, were "dent sensitive" and might have exploded on impact had Jon and another crew member not been able to tie them down.

You say: "I guess I'll learn the hard way." Maybe all learning is "the hard way." It stretches us. But in another way, you do *not* have to learn "the hard way"—not as much as I have, or your father or Jon. This is because you are gifted with a marvelous adaptability. You "ride with the punches" better than they, or I. And you have, allied to this adaptability, a sense of the medium you live in. *People:* you like them, they like you. You make friends wherever you go; you will always. You will never be alone. Like a boat whose natural medium is water, you will be carried along and buoyed up by the medium. I sense that also in your letter: that you like the men and they like you, even though they are different from you. This is saying a great deal and you have done well to accomplish this.

You probably haven't time even to read a long letter like this. I miss you. The news from the children is good, though Anne feels strange in the western atmosphere. Scott developed saddle sores the first day ("I'm goin' down the roa-ad feelin' bahad . . ."). Reeve is a duck in the right water.

I must run and get this in the mail. I wish you could come home before college. I can hear you swapping stories of your summer's trials with Jim and Jon and Father.

[SUMMER 1955, DIARY]

. . . It is my time to lose my parents—all of my parents—not only my Mother & Father but all those who took the place of parents. But this is not abnormal—or tragic. This is life at its most normal. It is their time to go. It is our time to let them go—in good grace. How to meet it without this terrible tearing up of roots?

One must no longer be rooted in the Fathers. What then can one be rooted in—one's children? Not exactly. One is the Big Tree oneself now—& others are rooted in you—find shelter in you. One can no longer look for shade, shelter, windbreak in others. One must *provide* it for others.

And yet—one needs roots of some kind. I find that losing one's parents seems to rob one of the future. I do not think this is simply a question of one more outpost down between oneself and eternity. Because I felt this same "loss of the future"—with other deaths & blows. Little Charles—Elisabeth. It has more to do with shock—all the connections having been shaken & loosed. The present is isolated—unreal—unconnected (numb & plodding). (It has been this winter.) And the future is non-existent—directionless. This is because the strands are cut from the past. One does not quite know how to go ahead.

"Walk *across*—not *down*" is a stage direction given to actors & dancers. I have been walking *down* all winter—numb, plodding—completely divorced from past or future. But to "walk across" one must have a sense of direction—to know where one is going—what one wants to do—where one wants to go. Perhaps the first step in finding a direction is not to strain ahead toward it but rather to find out where one *is*. To have & to refind a strong sense of place—of location—of here & now—of balance & pleasure in the present moment. Not a plodding treadmill sense of the present—as I have had all winter & spring. But a motionless & erect sense of it—a sense of joy & pleasure in the immediate—a stopping to look at it—feel it.

This is what I feel like doing now. To have a sense of my house & in making it comfortable—beautiful—peaceful (*creatively*—as contrasted to the destructive tearing down of a house I have done all winter). Also—very strongly—to make Mother's beautiful things fit into my house—where they can & as they can—differently—in a living sort of way.

Then to enjoy being alive again—to get up without a sense of pressure—or something that *must* be done—this day—this week. (The first weeks I was back from Englewood I still worked at this pressure—cleaning up, etc.) To swim before breakfast—to dress in shorts—bare-legged—& only scuffs on one's feet. To eat on the porch! Unhurriedly. To do a *little* cleaning up each day.

To enjoy weeding my mint garden & my chives—for mint tea & vichyssoise. To enjoy eating—& plan for simple summer meals. To enjoy baths & taking time to cream my face—brush my hair—*hard*. To lie in the sun & experience & use eau de Cologne—& wear pretty summer dresses at night. To listen to music on the porch at night. I have moved the radio to the window. To read again—the George Sand–Flaubert letters—Delacroix's journal—Marianne Moore's essays. Not problem-reading, running along reading—"Walking Across" reading.

To go each day to my Little House. The wasps had built nests in the eaves; the grass had grown around the door & spiders had webs in my desk drawers. But I cut & sprayed & swept. Put up a new blind. C. has been cutting the trees for light, which helps a lot.

It is very hot now midday but I have found I can work on a card table on the bedroom porch—a different setting but possible. I cannot work in the study or my bedroom—too many spider webs, back to household duties—but the porch is free again. I can be my writing self here. I am very pleased about it.

Make the *present* creative—then perhaps I *will* find a sense of direction for the future.

Later

At night I read over for the first time since Mother's death the whole of *Dearly Beloved*. The first chapters are crammed with introductions—descriptions—explanations. Strained, breathless & lacking in confidence & inevitable—they are self-consciously effortful & therefore lifeless. But it gets better—easier. Poetic interludes—*good!*

Little House
July 13th [1955] [DIARY]

We have just had nine days of intense heat-humidity and—for me—loneliness (I who long so to be alone!). It was a kind of let-down—a sudden let-down—the children and C. away, still masses of unpleasant jobs to do in the house, cleaning up of accumulations. I felt exhausted, uncreative and at loose ends. The heat and humidity and deadness of air made it impossible to do any but the most mundane physical jobs. (It is easier to push one's body than one's mind.)

Nothing one does seems to help. How does one get out of these states? Analyze it? I went down to Bucks County and saw Rosen and Dwight. I was happy he seemed easy and relaxed and warm and gay and I saw his new house and felt his joy and new security in it. Yes, it was good to do that. But when I came back to Darien I still was not lifted out of my Sargasso Sea. I did difficult jobs. The day after I got back from Bucks County I decided to go over and burn a lot of old papers: diary material, notes and letters about the time of and preceding the analysis. A hot job for a hot day: a solitary gloomy job, which made me feel even gloomier. The self-analysis and letters and copies to Rosen were not interesting or moving; I was glad to destroy them.

But the copies of my letters to Dana moved me and made me very sad. (He never keeps *any* letters and has destroyed all the originals.) Though they were the letters of a patient to a doctor, they were also full of beauty and wisdom, all the working out of my life, much insight that he helped me with and that finally made its way into *Gift from the Sea*. But also everything beautiful that I discovered or felt or saw—such a pouring out. I brought him all the flowers I found. "O to whom—to whom shall I present these flowers?" It was so easy to give them to him—and so safe—I suppose. My gloom and loneliness in rereading and destroying (I kept some for notebook or novel material) was the sense of loss of someone I could share all that with. I can no longer share the flowers with him. Partly because I have grown—and partly that he has retreated—from our mutual position. I know it is inevitable, but I mind, and I feel less creative because I have lost his ear, his marvelously subtle and welcoming perception and understanding. Perhaps the position is not lost, but shifted, and I have not yet discovered the new position, the new relationship.

I must give the flowers to the many—to writing—to books, not to the one.

Perhaps, it occurs to me, doctors are like artists in this: they also cannot give to "the one" because they must give to "the many." Is it an excuse for not being able to give to "the one"?

Saturday, July 16th [1955]
Dearest Con,

The weather has changed—*twice*—since I wrote you so gloomily. First to cool, sunny and dry* and now to damp again—fog-horn going, humidity 95 percent. But in the meantime it has been a better week. I think the weather has a lot to do with one's spirits if one is on the edge. Also, *we* are conditioned to summers' being sunny, warm and dry (Maine again). Those foggy weeks were the violent exceptions that proved the rule and we rather enjoyed them by contrast.

I love your letters. They are a great joy to me because I think we *are* going through the same thing. It is all part of the adjustment to the new state. It *cannot* be creative. It is uncomfortable, hot or cold, humid or dry. "We are not supposed to like it." It is part of learning to live again and enjoy it, which death blankets out temporarily. I think we just have to get through our summers and have our houses, our lives, and our bodies better on the other side of it. You, unfortunately, are living in pressure.

I saw Dana on his way to Newburyport. He seems much better and gayer and is going to write a review of a book, for *SRL*.† I think he is making, or will make, his adjustment to a new stage in life. (He will never be free but he will find a new way to forget his trap.) And I think I can also adjust to a new set of positions vis-à-vis him. Not lean too much—not expect too much. See his great quality for what it is. I feel it is like some gigantic Virginia Reel. We are back somewhere at the beginning again.

---

*Here AML draws a smiley face.
†The *Saturday Review of Literature*, a popular literary magazine.

In and out the window
In and out the window
In and out the window
*As we have done before—**
Stand and face your partners
Stand and face your partners
As we have done before!†

This week I have had CAL very pleasantly—some cleaning up and some swimming. He is busy and in good spirits—off again tomorrow. Also went to town to see Rosen and Jean Webster‡ for lunch. This was interesting: Rosen on schizophrenia. Sometimes he manages to be artic- ulate and lets one in, accidentally, a little, to what he does or tries to do. This is probably clearer at times like this since it is *not* about oneself.

What I got was this: most doctors try to dynamite all the bridges between the conscious and the unconscious because they are afraid of the unconscious (shock treatment, drugs, etc.). Rosen is afraid of the unconscious too, but fascinated by it. He tries to (1) keep the bridge open, even the most tenuous bridge—make *more* bridges, (2) be more permissive than most doctors about schizophrenic behavior, (3) give them what they want so they don't have to go on asking and asking for it in all those strange ways and strange words and images over and over again.

I also felt very strongly his love of and interest in all forms of life—wherever it may appear (curiously related to Schweitzer's "rever- ence for life"). Cannot bear to blanket out life in any of its manifesta- tions. This time I felt better after seeing him.

It seems to me, re your comments on the future (love or creative work giving a sense of it), that being in love obliterates the future (*and* the past). It simply wipes out all need for the future. This is enough. Or perhaps what it does is to make us see time less artificially. Past, present and future are all contained in it, all continuous. (This is also, incidentally, the sense of time in the unconscious. The unconscious, according to Rosen, has *no* sense of time; it is all co-existent.) It is like the movement in music called *sostenuto*.§ (How I love that movement and the word!) Creative work at

*Here AML draws music notes.
†AML slightly misquotes this traditional nursery rhyme.
‡A close friend of AML's.
§Instruction to play a musical passage in a sustained, drawn-out manner.

its best also obliterates the future. So does sex, of course. The *idea* of creative work, like the *idea* of being in love or the *idea* of what to eat for supper, gives one a substitute present and future. (When Mother was dying, you remember, we did not have or need a sense of the future. This was love, too. I sometimes think this period is reaction from that spiritual high and nostalgia for it—not so much for the past behind it.)

Well, so much for that rambling. I am struggling with the new air conditioner. It came yesterday and was installed. It was a *very* hot day and it took four hours to get the house cooled down from its noon-day heat. This morning we put it on *early* and I have been wearing a sweater and the windows are all fogged up and I have the light on!

Land writes it has rained every day in the mountains of British Columbia. They push three hundred head of cattle all day. It is very wet ("I guess I'll learn the rough way"). What a life you lead out there!

Love—love

A.

P.S.

Even geraniums, you know, will not bloom summer *and* winter. I try to make them, of course. I took them out of the summer window-boxes and put them in pots inside; they stayed alive but they would *not* blossom. Then I put them all back into their summer frames. It took them a long time to recover. They are just now beginning to bloom again. Don't you and I expect blossoms from ourselves all year round? (A little Vigoro* is needed!)

Little House

Monday, July 18th, 1955 [DIARY]

I think I am going to have to give up on finding "people" in July. C. has gone off again. Evie called this a.m. & cannot come until perhaps Thursday or Friday. I have written the Kennans & wired Yvonne & I shall try to call her tonight & also Kitty. But I feel it is no use. I had better relax. It is my month to be alone. There is a terrible irony in it with *Gift from the Sea* heading the best-sellers week after week, preaching "solitude—solitude!" Here I am, having *just what I say I want* & it does not seem to be the answer! Then is the book all "hooey" as I sometimes feel? I don't think so but the truth of it is not relevant to me at this moment in my life. (It is one of those half-truths Whitehead speaks of—the danger is when one takes them for whole-truths—"not true or

*Brand name for plant food.

false but *relevant*.") It is true if one feels creative & it is true, actually, that I *am* better, probably, alone—not happier but more relaxed & out of that relaxation, I hope—creativity will come again.

"*C'est de la terre en repos.*"* If I would only accept it instead of fighting it, condemning & judging myself always for getting so little done. If I work all day at tidying up (like yesterday—washing—taking down dirty curtains—putting up new—filing & sorting at my desk), then I can relax at night & listen to music & then I feel better. Or swimming before supper—or that still hour before breakfast. I don't have to justify myself doing these. Perhaps this is all I am supposed to do this summer—to get back to life—normal life. I am so greedy—I hate seeing the summer slip away with all this precious solitude wasted—nothing created out of it!

Evie was a help on the telephone this a.m.

"How are you?"

"Oh—I'm all right" (as Mother said it the last year of her life, rather grudgingly). "I'm not unhappy—I'm not happy—I'm just nothing—I feel nothing." ("A day without salt.")

Evie went on to say that she had felt for months after her mother died—after a period of sharp grief was over—simply numb. "The world was covered with dust & ashes." Almost worse than grief.

I think it *is*, because grief is so illuminating & vivid & one feels alive—if suffering—through it. But this is a kind of anesthesia—one feels not that *they* are dead but that *you* are. One is unalive—unaware—unseeing & unfeeling. Surely this *is* death. Are we punishing ourselves for their death, I wonder? One feels very unloved after the death of someone who loves one. That is where the purely & concentratedly religious are so lucky—God loves them & they never doubt it. "I know—he *cares*—my Jee-sus *cares*. I *know* he cares for meeee."

This doesn't seem to be enough for me. I lack faith—or I want a more human love—or perhaps I do not love (forgive) myself enough.

[DIARY, UNDATED]

I plan to have the Wolffs for the weekend—& have sent off to him some pages of the novel typed. I also work each day at the Little House—until about two–three when the heat from the roof comes down & overcomes the cool air from the air conditioner. I work at Don—slowly—painfully.

I write postcards to the children—I swim—I listen to music—I plan easy meals for the weekend.

*It is of the earth at rest.

Ernestine is back—I see her for a moment (when K. is there). She looks entirely different—refreshed by her trip—alive & positive again—she leaves for the weekend to see her boys at camp.

[DIARY, UNDATED]

We have quite a successful weekend. Though the heat continues to be appalling. I have bought from the delicatessen two cooked ducks—to have cold—also lots of fruit salad—cold soups—cheeses & cold cuts—& brioches & croissants for breakfast—so as not to cook much. Even so—just the preparing of salads—trays—iced tea—whipping up the cold soups—& cleaning up—keep me on my feet all the time & I get very tired & angry at not being able to do it better. All other women do!

Fortunately C. arrived Sat. p.m. & he was fresh & full of life from abroad & he could talk to the Wolffs while I did the necessary practical work.

The week-end is somewhat weighed down by the heat—the humidity & all of our weariness at the end of such a summer. Helen* has not slept enough—with heat & a bad sun-burn. Kurt is tired from the summer in N.Y. I am weighed down by the sense of Monte's wire—Ginny's letter—the Aunts, etc.—all Mother's dependents I cannot carry forever, & C.'s natural & proper resentment of them. Also just weariness with the unaccustomed work & not doing it perfectly & not being able to give myself up to conversation at the same time.

A few moments' clear joy listening to Wanda Landowska's[†] record.

Also a good talk Sunday a.m. with Kurt on the chapter of the book he has read.[‡] He is very encouraging & stimulating & asks rapier-like questions that show me where the chinks—*holes*—are in my thinking & planning.

Monday I get to his suggestions & write again—slowly on Don—it comes a little. I am at least thinking about all the characters & they are getting rounder—but on paper it does not go fast.

Monday is cooler—we had storms all Sunday night & it is suddenly clear & bright—dazzling—like Maine—Ernestine comes to swim.

---

*Helen Wolff (1906–1994) was a noted publisher and editor, and co-founder, with her husband, Kurt (see note on p. 103), of Pantheon Books in 1942 and of the Helen & Kurt Wolff imprint at Harcourt, Brace & World in 1961. She was renowned for introducing American readers to such eminent European writers as Günter Grass, Umberto Eco, and Max Frisch.
[†]Polish-born harpsichordist (1879–1959).
[‡]The novel *Dearly Beloved*, which was published in 1962 by the Wolffs, after they had moved to Harcourt.

[AUGUST 1955, DIARY]

. . . I went in to see R.* Tues. p.m. and discussed the summer's depressed period. Heat & humidity & let-down are much too simple excuses for him. Also all the rest of my analysis of it. (Don't want to be ECM & to be tied to the past—new person coming to birth & all the "past-ness" hinders that, etc.) He says I still have no confidence in being a woman, mother, etc. The book—success & letters make me nauseated because it is competition with C. (i.e. I still want to be a man & yet it doesn't bring happiness, etc.). All depressions are "anal." I want to punish myself. Yes—I want to punish myself. I hate myself—but for what? Why? For being so lazy this summer? For having stopped my compulsive busyness of the spring? I don't understand it really.

However—his animal good spirits & enthusiasm always hearten one somehow & make one feel there is more time—more space—more life—more opportunities.

Monday, August 22nd [1955] [DIARY]

Another hot weekend—broken by thunderstorms. C. and I meet Anne at La Guardia in the middle of the hottest day—Sunday. We barely get into the house when Sue and Bob Hatt arrive and we all go swimming and then sit on the terrace and drink iced tea. Then Sue and I go to the kitchen to get supper prepared: cut peaches, shuck corn, and talk. Sue tells me, quite accurately, that this is the wrong kind of meal for company because it keeps you in the kitchen up till the last minute. Casserole cooking is how she does it. She is quite right and I feel, as usual, inadequate in a household way.

She also talks to me about George,† who is getting married, and Nancy, his bride, and how she was influenced by my book (for the worse!), confirming my dim feelings of discomfort about the book. (Most women like it—for the wrong reasons, she fears; men *don't* like it. It's really a bad sign, its being so popular with women—shows how many unhappy women there are in America, discontented women who want a career. Nancy is an example.)

Much of this is true and I have said it myself. But this discussion rather helps me to say it out loud and clarifies what I feel. Actually it was written over a long period of time and *growth*, and has so many different

*Dr. John Rosen, AML's psychiatrist. See note on p. 77.
†George Eman Vaillant, M.D., Sue Vaillant Hatt's son by her first husband, the anthropologist George Clapp Vaillant.

layers of growth in it that people can find in it what they want—and they *do*! Among other things they respond to is my period of unhappiness or discontent with being a woman and my suggestions of ways, chiefly external, to counter this discontent. This discontent corresponds to the general malaise of the American woman with being a woman. I don't know enough to understand this profound malaise in this country or why it has become so wide, but I think it has to do with the fiercely competitive nature of our culture—certainly with the competitive struggle in America between the sexes.

Why does the American woman want to be a man? The English woman wants to be a man, too, but she just doesn't have a chance. She doesn't compete successfully. The American woman competes quite successfully—and unhappily! The Latin women are content to be women—why is this? Does it lie in some form of respect women get in Latin countries—*as women*? Is it due to our sexual repression, fear of sex, shame, etc.? Has it to do, as someone suggested, with the worship of the woman (the Mother Mary) in the Catholic countries—which we don't have in the Protestant countries?

I wish I knew.

In any case, the discontent of the American woman is certainly *one* cause of the popularity of my book. But there are other causes, some spurious, some not. It has an "even as you and I" popularity (like Eleanor Roosevelt's column), founded on the myth of CAL and me as a dream couple, idealized, worshipped. *She* has had trouble adjusting to housework, married life, etc.—"even as you and I."

Then there is the "Back to Simplicity" movement, always and perennially popular. This is partly sound, partly escape. Then there is the frank explosion of the American myth of "The One and Only"—always and eternally at the same level of happiness. Everyone knows this is a myth, but saying so out loud helps and relieves people. (Love is intermittent, etc.) This is true and helpful and popular.

Then there is the hope for middle age and a new period of growth, and maybe even a new and more wonderful relationship! "The one and only" in a *new* package! Also part true and part false. Middle age as a new period of growth is true—the new and wiser and better relationship—the argonauta? I don't know. I certainly believed it when I wrote it, but I don't know. Anyway, both of these are very popular.

Then there are other smaller bits of insight or wisdom scattered through the book which are somewhat true and helpful: on the nature of love, relations with one's children, on being insincere, on can't-say-no-ism, etc. It is also written (and rewritten) in polished prose that is near the poetic and therefore charges the thoughts with an emotionalism it would not otherwise have. This also makes it all sound *easier* than it is! One can praise the book for this, but it might also be called a fault. It was a personal experience frozen into a beautiful form at a moment of half-growth. So that in the beautiful form, one finds embedded both the true and the false, the eternal and the ephemeral. The beautiful form *changes* it, so that people read and get fired by it—either to love it or hate it.

I told Sue I felt it was like *The Wave of the Future.** She said she had thought so too but thought it would be tactless to say so(!)

Though I know all this I am quite deflated[†] by the evening—both my inadequacy in the kitchen & in the realm of the artist & thinker.

Dinner actually was quite good & everything done at the right moment—too much corn—too many peaches—a *little* too much seasoning in the peas—but on the whole a pretty good meal—for *me*—not for a Sue!

And the *effort*—I have expended *so* much effort—even for this simple meal—a good adequate meal. Finally, *after* cleaning up, we sit on the porch & sip white wine in seltzer & I get the conversation off of me & the book (What adverse criticism did I get from reviewers? Bob asks. I tell him about *personal* criticisms as C. launches on *no* bad reviews) & on C. & the movie[‡]—chiefly Sue & C. discussing. I get the men to discussing traits in unification & diversification in nature & man. C. is good & challenging on this & Bob is—somewhat—in his own field—& although rather conventional, open & interesting. I am pleased at this & to give Bob a chance to talk. Here I am successful & we have a wild thunderstorm—wind & rain which cools things off. Anne sits inside & plays recorder & writes letters. I feel vaguely uneasy about her.

When we go up to bed C. and I go in to say good night & she bursts into tears. She is tired—up all night on the plane & feels homesick for Camp & the nest of all those wonderful people! I put my arms around her & tell her I know how she feels & how I feel like that each time I

The Wave of the Future (New York: Harcourt Brace, 1940), AML's controversial third book, appeared to support CAL's isolationist views. In later years she would refer to it as a "mistake."
[†]In a footnote, AML writes: "Sue is—of course—& always has been a deflater."
[‡]*The Spirit of St. Louis* was eventually made into a movie in 1957, directed by Billy Wilder and starring James Stewart as CAL.

come back from Europe—strange & out of place & wishing I were back there & feeling no one here understands. But she wouldn't like to be there all the time—would she? No—she wouldn't. She likes it here—she said it's only the in between that is hard.

I tell her it always is, but that it is wonderful to *feel* & wonderful to care about people & wonderful to love them so much that you miss them. And you *do* find them again & more new people like them. The change is always difficult—she didn't want to change from Camp but when she did, she found the change wonderful & new & she was able to adjust to it & fit into the new western world & make new friends. And this was a real achievement & she had shown the capacity for adjusting to change which would serve her all her life. She would do it again & again. She was more of a person for this new experience & she would find more new friends because of it.

And I told her how *terribly* happy I was to have her home. This is part of it—of course—she was dropped into a busy adult world in which her all-absorbing world no longer counted.

She went to bed comforted & I also—feeling more alive—more adequate—more functioning than I have all summer. For *this* one lives!

Friday, August 26th [1955] [DIARY]

Monday night, as C. and Ansy and I clean up after supper in the kitchen, Land walks in the door—tall, lean, serious, in a wide western hat, blue jeans slung low on his hips on a wide studded belt: very tan, very man-like. Ansy shrieked, "*Land!*" I threw my arms around him. C. was too surprised to speak.

That evening Land tells us one story after another—in a slow drawl, half-western, half-Canadian—of his incredible summer: chasing bulls, roping, tearing through brush on horses, drunken Indians, strange characters talking to him, getting razzed. "Gee, I was green. I am *still*." I felt he had come to man's estate this summer, learned a lot about life, about ranching, about men, and about *himself*. A new confidence.

The next day Land and I drive in for Scott, who arrives, also tan and in a western hat, without his baggage (left locked up in some station), but holding a cigar box in one arm in which there were four horned toads! We are a strange trio walking down Madison Avenue: Land and his drawl asking questions of Scott, Scott and his hat and cigar box, and I laughing at the two of them, racing along.

It is curious, this summer, as I said to Dana. I feel as if there were a kind of permanent high level of despair in me and I fall into it at the slightest provocation. It is like an uncovered well. All sorts of irrelevant details throw me back into it again. I suppose the well is the unabsorbed grief at the loss of Mother. At night I dream back to the old house in Englewood. I am in her old room and find an old nightgown on her bathroom door; I realize she is dead, but when I get into the bathroom alone and see the nightgown I sob and sob (which I never do awake). And there seem to be unexpected trap-doors every day which let one down into this level of despair.

[August 1955]
Dear Kurt,

I realized that of course I would go through with the picture for the *Life* article and that I would certainly not let you down, or Pantheon. I felt badly not to be able to reach you until the evening, for this kind of misunderstanding is best cleared up immediately. On the other hand my—our—extreme sensitivity about press pictures and publicity may need more of an explanation, at the risk of making this small incident sound too serious, than is possible except by letter.

Perhaps we all have areas that are oversensitive to pressure, in which one sees thunderheads and feels threatened where outsiders can see no cloud or threat. Press, publicity, pictures seem to be such an area for us. There are reasons, of course, in the past, for this.

At any rate, at no time did I feel "angry" at you or at Pantheon, only at *The System*, and chiefly at myself for getting caught in this. By "The System" I mean that American tendency (of which Pantheon is remarkably free) toward commercialization of spiritual goods on an enormous scale in the same way as material things are commercialized. However, this *is* the system in America. One cannot operate outside of it. One must work with it and keep one's integrity somehow in the process, which I certainly feel Pantheon does. The fact that you have been able to launch a successful book without intruding in any way into—or without any exploitation of—our private lives or personalities is really quite miraculous, and we realize and appreciate it. I also realize that your understanding and protection of our attitude has involved difficulties and possibly sacrifices on your part, although I would not think it had actually affected the sales of the book. So it is *I* who should thank you, and also say I am sorry for the trouble this has caused.

Now, we can forget about this and take it for granted. I will wait to hear from you on the time for the photograph. The children are all home now—my youngest boy *minus* his baggage which he left locked up in some station, carrying carefully instead four horned toads in a cigar box.

The weather is autumn-ish and the cook returns Monday. Life hums again!

Darien
Wednesday, September 7th [1955]
Dear Mina,*

I write in pencil sitting on the terrace with my eye on the new moon-flower bud: I cannot miss another opening. Saturday, after looking at that bud in the rearview mirror all the way down from Ashfield, being sure the drafts were not too rough on it, etc.—then depositing it on the terrace and telling all the children we would watch it open that evening—it went and sprang open as I went for a short swim at four!

Now I shall keep watch, or set a child as ground Observation Corps when I leave this spot. Anyway, it was extremely decorative—unbelievable, really. "Like a moon," one of the children said, "and the round wire cage is the world," one of those rare beauties that seem to be quite natural in Ashfield but simply fantastic here on my porch.

That rare world seems far away in this bustling one of the first day of school. Sunday went to Charles's departure, Monday to going over the children's clothes in preparation for Tuesday which was an expedition to Stamford for fall and winter clothes. (Every other mother had the same idea—Best's was jammed.) But today the winter routine has started and the house is quite peaceful, after eight a.m. and before 3:30 p.m.

Anyway, I think my new year started in Ashfield. I don't believe I can give you an adequate sense of what it did for me. I have been trying, in my mind, to express it for Con. I suppose it is really a renewed sense of one's capacity for joy that it gave me.

(Anne has just come back from school. She had her first French lesson. "We learned to say *le professeur*!")

Joy in the external world first: the overflowing apple trees, the lush grass, the ferns, the pine needles, the birch trees on your hill in the middle of all those dark pines. Delight in sheer living too. The food. (How did you get shad roe in September?) The salad. The wood-fire,

*Mina Kirstein Curtiss (see note on p. 93).

the linen sheets to sleep in, and then the excitement of talking and listening to people.

(Scott has just come to give me his change from the school lunch. The moon-flower bud has bent its swan-neck in its effort to follow the sun across the sky.)

All this was true last year, of course, but this year I was hungrier and more grateful. Also there was more ease. I have decided, thinking about it on the way down, that the "needles and pins" feelings I have listening to M. Léger's* conversation is not really—or entirely—due to shyness or fear of being inadequate, but it is simply a feeling generic to poetry. Real poetry is, of course, not soft and flowery, but pierces intuitively to the naked nerve. That is why, whether he is talking about the frigate bird or his mother riding through a tropical storm or the diet of hummingbirds, it is always exciting. One is shocked to a new image in a flash of lightning. I must try reading his poetry with this kind of receptivity. One gets into the bad habit when young, when adolescent, of reading poetry in order to find mirrored one's own feelings or to be lulled into acceptance of one's own feelings, when it really should bring "not peace but a sword."

But there was peace at Ashfield too, given by you. I don't mean a pillow kind of peace; I think it is, among other things, the absence of trivia. You live, and you permit others to live, very vividly in the real things about you—the cats! the Brussels sprouts, the toadstools—so that one feels very rooted to the earth. Then one lives in the world of human relationships, ideas, books, etc. But that in-between world of mechanical trivia that occupies so much of most people's lives does not seem to exist. It really is an extraordinary atmosphere and does give a deep sense of "comparative and intermittent peace."

You, of course, as you say, are different in Ashfield. Or perhaps I noticed the difference more, or perhaps it was something new—a sense of being not afraid of being vulnerable (was this what the man waiting for the train with you saw?). I hope I can achieve it sometime.

The sun is now behind the trees. The moon-bud looks less strained. Perhaps it won't open tonight after all. I must stop this rambling and interrupted letter. (A chickadee is sitting in the moon-flower's world.) I hope Italy does for you what my time in Ashfield did for me.

---

*Alexis Léger (1887–1975), French poet, diplomat, and man of letters who wrote under the name Saint-John Perse. He won the Nobel Prize in Literature in 1960.

December 28th, 1955 [DIARY]

There has been a pressure on me all fall that makes me feel constantly uneasy & inadequate. It is, I think, a double pressure—trying to adjust to—or disregard (I can't decide which) the roles thrust upon me by Mother's death and by the great success of the book. Both these two public changes demand or *seem* to demand something of me which I am unwilling to give & resent being demanded. (Why should I carry on Mother's role—her public role?—I am not in the least like her.) (Why should I take on the role of "Foremost Woman of the Year" with its hypocritical saccharine overtones—just because of a book I wrote & meant—but have outgrown?)

I feel imprisoned in these two false pictures the world has of me—& yet unable to—as I should if I am honest about disliking the roles & believing I should *not* play them—disregard them. The unanswered & unfulfilled demands in both areas make me feel thoroughly inadequate & guilty.

Added to which—just practically—they take so much time to fight against—say no to—etc.—so much time—thought—energy—that they use up the extra time I have and the delicate balance of being wife-mother-writer is thrown again.

One needs *leisure* to write & leisure presupposes—demands—money—and the ability & free conscience to use it (I have the money but don't feel free enough to use it wisely enough to obtain the necessary leisure). Leisure also must be accompanied with a free conscience as regards the demands of family & friends—not to speak of the world—clamoring on one's door.

This I have felt all fall & resented. Fame (in this country) just practically makes it very cumbersome to live one's life. In a subtler & more destructive way it makes it very difficult to be oneself—to change—to grow.

One is frozen in the picture the world has of you. If you move out of that picture they resent it—much as a friend resents your moving out of his or her concept of you (or a wife or a husband). The artist—if he stays alive—has got to keep moving out of these picture frames set around him.* He must break picture after picture—frame after frame. Only the people who *don't* frame you, can you remain faithful to in any way.

---

*Here AML writes in a footnote: "It is not only difficult to do because you keep hurting people's feelings as you do it—& losing their 'love'—but part of you *wants* to stay in the picture frame. It is easier—self-satisfying—pleasant & you are patted on the back for it."

My discomfort in the frames has manifested itself all fall. The mail nauseates me—the requests—the letters asking me to speak—awarding me degrees, etc., etc. All nice enough—but basically all, or most of them, are fixatives to shellac me into *their* frame.

The sincere letters are sometimes different & interest me—if the writers tell about themselves & their lives—but there are too many to read them all—& the sheer mass knocks out the pleasure of finding the real ones.

All of it seems to me to *impede* life & growth & discovery—clog up the streams.

January 13th, 1956 [DIARY]

. . . Yesterday was a bad day for requests. We had a wire, an angry letter, & a request from Pantheon (besides 2–3 other requests in the mail for speaking). C. blows up at Kyrill*—so he told me later on—on the telephone, I go off to the house feeling paranoid about the wire, the sarcastic letter, etc. . . . I must either give up writing or get hardened—or live a life of constant escape—or write to be published after death.

Monday, January 16th, 1956 [DIARY]

C. has been laid low for three days with a fever & some kind of infection in the glands. His temperature is quite high—102—at night & he feels flat—very unusual for him. He is such a hard person to do anything for—comes down for meals—won't take medicine—or call a doctor. (Perhaps he is right—he seems to be shaking it off.) His inactivity somehow equates him with me & brings us closer in a strange way.

I have had a full weekend. Children's trips & always a difficult letter to write. Yesterday a.m. writing Leland Hayward† I could not help them with C.'s film. Kurt Wolff comes for lunch. We discuss the book of poems,‡ especially the last one, "On a Photograph" with his poetry editor's criticisms. Some helpful—some too literal . . . Kurt takes the two copies of "The Uncle" & "Aunt Harriet."§ He is bewildered, I think, that I do not get more work done on the novel. Here too there is pressure.

I try to explain—my ordinary life as a woman—with three children

*Kyrill S. Schabert (1909–1983) was co-founder and president of Pantheon Books from 1943 to 1961.
†Leland Hayward (1902–1971) was the producer of the film *The Spirit of St. Louis.*
‡*The Unicorn and Other Poems, 1935–1955,* was published by Pantheon in September 1956.
§Draft chapters from AML's novel *Dearly Beloved.*

at home & a husband demanding a certain amount—is so delicately balanced I can *just* find time to work if nothing else is thrown in.

But add just one thing—Christmas—the extra work due to problems of being an executor of ECM—or the extra mail & having to say *No* to a number of demands—the apple cart is upset.

Scott's Cove
February 9th, 1956
Dearest Land,

We have just picked up your letter, early, from the post office. Your father and I have both read it. There is not time for me to write you the kind of letter I would like—I will do that from Canada, I hope—because I have only 3/4 hour before we start to leave, but I want to drop a letter in the mailbox as we go so you can have our first reactions and not be wondering, "What the hell are they going to say to that letter?!"

There are many, many things to say. That was a thoughtful and honest letter and it brings up much to think about, and it shows that *you* have been thinking—churning things over, questioning, weighing, and trying to do it as sincerely and honestly as possible. I can't answer all of these thoughts here. It will take *me* some thinking. But certain things can be, and should be, said right off the bat.

You are *not* "disappointing" us and you are *not* "letting us down." Nor do we feel you have or are wasting our money. I am sure from your letter that you have "learned" many things—perhaps not just the things you expected, but you have learned certain things about life today, and you have learned things about yourself and other people which are invaluable lessons and which can help you all your life. I think you can learn still more by analyzing the situation and yourself in relation to it before you leave it.

We are not disappointed because we do not feel that college marks* are a criterion of character or intelligence or success in life. (I will have to come back to this point, because getting through college with passing marks may help one, of course, may be valuable in the world's eyes. But it is not an invaluable *criterion*.) We are both highly doubtful of the mass-production education of today, applied with pressure to the amassing of facts: knowledge, not wisdom. We are both of us very sympathetic to your reaction to the pressure routine of this year. I wrote much the

*Land was a freshman at Stanford University at that time.

same kind of thing to my parents my freshman year (and college was far easier then), and as you know, your father just left college. I felt there was no time for thought, for life, for any kind of creative work, and I got so I couldn't sleep, find time to be out of doors, etc. I was pressed by my father and mother who felt this was a "wonderful opportunity" and that "I would always regret leaving," and by the inner compulsion and humiliation that my sister had done well and loved it and been the perfect college girl ahead of me (more popular with boys too!). I was pretty much pressured into staying in college.

It is hard to say now whether it was a mistake or not. What I *do* know is that I should *not* have gone to the same college as my sister. I should *not* have felt I had to compete with her or live up to her, or to my mother and father in college. It took me many, many years to realize I had my own gifts and they were utterly different from either of my sisters. (And Con was *summa cum laude*, and Dwight was a scholar, Phi Beta Kappa. I was the poorest student of the family.) I am telling you all this because I think some of your feeling of "letting us down," "failure," depression, etc. (which worries me *much* more than your marks or your wanting to leave), is bound up with your very natural and similar feeling that you must live up to Jon!

Jon has his own gifts. You have yours—and you have great gifts. They must be used and you must, and will, find the environment that gives them scope. Jon wasn't so perfectly suited to Stanford but, as he once said to me, he was more of a conformist; you are more apt to question and rebel. Rebellion can be a sign of great strength. I am proud of you for seeing the shortcomings of your situation and facing the fact that you're not getting anything out of it—and that most people's shocked answers about the value of college education are merely conventional and have no thought behind them. Rebellion is often healthy and I feel it maybe is in your case. But it must be used wisely, like any kind of explosive material. It can teach you much. Ask yourself, with that incentive of rebelliousness as a spur, what it is you are rebelling *against*? And what *toward*? Don't let rebelliousness simply blow you out of a bad situation into a worse one. Try to make the transition smooth. It is a waste to use all that gunpowder to blow yourself out of college and leave a hole and broken bric-a-brac in the process.

If it is the best thing for you to leave—and it may well be—try, if you can, to tie things up so that your next step won't be too difficult or wasteful. A B and even a C can count for a lot; a finished course, even with a D, makes for a smoother transition into the next step you want to take—infinitely easier if you want to transfer to A&M or another college. Maybe you don't want to transfer. All this you must discuss with your father: the draft, etc. I hope you will wait to talk it over with him before taking definite action. I think he feels sympathetically toward your attitude and *can* help you toward the next step.

If you can, don't go on at this pace—let up a little—even the marks. Set a limit for yourself. Work just so hard, and then get out and away from it. Accept the fact that you're not an A-student or a B-student. It doesn't mean you have a lower intelligence—you're not in that narrow groove, that's all. Use your intelligence to live balancedly. I will add more to this—

Mother.

P.S. One more thing: you are *not* lazy. You have shown that you can work hard and long at difficult jobs—new and green and all-to-learn, as you did this summer on the ranch, when you felt the work was worthwhile and you liked it. You have that behind you and you can be proud of it. It is a good record. And we were proud of you. But, as you yourself know, the ability to take hard physical work is not enough to make one a successful rancher. It is not enough to escape into hard physical activity day by day. One must have some kind of broader vision of the whole project and the world into which it fits, what you are working toward. This is what you need some kind of broader education and/or training for. We—and you—must figure out how best to get this for you.

I could write you another long letter on the "unreality" feelings you describe, both at college and at home. I think it is a very natural feeling and it is really, I think, a sign of growth and great change going on in you. Actually, it is not the world which is an unreality, but yourself. You are going through such big changes that you are a stranger to yourself and therefore to the world around you. You do not know *what* to do because you do not know *who* you are. When you know yourself, then the course of action will proceed inevitably from that core—and not as escape action but action which expresses *you*. I am sure you will find this, dear Land, and I do not really worry. Only I know how upsetting these periods are and I would like to help you if I could. I wish you could fly back at the first chance and talk this all over with me—or perhaps I should fly out. Let me know. In the meantime, I love you very much and I believe in you and I am behind you.

Darien, Conn.
May 11th, 1956
Dear Monte,*

I didn't realize you were counting on my opinion of the *Reader's Digest* article. By the time I read it, it had already gone to them, so it seemed a waste of time to comment on it. But for what it is worth, this is what I think.

First of all, I see no great objection to it from our (the family's) point of view, but I think it is just as well it wasn't accepted, as it now stands, for your sake. It isn't, of course, *Reader's Digest* material. The *Digest* does not print poetry at all—which is your true medium. It avoids subtleties, delicate writing, innuendos, images, quotations. Your writing is full of these.

I don't agree with your friend's criticism of the title for the piece on Mother: "Her Victory of Happiness." It is, I think, as you thought, a good *Reader's Digest* title, and very true of her. Her happiness *was* a victory. But you do not make this clear. For this woman who wrote you, "I have had a happy life"—what was her life like? Have you ever stopped to think?

She started poor and in delicate health. Her twin sister died and they were afraid she would too. She wore clothes passed on to her by richer relatives and depended on them for vacations. She longed to go to college, but was considered too delicate, and it was expensive. But her desire for life, her hold on life, was so great that she got there (teaching school and tutoring for extra money). She did well and became strong and discovered her talents. She wanted to write, but before she could develop her talents and reputation, she married a poor and struggling lawyer. She put everything she had into housekeeping and budgeting and child care. Like all mothers, she was too busy to write. Later, she threw herself whole-heartedly into her husband's and children's lives. In middle life, when things had opened up for her, and her husband had become well known and successful and she might enjoy some of these hard-won benefits, she lost, in quick succession, her husband, her first grandchild, and her oldest daughter, and her son was stricken by long illness that was then thought (though she never believed it and it turned out not to be) incurable. But she did not write or act despairingly, or live despairingly,

---

*Margaret Bartlett "Monte" Millar, AML's secretary in 1935, when the Lindberghs left the United States to live in England in response to the relentless publicity that plagued the family following the kidnapping and murder of Charles Jr. and the threats made on Jon's life.

or even stop to feel sorry for herself. She went on with a life of service to wide circles of education, welfare organizations, etc. until her death. You were right in your title: her happiness *was* a victory.

As I write, I realize you couldn't have known all this. You only knew her in a very brief period and limited life, at Next Day Hill at the end of her life. What could you know of the struggle, except intuitively? You are a poet and your intuitive feeling about her is in your title.

Because I don't write doesn't mean that I don't think of you with sympathy and compassion. I simply do not write letters to anyone any more except my immediate family. Correspondence, like social life, is one of the things I have had to give up in favor of the things I feel a duty to concentrate on: my husband, my children, the wider family that has fallen to me since Mother's death—and my writing. Writing books must take the place of correspondence. You, who are yourself so dedicated to writing, must understand this choice.

Little House, Darien
May 15th, 1956 [DIARY]

I have not written all winter. Now it is full spring: apple blossoms out, a wren building a nest in the exhaust pipe of my little house, a phoebe nesting over the Ford in the garage, warblers flitting among the new leaved branches, the oak pollen flying, the maples and beech very green, the copper beech very pink. Even the oaks have passed the "squirrel's ear" stage ("When the oak leaves are as big as a squirrel's ears, then it's time to plant corn"). The spring has been slow—cold, wet, and very behind. (I say this each year but this year it is really true. Things are behind and have *just* come out.)

This year has gone fast and I feel sad to have it unrecorded. (How much of life is unrecorded!) But I have been trying to put my mornings into the book. It goes very slowly, probably because I am working out what I believe as I write. Yesterday, I finished the first very rough draft of Frances, the most complex woman. It has gone through weeks of outlines, then notes, then this first draft. It is a long essay on marriage. The whole book is that. I must now rewrite, condensing, smoothing, and making it less of a sermon. I am not sure I can pull it off. I am really writing essays, notebook or diary material, thoughts on marriage from the points of view of different characters.

I often feel I should give up trying to put this material (this "something to say") into fiction and just write notebook pieces or in my diary.

(Though a diary would be too personal and not give enough scope.) Fiction is not my field. These people just stand and *think* for pages at a time; they think in semicolons, in images, in philosophy, in sermons. They preach! However, I must go through a first draft of the whole thing and see.

[JULY 3RD, 1956, DIARY]*

I land in San Diego about 7:15 & there is a brown Barbara & a child in her arms—big dark eyes—dark wispy hair, her thumb in her mouth & a little red dirndl on—dancing about on the sidewalk as soon as she is let down. . . . Soon we are all driving back to their little house & walled garden in Coronado. It is a convenient little two-bedroom, one-story house, right next to another—with adjoining gardens (children & toys & gardens are shared—also juice & milk & picking up, at times).

Their house is now full of Japanese touches—a potted dwarf pine on their outdoor table—Japanese blue & white plates & bowls on the table—a paper lantern-doll in Christine's room, water colors on the walls & Barbara's flower arrangements. I sleep in with Christine—& wake to her gurgling in the morning from her crib (Jon made it, as well as her chest & a beautiful coffee table out of a polished stump).

It is a happy peaceful life in a small circle—Jon off to the base in the mornings—Christine in her high chair feeding herself or tearing around the rooms—or calling at the garden gate for Debbie next door. I drop into a life of relative inactivity. I am a guest in my son's home. I am a grandmother. It is strange, restful & delicious (see notes on being a grandmother written on plane). . . . And I am entranced as by a miracle in watching Christine. . . . Each move of the child is a miracle, something that never happened before & may never happen again—before my eyes. . . . First picture of Christine, dancing around, then sitting in her high chair—quiet & expectant for a few seconds. Feeding herself from the unbreakable cereal dish held onto the tray by suction (superb idea!). She does not like to be fed & is very independent.

I brought her a little blue dirndl with red apron that C. had bought for one of my babies. Big puff sleeves. It fit her perfectly. I also brought a book to sing to her ("Frog Went a Courtin' ") and it was a great success. I would sing & she would sit next to me on the bed ("Up! Up!") or,

---

*This appears to recount a trip AML took prior to July 3, to visit Jon, Barbara, and their daughter.

later, on my lap, & she would turn the pages, pointing out objects she recognized—with—often—unrecognizable words! Soon this book was her favorite. I was her slave. "Book! Book!" she would run to me & take my hand & lead me to the bed—or sofa—("Up! Up!") often dragging the big book after her.

Jon chasing her ("goin' to catch that baby!") & her ecstatic crowing delight. Jon giving her a bath & holding her in his arms—wrapped in a big towel—all damp—big-eyed & dark hair a little wispy.

She runs to Barbara a hundred times a day—not for anything in particular—but simply to express joy or to make sure her mother is there—"Mommee!" And Barbara always answers "Babee!"—& usually takes her in her arms. Then she goes down again happy. "Sometimes when I haven't time to love her with my arms I love her with my knees!" said Barbara, laughing. . . .

I cannot see what I have gone through until I write it down. I am blind without a pencil. And I cannot go ahead with new work until I know where I am. I resent life slipping by in unawareness. It must be savored, understood, analyzed as I go along. Otherwise, I not only walk unsteadily, I cannot work at all. I have no materials to work with, no storehouse of insight to draw from. But it does seem a slow and wasteful process. (Like walking, tapping with a cane.)

The process, though, of evaluating, allows me to simmer down from a life of action to one of contemplation and eventually, writing. I descend, step by step—page by page—deeper into myself, my core. When I reach the core, then I can write again. Creativity comes out of the refound core.

July 8th, 1956 [DIARY]

Perhaps people also connect you to your core, at least if they are close and perceptive adults with whom you can be yourself. This week, I had all those. I went in one night to have supper with Dana and then go to a stadium concert with him. This was relaxed and easy, as it is with Dana now, neither of us wanting or expecting more than the other can give. I had a feeling of detachment, sitting in the open air stadium and walking back with Dana afterwards. There was a wonderful anonymity about it, and casualness, as though we were in a foreign city, Paris or London, taking our time and enjoying life with no pressures and no constructions. Some of this was the actual physical aspect of it. New York on a summer evening has an utterly different quality from its winter aspect; it is spacious, less hurried, casual. (Only the poor or the serious are left in New York in the summer—and strangers, country people visiting it on a vacation.) Perhaps it is this last component that gives it its almost provincial character. Couples walk arm in arm, eat out of doors, linger at corners. The parks and public places like museums and stadiums are full of people enjoying simple pleasures, rather casually, as in Europe. Some of the intensity has left.

The spaciousness of the Lewisohn Stadium* separates one from the many people it holds. One is aware of the sky, a mackerel sky, dove-colored tonight. It seems to come down and wash through the interstices of city life and we are all bathed in another element. We are separate; we are freer; we move to quieter currents, easily, like fish on the ocean floor. Perhaps for Dana and me this was accentuated since we usually meet in his tight little office, sealed off from the world in a constricted segment of time, artificially walled off from the clamoring pressures of life. The peace of those segmented appointments is like the artificial tranquility of the carefully locked segments of a canal.

We talk easily—or don't talk—in perfect understanding. Dana tells me that his great French doctor friend has told him he is like Erasmus: his great gift is *illumination*. I laugh and agree—and add that Erasmus was my ideal in college, the personification of everything I believed in. I add, ruminating, "I seem to gravitate to two kinds of men in my life, heroes and wise men."

"And St.-Ex. came the nearest to being both," he adds, "and being both was what killed him" (or tore him to pieces). I agree and think more about it. The wise men, of course, are my fathers, but the heroes? Who are they? Where do they come from? Fairy tales? Rosen said they were both the same thing. But I think this is oversimplification and so does Dana.

We leave before the concert is over, walk part way back to my car and stop and have a limeade in a drugstore on the way. (This is *not* like Paris or London.) Home early—to C.'s surprise. This too is new leisure.

Then Thursday I have the Wolffs and Evie and Ammie† and Dana for supper. I want Dana and the Wolffs to meet, and Evie and Ammie know

*Lewisohn Stadium was an amphitheater and athletic facility on the campus of the City College of New York that hosted many notable events. It was demolished in 1973.
†Amyas Ames (1907–2000), investment banker, amateur pianist, and supporter of the arts. In the 1970s Ames served as chairman of the New York Philharmonic as well as Lincoln Center for the Performing Arts. He was the husband of AML's friend Evie Ames.

both and are a bridge. As usual, I somewhat wear myself out in preparation. We spend the morning preparing three guest rooms: putting away children's things, clean sheets, towels, extra blankets—it is suddenly cool. And I fix the flowers I did not do the day before. Mrs. Weber goes to shop for extras: brioches and croissants for breakfast, raspberries, cigarettes. Martha is baking a blueberry tart. The house looks quite lovely by noon: pale pink rhododendron in the big window, tiger lilies and blue shut-eyes in the big blue jar at the end of the room, the white man-boy and a white shell with pansies on the table, more rhododendron (I got soaking wet picking them) in the dining room, and—the best arrangement—three rhododendrons—low ones—in the black lacquer box (red inside) on the big red leather desk. I bring up the wine for the steak and put honeysuckle and roses and pansies in little pitchers by all the bedsides.

Then I go to the Little House for about an hour to simmer down before Evie comes, early, for lunch. We have a late but nice lunch alone, talking furiously as always of our women's lives. She has been in a three-ring circus of family activities. I think in a way she is like Con; her efficiency in too many ways tempts her into too many things.

A short rest, then I build a fire. Everything is ready. Evie meets Ammie at the train. C. comes home and goes for the Wolffs. Dana arrives.

Then the evening is under way. It takes off and I sit back, watching it go—and unable to join very much in it except in smoothing corners, passing or clearing plates, trying to join loose ends of conversation. However, it does go. I think everyone had a good time. Dana sparkled. CAL fenced. Ammie and Dana sparred and appreciated each other's foils. Evie was the beauty and dazzle, Helen and I quiet appreciators. The Wolffs thought Dana was a wonderful man. (Some envy on the part of Kurt, I suspect—both men specialize in understanding women.)

And the flowers and the food and the wine were, I hope, the good blending background. When we go to bed, I turn to C. for his comments on the evening. "Well," he says, as always, "I think that was quite a good evening."

"Say it again," I say, "in a great many different ways!"

July 9th, 1956 [DIARY]

A dog day—more showers—dark—*very* humid and heavy. I start off Mrs. Hart and Mrs. Weber on sorting out slip-covers (ECM's old ones—slowly the house and closets are clearing) and other odd clearing up jobs, then go off to the Little House. CAL comes up for lunch. He is restless and talking about going off.

"For how long?" I ask.

"I don't know."

"Where to?"

"I don't know." !

He wants to fly over the line on certain planes he has not flown on before. He will be gone at least two weeks, perhaps three or four. I find I mind, suddenly, being left alone, although I *could* have gone to Europe with him and stayed in one spot while he flew around. But I elected to stay here and "work." Now, I feel, irrationally, somewhat abandoned! I find I enjoy the summer slack season, alone with C., working in the Little House all day and clipping or gardening in the late afternoons with him and then supper and music with him in the evenings. I like *working* alone, but I don't like evenings alone.

For C. though, there is not enough action here, or stimulus. He can write better on trips. He needs the trips away; he craves the change. I used to feel this myself. (Though for me, it was escape from certain tensions.) He can work better when it is interspersed with travel and action. These are *too* stimulating for me, and too distracting. Good for in-between periods, when one is *not* writing. So I understand and yet cannot help feeling rather sad, let down. (I think this is a good sign in terms of our relationship but how it would startle all the readers of my *Gift from the Sea*! What! Not like to be alone?!)

I will, I know, get over this and work better, perhaps, after he has left. I usually do. But I find myself putting on my armor, retreating into the artist, the solitary person who does not need people: a strange transition, from woman to man. After I make the transition, I will, of course, find myself again—the other half of me. But the transition is painful. Is this so with all women who have a profession or creative urge? Or is it just I who am so inflexible, so lumbering about the shift? And then, of course, *if* I get into my work, I will mind the shift *back* when he comes home in August and I become a domestic woman again.

Sunday, July 15th, 1956 [DIARY]

A beautiful day. C.'s last here. I work the morning at the house. Back for lunch with C. on the porch sitting in the sun, then back to the Little House and work till four. Then C. and I go swimming. He has discovered a pure white bird, the size of a sparrow, in the bushes; it is being fed by a song sparrow. We watch it with glasses—looks like a sparrow but pure white, pinkish beak and feet. An albino? A little bigger than the mother and dependent on her. We lie on the seawall rocks in the sun and then go in for supper.

Then we sit on our chaise-longues on the porch and watch the ducks and listen to music. I feel quite sad. C. will not be here tomorrow night. I shall be depressed but I shall get over it. He reminds me that he planned this trip around my original thought of going abroad with him. Now I want to stay and work. Yes, too bad.

[From a letter to Alan Valentine]

Tuesday, July 17th, 1956

I have been sitting on the terrace, eating supper alone (to Almaden Grenache and French songs on the radio): an utterly beautiful evening, one of our few. The little cove was mirror still and luminous, a pearly sheen on the water. The far line of Long Island was clear and blue, and the near marsh grass very green in the foreground, with the evening light white-bright on the sides of two or three boats tied up at docks in between. I stayed out until the light on the boats had gone and the gnats had come! I know that Almaden Grenache and French songs lie, but even so it was a delicious evening. Would have liked to communicate it to you, since you like both!

CAL left yesterday on a rather long trip and I must say I felt quite sad to see him go. As you note in your letter, this is a new departure. Actually, I think living alone at one period of my life was a necessary escape from the anguishing difficulties and burdens of human relations. Now, I find them less anguishing, and the need to go off less necessary. Today, after yesterday's temporary loneliness, I find being alone quite pleasant. I can work later, not be interrupted, eat when I like, write in the evenings to friends, play music I like, drink what I like, etc. But I wonder, is liking to live alone not simply liking to have one's own way, bending to no one, listening to no one, planning and following one's own routine utterly, selfishly? Perhaps it is good for one occasionally, but I no longer think it a higher form of life.

Chiefly I wanted to talk to you about the *Letter* (naturally I have mentioned it to no one). I am convinced that you must write it as if no one were ever going to see it. Write it all, as personally and specifically as you can, as deeply and honestly as you can. A "generalized" letter will get you nowhere, because it comes from nowhere. Also forget any idea of publication or readers. One cannot write with someone looking over one's shoulder (though I do often enough, I am ashamed to say). If you write as honestly and deeply and, as you say, non-cleverly as possible, you will not only find out, I believe, much about your hurt and your own specific problems (the catharsis theory of writing; I don't really like that word because I don't believe it is getting rid of it that helps, but illumination about it; in fact, just the opposite of getting rid of it, seeing it; one can absorb it, understand it, live with it), but aside from this, I am sure from this boiling down, the essence will emerge. In fact, I think it is the only true way to reach the universal, through the knot-hole of the personal. So do, do go ahead and write it as it boils up: the hot lava from the unconscious. Don't stop to observe, criticize, or be "ironic." Just write it, like a letter, without rereading. Later, one can decide what to do.

I hope you are coming down sometime? It is so much easier to talk than to write, at least, when you are writing as much as I am these days. I find letters are anathema to me. After I leave my desk I only want to weed, water the chives, swim, listen to music, or wash underwear (what an anticlimax). . . .

[AUGUST 9TH, 1956, DIARY]

. . . I am somewhat thrown when I get back to the house to find I have lost my wedding ring! Why? Where? When? In the past two days somewhere. I search the bed. I have sometimes taken it off in my sleep. But I fear it came off washing—it is quite loose—or more likely still—in swimming. . . .

C. always *said* I would lose it—I have dropped it so many times (in a swimming pool & he dove for it! In a sampan bottom, etc., etc.). He said he had enough of the Central American gold saved to make several more! That helps. But oh I mind—I mind *terribly.* One fights down the waves of superstition & symbol that rise up like great threatening storm clouds.

Besides, of course, there is the special anguish of "loss." Any loss is *all* loss! The terrible sense of the loss linking you to all other losses—the sense of eternal deprivation. . . . Something you had is gone—& there is a hole in you—a pit.

I can do nothing in the evening—except wash underwear! . . . I wanted to die with it—to be buried with it ("a bracelet of bright gold about the bone"). But I misquote Donne.*

---

*The line AML quotes from "The Relic," by John Donne, is actually "A bracelet of bright hair about the bone."

[JANUARY 13TH, 1957, DIARY]

. . . All this means is that I am tired & oversensitive inside—concave instead of convex. It is at such a moment that one is hit by other things that aggravate one's concaveness—like the three page full-spread attack by John Ciardi—poetry editor of the *SRL*—on *The Unicorn*.* The criticism itself is not so unjust (I feel myself that most of the poems—though not all—are trite—jingly—old-fashioned—I have outgrown them) but the attack is so full of personal venom & hostility that I was shocked by it. I always am shocked by violence. And at this moment I felt in it a susceptible quivering core. Why should he attack me with that much personal violence?

I ought to understand such irrational resentment because I have both experienced it *on* and felt it *in* myself. I know it has not to do with the object at which it is directed but is related to some earlier unconscious object. That one does not strike with that much venom unless one is desperately hurt oneself.

And yet—I felt his attack on an old sore place.

Moreover, the general effect of the attack has made me feel again trapped—by my name, my fame, my money, my position, my marriage.

I suppose the *real* trap is my sensitivity—my inner vulnerability—my own weaknesses.

But sometimes the outer traps seem very real. How to live free of the pressures that beset the famous & the rich in America? How to be oneself in the frames the world gums down over you?

How to be oblivious of them? I know the answer really is being creatively occupied—*engrossed*—in your own work—so engrossed that nothing else matters.

Here again, the logistics of a bad ten days of overwork in a house with sick children & interrupting obligations have kept me from the one outlet that could help free me.

(Outside people who love you help, too, but I have been for the same reasons cut off from them.)

Next week I must start again. Work—and a few warm outsiders—if possible—to laugh with me (telephoning Dana helped).

---

*John Ciardi wrote a review of *The Unicorn and Other Poems* in the *Saturday Review of Literature* in January 1957, calling it "an offensively bad book—inept, jingling, slovenly, illiterate even, and puffed up with the foolish afflatus of a stereotyped high-mindedness, that species of esthetic and human failure that will accept any shriek as a true high-C." The review ignited a firestorm of criticism and controversy, prompting a rejoinder in the magazine a few weeks later by its founding editor, Norman Cousins.

[JANUARY 25TH, 1957, DIARY]

. . . How strange & isolated & unloved one gets to feel in those trapped periods & a review like Ciardi's is enough to make one feel that the whole world hates one! That, plus Monte's letters supporting him!

. . . How alone we are—C. & I—in the midst of our fame! He doesn't mind it but I do.

[MARCH 17TH, 1957, DIARY]

. . . I have found two small rooms in an old house on 19th Street*— the new frame for seeing people—& a place to escape to for a night—perhaps to write in? It is charming & I have now put some of my own things in it—& it gives me a sense of the summer person I am when I wake up in it—detached & whole—not torn into shreds by the myriad head-of-the-house duties. I walk up & turn the key in my door. No one sees me & stops me—as at the Cos. Club—where I cannot go now without people recognizing me, coming up & asking me something or telling me what they think of my book or books—or the Ciardi review.

This has gone on & on. His attack provoked an avalanche of angry letters back (most of them in exactly the same key as his angry & petty article)—which he then answered again in another long defense of his attack. (Some of this was interesting. I understood better *what* he was attacking in me—whom he sees as an example of "the genteel tradition.") Then letters coming to *his* defense, etc. etc. I feel the *SRL* exploited the affair & whooped it up—like a horse-race.

I think Ciardi is completely sincere but totally unaware of his motivations (this may make for a good poet—but it makes a bad critic) in attacking me & unaware of the penumbra into which his explosion fell. All of this has little to do, I think, with poetry or personalities but has to do with what Spender called "the pathology of literary success" in America. Also the curious phenomena of projection and negative & positive transference. I have become a kind of symbol—a Mother figure to the American public—because I married their Hero—is it?—or because I lost a child? Or because my other book offered women "a consolation prize" for frustration? I am gummed into a frame—*Whistler's Mother*, complete with rocking chair & folded hands. Ciardi couldn't bear *Whistler's Mother* & called her a bitch (I can't bear her either & I suspect she is a bitch)—but the American public don't like her called a bitch. She is *their* mother. They don't tolerate their mother being called a bitch. So

*146 East 19th Street, in the Gramercy Park section of New York City.

they rose in fury against him. He was attacking a false picture; they were defending a false picture. The net result has been one more coat of shellac over me—the false picture of me in a frame.

The criticism of the poetry per se I accept—it was exaggerated & unfair, but it had validity. But the anger was related to something else. He meant, I believe, to attack the phoney values, phoney praise, phoney sales of my books. If he had done it clear-sightedly he could have done a service to poetry, to book selling & reviewing, to himself as a critic & leader of taste, to the *SRL* as an instrument of good critical insight—& to me. But, as it was, he did it in such a petty & hostile way—attacking me with petty animosity—& so his attack illuminated nothing—proved nothing—& accomplished nothing—except to arouse the same kind of petty animosity in return.

Nothing has been worth the candle. My poems were not worth his attack; his attack was not worth the letters that answered it. And all of it—attack, letters of defense & counter defense—has been on this blind, petty, unenlightened level. A waste of his time & energies as a good poet, a waste of anger—which was unproductive—a waste of target in me. And there I am—gummed tighter than ever into *Whistler's Mother's* frame.

However, one must just keep on trying to break out of the frames that parents, teachers, husbands & wives, public & critics, put one in for their convenience & safety—by new action—new writing. It is hard to write when one mistrusts one's talent—but I am beginning again.

. . . I have put out feelers for new ways out of my ruts: the apartment, seeing people in town, the Institute in Phila., meetings. Not all of these will be fruitful, but one must *try* to break one's frames in many directions.

(Poor Ciardi does not know that I too am in revolt against the "Genteel Tradition"—it did not show in most of the poems but I am. How I have struggled against it & struggled for life! He too, poor man, is struggling, caught perhaps in the rut of revolt—one of the worst because one feels so self-satisfied in it.)

[OCTOBER 8TH, 1957, DIARY]
. . . My first look at Wendy* in Barbara's arms—a golden baby—golden-haired—round—fruit-like—warm & cuddly & smiling—one of

---

*Jon and Barbara's second daughter, Wendy, was born in September 1956.

the fruit-like babies like Reeve, Land, Scott. Christie, on the other hand, as I wrote Land, comes of the line of hellions—ECM, Elisabeth, Ansy & Eiluned.* Erect & angular, sharp-nosed, sharp-eyed, precise in speech & step—& look. Very sensitive, very strong-willed, very intelligent. A character! She has all the tenacity of all sides of the family—Jim R.'s chin, ECM's ("no-trump look") tip-tilted nose, Elisabeth's "sassiness," CAL's stubborn persistence, Jon's determination. She is made of dynamite & having her will crossed sets off an explosion. A dangerous child, but with Barbara's patience & love her heart will expand to accepting & living with the imperfect world & imperfect people & situations. I cannot help, of course, adoring her. Mother, Elisabeth, Ansy & Eiluned: I have always been in love with them. It is wrong to type them for their most essential quality is that they are unmistakably themselves. They have a good proportion of the masculine in them. (Ansy & Elisabeth were/are more feminine.) This child reminds me of ECM in that and in her erectness & her vitality. But her sensitivity & artistic qualities are like Ansy & Eiluned. . . . Wendy, I see as perfectly balanced, heart & mind—like Reeve. She is "loving & giving," gave all her food to Sigee.

[From a letter to Alan Valentine]

October 11th, 1957
Dear dear . . .

It was wonderful to find your letter in my pile of unopened mail last night, coming back from a day and night at Bucks County. . . . The first time I have been in the apartment since I lunched there with you, and the first time I had left home since the children and grandchildren came. (They have all, including C. and Uncle, just left!)

It has been a totally absorbing, very satisfactory and successful, but, to me, very exhausting three weeks. The presence and problems of Uncle, who is a darling person, added to its complications. I thought of our grandmothers, who certainly managed to have children and grandchildren, uncles and aunts in their homes for years without breakdowns. I did not break down, but I felt as if I was holding it all up, the load, on some tense part of the neck. No doubt this is some kind of God-illusion. One doesn't have to be such an Atlas, or to assume one is indispensable, or to get so emotionally involved with each person's set of values. (The indispensable something for C., Jon, and Barbara, Anne, Scott and

---

*Margaret Constance Eiluned Morgan, youngest child of Constance and Aubrey Morgan.

Reeve, Uncle [his teeth!], the babies: each one is revolving to a different sun, a different time, a different cycle.) I try to mesh in with all of them and get worn out. There is something wrong with this; maybe you can tell me when we meet. Or perhaps by then I shall have had enough perspective to know!

In any case, this is just to explain why I did not get a letter off to the Hotel Metropole, as I meant to do when I drove away from the parking lot, thinking so much of you as I drove out to Scott's Cove, arriving a half an hour before we left again (C. came back) for Idlewild and Jon's family. Also to explain my joy to get your letter last night, a joy, I suppose, compounded of many things selfish and unselfish. Partly because it spoke directly to a me that has been engulfed for weeks. I have been a faceless, eyeless, bodiless person. I know, of course, that this me that is a collection of functions as I have been this month (the functioning housekeeper-mother) is just as real as the artist-writer friend of Gramercy Park, but they seem like different people, and opposed; it is my life job to unite them. Partly a very real joy and relief to hear the released you that spoke in that letter. You cannot know how different the tone, and how relieved I felt to hear it, a weight off my heart. (Of course I carry *both* you and Lucia in my heart.)

Until such time as we can resolve, dissolve, or learn to live with our indissoluble problems, it seems to me that periods away, and the acceptance of them on both sides, is the first, perhaps only constructive step for our complicated marriages. (I will talk to Lucia about this.) C. takes his openly and constantly. They are always rationally for work, not for escape, change or refreshment, but I cannot but believe they are really motivated by these last needs. It seems more difficult for me to take them. But that is partly because I am a woman with children still at home, and partly because it is so hard for me to break my ruts, to break away as I feel, instinctively, one *must* from time to time.

Perhaps for movement, for life itself, for feeling, for awareness, one must continually break and break again one's habits, the minute they become thoughtless and easy, the minute they lie lightly on one. And we are wrong to try to plan for peaceful routine. (Is there not a parallel in electricity for this making and breaking of currents?) Women err in this much more than men. I resent and resist the breaking of my routine, but I am always grateful when it is broken, and renewed.

There is so much more to say but I must think it out. I have thought a great deal of the problems of women in the modern world just lately, in the last month! But it takes time and peace and isolation in my Little House to think it out. There has been none this fall so far. This morning's letter, or jotting down of thoughts, has run on and on and is, I feel, rather incoherent. The weeks in Austria seem so far away and unreal. Perhaps your present peace and creativity gives me renewed faith in them. Don't question them—take them . . . and my love,

A.

Wednesday, November 14th, 1957
Dear Land,

It is Wednesday evening. We have just finished the dishes. Father put his fish bones out for the coons but Sigee happened to be outside and cleared the plate. I have just corrected Scott's theme (on a *Camp Day!*) and told Anne how to refuse a Mt. Holyoke tea invitation. Reeve is getting ready for bed. I am very sleepy but I have been meaning to write you for so long. I must start.

Scott seems to have turned some corner and is doing better in school and seems happier in general. I have no doubt that your wonderful letter to him gave him a real boost just when he needed it. He was *very* pleased by it. Incidentally (not really incidental at all, but I was surprised at Scott picking it out) Scott said of that letter: "This is a very well written letter, don't you think, Mother? I mean—that's pretty good description there—Land is a pretty good *writer!*"

I think he was right and I was pleased to have him notice it. We have not gotten around to his *using* your room. (Incidentally, again, Scott never imagined more than *using* it while you were away. It *is your* room—and you should always have the use of it. It is here ready and open for you. But it still would do a lot for Scott to be able to use it while you're away.) We are about to line up the skis, boots, etc. in it to ship ahead for Aspen. We have a chalet—I gather the same one as last year.

I went off last week (the week of the flying dog)* to New Boston and sat in the sun and copied and rewrote the chapters I did in Austria last summer. The first chance I've had this fall! I'd like to get another chapter rewritten before Christmas if possible. I'm now through the first

---

*Here AML inserts a footnote ("soviet space dog") referring to Laika, who was on board the Soviet spacecraft *Sputnik* 2 when it was launched on November 3, 1957, thereby becoming the first dog to orbit the earth.

rough draft of this very short—but tedious to write—book. Some of it I *know* is bad, some I *suspect* is bad, and a little of it I am not ashamed of!

It is now morning. (I didn't write all night!) Your father is about to go off for three weeks but plans to go to Aspen and seems quite cheerful about it, though he doesn't expect to ski much!

I enclose a *New Yorker* cartoon on the Satellite Situation. Anne came back from Mr. Peebles' History Class with the latest gag on satellites—perhaps you've heard it? "They're going to send up cows next—and that'll be the herd shot around the world!"

I cannot understand why someone in the State Department didn't have the sense of form, manners, and statesmanship, or psychological insight, to *immediately* congratulate the Russians on their achievement. This would seem to me the line to take instead of this panic.

It will be wonderful to talk to you—about your new life—and about our old one here. (Your father and I get very tired of the pressures around New York and the lack of wilderness and lack of peace to work. But where to move to?)

Much love to you—

Mother

Scott's Cove
Saturday, July 26th [1958]
Dearest Margot,

Con has just forwarded your letter from Rome. (I have been home for five days from the island in Puget Sound.) Heavens, what a summer (yours)! I can only guess at it. And I can only contribute that our month of driving (C. and I, Land and Anne, last summer, with no one else and really *no* complications, was really also a *great* strain.)

It is true what you say: everyone reverts to an earlier stage of insecurity: Land was desperately impatient. Anne wanted to sit in one place. I couldn't make up my mind about anything. CAL pressed, lectured, criticized, and finally fled alone. But even after that it wasn't too good. I arrived in Austria, feeling it, and especially I, had been a total failure.

I just think adolescents today cannot be taken on trips abroad—as we used to be. They are too old, too independent, too interested in love and life and themselves to see anything else. The pre-adolescents are more open, more the way we used to be. I think Reeve and Scott would have been better and happier all summer than Anne and Land. (They did much better alone together.) Or perhaps one child *alone*! When I think of you with all seven—different families, all the extra pressures and insecurities that come out when you are away from home—I don't see how it worked at all.*

I don't know that there is any solution to those difficult problems of double families. I have just seen Ernestine (yesterday, here for a swim) struggling with hers. The adolescents of another mother cannot be reabsorbed. They have to go out and live and make mistakes and suffer and then, perhaps, if you are an understanding person, they will come back to you gratefully as adults—but not as children.

Since you *are* always—even in anger or impatience or tears—open and fundamentally loving and truth-seeking, they will feel that and will gain from it and learn to trust and come back to it. But I don't think they can *now*. The misery comes from that persistent illusion that you *can* make them yours. One sees small signs of improvement and says: *Ah, Now—Here it is!* But it isn't. It's only an indication of an openness it will take years to fulfill.

Anyway, the struggle to succeed all the time—to win through—is totally exhausting. I hope you have some time of *not* trying, of being alone with your own children—and here, being alone with John.

The crisis in the Mideast seems to be better—from what one can see by the papers here—so I hope your plans to leave the children and come back here alone come through. I must say, I long to see you. Just selfishly, I feel I've had two summers already—four days with Con and a week on Jim's island in Puget Sound (a totally wild out-of-touch beautiful spot in process of being organized as a farm-resort-camp), but this summer rather inadequately prepared to feed, bathe, clean up after the twenty-four relatives that turned up!

The four days with Con were wonderful, though we spent much of it in the kitchen because her two part-time helpers had been knocked out by a funeral. I had a much better and happier picture of her life there. Full, yes, but rich and peaceful, varied and happy. It has taken a long time but it is beginning to flower I think. Only she still has *no* time to write—or very little.

I then proceeded by Jeep with Land, Scott, and Land's dog Willy via *three* ferries (we missed one of them and spent the night in pup-tents in a campground) to Jim's most inaccessible island off Vancouver,† where he had gathered all the young Millers, Robbinses, Lindberghs, and oth-

*After her marriage to AML's brother Dwight Morrow Jr. failed, Margot married John Wilkie, president of Central Hudson Gas and Electric Corporation, and chairman of the Vassar College Board of Trustees.
†Samuel Island, one of the small "Gulf Islands" in the Strait of Georgia, British Columbia.

ers to work at setting it up. Ages ranged from a baby of six months to Great-Grandma Robbins. We were scattered about in cabins and farm buildings and ate at a central farmhouse. Anne and three other girls did all the cooking and washing up for twenty-four people for two meals a day. And let me tell you, this is the system. She learned more in three weeks than I have in a lifetime about cooking! Reeve and another girl did all the babysitting, washing, feeding. Became quite the experts too.

Everyone worked. It was the kind of disorganized first-summer-half camping place where you just worked all the time, but quite happily, to make things go. There wasn't much chance to talk or privacy but you shared the island and beautiful brilliant sunny cool weather. We were so self-absorbed and isolated that when I came out a week later, I discovered with some shock that the world had almost burst into war—without our knowing it.* I then came back to an empty house: very silent, very hot, very humid, and everything overgrown outside. The shock of the change from totally communal active extrovert life to this one of total let-down in damp silence is very odd and I'm not yet used to it. I go to the Little House each morning and turn on the air conditioner and try to get back into my *ghastly* book but haven't yet managed to get started. Probably it's good to let down and look at things.

Martha leaves for her vacation tomorrow. Anne comes back in a week, which will be lovely. *Please come back* and sit on my terrace and drink Dubonnet with me!

Love—love—(What a wonderful birthday letter you wrote me!)
Anne

Wednesday, December 10th, 1958
Dearest Con,

Right in the midst of *la vie triviale* of Aspen packing and Christmas shopping, we are suddenly immersed in *la vie tragique*. Jon called us at two a.m. last night to tell us that Jim Robbins was two days overdue on a flight out of Denver for Seattle. The weather was "good," his plane all right, and he had no "flight-plans" (no schedule of his route). He must be down somewhere in the Rockies or the Cascades—crashed, killed, or—a dim hope—making his way out of the wilderness, out of touch now for three days. CAL was on the phone half the night and this morn-

*In July 1958 President Dwight Eisenhower sent 14,000 American troops into Lebanon to support the pro-Western government of President Camille Chamoun against internal opposition and threats from Syria and Egypt. The forces were withdrawn in October of that year.

ing again getting in touch with Army Air bases, search and rescue opera-
tions, etc. But you can't search the whole Northwest for a small plane.

The only hope lies in the fact that Jim was an exceptionally skillful
pilot, experienced in that terrain, tough in health and ability to survive
in wilderness conditions. (He was an Alaskan bush pilot.) He has gone
down before, in Alaska, and last year in the Northwest, and walked out
(on skis last year). He has skis and ski clothes and emergency food in the
plane. So we are all hoping against hope he is down in some very out of
touch area and making his way out.*

In the meantime, we are back in this desert of suspense, that is always
the same—a territory one knows so well and feels instinctively in the
chest, in the dry throat. And the old impossibility of reconciling the frozen standstill suspense of *waiting* with the dogged day-by-day pressure
of *doing*—of going ahead in life.

It is impossible to look ahead. I did Christmas lists this morning, dog-
gedly, while Reeve sat red-eyed in bed, making presents. How to explain
to children these sudden meaningless tragedies? His three children are
carrying out all the details of the search with magnificent courage, calmness, and his kind of dogged determination.

As I witness this, I find some kind of compensation or reconciliation
linked to a phrase sent me in a letter: *He left no crippled orphans behind
him.* They are all brought to shiny independent maturity. It is hardest,
perhaps, on Dick, who has no wife, but has carried on Jim's brilliance in
engineering and is now launched in this.

I must put this in the mail and go back to Reeve who has had a bout of
the flu. The day is bitter cold and beautiful. Our first snow fell yesterday.
Again, so hard to reconcile the cruelty and beauty of nature. Will write
again—

Love—

A.

*Scott's Cove
January 22nd, 1959
Dearest C.,*

Your letter from Zurich has just come—on the areas in Switzerland.
It interests me very much, especially the new areas you have discovered
in French Switzerland in the pre-Alp country (north of Lake Leman in

---

*Jim Robbins was killed when his plane crashed into a mountain ridge in bad weather, just
east of the Tetons. His body was discovered the following spring by a sheepherder.

the Canton of Vaud). The variations sound interesting, and of course the greater availability plus the French language are an advantage.

You do not say anything about *coming home*! No hope of it? We are, I think, doing all right despite quite extensive weather. First very cold, the cove frozen out to the island—like the ice-pack—for about two weeks. Then, a thaw and fog and rain—just over. Tonight it is due to get *very* cold again.

The New York, New Hampshire, and Hartford had its bad wreck (which you predicted), which put it out of any regular service for a while. Fortunately, the overturned cars were freight cars and no one was hurt.

I went to bed after you left, trying to get over the Aspen cold or bug or whatever it was—chiefly exhaustion, I guess. It took about two weeks. (I was only in bed one whole day but for a week felt absolutely flat and kept going back to bed.) But I am all right now.

I have seen Kurt and Helen who are planning a big change in their lives and work: to move to Europe (Zurich) more or less permanently. This is to lessen the pressure on him, really. He will head the European side of the business, and instead of moving back and forth between the two offices will just stay there. He seemed quite pleased when I told him we hoped to be in Switzerland this summer. And I must say, it would be nice for me to be able to see them there, if we make any kind of return trips winter or summer.

I must let this go and get to my Little House. I have been writing this over two days. The sun is bright this morning and it is very cold again. I have already lit my Little House and it is warming up.

I have called B. and Jon on Krissie's* birthday and they seem to be all right. We also called your uncle last Sunday night. It has been very cold in Florida, but he seems to be in good health and spirits. I am ready for the Virgins!

Much love and *come home soon*
Anne

Scott's Cove
Monday, February 1959
Dearest Barbara and Jon,

Your letter made me very happy—the feeling that we can communicate what one is thinking—feeling. I don't think it strange (I wanted to

---

*Jon and Barbara's eldest daughter, originally named Christine, was now known as Kristina.

write this right back to you) that you felt far away from Jon during this period of shock at your father's loss. I can remember when my sister died, CAL wanting and trying to comfort me—and I felt I had turned to stone. I only felt in one direction, and I was close only to all the people who were going through the same thing, feeling my sister's loss very immediately. And the same thing was true at my mother's death. Only that was so prolonged it wasn't as acute. And I suppose, poor man, he felt the same way with me, when his mother died.

Tuesday morning

Your father, Jon, is still away. That makes the whole of January and most of December, too. "How does father *stand* being away all the time?" Anne asked me. "And how do *you* stand it?"

I don't know, sometimes I feel very abandoned and put upon. Then I think, this is the way it's going to be from now on—more and more as the children leave. (Reeve is *never* at home any more—always out with a friend watching TV and Scott is off, too.) It is just like being a widow and I should make up my mind to accept it and decide what to do to counteract it, as a widow would: live where I want and can get companionship, be near the people I love, etc. California? Halfway between Con and Jon and B.? San Francisco? Well, you never can tell, I might turn up out there! (Buying a TV might be *one* solution—not for *me*—but for keeping the children at home.)

Now, I must go to my Little House. It is a lovely bright cold day. I shall skate again this evening. That helps.

Friday, March 6th, 1959

Dearest Land,

Scott has just gone out, all dressed up in his tweed jacket, in the new blue Volkswagen. I assume to a dance! Or to take a girl out. Your father gave him a little extra money, I guess to make up for breaking one of his best calypso records last night (on purpose!).

I know it is hard to write letters—the real things don't get said and the other things don't seem worth saying. I also find it hard to write letters. After I've been at a desk all morning, I can hardly bear to go back to it in the evening, no matter how much I want to reach the person I'm writing to.

I hope you are seeing people. I think it is quite a lonely period when one has broken off a close relationship. One misses it even though one knows it wasn't quite right. This is painful and sometimes confusing too. I guess there's no way around it but time, and facing the disappointment in oneself quite honestly as one has to accept any kind of pain—not trying to escape or drown it in ways that don't help (but only force it underground—to come out explosively in other ways).

Also, I have the feeling you may be feeling about college the way I feel about my ghastly novel, which I keep plugging away at but which I have outgrown and now doubt the value of—but somehow want to finish—because I feel nothing is learned from one's unfinished books. The whole problem of going through the ritual, the discipline, when the vision has departed (going through the ritual when the God has left the altar; St.-Ex. describes it). One *did* have a vision once and it might be still there. Only one is blinded to it, temporarily. You must have outgrown parts of college, other parts not. I hope you can be seeing interesting people—both students, graduate students, and professors. This kind of stimulus one can never outgrow or have too much of.

I must stop—getting too sleepy. Don't you think you ought to come down to the Virgin Islands with us to look at sugar plantations or listen to African or Caribbean rhythms?

Love,
Mother

[From a letter to Alan Valentine]
Sunday, April 12th, 1959

Not yet back a week, I still feel deliciously loosed from my moorings, and in spite of three days of rain, snow, income tax, and a bad leak in one of the bathrooms which has come down into the dining room, I still feel rather light and airy. (Fluid, like one of those beautiful fish on the reefs, gliding with no haste and perfect ease, in and out of turreted coral castles.)

Even the book looks different now, and I have gone at it again with fresh eyes these first three days. How long this will last I don't know. There are, of course, real duties to be taken up and things to be decided before summer (family problems and decisions that cannot be ducked or postponed), but spring should be here soon and that should help one live from day to day, instead of guiltily in the past or apprehensively in the future, which I find weights me down and makes me live unfreely, unspontaneously, and uncreatively, as I do when I get into a rut like this winter.

How wooden I feel tonight, and letters are! How awkward and inadequate. So much to say. So little gets through. We must talk. I must go to bed and add a line in the morning. . . .

I know the discouragement of not having the response to what one has written. (With me it is because I am so infernally slow at finishing anything. So much that is written is wasted, must be discarded or cut and changed completely.) You write faster and perhaps must expect waste in other ways. There is so much waste in creativity, always. But there is something curious about creativity: the trying-too-hard for results seems to defeat itself. (The something-to-show pressure, I call it in myself.) I know this kind of pressure, for me, reduces what I write to a thin, weak trickle. It is only when I am "loosed from the moorings" of wanting a result that I write the most freely, and well.

Also books do ripen on shelves, I think. After an absence, or in a new environment, suddenly the knot, or the stale part, or the unclear section, clarifies and can be shaken into focus quickly. Remember that big creative act of taking hold of your life freshly and adventurously, as you have just done, takes much of the creative energy you have. It cannot help but use it up. One tends not to count that in the ledger.

Now I must go to the Little House to attack the end of the book for the hundredth time. . . .

Come home soon!

My love . . .

February 4th, 1960
Dearest Land,

I suppose you have heard from your father who has bought the new VW for you to take possession of, temporarily, in March? He seems also to have entered Scott in a school and is trying to get us a chalet for the summer above Vevey. Some practical steps.

In the meantime we have been carrying on here, skiing weekends. Scott has suddenly become phenomenally good at skiing, wedeling downhill with both skis together, waving his ski-poles carelessly. He looks like a long lean future champion. He is now so excited about skiing that he won't stop for lunch. However he makes up for it afterwards having a large tea at 4:30: three hamburgers, two glasses of milk, chocolate cake, pie, hot cocoa—and a cookie! I ski conservatively and stop often, surprised to still be on my feet.

I have also just seen *Wild Strawberries* in Stamford. I must say I think it is his* masterpiece. I realize it may not be as deep as *The Seventh Seal* or as provocative as *The Magician* but I think it is more perfect than either.

*Ingmar Bergman, the film's director.

Marvelously simple in structure, terrific in impact, and astonishing in its *economy*—every detail counts, nothing is wasted, like a pared-down intensely moving piece of sculpture. I am fascinated by it technically—as a stream-of-consciousness novel—in film. As such, it is meant "not to be read but to be reread." Bergman's films should be *reseen*. I couldn't get to sleep after it—he stirred up my unconscious so completely. I wish I could talk to you about it. He certainly is obsessed by Time, Death, God, and Love. But then, so am I—who isn't?

I have just sent you an odd book by a psychiatrist* who went through a concentration camp during the war and came out with a "meaning" to life and a new core of beliefs for his patients. I could not put the book down: a simple object but moving as a poem—as a human document—and despite the horror, somehow very positive. The last part is an outline of his "new" school of psycho-therapy in Vienna. It is really based on Nietzsche's statement: "He who has a *why* to live, can bear with almost any *how*." He feels man's life must have *meaning* or he goes to pieces—and that man's "will to meaning" is stronger than his "will to pleasure" (Freud) or his "will to power" (Adler).

I realize you are now on the last lap; papers and examinations must loom. No time for extra reading. Perhaps you can read it on the flight to Europe. It is a little book and easy reading. Have also been reading *The Biology of the Spirit*, by Sinnott†—a paperback—Compass Books—worth reading on the same general field from the biological approach. "The suggestion is offered that this tendency toward goal seeking, manifest in the activities of both body and mind, is a basic characteristic of *all* life, and that life is thus inherently goal-directed and purposeful."

Well, dear Land, you've gone into this more deeply and intellectually than I and I could take lessons from you. I would certainly like to have a chance to talk over these subjects and get your thoughts on them, and other things. It must be good to be almost through! I think of you often and so much love,

Mother

---

*Viktor E. Frankl (1905–1997) was an Austrian neurologist and psychiatrist whose book, *From Death-Camp to Existentialism* (later reissued as *Man's Search for Meaning*), described his experiences in a series of concentration camps and his groundbreaking psychotherapeutic method of finding meaning in all forms of experience, however horrifying they may be.
†Edmund W. Sinnott (1888–1968), American botanist, university professor, and textbook author.

*Harkness Pavilion**
March 18th, 1960
Dearest C.,

Where are you? I have been expecting you every day for the past two weeks. I know I made light of the operation but I did hope you'd get here in time to take me home. Of course, I can arrange to get Mrs. C. to do it—or a limousine, but *I wanted it to be you.* It would help so.

I am still in the hospital. The knee operation turned out to be much more extensive and complicated than I—*or they*—anticipated. The knee had deteriorated so much since the last X-rays last June. The doctor talked to me about it the night before: he said he didn't know that I would ever have a skier's knee again. Also the consequent pain, swelling, and retardation of healing were all geared to the more complicated operation. I also (you know *me!*) was so anxious to start exercising that I developed a huge blood blister on my heel which had to be lanced. More delay! Ten days after the knee operation, I had the lump taken off—a very small non-malignant growth. I'm glad it's over. But this soreness in my right hand has delayed my use of crutches, necessary to learn before I get out of the hospital. The doctors say my knee is improving very fast now—my muscles are good. The doctor even says, "I think you'll ski again too but don't ask me when!" Please come home as soon as you can. This is a time when I need you.

All well—love,
Anne

Norwalk
June 7th, 1960
Dearest Jon and Barbara,

I am sitting in the lobby of the Norwalk Hospital where I go for therapy three times a week for my knee—which is *much* better.

Saturday morning, June 11th, before breakfast
That start was interrupted by Scott and Reeve coming for me, Scott to take a chest X-ray, and both to have shots for Europe. This last month has been terribly full packing up things for storage, moving out of the apartment, etc. It is one of those times full of packing-boxes, extra fur-

---

*A building in the complex of what was then known as Columbia-Presbyterian Medical Center.

niture, CAL running up and downstairs from the attic, *everyone* clearing out. Last weekend was a holocaust (if that is the word) with Land going over everything he had ever had, throwing away and wrapping up. (Susie* is going to be surprised when she unwraps some of those brown paper parcels: old Navajo dolls, bits of petrified wood, Mexican hats, African slave bracelets, etc. So useful around the home!) His cleaning up was catching: Reeve went through all her cupboards and closets, including the one Land called "The Doll Morgue," and Tommy,† intoning a funeral march, helped carry cartons of dolls down to a funeral pyre. Anne turned up with her latest beau and a Volkswagen crammed to the gills with her things from college, also dumped into our house. Uncle has also been here, polishing cars and digging up the garden.

I felt dreadfully gloomy seeing Land pack up his treasures of twenty-three years and feeling the family was breaking up—though, of course, it could be said it was doing the opposite—getting closer and closer! But Land did seem very serene and sure of himself and we are all very happy about Susie.

I certainly shouldn't feel sad about Land's leaving the family when I realize what Jon's marriage brought us: Barbara, the children, and greater closeness for all of us! I feel now I couldn't love any daughter-in-law as much as Barbara, but I'm sure I'll love Susie, too. (Anyone that means as much to Land, Barbara, and Krissie must be something very special!)

I am firmly hoping to get to San Diego for the wedding (though I wish it were two weeks later. CAL says it's the worst week of the year to get transportation back from Europe—the end of August). I can't very well come earlier, as I must get Anne some "safe" place in Paris for the winter—at least reasonably respectable! And also must get Reeve a school and us an apartment or small house for next winter. I can't put this off any later—should have done it *this* winter—but couldn't because of the knee.

At the moment I can only look a week or two ahead at a time—I suppose it will all get done—somehow.‡

This is long past breakfast and I must get to the day's work. I hope this last month is not too hard for Barbara. It is so long and difficult and exhausting to be on one's feet.

---

*Land would marry Susan Miller, a classmate at Stanford and a cousin of Jon's wife, Barbara, in August 1960.
†Tommy Miller, Susie's brother, then a student at Yale.
‡Here AML draws a smiley face.

I keep saying to CAL, "I think they've had enough, now, for a while. I think Barbara needs a rest."

And he always says, "Now you leave them alone—they know what they're doing!" I'm sure you do—but I worry anyway—I miss you and love you—will try to write again—will call anyway before we leave—

Love to all,
Mother

Locarno [Switzerland]
Tuesday, February 14th [1961]
D.D.

I am here in Locarno—still rather giddy at the change. Charles drove me down Saturday—just for one night—but it was such a happy day and evening, I quite forgot my pain at missing the weekend of skiing. I guess it wasn't really the skiing.

Kurt and Helen had visiting them here William Jovanovich, the present head of Harcourt Brace, with whom they have *just* signed an agreement! He is young, vigorous, intelligent (young man on his way UP!), evidently appreciates Kurt and Helen for what they are, and has offered them enormous freedom to publish their special books within his firm.

By a rare combination of luck we were all here together and Charles was much impressed by the man. They got on very well together. W.J. is an example of one of those extraordinary myths in America. His father was a day laborer in Yugoslavia. They came to America "with tags on them," according to W.J. (that is, they could speak no English) and lived in Colorado. W.J. worked his way up into Harvard and Harvard graduate school, became a book-seller at Harbrace, and very swiftly worked his way up to be head of it—in his *early* thirties. Rather fantastic story. As you can see, he has tremendous energy and imagination and—what one wouldn't expect—perception and sensitivity.

I do hope it is going to work out for Kurt. At the moment, everyone is in a honeymoon stage of excitement over each other. Kurt looks like a different man: alive and back in his world again, with power behind him. And Helen has lost that really painful look of worry and responsibility over Kurt. Charles, of course, was delighted to have it work out that I should return to Harcourt Brace ("The homing pigeon!" as Helen said), and it all seems rather too good to be true.

I have hardly gotten to work in such an atmosphere, but will soon, I hope.

I do eat at my table each morning, but feel almost too giddy: with the sunshine, beauty of the mountains across the lake, the sudden lifting of housework and responsibility, and the general feeling of spring in the air. I can hardly bear to stay indoors and walk for hours up mountain roads with yellow primroses dotting the rocky slopes and violets in crannies and frail pink blossoms suddenly surprising you around a corner. Also the people one meets on the roads are really such a different race from those around Vevey. They are really Italian: warm and relaxed.

The weather cannot last—nor my mood—I know—but it is fun for a change.

Anne is coming Thursday for a scant week—and will play the piano in the mornings (in the ballroom) while I work. Sightseeing or walking evenings.

I am at last attacking the problem of *sequence*—or *cohesion*. So far see *no* solution, but perhaps we can work out something together. I cannot see it *whole*.

Reeve, whom I called last night, sounded very happy in her pension ("I like it, Mother") which is a relief. But, as Jean said, "She just seems to have a music-box playing in her all the time"—Must dress for dinner. . . .

A.

February 15th [1961], a.m.

Just a line to record quite a delirious evening out at a restaurant—supper with Bill Jovanovich (we are all suddenly on first-name basis!), the Wolffs and Erich Remarque.* It was very gay and I refused no "cups." I wish you had been there to sparkle.

Erich Remarque came in rigidly and punctiliously drunk—if you know what I mean—but loosened up with the steak. Kept calling me "Baby" across the table, with an occasional polite question: "Are you married, Madame?" All of this was so deliciously funny for the rest of us and never annoying—as drunks usually are. Bill J. is very sympathetic and electric—too young for me, though!

Your giddy

A.

---

*Erich Maria Remarque (1898–1970), German-born author of the novel *All Quiet on the Western Front* and of later novels that examined the struggles of individuals in Nazi Germany.

Locarno
Wednesday, February 22nd, 1961
D.D.

Your letter to Locarno from the midst of blizzards and catastrophes (two friends *very* ill and your little Vassar girl with a concussion) made me feel quite sad—what a profession! Yet, of course, it is balanced by the times when you bring the miraculous about, when healing, happiness, usefulness, flowering, springs from your hands. Perhaps the mixture of joy and sorrow, the proportions, are no different from ordinary life (and professions?) but the *responsibility* is so much greater. And in February it weighs more heavily on you. Are you not going to take some vacation? How about flying over to Paris with Margot! Not impossible, you know, at all. I would come to Paris to see you and what fun we would have!

Of course, I rather feel I've had my vacation. We had ten days of dazzling sunshine—warmth, spring flowers opening. The last two have been bad, and today a wet snow is falling suddenly, blanketing out mountains, lake, everything.

Anne leaves tonight after a scant week. It has been a joy to have her and satisfies me that she is getting along all right now in Paris. I have also worked each morning, part of the time alone, and partly with the Wolffs, reading and criticizing the book (we have now finished reading it together—I read it aloud).* A great many things have come out—come clearer. I have not really done much *writing* here, but living and thinking and reading in such an atmosphere has given me new vision on the book. I see it again with "the eyes of love" since they do. And this—*whether it is right or wrong*—is more constructive and stimulating.

I feel now I must go back and work over, implement, the insights gained here. Of course, I don't *want* to go, and yet I feel the time has come for me to "fly alone." One knows when one must go back into one's cell and work. I have, however, kept open in my mind and plans the possibility of coming back sometime in late April or May for a new "shot in the arm," when I get all blind and unbelieving again, as I do periodically.

Also the possibility of taking two weeks in the summer with them somewhere to "finish it up"—God willing! I do feel very strongly that I

Dearly Beloved would be published under the newly established Helen and Kurt Wolff imprint at Harcourt, Brace & World in 1962.

must finish this book before I go home to the U.S. sometime this summer. (It will not survive another *moving*!)

The new head of Harbrace (Jovanovich) also read the book at one reading the day before he left, a fresh eye and ear. He is perceptive and very intelligent, if in some ways perhaps naïve, rather non-introspective: I would think a rather healthy active American executive. I was very nervous and still do not know exactly what impression it made on him (I think he was anxious not to hurt either the Wolffs or me). But he said about the same things to both of us: *some* of the things please me, others troubled me. He was very moved by it (he said), did not find it monotonous at all. "It was static," yes, but it had "inner movement" so it carried you along. Found the characters real, except for Aunt Harriet, who was unconvincing to him. "And once there is a character in a book that is unconvincing, it makes you doubt the others." (Quite a perceptive comment. I always felt she was a stock character, so this doesn't bother me.) It made him feel terribly sorry for women—all women. He was so glad he was a man! "All the women will cry over it." (Oh dear! Have I written another feminist tract?)

Well, the only thing I'm going to do on his criticisms is to try and revitalize Aunt Harriet, or cut her down drastically, or cut her out entirely. There are other things to do, of course, at least three or four months of work—as I work, if only I can keep my vision.

But you, now, you *need* a vacation. Is there no excuse you could use to get abroad between now and August? Some ailing Maharaja or King? No important conference to attend? Don't say *impossible*, try to think of an opening. How good it would be if you and Margot and I could meet in Paris! It's been such ages since I saw you. But for me to fly back to N.Y. would be too fragmenting, I feel.

*Le Coteau–La Tour [Switzerland]**
[Spring 1961]
Dearest Con,

Back in La Tour to my great relief. We got in Sunday night late, driving all the way from Venice (ten hours—Anne drove half of it). Monday was spent recuperating and getting Reeve's hair cut and some clothes for Paris (Reeve). Yesterday the girls left for Paris—Reeve to

---

*With Anne and Scott living in Europe in 1961, the Lindberghs had rented an apartment in La Tour-de-Peilz near Lake Geneva in Switzerland for the year. Reeve attended, as a day student, a British boarding school in Clarens.

have a week with Anne alone, I to be here a week alone, recovering from the worst cold I have had in years (caught in that badly heated fourth-class hotel—*that* was what was coming on when I wrote you that complaining letter!). Since I haven't had a cold all winter I really can't complain, but ten days of sightseeing in Italy is not the way to recover from the flu. It wasn't warm enough to sit in the sun on a beach, and the hotel rooms were so ugly and gloomy. I couldn't have borne going to bed for a day even if I'd been urged to. Actually it turned out not to be such a bad vacation (though *not* the sun-on-a-beach-in-Sicily we had originally planned). CAL stayed with us the whole time—quite a triumph. *He* must have enjoyed it.

The day with the girls alone here was good, and I had a chance to talk to Anne about going back to Radcliffe next year. After I took them to the station, I bought a new dress and then lots of flowers (quince blossoms and tulips) to make the apartment look gay for Helen Wolff, who arrived from Locarno for the night. I did not realize she had come on an errand of mercy: really just to see me and tell me about the book *Kidnap* which is coming out in June.* (I was really so moved that Mina and the Wolffs should be so concerned.) Of course I am concerned too. It has such nightmarish explosive material and is hard to gauge what its effect may be—on CAL, the children, the grandchildren and even on me.

I felt chiefly that it was an extremely dangerous book, not so much for us now as for others more in the limelight (the Kennedys, etc.) to publish and sensationalize in the way they are evidently trying to do. There are too many crazy people wandering around to whom such a book and such ideas will appeal. Everyone is endangered by sensationalism in the field of crime.

Of course, this is what the publishers are *trying* to do—to make sensational headlines, sales, impressions in everyone's minds. But they may not be successful at all. It may just be a flare-up that burns out quickly. We are now reading their publicity plans. *Reader's Digest* and Book-of-the-Month Club talking it up really shocks me. I am, of course, shocked in the way I was originally, shocked at people using crime, tragedy, suffering to get themselves a little attention, as if it were gold instead of blood. It is still incomprehensible to me: politicians stand-

---

Kidnap: The Story of the Lindbergh Case, by George Waller, was published in 1961 by the Dial Press.

ing up beside the ladder to be photographed, etc.* My resentment that tragedy should be smeared by the feet of men. But of course, we have seen much worse examples since our private tragedy: the war, the concentration camps. What horrors were opened up by those years and for so many. It became not the exception: it was the rule.

Tragedy of course passes—or rather the person who suffered it dies and another person lives on, and remembers it as in another life. This does not change what one feels at the exploitation of crime and evil for gain—gain that may cause more crime and evil.

And there are the practical aspects of it—the publicity of such a book. Any publicity makes living in the U.S. more difficult. This is worse than "any" publicity because it heightens to an enormous shadow something that was a part of our lives, now over. How will the shadow affect Jon and his children, Krissie going to school? Reeve back in Darien High School? Anne in Radcliffe? And that store of bitterness built up for so long in CAL? I don't really feel I can estimate.

Fortunately, neither Jon nor Land has had much publicity. But Jon was brought up in the shadow and it could affect him—perhaps should. . . . If there is much publicity Krissie should be watched, etc. We will be over here till late August or September and it may easily all have evaporated—or never even come to much.

At this point last night Charles came in the door unexpectedly from Uncle (about whom he is worried and wants to get to a clinic)† and we discussed this book and many things. He relieved my mind quite a lot—doesn't think it will make much stir. There have been other books on the case.‡ Books don't touch the publicity of newspapers and he doubts if it will get much newspaper or radio and TV publicity. He sent a note to Jon, but didn't think it would affect their lives at all. I hope he is right. *He* doesn't seem upset about it and says, in any case, *nothing* can be done about it. To try and stop it brings more publicity to the book.

This letter is already much too long and has been interrupted. I expect to have a quiet week alone (C. will try to get Uncle to a Zurich hospital)

*Following the kidnapping of Charles Jr. in 1932, a number of politicians appeared at the Lindbergh house in Hopewell, New Jersey, solely to have their photographs taken beside the broken ladder used by the kidnapper.
†Eighty-two-year-old Charles Land was in failing health and was placed by CAL in a sanitarium in Switzerland.
‡A bibliography assembled by Sam Bornstein in 2004 lists 210 published books and articles about the kidnapping.

until Reeve comes back from Paris. It suddenly seems like home to me, and if it is good weather I can think of nothing nicer than to sit in the sun on my balcony looking out over blooming fruit trees.

I must not go on—C. is off tonight for Zurich.

From Montreux → Venice
April 22nd, 1961
D.D.

I am on the right car on the right train (something I always doubt!) on my way to Venice for a week (with Helen and Kurt and Bill Jovanovich, Hotel Monaco, Grand Canal, Venice). There isn't time for a letter but that is the address. I will be back in La Tour a week from today.

CAL called me last night from Zurich where he has got Uncle in a hospital undergoing tests. Uncle, now that he has capitulated, is simply delighted with the hospital, doctors, nurses, treatment, etc. (He is getting all the attention he wants, *and needs*, and always refuses, now forced upon him.) CAL fears he may have something seriously wrong with him.

Scott spent the night in the apartment last night. We had supper and talked a little. He's quite enamored with Europe—wants to come back. He and Reeve drove me to the station at 7:00 a.m., and Scott keeps the car for the week I'm off ("convenient for dating"!). It is raining—too bad—but I have my rubbers and rain hat (you'll be glad to hear, I know!) and am sitting in a first-class compartment (Wow! as Anne would say) and am going to stay at a reasonably comfortable hotel. "Not a deluxe hotel," Kurt writes, "rather bourgeois." But I'm sure it will be deluxe to me!

I have been buying newspapers furiously (yesterday and earlier) to try to find out what is happening on the U.S.–Cuba situation.* How can the world survive so many appallingly rocky situations!?

April 26th, Venice
Since writing this we have been startled by what Kurt announced to me as "civil war in France." The French papers are hysterical, the American ominous. It seems most fantastically unreal here in glass-perfect

---

*On April 17, 1961, some 1,400 Cuban exiles, trained and backed by the U.S. government, landed in Cuba at the Bay of Pigs in a failed attempt to join with local rebels to overthrow Fidel Castro. The operation was a great embarrassment to the Kennedy administration and led both to the long-term disintegration of American relations with Cuba and to a strengthening of ties between Cuba and the Soviet Union.

Venice (the sun has come out today!). Or rather, this shimmering world is the unreal one, I am afraid.

April 26th

The latest news today is the collapse of the revolt* and a totally unified France behind De Gaulle. The newspapers of the response in France were quite thrilling to read. Perhaps Anne has lived through a historic moment. At any rate it must have given her a sense of France and of living history that nothing else could do.

April 28th—Last p.m.

Our days have been very full of sightseeing with Kurt or Helen— *marvelous* guides to Europe. I feel the world of Venice, indeed of Italian art, has been unlocked for me—not to speak of delicious meals, trips by boat around Venice, walks and gondola rides. Bill J. left after three days. He is great fun and we are an easy and sympathetic four. Kurt survives extraordinarily well and plans to go back to the U.S. for a visit in November. Helen has heard of an intricate heart treatment—operation—inserting a wire in the heart . . . ? this is as far as I can follow. They want to go to you for advice on it.

In fact, we have spoken often of you, Helen suggesting, "Couldn't he be persuaded to join us on one of these trips?" (Kurt has planned out my Italian education—Florence is next.) How lovely it would be! I have been deliciously spoiled on this trip. Breakfast in bed and wine at every meal! It has been a real vacation.

11:15, Saturday, April 29th

We are now on the train bound home. I leave Helen and Kurt in Milan and get to Montreux at 7:15 tonight where I hope Scott and Reeve and perhaps Charles will meet me. It is again lowering and rainy as it has been much of the week but we have had some nice days. It hasn't mattered too much—churches and museums to see. It makes such a difference to see a painting *in* the church for which it was painted instead of in some museum in another country. (pause for lunch)

---

*The revolt of Algerians against French colonial rule triggered a revolt against the French government itself by the French Colonial Army, which was quelled after the appointment by the French parliament of Charles de Gaulle as president.

6:00 p.m. Back in the Rhône Valley

We are at least a half hour late. I have left the Wolffs at Milan and got on the train for Lausanne: a very crowded train—four Swiss women and an Italian man in my first-class apartment. He is by far the most interesting and charming. I have talked to him a little while the four buxom Swiss look on with some disapproval—or envy? He married a Swiss. I wonder why?

I must finish this scrawl and mail it in the Montreux station. Have been reading Bill Maxwell's book, *The Chateau*, about two Americans visiting France after the war. Pleasant, perceptive, and to me very reminiscent of my own over-prickly sensitivity on being a foreigner in France (or Switzerland). But also a bit wispy. Margot says it has had good reviews. It is pleasant reading, as if I'd been with them and been in the company of very nice, sensitive, perceptive and witty people—

A.

P.S. B.J.'s bon mot on Princeton: "The leisure of the theory class."

Little House (Cooler on!)
August 26th, 1961
D.D.

I am very glad to have the galley*—and the little note tucked inside—and have been reading it in the evenings. It reads very smoothly and swiftly, though one wants to reread the succinct and wise bits, like that on medical education—the *whole* of education, it is. I am aware, reading it, of your wisdom and how rare the really wise are—like Judge Hand,[†] who is now gone. So few like him, and you, who are wise *and* gay.

I am back at my desk again and it is a great relief. I go each morning, with interruptions: trunks arriving, children coming or going, men to cut grass, etc. It took some time to get into it again. I am struggling with some positive final conclusion for Francis and it is difficult. However it is good to be struggling!

It is very hot and humid here and one wakes as if one hadn't breathed enough all night. However it gets better as the day goes on and gets hotter but less humid.

I have also accomplished quite a lot, in and out of the house. Reeve

---

*For Dana Atchley's book, *Physician, Healer and Scientist* (MacMillan Career Book, 1961).
[†]Learned Hand (1872–1961), noted American judge who served for many years on the U.S. District Court for the Southern District of New York and then on the U.S. Court of Appeals for the Second Circuit.

and I saw Rosemary Hall. It is a top-notch school with a good young alert headmistress who came from Concord Academy. She seemed fresh, spontaneous, sensible, warm and friendly, as well as awake to all the best in a scholarly approach. It is only college preparatory—and *nice* girls. Reeve will have to commute by train or car but is *so* relieved not to have to go to Darien High. I said I hoped her father would approve. "It's expensive, you know."

"Oh dear," she said. "Then he won't let me go." I said I thought he *would*. (I am determined that she go, but want his approval if possible.)

"What can we say?" she went on.

"I think he will understand in terms of the environment," I said.

"Oh, I know," Reeve said suddenly. "I have a friend—a very nice girl—who's been seduced three times!" I must have looked shocked, for she added, "She *used* to be a nice girl." I agreed this would be a telling point with her father!

Scott has made his college tour and seems quite interested in colleges in the U.S., especially since the draft board says he's less likely to be drafted if he's in college in this country. Anne arrives Monday. Her letter says she feels much better and less panicky.

This must go—I am stealing morning time to write and shouldn't. The big house is full of young: Scott and a friend, Reeve and a friend, and the Victrola going all day and night! I let them do their own breakfast, picnic on cold things, noon, and cook a hot easy supper at night. Ernestine came for one night while the children were away. We had fun and laughed.

Last night we (children and I) swam under the half-eclipsed moon, phosphorescence streaming from our fingers. This is reviving and my knee feels better.

I hope you are getting a rest and some fun?

Fall 1961 [DIARY]

Weeks have gone by again. No diary writing. Life becomes less vivid when I'm not writing in my diary. And yet I don't let myself use "good writing time"—that is, mornings, for diary writing, except when I've come to the end of a period of book-writing, a temporary surcease, like this weekend.

I have been revising chapters steadily to get them in shape for Helen to see. She is now over here from Europe for two or three weeks. I need a fresh eye on this book very much. It's one's vision that flags, not one's will power. As long as I can see something to do, to change, insert, or rewrite, then I'm hopeful. ("This will change it, this will make the difference!") But when I can't *see*, and feel it is all uniformly poor, then I am depressed. Compared to the vision I had of it originally, so many years ago, it seems like a total failure. But then, I always feel this way at the end of every book. One outgrows books in the process of writing. One outgrows the problems in them, which become stale, bromidic, unimportant. As Jung says somewhere, we don't solve problems, we outgrow them.

I have certainly learned a great deal in the writing. It is not a novel, of course, though it is fictional. I have written a series of essays on love, marriage, relationships, etc., and put these into the mouths of not very real characters, speaking for me. But neither the characters nor the situations are real ones from my life. They are extrapolations of characters and situations. The writer of fiction extrapolates from tiny items in his own or other people's lives, observed around him. Sometimes extrapolations are false, even in the scientific world; how much more so, then, in the world of fiction? Yet it is also true that you do not need to drink a pitcher of water, wine, or milk, to know the taste.

At this point of despair in writing, one says to oneself: *Then, if it is so poor, why not throw it away? Why finish it?* The answer to this, I suppose, lies in that saying of Isak Dinesen I have thought of so many times in the past three or four years, "When you have a great and difficult task, something perhaps almost impossible, if you only work a little at a time, every day a little, *without faith* and *without hope*, suddenly the work will finish itself." One goes on working "without faith and without hope." And yet, if one works like that, "every day a little," surely, that *is* faith?

I wonder always when I reread the quotation if she didn't mean "without fear," and often substitute "fear" for "faith." (But perhaps Isak Dinesen was one of those people who have no fear?) It is fear that is so crippling to me: fear of failure, fear of mistakes, fear of criticism. One must work without fear as well as without hope. Perhaps both are pride, and certainly external to the heart of work. One shouldn't think externally, in terms of results, rewards, or punishments. One ought to be immersed in the process and not dissipate the focus by imagining someone looking over one's own shoulder: reader, critic or family, or even one's own self-conscious self.

Another way of saying it would be that the writer must stay centered in the moment. Both fear and hope are in the future and one should not be thinking of the future. To write one must be steeped in the present. Is this what she meant?

Helen came out last week to go over the manuscript with me and took the copy in to Harcourt Brace for another editor to read. She feels I should stop working at it and put it into galleys. She says I am just afraid to let it go. This is true, of course. While she was here I felt buoyed up by her presence: such a rare person, understanding, sensitive, perceptive and yet very strong and direct.

But when I put her on the train for New York, I felt sunk. To lose both Helen *and* my manuscript, both the mother and the child, in one blow, was an amputation, almost a physical one. I did not know what to do with myself, and could hardly get through my day.

Christmas at Aspen 1961 [DIARY]

I am sitting on my bunk bed on the top floor of the big ski-barn at Aspen. The young have gone out skiing despite the snow which is gently falling—breathing, I want to say—around us, shutting us off from the outer world, muffling all sounds, enclosing us in a world of our own, like sleep or night. I am waiting for the snow to ease off slightly before I venture out. I'm afraid I've become a fair-weather skier. I have to *see* to ski, and am not limber enough to take the bumps blind, as the young do. But what a joy it is, still, to feel oneself dancing downhill on powder snow, a delight in being alive, a sense, or an illusion, of being young and free. How can the young appreciate this? They have it anyway, daily.

We have been here a week. CAL delivered the manuscript of my book, ready for galleys, on the way to the plane. How quickly all those weeks of work dropped behind as the plane roared off. I haven't had a minute to think of it since, immersed in this intense family atmosphere. We met our two older boys and their wives and families in this halfway point for a Christmas reunion.

After the cloistered cell of the writer, this is a plunge back into the world of motherhood and grandmotherhood, acting as housekeeper, shopper, cook and babysitter—with many helping hands. We are thirty relatives in all, in a huge rented barn: seven small children, four grandparents, two grand-aunts, fourteen to fifteen young adults, a great-grandmother and an infant baby. This last, my latest grandchild, only two weeks old, spreads a glow of divinity from her basket in the center of the turmoil.

This huge family reunion is, in a way, a grandmother's dream. (Also, I may add, occasionally a nightmare!) How we long to have our grown-up family again under one roof for celebrations. It is the dream of the old family homestead that some of us had in our youth, the tradition of welcoming the children and grandchildren back for Christmas or Thanksgiving. "Over the hills in an open sleigh, to Grandmother's house we go," I used to read in my childhood primer.

It is now only a dream because it has become almost impossible. Family homesteads large enough to welcome several families are rare. Grandmothers no longer have "hired hands" to help them. Children are scattered too far for a journey home by sleigh. Travel is expensive and cumbersome for the young. It was different in my mother's childhood. She lived in her grandmother's big house until she was nine. And when *she* was a grandmother, she was still able to carry on the tradition, welcoming her children and grandchildren back into a big house. Even then it was rare; in my generation, it is almost unknown.

But the tradition remains, a nostalgic memory to be lived out on special occasions like this.

Three or four years now, we have repeated our family reunion at Aspen. I begin to realize how short is the period when one can unite one's grown-up family. In a few years the new families become too large and too scattered. Even their interests become too scattered. As time goes by they have no longer as much in common to unite them. They cease to feel as strongly about the old family homestead; they are creating new centers of their own. Is this why we middle-aged mothers make such an effort to create this kind of occasion—because it is something that is slipping from us?

January 16th, 1962 [DIARY]

We flew back from Aspen on January 1st, to find the galleys waiting for me in the piled-up mail on the hall table, along with masses of unopened Christmas cards, bills and letters. The bills I pulled out, and a few letters, but the Christmas cards are still unopened. Everything had to be pushed aside to correct the galleys and return them as soon as possible to the publisher. Another two weeks of intense work: reading, cutting, changing.

It is strange how different a book looks in galleys—actually, the first time you see it in print. All kinds of faults, passed over in the typewritten manuscript, jump out of the printed page. CAL has gone over the galleys, page by page, making lists of technical errors, thousands of small details, commas, repetitions, roughness in sound or construction. His eye and ear are very good, and his lists stimulate me to make ones of my own. In the end one no longer sees the book as a whole. There is nothing left but shreds of fiber. Fiber by fiber, one has torn it apart.

In periods like this, time seems suspended; life held at bay. One does not look ahead either with dread or anticipation; one simply lives from day to day, from galley-page to galley-page, those long flopping scrolls rolling over the desk. Then there comes the day when one goes over the penciled corrections in ink. No more rubbing out and changing, now. One glues down the last typewritten inserts, seals the big envelopes and drops them in the mailbox. One can do no more. At this point I have become completely blind and have no idea what I have written.

Amey* called me up two days after the galleys were mailed. She had seen a big advertisement in the newspaper for the magazine serialization. "Well, I see you're splashed all over the papers again," she started out acidly.

I cringed. "Yes," I said, "I nearly fainted myself when I saw that ad."

"What kind of a book is it?" she went on curiously.

"I really don't know," I said truthfully, groping for a label. "It's a lot of people's thoughts at a wedding."

"I hope they're *nice* people?" she asked crisply.

"Some of them are," I ventured.

(With alarm) "It's not a *nasty* book, is it?"

Oh dear, I do dread her seeing it. It isn't only that she may think she is the model for "Aunt Harriet" (she isn't). Even if none of the characters are taken from life, there are always a certain number of scrips and scraps from the past that offend relatives. And the talk about sex and morality, coming from me, will shock her. ("She knows better," I can hear her comment.)

Well, it's too late now. The manuscript is in the hands of the publisher. I always want to hide in a hole at this point. But it isn't that I am ashamed of what I have written. It's partly the old business of having been brought up to "be a good girl" and to want to please everyone. One knows, at fifty, that pleasing everyone is not only impossible but undesirable. But the old conditioning remains: dreading people's dislike, scorn or disapproval. And with me there is another subtle illogical factor. Instinctively, I find myself feeling that all publishing is indecent exposure. If one could, one would like to write and write and never have

*Amey Aldrich, a college friend of Elizabeth Cutter Morrow's, known affectionately as Aunt Amey to family members.

it seen. Or perhaps the artist wants to publish and the woman wants to hide.

I remember once seeing an explanation of this odd feminine reaction in a book by a Jungian. The writer said that woman so instinctively wants to be veiled, hidden, in the background, that it is almost a violation of her nature to expose herself as she must if she comes out openly with a work of art. Rilke touches on the same theme, less clinically, when he says of woman, "She, whose strength has always lain in her being found."

January 30th, 1962 [DIARY]

These last weeks have been a hiatus, one of those desert stretches in which nothing happens or grows. When the galleys left and CAL went abroad at the same time, I felt a sudden let-down. The pressure of the last weeks—even months—has been constant working toward a set goal, finishing the book.

Now the goal is reached, the book done. Where am I? Nowhere, I find, to my surprise. My husband is away, my children back in school, and my book off my hands. I feel lost, at loose ends. With no mark ahead, I walk unsteadily.

I remember once, on an early flying trip out west, we landed on a flat mesa above the De Chelly, Del Muerto Canyon. We walked along the plateau until we found a trail we had seen from the air, followed it, clambering down a steep serpentine gully and along the river bank below to the cave dwellings under the cliffs. After spending the day exploring caves, we climbed back up the cliff and retraced the trail toward our plane. It was a long day and I was tired, but I was able to walk swiftly and steadily as long as there was a trail. When it petered out at the end, I hardly had the strength to lift my feet, and kept stumbling over mesquite and stones. It is like this now. I am off the trail and keep tripping over small stones and weeds. I do not clearly know where I am going.

I have tried, putting on city clothes, going into New York, seeing friends for lunch, accepting every invitation that came my way. A great success at first. It seems helpful to externalize oneself. (See, I look like a different person, one says, glancing in the mirror.) In reality, one cuts oneself in half. One locks up the unhappy goose girl in the cellar and then, putting on a new face and new clothes, goes out into the world. One talks and laughs, takes interest in other people. (See, I'm being quite gay—I'm fine!) But all the time the goose girl is crying in the cellar.

Finally, one realizes that friends can be just as much of a distraction as duties. One cannot find oneself here, either. Neither duties nor distractions cure the rootless feeling, and I find I need roots very badly. I try to find mine in home, children, and writing. But with only one child left at home, my husband away, and no work at the moment, I feel very adrift.

One cannot root oneself in friends, although old friends do give one a temporary sense of home, a substitute for roots. But it is not fair to use them as lifelines. It is an exploitation of one's friends, a denial of friendship. Sharing is permissible; leaning is not.

But actually this is just as true of the relationship with husband and children. You cannot demand that they give you security. This too is exploitation. Perhaps we are not meant to find roots in anything or anyone outside ourselves.

Of course, there are always the small daily joys that keep me alive. I make a game sometimes of counting them: waking in the morning to the sound of wood-doves, lying in bed a moment longer watching the patterns of sunlight rippling through the Venetian blinds onto the opposite wall, golden coins piling up and spilling over endlessly. The first cup of coffee and the walk to the Little House; the glint of bare twigs against burnished winter sky. Skating in the afternoon on a neighbor's pond, bright figures spinning on the slatey ice. The paper narcissus in the living room that has just flowered and smells like spring. Reeve playing her guitar in the kitchen as I make supper or clear up. Listening to a radio concert at night, propped up in bed, or reading a good book before I go to sleep. I'm in the middle of *An Experiment in Mindfulness*, by Shattuck, the account of a British admiral who spent a month in a Buddhist meditation center—a very precise, practical, unfuzzy investigation of attempts to control and observe the mind. One realizes how little control we in the West actually have of the mind (as opposed to how much we can cram into it) and how much we could learn from the East, especially in the realm of intuition and the unconscious. How to use the unconscious and keep in touch with it. I am certainly out of touch with mine.

Kennedy Dinner
Sunday, May 13th, 1962
D.D.

We came back yesterday from Washington. I still feel a bit dizzy from the party. It was really quite a lot of fun, though not at all what I expected. It was an *enormous* party—about two hundred people—very well managed and quite gay and beautiful. There were really so many people that it was like a large reception, and when you saw someone you knew you felt like throwing your arms around them. I practically fell into the arms of the David Rockefellers, the MacLeishes, the Légers (St.-John Perse), René D'Harnoncourt, Alfred Frankfurter (editor of *Art News*), Thornton Wilder, etc.*

CAL and I took a taxi to the White House after taking the shuttle down from New York, and after picking up CAL's newly made "black tie" outfit on Pennsylvania Ave. It was about five p.m. and the downstairs rooms of the White House were full of people arranging flowers and moving chairs about. We waited in a small reception room (it had two Cézannes in it) next to the big cleared ballroom where the Isaac Stern Trio was practicing in their shirtsleeves for the concert they were to give after dinner. Mrs. Kennedy's secretary then came and greeted us—a gay, informal, pretty woman with quite a line—and took us in the elevator up to our rooms: "The Queen's room for Mrs. L. and the Lincoln room for Mr. L."

"So far away!" I cried out in dismay, so we were both put together in the Queen's room.

We then had tea, brought us by a nice Negro maid who took my dress to press it, and I sewed some brilliant buckles on my new evening shoes (bought in Stamford that morning). I was handed the list of guests to look over and decided there was no use trying to read any more Malraux—I would never get to speak to *him*!† There were at least a hundred people listed from the art world: museum directors, artists, theater, writers, poets, dance (Agnes de Mille), music (Leonard Bernstein), etc.

We dressed and were ushered ("Call Usher's Office") to a small private upstairs salon where the house guests and French Embassy were having cocktails. M. and Mme Malraux, the French Ambassador and his umpteenth wife (he urbane, intelligent and very smooth; she blond, beautiful and hard as nails), Vice President and Mrs. Johnson, and various members of the French Embassy, the Kennedys, etc.

*David Rockefeller (youngest son of John D. Rockefeller, philanthropist, and president of Chase National Bank) and his wife, Peggy; Archibald MacLeish (Pulitzer Prize–winning poet, lawyer, journalist, and adviser to Franklin D. Roosevelt) and his wife, Ada; Alexis Léger (see note p. 143) and his wife, Dorothy Milburn Russell; René D'Harnoncourt (director of the Museum of Modern Art in New York City); and Thornton Wilder (Pulitzer Prize–winning playwright and novelist).
†The guests of honor at the dinner were André Malraux (1901–1976), the French novelist, diplomat, and explorer who at the time was the French minister of culture, and his wife, Marie-Madeleine Lioux.

The President was very natural, charming, and easy—no mask or pose—quite impressive. The French ladies were all dressed up and made up like mannequins—rather terrifying. M. Malraux, a nervous and interesting white mask. Mme Malraux less mask-like than the others, quite sympathetic. Mrs. Kennedy swept in like a queen, looking extremely beautiful in a long pink stiff gown, hair high and stiff—rather Japanese—with a diamond star set in it! I talked in English to Mrs. Johnson, who was kind and quite natural and American, and in French to the French women (not too well—but they were surprised to have me speak at all).

Then we went downstairs to the main reception hall—where all the other guests were. I was shown my place at dinner (there were eighteen smallish round tables) between Alexis Léger and Vice President Johnson, and C. was at Kennedy's table on the other side of the French Ambassador's wife. We lined up (alphabetically) and passed by President and Mrs. Kennedy and then sifted our way into our separate dining tables.

It was a little like "heaven" in that you kept seeing people who looked rather familiar and you had never met: Is that Tennessee Williams? Or Arthur Miller? Or Edmund Wilson? (I would like to have met E.W.)

I was at a table with Thornton Wilder, Robert Lowell and Alexis Léger. I loved talking to Alexis—and Vice President Johnson was sympathetic and very, very tired! (He had just flown in from Seattle where he had opened the Fair!) After supper (there were speeches by Malraux and Kennedy, given and translated over loudspeakers), we went into the ballroom to listen to the concert. I found CAL, who was much disturbed by the numbers of press around and would not sit in the front rows as we were intended. We sat in the back rows and the music was heavenly, but I was concerned about C. and not entirely at ease.

After the concert, people began to leave and we found ourselves being ushered upstairs to the same private salon, where about the same group were gathered as before supper—chiefly the French set. C. and I talked to the French Ambassador but nothing very real was said. And rather quickly, goodbyes were being said again. We said goodbye tactfully and went to our rooms though apparently Isaac Stern went on playing the violin until late at night. I wish we had stayed up.

The next morning, after breakfast in our room, Mrs. K. came up with the children and we talked informally in the hall—without a mask and quite real and simple (I must tell you about it). The children were refreshingly children and she was quite real and still beautiful. Caroline skips down the great halls happily and John Jr. crawls and climbs and collapses, overturning cigarette boxes on the carpets. We also saw the

President in his office as we left. You have a sense of great integrity and naturalness—no pose. We were both impressed.

Scott's Cove, Darien, Conn.
May 15th, 1962
Dear Mrs. Kennedy,

Despite the enormous burden of your mail—even your personal mail—I must write to thank you for the great kindness you and the President showed us in inviting us to dinner in honor of M. Malraux, and especially for your consideration and thoughtfulness in wanting us to stay at the White House.

It was an extraordinarily beautiful and stimulating occasion, which is not surprising. All parties—even big parties—I believe in some measure reflect the spirit of the people at their center. From this core radiates the beauty, vividness and good feeling which spread to the guests. That such an atmosphere was created, at such a party at the highest point of our government and in a formal and dignified setting, is a great tribute to you both and an inspiration to the people who were privileged to be witnesses.

On the private side, I must add how much my husband and I both enjoyed the personal glimpse of you and the President and your children. We were very touched that you should have found time for this in the midst of the many pressures that surround you. Aside from our pleasure, it is a heartening thing to find in the First Family of America the personal touch, the simple directness and the sense of clear integrity that one feels to be particularly an American heritage.

With the warm thanks of both of us

[From a letter to Alan Valentine]

Scott's Cove
Saturday, October 20th, 1962

Here I am in my Little House, about the second or third time this fall, on a beautiful fall day, alone. Reeve is out with a school friend; Scott has not yet appeared from college for a weekend. And quiet! The constant whine of buzz-saws and grinding roar of tractors plowing up our house-site* is still because it is Saturday. There is so much to say. How

---

*In 1962 the Lindberghs subdivided their property in Scott's Cove, sold their house, and had a smaller house built a little farther up the cove. The smaller house was eventually named Tellina, after the "Double Sunrise" shell described in *Gift from the Sea*.

disappointed I was, truly disappointed, not to see Lucia or you on your way through, but there was no choice. It was the most difficult week in a hard month. Everything has now subsided, I hope. Reeve is finally back in school on a half schedule. CAL is off on a world trip of some kind. Land and Susie and Erin back in Portland, and Ansy, at the moment on a leave of absence from Radcliffe, is living with Connie Morrow* in Bucks County, having fled Boston and the beau—catching her breath and seeing Rosen.†

It has been a stormy fall, but still not as difficult as last year, chiefly because Charles, arriving in the midst of it (the week I hoped to see you and Lucia), although much upset by Anne's plans (to leave college while considering marriage, etc.), was much more understanding of her state of mind and heart (while not approving), and much more concerned, and therefore much more open to her having some help from Rosen, which she is now getting. And though the present arrangement seems to me not perfect or sure, it is so much better than the alternatives that I breathe a sigh of relief and hope she'll be back in Radcliffe by next term.

But I meant not to embark on all that, but to tell you how I blessed you for your letter to Reeve which arrived while she was still in bed and rather down.‡ In fact, I had left her to go and shop for groceries that day and she had said, a little sadly: "Uncle Alan has not answered my letter." I said firmly that you hadn't had time even to get to England—no time for a letter. But to my delight, when I came back from the store with bags of groceries in my arms, there was a letter for Reeve from you on top of the pile. (I did not wait to find the letter for me in the middle of the pile!) I tore up to Reeve's bedroom and gave her your letter. She smiled and said, "Never mind about the rest of the mail," and settled down in her pillows!

Then I had the extra reward of finding your letter for me, and went out and sat in the sun and read it, and did not realize until that moment how much I needed *that*. Someone at last speaking quietly and perceptively to the inner me. I felt very restored and quite caught up with you and your life too, and this was a great alleviation of the pressured and somehow impersonal life I had been leading. Impersonal is not quite the

*AML's niece, daughter of Dwight Morrow Jr. and Margot Loines.
†Suffering from depression as the result of several difficult romances, Anne lived in Bucks County, Pennsylvania, for a short time, to be treated by Dr. John Rosen.
‡Reeve had hepatitis and was in bed for several weeks.

right word since what could be more personal than being a practicing wife-mother? And yet one feels so much of the time that one is living under a mask, or under *one* of the masks that is oneself.

Then came the week, or weeks, just before CAL's take-off, full of the pressing last details of the new house just starting and all those other chores which, for CAL, have to be compressed into the single month he is home out of three or four.

With his take-off, Reeve and I have just begun to relax into our quiet life *à deux* in the big house, while blasting is going on for the little house. This week would have been "normal" had it not been for Anne's sudden flight from Boston—almost like a war refugee's, escaping so fast (lest she change her mind?) that she brought with her (rather typically) a bird-cage, a guitar, and her best evening dress! (These were all "brought for morale" and for aesthetic purposes, not practical ones.)

(The tractor is inexplicably going again—and on Saturday! I have fled and am now in the big house.)

I can understand your sense of relief at getting off and getting back to the peace of Oxford. (I can picture you working at the Brussels sprouts in your faded Swiss smock! And Lucia at her rock garden!) I think (re your description of the summer and my thoughts about my own fall), that one really needs a very different rhythm at our age, and it is difficult to reestablish it in the old place—be it North Haven, Darien or whatever. I cannot look on this new smaller house here with very much zest, though I approve and can see no better alternative. We must have a base here, and I love the sounds and sights of the cove. It is quite different with the chalet above Vevey, which is almost built, if bare and empty.* I feel I will be able to live the way I want—or the way I believe—there. Perhaps this is an illusion, the dream of the free unattached-to-responsibilities place.

Still, it is easier to live a "new" life in a new place. I think all of us by middle age have lived so many compromises and so much unsuitable insincerity, and if we have grown and grown more perceptive, less ambitious, and closer to the truth of society and outer pressures, we feel at this age very impatient of the frustrations of living what we don't particularly care for or about. Also time is precious. Why should one

---

*In 1962 CAL bought several acres in the hilly farmlands—Les Monts-de-Corsier—above the village of Vevey and Lake Geneva, in French Switzerland. There he and AML built a compact but practical chalet, which they called Planorbe, where AML spent most summers until the last years of her life. CAL used it as a European base throughout the year.

spend it on dull neighbors who happen to drop in, or old beaux of one's children, or their fathers and mothers, etc.?

I resent the waste of life more than I did. There is less time. There is less energy. My time for going to school teas or being nice to my children's old teachers or friends, I feel, is over, and I have earned the right (by "being nice" for three decades or more!) to see only the people I like. Useless resolution: I succumb again and again to the accidental doorbell or call!

Just the same, one can choose a spot—like Oxford or Vevey—where one can start relatively fresh and make adult friends for the inner real person.

At any rate, all this was supposed to tell you that I have hope of a very simple, pleasant, relaxed life for at least some months of the year in Switzerland. I'm not so sure about Darien. And, of course, once one starts to live closer to the bone of what one believes and feels for a few months of the year, it makes the other months seem rather more unbearable than they were before, which is perhaps the hitch of living half the year in different places.

We have at present *nothing* in the chalet, but we have packed up one of the VWs with a sleeping bag and a few indispensable cooking utensils, towels, soap, old shoes, and have ordered four wooden chairs from a carpenter, so we could set up house with these at any moment!

I hope now to be able to get quiet enough to find the threads of a new book! I wasn't able to this summer—too busy, perhaps intentionally too busy—with moving, housework and details to get to and by myself. And this fall has been worse because it has involved the emotions as well as the hands and legs.

I must let this go. Do write again if you can; it means so much to me. Do give my love to Lucia. It was a wrench not to see her—not to talk. Time is short for friends too. My love to you, from Reeve and especially,

Anne

N.Y.C.
Tuesday, October 23rd, 1962
Dearest C.,

I came in town to have dinner with Margot and John, but am now probably going back to the country with Ansy. I'm just as glad since Aubrey, Con and I were up too late last night listening to the news on Cuba and the rebroadcast of the President's speech about the "quarantine" on Cuba.* Reeve came downstairs and snuggled into a corner of the sofa and said in a small voice: "I wish Father were here, I'd feel safer with Father."

In the meantime—Con and Aubrey are on their way back to Portland, and N.Y.C. is noticeably emptier (quite pleasant) because of the war scare. Ansy and I will drive back for supper (because a man has dropped out of Margot's party and it makes it uneven to have an extra woman), and she will be there tomorrow and then go back down to Bucks County.

. . . I got your note from Suisse saying that no more letters to Vevey—that you were off to Johannesburg and then Nairobi, so I assume Bell is in Johannesburg and have addressed this letter there—as well as to Kenya.

Must stop. I do hope nothing blows up in Berlin. I don't suppose Russia will fight over Cuba—not only Reeve misses you!

Ashfield, Mass.
November 11th, 1962
Dearest C.,

This letter will hardly be an answer to your long one to me about Ansy and psychiatry, which I got last week—much of which I agree with and hardly can answer, and where I differ with you can only, perhaps, be gone over by word of mouth.

I have been reading an article in the *Times* magazine called an analysis of psychoanalysis. Not very deep, but rather good and objective—admitting the impossibility of any precise data about "cures" in answer to some of your questions, without arguing too deeply—or at all—just my opinion.

I don't think Anne is going to Rosen because it's "smart" or "convenient," and I really believe she believes she needs him—how "desperately" I don't know. She is certainly a different person now than she was two or three weeks ago when she left Boston. She even *looks* different and is leading a fairly quiet and normal life there: keeping house in a very inexpensive apartment, studying German and guitar and riding horseback and walking and seeing Rosen rather regularly. It's a good deal more normal than life in Boston was—or even Radcliffe life—and I think she sees more normal people and can come up here for weekends.

*Nikita Khrushchev's attempt to install nuclear weapons in Cuba resulted in a U.S. military blockade of the island in October 1962, which was lifted after Khrushchev agreed to dismantle the missile bases and ship the weapons back to the Soviet Union.

Some of it is certainly "sugar pill"—or just being away from pressure and a pressured environment, and feeling she doesn't have to make any decisions on her life for the moment and can look at the way she's been acting, and certainly feels it's been—some of it—a great mistake.

I don't think Rosen is equally good with everyone, as he has certainly had his failures. I don't happen to feel that Anne is one of them. I do feel that she has been helped—that she is stronger than the spring in France or last fall. These states are hard to measure—I know you disagree. I don't think the improvement is spectacular or fast, but I don't see any retrogression. On the contrary—a slow and persistent growth and improvement. In the face of this, and in the face of the alternatives (in Radcliffe or in France), and in the face of not knowing anyone any better than Rosen (imperfect as he may be and certainly is), I would be hesitant of separating her from Rosen at this point.

I would hesitate to take this responsibility on myself (after all, it was *her* choice and *is* her choice). However, you feel strongly about it and if you feel you want to take the entire responsibility for Anne, you might, when you get back, look around for a new psychiatrist, urge Anne to go to him, and stay around to make sure the reaction is good between them, talk to him regularly, and keep an eye on it, etc. You have certainly every right to do this. We would have to do this if Rosen died, and I am sure there are other good psychiatrists—perhaps better—for Anne. I also think there are a lot of worse ones.

All this we can discuss when you get back. Our frameworks *are* very different but, as you say, even though they may clash, they seem to want to stay together—balance each other.

Incidentally, I feel Anne—and perhaps this is the *you* in her—has quite a lot of objectivity about Rosen and the troupe down there. She is humorous about it and really not a hopeless devotee (Thank God) and doesn't *want* to stay down there too long or too closely, and says she can't bear to go to Florida with them. I also agree with you that "each year brings a decided advance in the judgment and emotional reactions."

Enough of Anne. I liked your letter very much re the ranch and am sure it was invaluable to the boys. I hear (from Con) that they have decided not to buy that Montana ranch, which relieves me. I think it was too soon and too heavy an investment—and Land is not sure enough—and it also seemed to me too isolated. Now I must go upstairs. Your descriptions of Africa—in flux—are very vivid and interesting. It will be good to hear all this from you first hand. Reeve and I miss you very much.

November 29th, 1962

Dear Lonnie,*

I was very glad to get your letter but sorry not to see you over the Thanksgiving weekend due to all the misunderstanding. I missed your telephone call since I was having my arms (both stupidly scalded with hot water) dressed at the doctor and it took longer there than I expected.

You must try to forgive your mother—and perhaps me too—for being overprotective. This is a common failing of mothers. I think your mother was trying to protect you—perhaps me, as well, but mostly you, I think. And it was true we would have had no chance to talk Saturday since I was cook *and* hostess *and* dishwasher.

That's all I'll say about that except that, though I'm fond of your mother and have known her a long time and feel desperately sorry for her (she has been through a lot), and though I knew and liked your father and valued his gifts, I am interested in you not for their sakes but simply for your own sake—as an interesting individual who has also gifts and sensitivity and courage and hope.

Now—that's enough about that. As to the paper: I wrote out before Saturday, in expectation of seeing you, some notes that I hoped to go over with you on some of the facts of my life and my points of view. They may not be at all what you want and they may be illegible, unexplained by word of mouth.

On the questions in your letter about "why certain people write certain books," one could write a book alone. The spurs to writing are infinite, as you must know. Some people write as a protest against the imperfect world and all they've suffered in it. (Your father wrote sometimes this way—critical of the society he had lived in.) Some people write out of love of the world—poets chiefly—praising it. (Do you know the poem of Elinor Wylie on the earth, ending up "I kiss the scars upon its face"?) Katherine Mansfield wrote driven by illness and death, feeling she must capture life in writing. Proust wrote in the same way to recapture the past. (Everything changes, everything passes—except art.) Chekhov and Tolstoy wrote out of love and compassion for human beings (Chekhov was a compassionate doctor as well—Tolstoy, a reformer), etc.

I think, too, that women write for different reasons than men. (That is, true women—who fulfill women's roles as well as write—not masculine women who are in another category.) There is a creative urge

*A son of John and Adelaide Marquand (see note on p. 60).

in men which I think is not as strong in women who, after all, satisfy that in having children. It seems to me that true women often write out of an excess of the mother instinct in them. They write to give more milk-of-human-kindness and more wisdom and more insights than their children can take. They write for other "children" in the world. (And I don't mean literal "children" waiting for child-stories.) They have garnered a certain amount of honey in their hives—more than enough for the family around them—and they must go on giving it to the wider world because it is in their nature to give.

But to come down to the particular: Why did I write? Why do I write? I think one must distinguish between the incidental accidents that turn one to writing (in my case, feeling inadequate in the world of conversation as an adolescent, or as in the years after losing my child, in sorrow, as an expression of and escape from the difficulties of life), and the deep inner spurs to writing that lead one on, no matter *what* the accidents of one's life.

I would write even if I published nothing. I wrote for years in diaries and notebooks and poems before I published anything. I believe I write to analyze, clarify, understand and perceive life. I write in order to see more clearly. If I did not write, I would be blind and deaf—as well as dumb. It is my lens through which to see myself and the world.

Writing is a glass-bottomed bucket through which one looks to the still world below the ruffled surface of the waves. It is the blind man's stick with which I tap my way along the pavement. It is also my keel, which keeps me steady in choppy waters and gives me direction. So you see I write because I have to. And incidentally it happens to be all I have to give (outside of what I give to my family). I give dates because I am a date tree. Not everyone likes dates. I tire of them, too. I would like to give oranges, pomegranates, or coconuts. But I don't happen to grow anything but dates, unfortunately.

Well—I cannot write you a letter like this every week and it would be simpler to see you. I would love to discuss related problems, as I think you may write in the future. Your poem *is* deep and also moving, though not completely clear. It doesn't quite come through as a whole. "Anchored depths" is the best verse. I think you can write. I wish you would read, if it is in your college library, Rilke's *Letters to a Young Poet*. It was a kind of writing—and living—Bible to me for many years, and I think you would like it. It would speak to you. Forgive pencil—but I write more easily with one.

My love—

AML

If you quote anything from this letter in your paper you should say— "From an unpublished letter of AML."

Scott's Cove, Darien, Conn.
February 4th, 1963
Dear Mrs. Johnson,*

I came back from town last night to find your very nice letter to me with its cordial invitation to come to the luncheon you are giving for Señora Betancourt, wife of the President of Venezuela, and to have perhaps an hour or so afterwards to talk to you.

I was very pleased by your letter on many counts, for your kind words about *Gift from the Sea*, and because of the directness and honesty of contact I felt talking to you for a few minutes the night of the White House dinner (I was more grateful for this than you can know). Naturally, also, because of the honor of the invitation to lunch with the wife of a head of state of a neighboring nation.

But I must admit, especially because of the opportunity for that hour or so afterwards to talk to you about what you learn from and say to women in America in your various talks. I don't know that I could offer any suggestions to you in your difficult task (I myself find talking to more than one or two women a most unnatural role), but the subject of women's interests, needs and problems in America today is close to my heart.

Before I go further I regret to say that, much as I am honored by the invitation to lunch on the 20th of February, it is really not possible for me on that date. We have a long-standing and traditional family ski-trip planned for that weekend. It involves three families, two generations of skiers, sisters, cousins, nephews, and nieces. I fear I cannot disrupt the occasion at this moment.

I do, however, want to express my sincere thanks to you and to add that I would really like to see and talk to you if the opportunity should arise easily for you in your very busy and scheduled life. Perhaps in New York, or I could take the shuttle to Washington for a few hours possibly sometime.

I will add our (unlisted) telephone number in case a moment should

*Lady Bird Johnson (1912–2007), wife of then vice president Lyndon Johnson.

open. I do plan to be abroad (where my oldest daughter is this winter) for several weeks in March, but otherwise expect to be right here. I lead a rather unsocial life, since social occasions interfere so greatly with any kind of peace for writing. So I am, or can be, fairly flexible.

With my sincere thanks and regret that I cannot be with you on the 20th.

A cold Sunday, May 26th, 1963
Dearest C.

I cannot send off this license to you without trying to add something on Scott and the voluminous correspondence now going on between you and him, me and Ansy, Scott, etc. (I have a whole dossier on Scott on my desk.) It is hard to write about it. I wish I could talk to you, and to him, and that you could talk to him. At the moment, I tend to feel (with the little fox in St.-Ex.'s *Little Prince*) "Words are a source of misunderstanding." And yet one must try.

I felt, as you know, extremely upset by your original letter to Scott, written and sent off before I had a chance to read it, while I was off in Bucks County. I felt it was a very destructive letter, even though the facts as you laid them out to Scott (on his account-keeping, on his college and school records, on his managing his finances, on his plans for the future, on his taking the apartment without any money to pay for it and without letting us know—i.e., being generous at someone else's expense) were irrefutable. When I wrote Scott a day or two later (waiting, as you asked me, so that the two letters did not reach him in the same mail), I covered a lot of the same ground and more. I told him that the things that you had said, the facts you had presented, were true and I could not argue against them.

Nevertheless, I feel your letter to him was written in such a way, and couched in such terms, as to *appear to be* harsh and humiliating and dictatorial. ("Words are a source of misunderstanding.") Perhaps you did not mean to be any of these things, or perhaps you wrote it in anger, or perhaps you felt, as I think you expressed to me, that it was a good thing to jerk him short—to make him think, to have him a bit pinched, etc.

My own feeling was, and is, that this was not the kind of letter to send to anyone, least of all an adolescent (I realize Scott is a man and is old enough to be in the Army, but he's still adolescent) boy alone in a foreign city who has had a discouraging year (due to his own failures, agreed) and a recent blow to his plans and hopes (of getting into Cambridge). These failures and setbacks speak for themselves. You don't have to rub it in with harsh words, a history of failures, and withdrawal of support.

Also, it is ineffective as a letter. When you write a letter in that tone, the effect is, rather than bringing someone around to reason ("snapping them out of it," to quote your letter), it tends to stiffen their resistance and persistence in a course which may well be unreasonable and foolish. Any person of spirit and *any child of yours* with that inheritance of spunk and independence is bound to react with fight. (You won't support me? OK, I'll do it alone. I don't need you and never will ask you again. There are other people I can turn to.) That kind of letter was bound to turn Scott away from you and to others for help, support and guidance. That is why I think it was a mistake, and I regret it.

You have sent me Scott's answer, which was what one would have expected. It is a rather wordy and sometimes vague letter, but certain things stand out: along with an acceptance of your criticisms and acceptance of his failures, a certain pride, dignity and courage. There is no sign in that letter (you may have a later one) of his reasons for the stand he is taking—i.e. of staying on in Rome, or of how he is going to meet his very real problems of finance, of schooling, of the problems of everyday life that he has not, up to now, handled too responsibly. But there is every sign that he intends to do it alone without your help or guidance—or mine.

My guess is that he will flounder around quite a bit this first year, and then pull himself out of it—not without quite a few mistakes, pitfalls and heartaches (I hate to see it). But he has, if I read him right, chosen his stand. He prefers to learn from the world than to learn from you. It may be the harsher way to learn, but it may be the best way for Scott to learn.

I do not know whether I can explain it to you, or even if I can put it in words—or even if put in words it would convince you. It takes a whole other way of looking at Scott and listening to him. To understand Scott's pattern you must look back at him, as far back as you can remember. (I am now just talking in hints and clues. This will not be clear or perhaps convincing.) I see Scott as an unusually independent child ("I listen to *myself*") and also an unusually sensitive child, idealistic. Also stubborn and persistent. His independence may come from you, his sensitivity from me, his stubbornness from both of us! But the non-conformity has been there a long time.

Scott has to do it differently. Why? I would try at the answer by guessing that he had to rebel early to hold his own—against his brother, his father, his older sister. In any case, I think he is and has always been fighting the *authority*—in school, in college. It is normal for children to rebel against their parents, especially their parent of the same sex. Ansy rebelled against me. Reeve in a quieter way. The older boys did it more normally. Land had his fling, but Jon's rebellion was just emancipation—one hardly noticed it. Scott, however, goes at it in a big way, and has been the rebel for a long time—but not against *you*. He has rebelled against orderliness, against being on time, against doing well at school, against examinations, regulations, accounts—but not against you. Perhaps he always admired you too much. You are a tremendously strong person; it is hard to rebel against you. Also, you are always right, or almost always right. It is almost impossible to rebel against someone who is always right, who is reasonable, who is infallible.

Of course, he is going to flounder around. I'm afraid he will flounder around a lot for a year or two, but I have a feeling he will be able to take the real beatings of his own blundering from the world better than the fake beatings from his parents' disapproval.

Actually, I do not think we can help him much here. This makes me sad and I feel sadness in your letter. But I feel Anne can help him more than anyone. She is the closest to him, and she has been through a long adolescence too—and she had to leave us. She had to find a new family, a new life, a new country. (This is rebellion, too. I ask myself why she can take from the Feydys what she couldn't take from me—from us?) But she is finding her way to strength. Paris is not Mother. Cambridge is not (for Scott) either Father or Mother, and he did better on his own in England than anywhere else so far.

Anne has been in touch with Scott and has written me and will see him sometime during the summer. She sounds quite free and strong. She has a part-time job for next year doing translating and as a guidance counselor for Sarah Lawrence girls in Paris.

Scott's Cove
Late at night, Sunday, June 9th, 1963
Dearest Scott,

I was very happy to get your letters of May 29th and June 2nd (one describing your routine and apartment, the next describing John's mother, Baroness Backhoven—also the ants!). Both letters sound much more real and easier and like you. I am also delighted I can see you on my way to Como. I have not yet got my reservation since I have been waiting for your father to get it through Pan Am. But I will cable you when I do.

I understand much more about the apartment now, and think perhaps it was the best thing to do. I really—as you guessed—*don't* approve of your rigid austere routine. *Too* rigid. You don't have to prove your worth to me by any such Puritan austerity. But perhaps you're proving something to yourself or Father. A more moderate schedule works better, and is more natural to you, and will last longer.

However, you said you were going to relax it in a month. I do approve of the Italian and Latin. Rome is a good place to study Latin and it may well help you. Also am delighted you may be able to take the exams in December and that you've written other universities in England (good reasoning here).

The letter about the Baroness delighted me. I wish I could meet her. Never lose an opportunity to meet or see or talk to someone like that. They have their wisdom of life and can sometimes help you to find yours; just by talking to them, one is more oneself.

Sorry about the ants! (I find flitting the surfaces helps—also one can buy "ant powder" or traps.)

I have had a short letter from your father, very full of praise about a letter you wrote him, on your plans (since I didn't see the letter, I can't comment). I do find it hard to bounce up and down with the sudden changes. You are the same person you were three or four weeks ago, and I found much to admire and praise in you then—still feel the same. Though perhaps this means you have *communicated* yourself and your plans better to him in these last letters. That is something.

We must talk about communication and its difficulties.

Scott's Cove
Monday, September 16th, 1963
Darling Reeve—

What a cold goodbye I gave you on those granite steps at Harvard! Not even a hug and a kiss, but somehow I felt I could not prolong that moment by *anything*—that it was best for you to go to Sarah and the unpacking, and for me to go back as fast as possible to Scott's Cove. Then the new life—new lives—could begin.

I suppose one isn't "meant to like it"—leaving one's child or one's mother—and so it hurts. But it is a "normal" hurt, so to speak, one that goes *with* life so one can find one's way out of it. I think it will be so for you, too. It is normal to be meeting and parting at your age with those one loves and feels close to. And you cannot find—at Radcliffe—quickly others to be so close to.

But you will find them. You did at Château-d'Oex and you did at St. George's and you did at Rosemary and you will at Radcliffe.* But at first it will be all queer and uprooted and just practical, dry, confusing-on-the-surface things that don't feed you *inside* (the astral body!). But they are a help, too, and they are to become routine, and routine tides you over until you can go deeper—find real friends or real interests. The *beginning* of things is always superficial. It takes time for the deep things to grow. But you are wise and patient and know how to have faith and wait and watch for the real things to come.

They will come, even right away, in little spurts—little sprigs of green. You will find someone who likes Handel's Water Music or Rilke—or you will see Rhidian,† someone you can be honest with and admit how confusing it is. (Just *admit* it's confusing—don't try to make order out of it immediately. Just go along with it—gradually, it will sort itself out.)

Well, you will work it out. Try to get enough sleep.

I miss you very much. It has been so wonderful to live along with you for so many years. But it is a normal loneliness and I will recover—I will find a new life, too. And I have complete faith that you—if you follow your deep and very true instincts—will find a great deal of richness wherever you are.

Much love, darling. I think about you all the time.

Darien
October 21st, 1963
Darling Ansy,

It was wonderful to get your letter, plus pictures, plus sample of the (I assume!) wedding dress material.‡ I think it is *very* lovely. When did you get the material? And the sketches look as if it would be very *practical*, too (not exactly what one expects from a wedding dress, but we were a

---

*Château-d'Oex, a town near Gstaad, Switzerland, where Reeve attended a one-month intensive French program; St. George's School for Girls, in Clarens, which Reeve attended as a day student in 1960–1961, when the Lindberghs spent a year in Switzerland; Rosemary Hall, an independent boarding and day school then located in Greenwich, Connecticut, which Reeve attended for the last two years of high school.

†Rhidian Morrow Morgan, son of AML's sister Constance and her husband Aubrey Morgan, who was then a freshman at Harvard.

‡Ansy had become engaged to Julien Feydy, a French law student and son of Hélène Feydy, who taught American students in Paris, and Jacques Feydy, a painter and professor of art history at Sorbonne University. They would be married in December 1963 in the Dordogne village of Douzillac, where Julien's parents owned a large, rustic summer house called Les Rieux.

sentimental generation). It is exquisite and romantic and you will look lovely in it. I don't think $336.00 is too much for a wedding dress which is also a suit and has three tops and is an evening dress too. Your drawings were a great deal of fun. I did not show them to your father (but will to Reeve) because I thought they would conjure up the image of a formal wedding which would scare him away, maybe!

I think you should, unless you have already, write him a letter and tell him exactly what the "wedding" will be and urge him to be there, for part of the time anyway. (I showed him all the part of your letter about the wedding date, etc.) I have already told him that I don't think there will really be any "wedding" in our sense of the word. Tell him he doesn't have to "give you away" as fathers do in U.S. weddings. No minister, no church, no aisle, no white wedding dress and veil, etc. Just going to the Mayor's office (Is that formal? How many people?) and then a small reception at the Feydys afterwards. Just the same, he said he didn't know whether he'd be there or not—said he'd like to come and see you and Julien and the Feydys but wasn't sure he'd be there for the wedding. Try to write him what it will be like and that he doesn't have to stand around all the time, meet a lot of people, etc. Perhaps he could be there for the most private part.

You will just have to explain to the Feydys that your father never goes to any ceremonies of any kind, *hates* them, etc., didn't go to my sisters' or his own son's wedding (Land's). And it wasn't that he didn't approve of Susie and her family. That wedding could hardly have been more simple: out of doors, no one there but family and a few of Land and Susie's young friends in Barbara and Jon's garden. I think it is hard, and will be hard to explain to the Feydys, that it isn't that he doesn't approve, or like Julien etc. But perhaps, if he makes a visit first, they'll understand better. But anyway, *write* him and do your best to persuade him. . . .

Scott's Cove
Saturday, October 26th, 1963
Darling Ansy,

You wrote a beautiful letter to your father. He was pleased and said it was a lovely letter and very thoughtful and considerate. He did not give me his verdict but my prognosis is *good*!

I also talked to him about the announcements (as well as to Aunt Margot, who said you couldn't invite people to a wedding unless you expected them to turn up. Father also feels this way, feels "announce" is

OK, especially since you are so far away, etc.). Father said he would like to see anything that went out under his name, to check it: would like it *very* simple and no title (Mr. and Mrs. Charles A. etc. announce the marriage of etc.), something like that. He will send none to his friends but complies (to my surprise!) to your desire for it. Otherwise thinks it in the unnecessary complication dept.

I feel quite shaken by the sudden death of Kurt Wolff in Germany due to a traffic accident.* He was taking a walk and was pinned to a wall by a truck-trailer turning around. He did not, however, suffer very much—was rushed in a stretcher to the hospital (next door) where, lying on a bed, he asked for a glass of brandy and for them to telephone his wife at the hotel and tell her that he was "all right." He died within three hours, in her arms (unconscious for all but the first half hour) of "internal injuries" (probably internal hemorrhage).

It seems a very brutal death for such an extraordinary gentle and elegant man (elegant *in the spirit* as well as mind and taste), and terribly tragic and ironic for Helen, who has for years protected him from the effort of opening elevator doors or uncorking wine bottles! Helen will leave Locarno and come back to the U.S. and continue her work as an editor for Harcourt Brace. She was, of course, prepared for his sudden death for years, but not this way. How strange life is. He was buried there in Marbach where they had stopped for the night—an old university town Kurt was fond of (he met Pasternak there). It was Schiller's birthplace and he died in the Schiller Hospital. Helen is, as one would have expected her to be, magnificent about it (according to Bill Jovanovich, who flew over for the service). I have asked her to spend Christmas with me—us—in the chalet, but she may be in the U.S. by then.

I think of you all the time, darling.

Saturday, November 23rd, 1963
Dearest Ansy,

I have just received your letter of November 21st (so fast!), relieving my mind and heart very much about you. I suppose I got too worried but Reeve's message, somewhat garbled over the telephone, came on me with a double weight since I was already very worried about your depressed note to me. And also since I was in the midst of one of your father's "last weeks" of instructions and warnings, and we disagreed so strongly about the wedding expenses. Actually, now that I have said firmly—in fact, I

---

*Kurt Wolff died on October 21, 1963, in Marbach, Germany.

fear, *stubbornly*—what I want to do (it always comes down to that—I can never argue it logically), and now he has written you how and why he disapproves, I think it will all simmer down (as Scott's crisis did last summer) and actually he won't object very much to what I'm doing on the expenses (which God knows are not high for such an occasion). He will feel better once he is off, and once he talks to you and meets the Feydys.

I want to take this down to the post office immediately, so I can't write much. We are all *reeling* with the shock of President Kennedy's assassination, barely twenty-four hours old. One cannot grasp that it happened, and happened here in America. Although the violence in America is just under the surface, happily covered up most of the time by our mystique of the great big happy welcoming generous open-armed nation. When violence erupts as it does in murders, bombings, etc. in the South or stranglings in Boston or muggings in New York, we are terribly shocked. The nation is terribly shocked by this, and the shock is right and perhaps therapeutic for us. We *should* look at our violence with shock and recognize it and deal with it.

I am anxious to come over early anyway—if it fits into your plans—but *not* if it stops you having a holiday with Julien in Les Rieux.

I think it is very natural for you to feel depressed there in Paris, making all your preparations for marriage all alone—or at least without your family. (And to be looked at always as a foreigner and stranger gets very depressing, if it's done with such a sense of stigma: "You are so different"—"This is so difficult"—etc.) The only thing I can say is you would, I think, have been just as unhappy in a different way had you been preparing for a wedding *over here* with your family but separated from Julien. As it is, everything you are doing now is getting to know your in-laws and the setting you must deal with *better*. It will all *help* you in your life in the future with Julien and his family. It is a plus and not a minus in your new life.

It is sleeting outside. Reeve is here with a Harvard freshman to go to the Yale-Harvard game (now called off because of Pres. Kennedy's death). The paper didn't come today and since I don't like listening to the radio all the time, I feel quite isolated.

New House
Day after Thanksgiving 1963
Dearest Ansy,

I have now received a very nice letter from Mme Feydy in answer to mine, and your letter enclosing the checks. I can see how you were startled by the total disagreement between your father's letter and mine. And it certainly *is* unpleasant to be juggled back and forth between your parents just before your wedding but there seemed to be no alternative except that of *my* agreeing when I felt he was wrong, which I could not and cannot do. So here come the two checks back again! You have done what you could to set things right and I am sure your father will be pleased by your action. But I am going to be stubborn and sentimental. I want to pay for your wedding expenses and please keep your money to pay for a trip home next year. You will need it. I really think, now all the proper gestures have been made, your father will feel it is all right, or at least not mind too much.

We had a quite peaceful Thanksgiving in the new house with Uncle Dwight, Rhidian, Reeve and Jimmy Miller.* That is all. We were saddened by a wire telling us of Aunt Amey's death (she died Thanksgiving morning) and yet I could not help but be thankful *for her* that she could go swiftly and peacefully. We are all going to a service for her tomorrow in New York.

This letter keeps being interrupted. Reeve, Rhidian, Betsy O'Hara,† and a roommate have just all come into my bedroom. (There is *no* privacy in this house!)

The country is beginning to breathe again. For four days everything seemed to stop. Time stopped. People couldn't do anything. It was like a paralysis. One could do nothing but watch television or listen to broadcasts. I watched the funeral cortege at Mina Curtiss's for four hours!‡ And I only saw half of it. It started at 10:30 and went on till 4:30. As well as the procession, one saw the service inside the Cathedral and the graveside service. Despite the television and radio commentators, it was very moving and done with great dignity and beauty and real feeling. Mrs. Kennedy, who has a great sense of form and beauty as well as dignity and feeling and sensitivity, was responsible for this, one feels. The form was infused with a reality and was not just pomp and show. She was quite magnificent.

Everyone feels that Johnson has taken hold with strength, vigor and dignity. And there is a sense of unity that followed the shock, that he has drawn on. He is not as brilliant as Kennedy, not an intellectual, but able and courageous and experienced, and since he is quite a simple, direct

*James Miller, Susan Miller Lindbergh's younger brother, was then a student at Yale.
†Betsy O'Hara was a close friend of Reeve's from Rosemary Hall.
‡The Lindberghs didn't own a television set until years later (though the cook, Martha, had one in her room and allowed Land to sneak in to watch the 1954 Army-McCarthy hearings).

and warm man, may be able to put through some of the things Kennedy envisioned.

This is a somewhat distracted letter. It is pouring outside—a sodden dark and quite gloomy day. But we need the rain.

Monday after Thanksgiving 1963
Dear Helen [Wolff],

We have moved—hence this long silence on my part. Also, of course, the events of the last fortnight have had a paralyzing effect on everyone. It is almost impossible to convey the impression of shock and stupefaction that overtook everyone at Kennedy's assassination. (I cannot write you a long letter about this, but we will talk about it soon, I hope. I thought about you, because it must have been hard to be out of the country at such a time—bearing the shock, horror and uncertainty all alone, with no American to talk to—but, of course, really, *no Kurt* to talk to.)

Despite the silence, I have thought of you so very much—even through all the throes of moving (what one loses—what one finds!). The sense of uprooting, the sense of the meaninglessness of possessions (when not grouped in a living room—expressing a spiritual reality). The painfulness of the dismantling is only bearable if one is doing it *for* someone else—to create a new home. For you it is so much harder. You *will* create it again, and it will be a haven for Christian* and your many friends, but it is a heartbreaking task.

People write letters of comfort or condolence when death first strikes, but it seems to me this is when one needs them least. One feels so very close to the person who has gone in the first days. One is almost buoyed up by them, and by the sense of all-pervading love poured out for them and for you. But the long bleak months follow, of learning to live alone. I wonder one can even *walk*—like a new baby. Part of one has really died with the other and one must learn all over again—how to walk, how to speak, how to think, alone.

I know that you will learn. Kurt envisioned this, I am sure, and what you would do—what ability you had. He once spoke to me (at the time of the break from Pantheon) of what a young woman you were, and what ability you had, and how you had a career ahead of you—should not be stopped and restricted.

The closeness of your relationship with Kurt—humanly, profession-

---

*Christian Wolff (1934–), son of Helen and Kurt Wolff.

ally, every way—makes (or must make) these months agonizing. An amputation has taken place. But this very closeness will perhaps quite unconsciously make the work easier—(or perhaps that is not the right word). The grafting that took place will enable you to carry on his work far better than you can envisage and your own work will be enriched.

I think of a line from C. Day Lewis in *A Time to Dance*, a long poem in memory of some fallen airmen. Do you remember it? One line I particularly loved and have said to myself at times, I repeat for you though the *adjective is wrong:* "He bore transplanting into common ground." You are very uncommon ground, Dear Helen, but the spirit of what I mean is in that line.

I have not thanked you for your wonderful letter—which came so swiftly and comforted me so much—both for you and for him. How like Kurt are the lines from his notebook. No, I didn't give them to him, but I know them. He certainly lived them. Maria's* words, scribbled on the back, allowed me to cry ("And I knew he was gone forever and we must go on living without his warmth and gentleness").

I am grateful that you could sob and laugh and be angry and make jokes and listen to Bach. It is the only way. Kurt was the completely rounded person—grief for him must be as rounded and complete as this.

On our plans: I am expecting you for Christmas and you will put no one out. The chalet is warm and cozy and plenty of hot water etc. Perhaps there will be a service and some music in Vevey we could go to. Perhaps we could walk in the woods behind the chalet.

A heartful to you—
Anne

Chalet—Monts-de-Corsier
January 1st, 1964
Dear Barbara and Jon and Susie and Land,

I will have to resort to a joint letter since I will not have time to write all of you—or in fact to write adequately all I would like to about Anne's wedding even in this letter. This is about the first time I have sat down since I arrived on this side of the ocean December 16th. Your father met me in Geneva. No sign of the mountains, very cold, and snow on the foothills. We picked up provisions on the way to the chalet which was warm and cozy, though still without rugs. Your father got a wire the next

*Maria Wolff (1918–), Kurt Wolff's daughter from his first marriage to Elisabeth Merck.

morning and was called to a Pan Am meeting in Bordeaux and took off almost immediately in his VW. We called Anne in Paris and arranged to have Scott come and drive me to the Dordogne three days later in the second VW.

Friday a.m. I set off for Lausanne in the VW and met Scott who had come on by train—all the planes were full. I was very grateful to him for coming since it was a long snowy and icy fifteen-hour trip across the Jura mountains and the Massif Central to the Dordogne. Also, it was a wonderful chance to talk to Scott, which was worth a lot to me.

It is such a good chance to talk in a long car drive. Actually Scott and I did all our talking in the first hour—and very good talking—and hardly said anything after that. It was a long, hard, and slippery drive, and we saw almost as many accidents as cars.

We did not reach Les Rieux that evening, which Scott had planned, because of bad roads all the way, but stopped en route in a snowy French town and continued the next a.m. The snow continued until about an hour from Perigueux (their nearest big town) and then it seemed quite springlike in looks: grass was green, cabbages in the fields. We had elaborate instructions and a hand-drawn map from Anne. When we got to the dirt road there was a huge cardboard sign painted by Anne with an arrow, "Les Rieux → Father & Scott turn here!" Looking up the dirt road, we saw two figures leaping up and down: Anne and Jacqueline.* Anne was in corduroy riding trousers, Robin Hood–ish boots and a heavy fisherman's sweater, yellow with blue trim, and a tight knitted cap pulled over her blond short hair. Julien, Jacqueline, Pierre (their brother) and Hélène (his fiancée) all came out. (Scott had met them in Paris.) It was sunny but very cold.

It is a great big yellow stone manor, with two wings, a courtyard, some abandoned barns and sheds, making an L-shaped house. It looks out over sloping fields, old orchards, vineyards that have been let go and the gentle valley and hills of that part of the world. Inside: big high-ceilinged rooms, wide stairs, open fireplaces in every room—*No heat at all!* Floors wide—old oak. A big bare summery house. Big windows, lots of light, no rugs, not much furniture, but some very beautiful pieces. Our bedroom had in it a huge old Spanish bed, a built-in armoire, a table, one old chair, an eighteenth century harpsichord (all painted with flowery scenes, Watteau-esque painting), and a fireplace! (Thank God!)

*Jacqueline Feydy, Julien's sister.

The rooms were bright, reminding one of the kind of rooms that must have been *behind* those window paintings of Matisse (you know, one always has one's *back* to the room, in those paintings, and one is looking out of the half-open French-door windows)! Also there were many glints of memories of other places (only Jon will remember): Illiec,* perhaps, the sense of a little chateau lost in the country or St. Gildas (where the Carrels† lived) with its walled garden. Only all bigger and more generous. But not formal at all. Open, careless, warm and welcoming, and all (the grounds) slightly neglected. The kind of a house children run through dropping coats and hats and boots and baskets in the hall (like North Haven).

Also the kind of house one hears music echoing in. There were three or four pianos in the house. We followed the music one night and found Julien playing a piano, Anne accompanying him on the flute, and Jacqueline curled up on the bed (the only piece of furniture in the room besides the piano) listening. There was an enormous old tuba on the mantel of the fireplace.

Then M. and Mme. Feydy arrived with their huge Egyptian cat. Fires were lit in every room. The boys carried up wood. Supper was started in the big kitchen. This was covered (on the floor) with rough old bricks and had a huge fireplace one could get *inside* of. A big spit for turning roasts, etc., and a rack for drying towels.

Anne and Julien got in their VW and went off to Bordeaux to meet Reeve and Connie who were (supposedly) arriving at 6:28. I asked to help in the kitchen but was not (yet) allowed so went up to my cold room and wondered *what* I could do till suppertime. The bed was too cold to get into and the bathroom was an icebox. I couldn't feel my hands when I washed them. I finally put blankets on the floor in front of the fire and lay down on them and under them, where your father found me about 6:30.

Your father was delighted with the house: its isolation, its primitive quality (B-r-r-r-r!) ("Like Minnesota!") and the challenge was a spur

*The tiny private island off the coast of Brittany, France, which the Lindberghs bought in 1938. They lived in the nineteenth century stone manor house there (with no plumbing or electricity) for much of that year.
†Alexis Carrel (1873–1944), French doctor, scientist, author, and controversial eugenicist who received the Nobel Prize in Physiology and Medicine in 1912. He co-authored, with CAL, *The Culture of Organs*, and the two men worked together to create the first device that allowed organs to function outside the body during surgery. His wife was Anne-Marie-Laure Gourlez de La Motte.

to him. He rushed down and brought up wood, built an enormous fire, got a basin out of the car so I could wash in front of the fire, got more blankets out, and soon we went down to supper at a big table in the living room. The women all sat with their backs to the fire, men opposite (in heavy sweaters!).

Supper was interrupted by a call from Julien from Bordeaux, the message being that Reeve was *not* on the train. Then it came out that Reeve and Connie were both on the train, but it was very jammed. Connie got out first and Reeve stayed inside to hand the baggage, including skis, out of the window. But before she could get out, the train started moving and they wouldn't let her off. So on she went to Bayonne, the next stop—some three to four hours ahead—without luggage or even a pocketbook—no money! Julien and Anne got hold of the station master, wired Bayonne, had Reeve paged and told to take the next train back—and all expenses paid! Actually Reeve was befriended by four Spanish soldiers who told her to go right on to the border and they would put her on a train back! However, as she sat in the train in the Bayonne station, her friends heard her paged and rushed her off the train back onto a Bordeaux one. Some seven hours later she arrived back in Bordeaux. Anne and Julien and Connie greeted her and rushed her back to Les Rieux. They arrived at dawn and slept till lunch time.

Sunday your father and I were taken to see, in a nearby cave underneath a friend's house, a small but quite rich cave in paintings and drawings. I had to translate, like a bad French lesson, while the wife pointed with a stick: "*Un autre bison—les cornes, le dos, les pattes postérieures—les pattes antérieures—le ventre,*" etc.*

This was the evening we followed the music to the little bedroom where Anne, in a long plaid wool skirt and sweater, was playing the flute to Julien's accompaniment on the piano. I realized afterwards that this little interlude was a great relief—since it was one of the few incidents that was not *translated*. All the time during those two days I had the curious sensation that I was watching something very familiar to me, but all translated into French—into French language, French place, French setting, character, furnishing, etc., like a dream. Never had I seen Anne so gay, so spontaneous, so natural—but all "translated" into French! (Like seeing a familiar play—*Midsummer Night's Dream* or *A Christmas Carol*—"translated" into French!) It gave the two days a curi-

---

*Another bison—the horns, the back, the back feet—the front feet—the stomach.

ous dream-like quality hard to describe and yet it was not separating as I might have imagined it.

Anyway, the fifteen or twenty minutes I heard Anne and Julien playing together was neither French nor English but just music and gave me quite a sense of their relationship, almost better than when I listen to them talking (in French) or to Julien talking (in correctly slow English). I could feel: yes, they really are well suited to each other. He gives her strength and solidity. She gives him élan, flight, and a kind of lyricism. In fact, lyrical seems to be a word that comes often to me in connection with this wedding. It was a lyrical occasion.

The next morning (the Wedding Day) right after breakfast (big steaming bowls of café-au-lait as in Brittany), they all started moving tables around to see how they could get twenty-three people seated at three tables in the living room. Then the village caterers came to set their things up and we went to dress for the wedding. Anne dressed in front of my fire. She had a lovely dress (short) of Venetian brocade, a pale gold-green with an embroidered figure on it—delicate green vines with tiny red flowers. She would *not* wear wool underwear under it (as I suggested!) and must have kept warm by love alone. The rest of us wore wool dresses or suits and coats (on top of our woolen underwear!). She looked very lovely—rather Botticelli with her blond hair, in that flowered dress. She did wear a coat, black silk quilted with fur around the collar and down the front (sort of a Gay Nineties coat) and red shoes!

"*On y va!*"* she shouted from the door, and we all came down and piled into three cars and drove through the little town of Douzillac, past the thirteenth century church to the *mairie*.† Douzillac is about the size of Bugueles in Brittany, which Jon may remember. There is only one store in it—plastered with banana yellow shutters—on a cobbled street. People were at the doors and windows as we clattered downhill from the church to the *mairie*. Someone took pictures of Anne (in her hour-glass coat) and Julien in the doorway.

Inside, a plain bare room with a table in front of the fireplace at which M. le Maire and his secretary stood. M. le Maire put a tricolored ribbon over his portly front and the ceremony began. Someone tried to shut the door of the *mairie* as it was very cold, but the *maire* said no, it wasn't allowed. The door must be left open until the couple were legally married. (In case one of them wanted to escape? Or in case someone came in

*Let's go!
†Mayor's office.

to protest?) The *maire* read the civil service, stumbling over the bride's middle name ("Spenssaire"), and the couple raised their hands in assent.

When the civil part of the service was over, the door was closed and M. le Maire read a very short little speech of his own. It was quite charming and short. (And, as M. Feydy had remarked at breakfast, "One can be sure of one thing—the Mayor's speech will be well constructed, because he is a mason!")

Then Anne kissed everyone in the room, starting with the Mayor who was delighted, and we all filed out again. Then we all shook hands and climbed back up the cobblestoned street to the cars. The church bell was tolling noon. And we drove back to Les Rieux.

We finally sat down, about one, to an enormous T-shaped table with Anne at the intersection, Julien on her left and the Mayor on her right, and had a tremendous meal that lasted until five p.m. I don't quite know how the time passed though we progressed slowly through *paté de lièvre* (paté of rabbit) to *brochet* (pike covered with sauce) to *dinde aux marrons* (turkey with chestnuts) to *salade* (all with appropriate wines!) to *gâteau de mariage* (a kind of pyramid of hard caramel-coated cream puffs) set down before Anne. She used huge gardening shears to cut off layers for the guests, handing them out with witty little comments on each person.

Anne called on various people to speak, or sing. Reeve and Jacqueline sang "Try to remember the kind of September . . ." It was impossible to think of crying. Anne herself was at her gayest, most happy, most spontaneous.

I wish you all had been there. And so, I suppose, I had to write you a firsthand account of it—much too long and too hurried but at least to make *me* feel you were part of it.

Much love to all,
Mother Mouse

Sunday, January 12th, 1964
Dearest Con,

Wonderful to get your letter yesterday—so articulate on things that are difficult to be articulate about. I have thought about you every day—been too sleepy at night to stay up to telephone and a bit too hectic daytimes to write (will explain later). But there were so many afterthoughts. I feel we hardly *said* anything to each other during the wedding days* but com-

*Con's daughter Saran Morgan was married to Robert Hutchins on January 4, about two weeks after Ansy married Julien.

municated on some other inarticulate level. For you sheer exhaustion and for me general unsettledness made communication, except on top levels, impossible.

No, "one can't go home again," and home becomes more and more of a will-of-the-wisp. I think this is new to our generation. Of course Mother had many homes, moved many times (more than Grandma who lived all her life in Cleveland), but still, the concept of a *family home* was still there, in the mind and in the stones and mortar. Children came back to the family home, lived near parents or returned for vacation. In the second half of your life you knew *where* you were meant to be and what your function was, to hold down the family home, expecting children to come home to you. This gave root and a purpose to the middle-aged and some sense of security to the young.

No, one cannot live in old homes, careers, localities, niches. One becomes a ghost with the other ghosts. But the solution of modern apartments (no care, no responsibility, no roots, no patina of the past, and older people being thrown into a young person's rhythm is *wrong*, I am sure, and very unfruitful for people of my age) or taking cruises year after year, living homelessly, is no answer. I am only *feeling* for answers. Somehow, one must retreat into the simpler life, but *not* a young-marrieds life and setting. (At times, there doesn't seem to be any other. No place for the aging middle-aged in America.)

I have always thought *work* would be the solution: at last, free to work at one's "career"! It isn't enough, and one has lost the driving ambition to write a best-seller or make one's mark in the world. One is beyond it. Gratefully, I note this. One does still have something to say and to give, and to learn. I don't think it is to be found rushing out and taking a real estate job or even a teaching job (this is better) or jumping into causes. This is all too imitative of the young. It is a reversion to the past. We are bound to lose at that game, and it is not *fruitful*—no fruit of wisdom will come from it.

I do think (like E. M. Forster on old age) that wisdom is the fruit of old age and we should cultivate it, treasure it, and dispense it. But *how?* Maybe writing (some people can—you can write and should write because you are *very* wise and have lived and watched and studied and *served* women's lives, and the life of Mother could offer you an opportunity to put some of this wisdom on paper). Maybe in occasional help, advice, talk, etc. to our children. We have to be perpetually *ready* to give this—so can't throw ourselves into competitive careers again (another difficulty).

Charles and Anne
Morrow Lindbergh, in 1948

Anne with *(from left to right)*
Reeve, Ansy, and Scott, in 1950
(Photograph by Lucia Nebel White)

At Jon Lindbergh and Barbara Robbins's wedding in 1954.
From left to right: Janey Robbins, Wendy Robbins, Reeve, Dick Robbins,
Barbara, Jim Robbins, Jon, Anne, Charles, Scott, Land, and Ansy.

In 1952, Jon was a member of an expedition to gather data from the ocean floor off New England. It was sponsored by Columbia University, the Office of Naval Research, the Navy's Bureau of Ships, and the Woods Hole Oceanographic Institution. This photograph originally appeared in *Life* magazine on October 27, 1952. *(Copyright © Bettmann/CORBIS)*

Anne and Ansy in Darien, Connecticut, in 1955

Susan and Land Lindbergh with their daughter, Erin, in 1963

Lucia and Alan Valentine
(Courtesy of Garry Valentine)

Dana Atchley

Anne at Little House,
in Darien, Connecticut

Anne and Charles with Vice President Lyndon Johnson
at the White House in May 1962, at a dinner in honor of French minister
of culture André Malraux and his wife, Marie-Madeleine Lioux.
(Courtesy of the White House)

Ansy with her son Charles Feydy
in Paris, in 1965

Anne, Reeve, and Charles at Reeve's wedding
in Montana, in 1968

Anne with Reeve's daughters,
Elizabeth and Susannah Brown, in Vermont, in 1979

Anne with Susannah outside Argonauta
in Maui, Hawaii, in 1978

Anne at work at her desk in Little House
(Copyright © Jill Krementz)

Anne and Charles, in 1968
(Photograph by Richard Brown)

At the Lindbergh Foundation Award Dinner in 1995.
From left to right: Jim Newton, Land, Anne, Scott,
and award recipient Queen Sirikit of Thailand.

Ready for takeoff in
Franconia, New Hampshire, in 1990

I am feeling for another way of showing wisdom—perhaps by simply showing the young how to live more fully than they possibly can at the moment. This seems like a contradiction but I don't think it is. One must live in the smaller circle, much more richly. Cultivate the balance they can't have: beauty of setting (even if small), richness of friends and conversation, richness of reading, music—all that goes under "culture"—good talk about not the past but the present in art, politics, statesmanship, etc. This can have a profound effect on the young. God knows they need it and if given a chance, relish it. You and Aubrey have done this for Susie and Land—also Jon and Barbara.

In other words, the family homestead we have to create is now chiefly a spiritual one. It must create and cherish serenity, wisdom, values. This seems, on paper, at first blush, very selfish, very hedonistic, but I think it is healthier than going out looking for distractions or activity or jobs. (The young don't want us out there.) I do think it is very hard in America with its worship of youth and activity. Other cultures have respected old age, used elder statesmen, revered the grandmother, etc. Also, we no longer have religion to help us. Basically, I think I believe that the second half of life is a preparation for death, not in a rigidly orthodox way of "laying up treasure in heaven," but in acquiring awareness and acceptance of the life you have led and will leave. What can you hand on as your last gift to Earth?

Tuesday, still reeling from traveling and weddings, I got a call from the White House from Mrs. Johnson's secretary. Apparently *Look* is doing a "spread" on her called "Wifesmanship in the White House" (what a title and *word*—Grrrr!) and Mrs. Johnson said, "I don't suppose she'd do it, but the person I'd like best would be Anne Lindbergh." I was somewhat stunned, and fenced for time and stayed awake all night and wrestled with the idea—writing for a deadline? Interviewing a President's wife—writing a blurb—a sort of biography—what did they want and could I do it?

After a day of calling (Margot, Bill Jovanovich [a great help], and Dana), I decided I *was* interested in writing something but couldn't write it in a week and would have to have more time. I am scared to death but I am *interested*. I was very much impressed with Mrs. Johnson when I met her and felt I could talk to her, and feel, somehow, if something intrigues you, you should not turn it down out of fear, lack of confidence, etc. It is, of course, *not* a world-shaking event, but might be interesting (maybe just *impossible*—one must take that chance!) and will certainly pull me out of *my* rut of moving, dismantling, and waiting around for children and husband to turn up and say what they want to do or *me to do for them.* Perhaps this is why I accepted—grasping at a straw!

I am thinking of you. Do let's meet at Washington's Birthday!

Love-love

A.

Darien

May 20th, 1964

Dear Francis,*

I had a lovely time last night and felt how grateful I was to you for backing me up in it, and carrying it off so exuberantly. I drove home swiftly on the dark uncluttered highways, thinking about you and still talking to you.

The first observation I made was the thought that you were probably younger than the rest of us, not in experience, mind, etc. but in vigor, hopefulness, spirit, perhaps even physiologically. I have a feeling you'll live to be a hundred, have another marriage, another life, and enjoy *and* fume about it all, perhaps long after the rest of us have settled down to philosophical acceptance.

Then I went on talking to you, lecturing to you really, analyzing— which I really should wait till June 22nd to elaborate, or even the Villa—but I'm afraid it may evaporate by then, so I feel on this clear and blowy spring morning I must jot down a few notes on it (preliminary sallies!).

Part of the youth is a romanticism. You like to rescue Damsels in Distress. Why, I asked myself, and you, does he think that once he has severed the chains and rescued the damsel from the dragon, that the damsel will be free, or even grateful to him? Damsels (for the most part) get chained because they are weak; they aren't weak because they are chained. Also why does he think the unchained damsel will turn to him in gratitude and desire? Damsels chained to rocks *like* dragons; that's why they let themselves be chained. They like tyrants, and seek them.

You are *not* a tyrant. Why should they run to you? You are a strong, normal, sanguine, positive, loving man. If that was what they wanted they would have chosen someone like that in the first place. They're not looking for someone like you; they're looking for another dragon and another set of chains.

You complain that after you have given and given generously of yourself to free them, they don't give back to you. What have they got to

*Francis Randolph, a friend of Margot Wilkie's and AML's.

give—these damsels in distress? In the first place, they're exhausted by the struggle and haven't the strength to give anything. Then, as I said, they are weak. The weak don't give—only the strong can give. You keep asking for something from the weak.

Yes, I know, it *looks* as though they gave to that dragon. But you are fooled (or romantic). It isn't giving, it's self-immolating—a very different thing. If you were a dragon they'd give to you in that way. But you wouldn't really like it because you don't like to trample over people. It's a neurotic kind of giving and wouldn't fill the hunger in you. It isn't giving from strength, but giving from weakness, and it doesn't nourish.

When you help the strong, they can use it and help themselves and give you something back. The weak don't really want to be helped; they want to complain. They want eternally to be chained to that rock so that they will incite the pity and attention and nobility of the brave prince—so they can cry on his shoulder and be always certain of a shoulder and of attention. But they don't want to be freed. If they are freed, they look for another rock and another dragon—not for a prince.

Moral? You are wasting your time rescuing damsels in distress? I can't quite be that cynical or didactic. I know this is all very much off the top of my head and dangerously oversimplified. You have to help them because it's your nature and makes you what you are—or at least, expands what you are. All giving enlarges the heart and helps the giver, whether the recipient is permanently helped or not. Probably the unrealistic quality comes in expecting something in return—some action or initiative on their own, some kind of equal giving on their part, some kind of equal relationship you are looking for. Probably you should expect nothing. This perhaps is cynical of me, but you see this in the business world because you once talked to me about it in terms of a loan of money someone made to help a friend that never bore any fruit. Why does it bother him so? you said. Why did he expect anything from it? Most of the time this is the case. One gets used to it.

(In the personal realm, you have *not* got used to it, and you do still expect results, and you do feel let down when they don't produce something.)

Now let me be plain in saying: all friends to whom one loans money do not let one down; they produce something. They pay back the world at least what has been given them. This is true in the personal emotions field too. Distressed damsels can change (with analysis, help, time, suffering, love and effort) their pattern. The weak can be strengthened. People do become wiser, learn something. But these damsels are in a minority, just as the people to whom you lend money and are able to fructify it are in a minority. (Or perhaps you don't agree with me?)

It's excruciatingly difficult to change one's pattern. You also know this. You've said to me hundreds of times, "he's not going to change," of some dragon. What makes you say this with such certainty and yet cling so desperately to the illusion that the damsel can change? She's usually just as irrevocably tied. Sometimes—a crack!—she's aware. Awareness can lead to self-knowledge, reorientation, and learning to walk again. But don't think it can be done simply by severing the chains, or by exhorting the distressed from the shoreline.

It is more like the ordeal of the little mermaid who learned to be an earth maiden, but every step she took was as if walking on knives.

There is, of course, the final question: why do you want to rescue damsels in distress? But this I couldn't dream of suggesting an answer for. Besides, perhaps it's impertinent. Perhaps the whole letter is. It isn't meant to be, but grows out of a very real and deep feeling about and concern for you. Take it as that and ruminate about it in off hours. We can talk in a more leisurely and rational way—in Balbienello—or the chalet.

My love and thanks always—

Anne

P.S. I am well aware that a lot of this can be said back to me. I know . . . I can see myself in the mirror. All I can say is, life is easier to write than to live, or to see. But seeing *helps*. One then makes some efforts to change the patterns, one realizes the patterns are of one's own choosing, and one doesn't blame others for them. One is less likely to feel abused and perhaps a little freer to adapt within the pattern—to change it a little and not be frozen in it!

Chalet Les Monts-de-Corsier
July 8th, 1964
Dearest Jon,

I am terribly glad and relieved to learn through my friend in Vevey who had seen it in a newspaper that your experiment* in living three hundred (?) feet underwater has proved a success and is over. Not that (I suppose) there won't be more experiments! You, with your inventive

---

*Jon and another diver had taken part in one of a series of experiments devised by aviation and ocean engineer Edwin Link. To explore the viability of living and working at great depths, the two men stayed for forty-nine hours at a depth of 432 feet in Link's "Submersible, Portable, Inflatable Dwelling" off the Bahamas, breathing a mixture of helium and oxygen.

genius and spirit of adventure, will, in all probability, not be through with new explorations in this pioneer field. Your father assures me that, though it is a dangerous field, you are at the top of it and you take very good precautions, as well as being extremely experienced—as experienced as anyone in this new field. Nevertheless, I am glad *this* one is over. I know no details. We have been in Europe just a week, three days in Paris where we saw the enclosed clipping about what you were *about* to do.

I gather you broke a record and that it was successful. I can't figure out whether just the three days underwater are over, or whether the three days in decompression are over too. I rushed down to Vevey and bought two papers, an American (*Paris Herald*) and a Swiss one, but found nothing. I will look again today.

I somehow felt there was no use writing you until this experiment was over and you were back in the world of average human beings. I read, out west, the speech you gave on the underwater work which was extremely interesting, clear and well written. Better written I thought, than the *Geographic* article (which I also read with interest), and gave one quite a good, lucid and vivid idea of the field and some of its problems. You appear to have the gift not only to think clearly, but to be able to translate what is not clear to other people in understandable and vivid and simple terms. It was a very good piece of work.

So much love to you Jon. I am still hoping for Christmas at Aspen— I'd like to see you—twice a year if possible! And those wonderful children—much love to B.

Mother

Nairobi
February 14th–15th [1965]
Darling Reeve,

We are about to start off on our safari—Father and I alone in a Land Rover which looks a little like a square battleship and holds camping equipment: tent, blankets, folding chairs, and boxes of cans, food, etc. We will be gone about ten days—going to animal country in Kenya and perhaps Tanzania—camping out most of the time. The game wardens have marked your father's map for places to camp and given us instructions as to how to cope with army ants, rhinoceroses, lions and jackals! (of which rhinos are the most dangerous).

The country is very beautiful: great plains and distant gentle mountains and lots and lots of sky and quivering hot air. It looks a little like California or Mexico and has the same trees—eucalyptus and pepper and acacias and bougainvillea and jacaranda. Father took me from the airport straight into the Nairobi National Park, small but full of animals: giraffes, ostrich, wildebeest, gazelles, impalas, lions and cheetahs and monkeys and baboons. Wildebeests are gnus and look like gray water-buffalo ("Gno Gno Gno—not a gnu!").* I prefer giraffes, who are very graceful and have velvety faces with great eyes and nibble all the time with their wrinkled camel-like mouths, or zebras who are round and sleek and skitterish, or, best of all, the gazelles.

Weather is like Mexico or California—cool in the morning and evening and very hot (dry and dusty) in the middle of the day. Now we are off to the really wild country. We will be back in ten days or so. No time to write more just now. Father is packing up the Land Rover. Africa *is* another planet but beautiful. I hope you are all right darling.

XOXOXOX—

Love, Mother

Scott's Cove, Darien
January 22nd, 1966
Dear Sue,†

I am just back from over a month in Africa on an incredible safari reunion, organized by Charles for all the members of his family that could get there.‡ We were seven—at times eight. Two Land Rovers, four tents, all our food and water taken with us, no guides and bearers—or comfort! But lots of wild animals—beautiful country—too much driving, heat, dust, and putting up and down of tents. Cooking over campfires and lots of arguments. Only Charles would attempt, and succeed in carrying off, such an expedition! It was quite rigorous and exhausting, especially for the girls (Reeve, Ansy and Barbara). I am relieved we are all safely back home with no mishaps or serious illnesses (Ansy is having a baby and was quite uncomfortable—should *never* have gone—but is back in Paris and OK, I think.)

I have just recovered from the exhausting twenty-one-hour flight: Nairobi–New York (direct new Pan Am line—stops at Lagos, Monro-

---

*From "The Gnu Song," by British singer-songwriters Michael Flanders and Donald Swann, popularized by Tom Lehrer in 1958.
†Sue Vaillant Hatt (see note p. 96).
‡This refers to a second safari, in October 1965, in which the Lindbergh children and their spouses (except for Land and his wife) participated.

via and Dakar and flies the South and North Atlantic on the bias) and feel, as I always do, that I never want to fly again. I don't think I can get another trip in this spring as I'm anxious to get back to Europe and see Ansy and what her arrangements are for the baby (not due till August). It is somehow different to have a daughter having a baby—so far it's been the sons. I'm quite excited.

I did find Africa and the wildlife a very moving experience again (we saw the big migrations of wildebeest in the Serengeti this time) although I saw the game through a slight haze of mother's anxiety about my family, especially Ansy. I do wish sometime you and Bob and Charles and I could have an evening together talking about Africa and conservation. So new to me—I have many questions I'd like to ask both of you.

Scott was with us in Africa for Christmas. He has been told his student's exemption will not be extended and he will be drafted next year. This means he will miss out finishing his last year at Cambridge. I suppose it isn't really a tragedy but he worked so hard to get into Cambridge, it is a great blow to him and I can hardly bear it for him. And this war* seems so senseless—and so endless. It was a relief to be away from newspapers for a while and not to read about it. One keeps hoping that somehow it will be settled—that it *is* being settled—under the dreadful news. But now this truce seems to be over and that hope gone.

This is an unfocused letter. Do let me know if you come through N.Y. on your way to Barbados—I might be here.

Much love and many thoughts. . . .

Darien, Conn.
Monday, June 6th, 1966
Dearest Land,

I can see why you love the West and want to ranch.† It is beautiful country where you are. One has a wonderful sense of space, wilderness, and animals—also, somehow, of time. We did feel very far away from New York and the overcrowded East. I loved the sense of the mountains and the elk who didn't run away.

We had a really wonderful week, as you must know, since we stayed

---

*The Vietnam War.
†In 1965 Jon and Land bought a 4,000-acre cattle ranch in the Blackfoot Valley of western Montana.

longer than we expected. Your father had a marvelous time, and it was something for me to watch him—I've never seen him on a ranch or a farm. He falls into it like a duck into water. I never realized how deeply ingrained in it he was.

To me it was a new language, but I loved the sense of space and wildness and the mountain quiet and the elk.

I wish you hadn't apologized for its being "a little unorganized." Actually I think it was miraculously well organized for the first year. I remember Aunt Con saying once that a ranch or farm is the man's equivalent for woman's work in the family since it deals with animals, weather, crops, pests, disease—all unpredictable things. Because of this, it cannot *ever* be perfectly organized like a business. There are too many variables not under one's control. Anything as close to life is going to be as unpredictable as life. But you chose it because it was close to life, and not removed like academic life or business.

We came at a busy time and I hope it was not too much for you and Susie. I thought the house very attractive—a wonderful combination of both of your pasts and present: your pots and rugs, Susie's weaving. I won't be quite happy about Susie until she has a shack of her own to weave in. It makes such a difference to a woman to be able to work somewhere *outside* of her full-of-duties house (out of that kitchen!).

Erin* and Peter were enchanting. I felt close to them, particularly Erin this time, because she communicated so much to me and seemed in the direct line (like my sister Elisabeth and Ansy) of my family, though her marvelous artistic color sense is like Susie—much else, too. The ranch is a wonderful place to bring up children and they show it. Your father was much impressed with them, as he was with everything at the ranch.

I am glad you have those cabins on the river and so glad we had that lovely evening around the campfire, with the vapor trail circling the sky. No sound but the rushing river.

Much love, Land, and thank you for all you did—
Mother

---

*Erin Lindbergh, Land and Susie Lindbergh's daughter.

Scott's Cove, Darien, Conn.
November 6th, 1966
Dear Nigel Nicolson,*

I am distressed to have to write you this letter about the letters and diary of your father which you have just published and of which you sent me portions last year to comment on.† You were considerate and meticulous in sending me all the pages in which the Morrow family were mentioned "for my perusal and possible deletion."

Although there were a number of inaccuracies, I felt, in the context of a diary, they were not of great importance and I wrote you that I did not find anything which needed to be deleted from our point of view, from these excerpts.

I also wrote that, though my husband was away, I was sure he would not wish to change anything in your father's manuscript, for I know that he feels strongly, as you do, that diary entries should not be changed. I did not mean to imply his approval or verification of the entries made by your father, which I had, of course, no right to give.

Reading the whole book now I am shocked to come on passages such as the one on p. 343, describing my husband as believing in the Nazi theology and hating democracy as represented by the American public. It is hard to believe that I could pass over such statements without saying how untrue to my husband and his feelings I know them to be.

However, I have checked the pages you sent me and the statements are clearly there. I must have concentrated entirely on the portions of the diary that were directly concerned with the Morrow family, which I felt was my province, and passed extremely lightly over the political or official sections in which I felt less competent to remember or judge.

I am afraid that my carelessness in this respect has contributed to a difficult situation for both my husband and you, as well as for your father.

I am deeply sorry.
Very sincerely yours,
Anne Lindbergh

---

*Nigel Nicolson (1917–2004) was an author, member of the British Parliament, and co-founder of the British publishing house Weidenfeld & Nicolson. He was a son of Sir Harold Nicolson (biographer of AML's father) and Vita Sackville-West; the Lindberghs rented their house in Seven Oaks, England, from 1936 to 1937.
†*Harold Nicolson: Diaries and Letters*, 3 volumes, edited by Nigel Nicolson (London: William Collins, 1966–1968).

Scott's Cove
November 26th, 1966
Dear Scott,

You did *not* owe me a letter. I owed you one, so scratch that guilt off! I owe a great many letters at the moment. Some of them spring directly or indirectly from the African article.* This is a good weekend to get at them. (Thanksgiving weekend with nobody here. Reeve went to North Haven with the Morgans but I decided to stay home—less "hassle.") But I think I'll try to answer your letter first.

When I first read it, I was aghast and thought, "I can't comprehend this at all. It is pure philosophy. Scott is way beyond me—I never learned what words like 'syllogism' meant, etc." But I persevered and have now read it four or five times and found it extraordinarily interesting and challenging and not as far from the things I've been reading as I first thought. At first, certain key sentences jumped out at me and I underlined them in red, and then I began seeing the whole thesis (which hangs together very well). Then I began to look up relevant passages in the books I have been reading (Martin Buber and a book on Buddhism).

The first sentence I underlined was "At least I have learned that no struggles are real that are not internal." The next one was: "Philosophical method is not helpful to the problems of the self, and I can't find the opening to religious method." Then your statements about the possibility (or solution) of the self being nothing but a myth—*or* the non-self being nothing but a myth.

Then in the book on Buddhism I found "To the Buddha the idea of a separate self was a mere intellectual invention, corresponding to no reality at all. The self, he argued, was plainly 'a process in time' not a single solid 'thing' or 'fact.' The term 'I' is merely a convenience for designating an ever changing combination or bundle of attributes of the body—sensations, perceptions, mental formulations (ideas, wishes, dreams) and consciousness. There is a constant interplay and interconnection among [these] which may give a sense of personal continuity and identity but which, in truth, preclude the possibility of a definite 'I' existing by itself, totally independent of and unconnected with the constantly shifting relation between physical and psychic forces. . . ."†

---

*AML's article "A Safari Back to Innocence" was published in the October 21, 1966, issue of *Life* magazine.
†From *The Three Ways of Ancient Wisdom*, by Nancy Wilson Ross (New York: Simon and Schuster, 1966).

Rather like, it seems to me, the physicists of today, who say there is no such thing as "matter." A table is just an aggregate of negative and positive charges, etc. (This is probably not accurately stated, but I am not a scientist.) However, one has to deal with the table as if it were real solid matter, and it does not disappoint us. One can set a tray of coffee and eggs down on it and it doesn't crash to the floor. The set of relations between the *energies* within the table are such that one can act as if it were solid matter.

I wonder if Krishnamurti's "awareness" is not what Buber means by the direct "I-thou" relationships. "Awareness" is certainly *not* just passive "reception." It is also very close to Buber's search for truth, as in this quotation:

"Is there a truth we can possess? Can we appropriate it? There certainly is none we can pick up and put in our pocket. But the individual can have an honest and uncompromising attitude toward the truth; he can have a legitimate relationship to truth and hold and uphold it all his life."*

It seems to me that what you are doing in your study of philosophy is not solving the problems of the self, or learning to apply yourself fully to something, or finding "The Truth." It is learning to have "a legitimate relationship to truth." Much of this seems to me to be learning to use a tool—or tools. Tools of the mind, of logic, of precision, of nomenclature. I would find it excruciatingly difficult, like mathematics—abstract and, I fear, dull—unrelated to life. Perhaps it seems sometimes like this to you and this is why you feel you cannot apply yourself fully to it. One cannot dedicate oneself to something one thinks is dull or unrelated to life. One cannot *will* dedication. This is a contradiction of terms. One can will oneself to application, goaded on by the desire to succeed, to compete with others, or to prove something to oneself or to others, or to gain a particular benefit. This is legitimate motivation, but don't let's call it, or wish it were, dedication.

You haven't yet found the thing you can be dedicated to, but you have considerably sharpened your tools so that when you do find it, you will apply yourself far more effectively and with less hindrance. Among other things, you are learning to express yourself very clearly and sometimes very beautifully. I like your image of "the vitality of the self . . . like the sea breaking on a beach, some things going out as the wave draws back, others replacing those as the wave surges in."

*From "The Prejudices of Youth," a speech delivered by Buber in 1937 and reprinted in *Israel and the World: Essays in a Time of Crisis*, by Martin Buber (New York: Schocken Books, 1948).

I have written all morning and I must go back to the house and feed the puppy who is now a miniature lion, bouncing around the kitchen floor and making puddles every six minutes and yipping with high insistent yips.

It has been a beautiful fall and now is bare and cold and gets dark very early—after a glittering cold sunset—copper sky and etched skeletons of trees.

Much love—how I hope we *do* meet for Christmas—

Mother

Scott's Cove
February 17th, 1967
Darling Ansy—

Such a long time without writing you! It was impossible to write on the boat, which was rough, windy and cold on the trip down from San Diego,* and very busy and active once we were in the lagoons, with whales spouting all around us. (We didn't see anything eight feet long, but lots of mothers with babies on their backs. And one baby whale played around Jon until his mother [the whale's] chased him away.) It was very much a man's trip—strenuous and adventurous. Jon and your father did a lot of diving in wet suits with tanks on their backs. And Land chased whales in an outboard motor skiff. (Jon and Father also.) These whales are gray and not too big—but still, pretty impressive.

Jon ran the expedition and did it very well, and Father was magnificent, taking second place. (The first day, it was a real effort. Land remarked, "Father's having such a hard time *not* running the expedition.") He kept tripping himself up and saying: "Well now, Jon, this is your expedition. What do you say?" In the end it worked beautifully and Father and everyone else had a wonderful time (really better than the African trip). No one was sick (though Susie doesn't like rough weather). Susie and I cooked, and there were some of the same problems: washing dishes in salt water, not enough fresh water to wash dishes or ourselves. (Our hair got zombie-ish.) But it was quite a happy trip, and a change for Susie and Land. Rather cold night and morning (I wore ski long johns to bed), but sunny and hot midday.

---

*In January 1967 Jon chartered a forty-foot sport fisher so the Lindberghs could study the "whale nursery" in the lagoons of Baja California for an article that would be published in the December 22, 1967, issue of *Life* magazine.

The boat was fairly comfortable though not roomy, and Father, Jon, Susie, Land and I all slept in one small cabin, in layered bunks like a filing case. We gave the one partially private bunk to the photographer. The captain, a friend of Jon's, slept in the wheelhouse, when not at the wheel. It was very wild desert country—sand-dunes and cactus and purple mountains in the distance, the sea teeming with life: ducks, geese and pelicans, porpoises, seals, and whales. We stopped to refuel in two small Mexican ports, little collections of gaily painted shacks climbing up dry wrinkled hills. Land and Susie used their Spanish and we ate tortillas and freshly caught lobster.

I flew back via Seattle, stopping to see Barbie who is having another baby (a deep secret kept from everyone) in less than a month now!

Reeve was down Tuesday to collect her skis. We went to the pet shop to buy a collar for Davin* and she saw these monkeys in a cage and bought one small wizened one! ("It's your res-spons-ibilit-ee!") She has named it Roger, and she took it up to Radcliffe in a small carrying box like a workman's lunch-box. It kept squealing and putting a long thin hairy arm out of the breathing hole. During supper we let it out in her bathroom upstairs. It was terrified and leaped all over from fixture to fixture, slipping from slipperiness onto the floor. In an hour it was the dirtiest place I have ever seen: monkey droppings, grapes, and banana remains over every inch of floor—and *wall*. Whee!

Reeve left with the monkey and a large cage she expects to keep it in. And I cleaned the bathroom so Mrs. Swanson wouldn't know—or have to do it. I'll keep you posted on it. She says Peggy's family will keep it weekends!

Much love Darling, I hope things are getting settled and more peaceful—

XO

Scott's Cove
Darien, Conn.
June 1st, 1967[†]

Mr. and Mrs. Lindbergh regret that, because of the absence of Mr. Lindbergh from the country and Mrs. Lindbergh's lack of knowledge of

---

*AML's cairn terrier.

[†]This reply to an invitation from President and Mrs. Lyndon Johnson was handwritten in formal (centered) style.

the date of his return or where to reach him, they are unable to accept the very kind invitation of President and Mrs. Johnson for dinner Monday evening, June 12th.

Les Monts-de-Corsier
September 12th, 1967
Dear Mina [Curtiss],

It was so good to get your rich letter. It is interesting how much richer letters from writers are. They are somehow three-dimensional as compared to usual flat one-dimensional ones, even from people one loves, who are not writers.

I have felt very cut off from people this summer. Partly it was just the flu–sinus–ear episode in August, which wasn't that painful but left me almost totally deaf for three weeks. (I only have one good ear and that was the one affected.) It was especially frustrating because Scott was here for ten days of that time, going through quite a crisis on the draft problem, and I had such difficulty *hearing* what he was saying. It is interesting how much one counts on the little asides, or the drop in voice—the hesitations and mumbled words. These are the important clues to communication.

CAL was here part of this time too, and it was rather an intense week. I don't know yet what Scott will do. He feels very much opposed to the war in Vietnam and, after eight years abroad, really more European than American. Also, he feels behind in his getting into a career and would like to go on into animal psychology and behaviorism. His deferment has been cancelled and he will certainly not get another deferment for graduate work in a new field.

Charles was very concerned about it, and I also (for somewhat different reasons), but there was very little we could do except listen (and I could hardly do that!) and, in Charles's case, point out the dangers in jumping too fast into a solution that might not turn out to be satisfactory in the long run.

I am glad you are going off on a trip. Even if one works (I have worked quite steadily all summer except for the week in bed), one gets so bogged down and ingrown on a writer's routine, particularly in bad weather. I am going off for two days next week with Helen Wolff to see Basel and some paintings Kurt loved. It will be good to get away. I have decided that I have become rather bored with Switzerland. I miss my sharp-tongued old lady friend who died last fall, whom I used to see once a week. I remember Amey saying (in her eighties), "Switzerland is all right for a month or two, but then you get so bored you want to go out and get drunk!" There hasn't been anyone around I could get "drunk" with, and anyway, I felt so flattened out by August that I couldn't do much.

It has been beautiful weather, however, and I had a lovely visit from Anne and the baby in July and hope for another short one before I go home (the first week in October). Now autumn has fallen quite swiftly. Foggy mornings, overcast skies, cold nights, and the wet meadows dotted with lavender autumn crocuses.

I think of you a good deal, often at that hour between tea and supper when one minds most being alone. (In July I used to walk then, but now it is too dark.) It's particularly hard if one can't have a glass of sherry. Grapefruit juice is a poor substitute.

CAL had a letter from a friend in the U.S. that must express what you (and I—so many of us) feel about this summer: "It's been a depressing summer, and I begin to think that something *must* be done soon about Vietnam to keep American society from becoming unhinged by self-doubt and worse, self-hate."

Much love, Mina. Your letter was a great joy and it will be wonderful to be talking to you soon.

Anne

Les Monts-de-Corsier
Wednesday, September 13th, 1967
Dear Pixie,*

I find myself unable to stop thinking about you and your painful predicament. I keep wishing I could have said more to help you, the afternoon you and Eglantine† were here for tea, in the ordeal you face those next days in your interview with your husband. I have finally decided to put down some of these after-thoughts that should have been said more clearly, that I would say now if you were here another afternoon. Think of it as a continued conversation:

No matter what he says—much of it may sound reasonable—he cannot answer for *how you feel*. If you neither love nor respect him, you cannot carry through a marriage successfully. It would be acting out a lie, which would be the worst possible thing for your children, for yourself,

---

*A friend who lived in Switzerland.
†Eglantine Moreillon, a friend who lived in Vevey, Switzerland.

and even for him. A relationship that is wrong for one person is wrong for both. A marriage founded on a lie is immoral and will fail.

The marriage vows, in such a case, are only the dead letter of the law and not true to its spirit. I think it is barbaric to be bound by them. To live a lie will be destructive to you, to him, but chiefly to the children. It has been demonstrated by psychological studies that the worst thing for children is to be told one thing and to *feel* the opposite is true. Children feel the lie and the pretense, even if it is unspoken. Many doctors feel this is a frequent cause of schizophrenia: children cannot deal with the two surfaces. It puts an impossible burden on them. The argument of "self-sacrifice," and "Christian charity," etc. falls flat before the rock of integrity and honesty.

The argument that your children need a father, a man: yes, but they don't need a man they don't respect and whom you don't respect. They will respect him more if he breaks loose and makes a new life on his own. It is his only chance of winning their respect.

Actually, I think you can and do feel Christian charity. It is not inconsistent. You feel sorry for him; you would like to help him; you believe he can start a new life on his own, free of you and the children; you would like to make it easier for him. If he does not fight the case, you need not bring up all the horrible details that you have against him. You prefer to bury them and will only expose them if forced to it.

Don't try to argue with him (the arguments I put here are only to strengthen you). He is desperate and will use any weapon to try to break you down, but this should only strengthen your resolve to leave him. If you can do nothing else, just try to remain there as quietly as possible, listening to him and saying only something, in your own words, like: "I am terribly sorry, but this is the way I feel and nothing you say can make me feel any differently."

Don't be afraid. He really cannot hurt you. He *has* hurt you, of course, but it is all in the past. You are now stronger than he.

It is only the memories of the past that undermine you—the memories of being afraid and of being hurt. And your false sense of guilt and your false sense of good manners. (Having been brought up not to hurt anyone, to want to please people and be nice—I know it only too well; I was brought up the same way.)

Remember you are doing this for the children more than for yourself. It is not right to sacrifice their lives for him. Your freedom from him is their only chance of healthy survival.

Forgive this outburst, but I had to write it. I will be thinking of you. I am sure you can, and will, carry it through as you have the earlier ordeals, and your son will certainly be a great moral support by your side.

You might surprise yourself by waking up to find how very strong you have become. Other people know it; it is only you who don't see it.

With my love and my very real faith in you—

Anne

Cuckoo Clock*
Sunday a.m., September 17th, 1967
Dear Scott,

This is the first time we have seen the sun here for at least two weeks. Ernestine and John Chamberlain[†] are here, came late last night from Vichy where John attended a conference of economists. John is now typing on the balcony, and Ernestine writing in the "baby's" room at the card table.

We had a long late breakfast sitting over the counter. I wish you could have been here to hear some of John's reflections on the state of the world. One thing he said interested me very much. He wrote a piece (published last year), written in the Beirut airport appropriately, where he said he had a sudden view of U.S. policy and the war in Vietnam as not a struggle for democracy, the Free World, our friends, etc., but simply to maintain control of airports all over the world, much as England fought to keep her seaports open. Air power is what ultimately matters; as long as we can maintain bases, so his thesis runs, we don't care too much about the politics of the country (e.g. Spain).

He thinks Johnson is trying very hard to end the war before the election, and that if the Republicans get in, they will press to "win or get out" as quickly as possible so that the Vietnam struggle might fold up rather quickly. There will probably be others, of course (to maintain our bases around the world?). He also said there was considerable pressure

*The one-room chalet built uphill from the Lindberghs' home in Monts-de-Corsier, which AML used as a writing retreat.
[†]Ernestine Stodelle (Mrs. John Chamberlain), an original member of the Humphrey-Weidman Company, modern dance troupe. She wrote about dance and philosophy, founded the Choreo-Lyric Dance Company in New Haven, and taught dance technique in Connecticut and at New York University. John Rensselaer Chamberlain, book reviewer, journalist, and longtime contributing editor at *National Review*.

from responsible sources to end the draft entirely and maintain a voluntary army (and professionals). This would be more efficient for the Army and for the country, too, economically. As it is now, it is very wasteful of man-power and the potentialities of the men concerned. I keep feeling, in the light of this constantly shifting picture, that it is too bad for you to jump too quickly into nationality before you have had a chance to try out your new work life, etc., and know exactly where these are going to lead you. (Perhaps you feel you *do* know?)

And I keep remembering your saying once that you'd prefer to be an "exiled American." If you really still would, perhaps that is what you should be. (Your father would probably not agree.) My feeling is that whatever you do now (unless you go home), you are going to get bad publicity about draft evasion, even if you announce you are changing your citizenship. And changing one's citizenship is not like marriage, where you can get a divorce if it's a mistake, or like divorce, where if you feel that's a mistake you can get remarried. It's pretty irrevocable.

True (if you remain in exile), you run the risk of arrest (if you go home), losing your freedom to travel, and possibly restrictions on your income (your lawyer or banker could advise you on this).

And I would think you would have time to write your draft board *something*, telling them their notice was delayed, as it unfortunately was. Perhaps just how you feel about the war in Vietnam. In other words, taking a position as a conscientious objector (on the grounds of *this* war). This would be an honest course and there are plenty of people like you.

And of course you *can* change your citizenship later, if and when you know exactly where your work will lead you and where you really feel you could live.

It seems to me that so often in your life you choose the hard way. What you are choosing now is infinitely more difficult than going home and getting into the Coast Guard or the Navy, say. But in the past you have shown that once you *choose* "the hard way," you have the guts and the persistence to follow it through successfully so I have faith in your being able to do it here.

I would like you to be free in your opportunities and in yourself—to really get ahead in the work you have chosen. It is a wonderful field and you can do a great deal in it. It will be good to be working on a "terrestrial plane" and not on just a political one. More seems to be able to be done here than in the human political one.

Much love Scott, and have a good trip to Ireland—
Mother

6:30 a.m., Monday, January 15th, 1968

Dearest Ansy,

I have been home a week but still wake at 5:30 or six—still, that is an improvement on two or three—and the first week, which is always difficult, is over. I have been through the accumulated mail, bills, and telephone calls (but not the Xmas cards). Your father was here for just three days, very busy ones: one in town, and the others spent on mail, telephone calls, files and lists. He is now back in England on Wildlife meetings.*

There is quite a lot of talk, confusion, and resentment here as a result of the President's recommended travel restrictions ("to the Western Hemisphere" was what he said, and that meant the Americas: Canada, Mexico).† Apparently Mrs. Johnson made an impassioned radio plea to American women not to travel to Europe for two years. And they are talking of taxing airfares or travelers six dollars each day they are abroad. Congress reconvenes today and there will be stiff fights over it. The travel industry is so enormous in this country that if it is slashed it may have some effect on the national economy. Also, people resent travel restrictions. There are many rumors: that travelers will be limited in the amount of money they can take out, as in England; that private investment abroad will be restricted; that this is the start of a controlled economy, etc.

Your father feels that your position will not be affected—or will be the last to be affected. And some suggestions are that people with relatives abroad have some laxity in travel. I hope so! Anyway it's too early to tell what will be hammered out. It is a world I do not understand very well.

I must now turn on television since Mrs. Swanson‡ has told me Jon will be on some program between seven and nine this morning. I doubt if I can look at it that long, but at least I'll turn it on. It has been terribly cold this week, so cold that you put a scarf over your face when you went out. It was hard to breathe, snow everywhere, and the cove was frozen over. It looked arctic, with ice pushed up in frozen chunks and waves.

---

*CAL began working with the World Wildlife Fund's parent organization, the International Union for Conservation of Nature and Natural Resources, or IUCN, in 1962, reporting on and cataloging threatened fauna around the world. As time went on, his involvement with the WWF grew, and in 1966 he became a member of its board.

†In an effort to increase tourism in the United States during the late 1960s, the Johnson administration pushed a voluntary "see America first" strategy, asking Americans to defer overseas travel.

‡The Lindberghs' housekeeper and cook.

Jon *has* been on my TV, talking on the resources of the seas and the dwindling whale population. He talks very well, slowly, with quite a western accent (surprisingly!), and smiling quite naturally—using his hands somewhat squarely, if you know what I mean. I guess it's over. It is now 7:25.

It is now after breakfast and bath, and I am going out to the Little House. The snow has melted some, but it is hard and icy and branches are down everywhere. Last night it blew and banged, and snow kept sliding off the roof with a roar that made Brenna bark angrily and made me nervous.

You communicate so marvelously that I get the quality of your daily life much better than I could hope. (That doesn't mean you have to write me immediately!)

There was such joy in seeing your gay happy baby. I think of the sheer joy of that beautiful walk, dragging Charles Feydy on his tiny sled through the lacy-with-snow beech forest, pink cheeks under his blue bonnet. Do take care of yourself and keep up the writing and the hours off. Reeve and Richard* will be here next week after exams. I will write again.

XO—XO
Mother

Scott's Cove, Darien
Sunday, March 3rd, 1968
Dearest Ansy,

Your letter from the Dordogne was a joy and was here waiting for me Thursday night when your father and I drove back from town in a wet blanketing snowstorm. (The windshield got packed with slush and the VW slithered in ruts made by trucks.) It was lovely to think of you in "light sweater" weather with "almost sun-bathing sun" and violets (plucked off at the head by Charles), primroses, and dandelions. Is Charles really offering you violet heads? How grown up he sounds. I loved the description of him in the plane. One wonders what he really saw out of the window, and how he translated it in his mind. Will he remember and tell you someday?

I am glad you are writing again, and your illustrations are delicious. A *good* idea for a book (remember St.-Ex.'s illustrations for his *Le Petit Prince*?).

*Reeve would marry Richard Brown, a photographer and teacher, in June 1968.

Your father asks, each time he comes back from Washington or each time he sees a letter in the mail, "Any news of Scott?" Reeve says the present draft regulations are actually better, since more individual choice is left up to the local boards. It seems that Richard will be allowed to teach as "essential to the community." But elsewhere you hear great criticism from the graduate schools, which will have almost no able-bodied male students next year.

Reeve is very anxious to have you and Julien and the baby for her wedding on the ranch. She is not having anyone except immediate (grown-up) family. No aunts and uncles or children, except for Erin and Peter who are *there*. So Charles would not be overcome with relatives. Only Richard's immediate family will come, and they will probably live at "The Homestead," entirely self-sufficient. Life on the ranch is somehow easy and not regimented and everyone goes his own way. Very simple.

Your father is very busy with his many lives: down to Washington for work and the Naval hospital, World Wildlife activities, Pan Am meetings and, in between, seeing people who are writing books about various aviation personalities or companies. This last can be taxing. We had eight people for supper last week on two such books. Mrs. Swanson and I had planned chicken and peas, when two of the guests telephoned me: "We can eat anything but meat and fish"! What else *is* there, I thought wildly? We added macaroni and cheese to the dinner. We're still eating up the chicken. (They were Seventh Day Adventists—I dimly remember that Scott was ill in one of their hospitals in the Middle East, and had vegetarian meatloaf and chips to eat.)

I must go back to heat up that chicken for Sunday lunch. Do stay well and go on writing.

XOXOXO
Mother

Monday a.m. before breakfast
Everyone left me at the same moment yesterday after tea. It is hard to be *left* alone—not so hard to *live* alone, once one adjusts. I wonder how your days without Julien, alone at Les Rieux, went? Dogs do help tremendously—also it is easier to be alone in a smaller house. One feels snugger. Bigger houses are full of noises and empty spaces, vacuums into which rush one's nostalgia and apprehension.

The newspapers are also loaded with bad news: the war, the predictions of more serious trouble in race relations here. Your father is very gloomy on this situation (and the state of the world in general). He argues with Reeve (Richard is *not* an arguer). Reeve says: "Throw me no exponential curves."* I feel, when we get into the argument, that we're going through the washer, no cycle can be omitted and they're irreversible and grind on.

Scott's Cove
April 5th, 1968
Dear Scott,

Your father and I came home last night from dinner at Fairfield Osborne's (head of the Natural History Museum, an old man but tremendously vigorous and alert and gay—a scientist and writer and great human being) where, mid-evening, we heard the shocking news of Martin Luther King's assassination, a great tragedy for Negroes and whites alike in our country—possibly a tragedy with even more ominous implications than the murder of Kennedy. We came home to read your letter to Father and your letter addressed to me but written to both of us, about your marriage to Alika† and your plans for life in Europe, and your immediate attitude toward the draft.

Your letters were gentle and sincere and direct and I am grateful that you wrote us this way. I suppose it is inevitable that they were also somewhat of a shock. It is not that I have not had some preparation for your marriage by meeting Alika, and it is not that I did not like her. As I told you, I found her sympathetic and, from those brief meetings, had the sense that she was warm, generous, intuitive and devoted.

I know that Alika has supported you loyally in your work and life. I am grateful to her for that. I remember how terribly lonely you were in the midst of your conflicts and problems last summer on the draft and citizenship. Now you have Alika and feel less lonely. Although loneliness is really not "cured," it is only covered up, filled temporarily. And I am not sure we should try so hard to cure it or cover it up. Loneliness, if one comes to terms with it, is one's good daemon: out of it come one's creative powers—and you have those, though they have not yet had the opportunity to express themselves. Alika, being a creative person herself, will, I hope, understand this—the *need* for loneliness. I hope you can protect each other's loneliness; it is precious.

---

*This is a reference to CAL's concerns about the world's increasing population.
†Alika Watteau, Belgian painter, novelist, actress, and animal rights activist.

I hope you will be happy, and I hope you will grow, and that the confining world of scholarship and a small circle of like-minded people will crack and open up for you so that you are liberated to ever-widening work and worlds and people.

We have just come back from Hawaii, a world in which I thought a great deal of you. It is freer, wilder, and less overlaid than the U.S. or Europe: very beautiful—still expanses of wild land to ranch or farm, still opportunities for new research; some of the rawness (but not the crudeness) of the Old West; isolated from the rest of the world, an island culture and civilization tinged with a fragrance of the Orient—not a heavy fragrance, though; washed by sea winds, fresher. Like Mexico, it seemed to me one of those rare blends of the primitive and the cultured. A man could start a new life there, I felt. We have done the best we could to ruin Honolulu, Waikiki Beach, etc. But there are still unspoiled islands. (No wonder Gregory Bateson wants to work there.)*

There is also, surprisingly, little color discrimination. Hawaii is a mixture of Polynesian, Chinese, Japanese, etc. and missionaries and whaler stock. People of all colors and mixtures (no Negro) walk the streets unself-consciously, with grace and pride. Life is informal, out of doors, healthy. A love of beauty and music, characteristics of the early Polynesians from Tahiti, still hangs over the islands, as I said, like a fragrance.

Don't try to answer this. There isn't much to say. Ansy will give me your news. We will miss you at Reeve's wedding but she may go abroad in August—

Love,
Mother

Scott's Cove, Darien, Conn.
May 20th, 1968
Dear Florida Scott-Maxwell,†

I have just written Mrs. Jones‡ of Knopf to thank her for sending me your last book, *The Measure of My Days*, and to tell her of my great admiration for it. I am painfully aware of how inadequate my letter was to express what I felt, and how inadequate this one to you will also be.

---

*Gregory Bateson (1904–1980), an English anthropologist, social scientist, linguist, semiotician, and cyberneticist.
†Florida Scott-Maxwell (1883–1979) an American psychologist who also wrote fiction, nonfiction, and plays.
‡Judith Jones (1924–), an editor at Alfred A. Knopf.

And yet I must try. In a way there is a kind of comfort in the inadequacy; it lets me understand better why I have been so appallingly silent over the years since I saw you. Not a word to you to show how much I have thought of you and carried your words and ideas around with me and shared them with others. As one gets older, I now realize, one goes deeper and it becomes increasingly difficult to plumb the depths and put the findings on paper.

But, the fact is, you have done it in this little book. You have brought up things from the depths, clarified, ordered, and put them into a form that can reach us, simply, vividly, beautifully. They are not tortured or strained, like thoughts that have been struggled for, or tangled and confused like unripe ideas, but whole, bare, beautiful, like something organic—shells or branches of coral, perfect in their growth and completion, rescued from the dark sea bottom.

They speak—as all you have written does—to my condition, but much, much more. You are speaking here not simply to the old, or to women, but to men and women, young and old, to anyone in any society or culture who is aware of the struggle of man's spirit toward maturity and wholeness. You speak, you say, from a restricted circle, but you seem much closer to humanity's struggles than when you last spoke. If this is what it is to be old, it is to be at the pulse of life. But few reach it at any age.

I am not being irresponsibly enthusiastic. I will try to be more explicit. When I opened the package from Knopf, I had a leap of joy to see a new book of yours, and with your card in it for me, as if my long silence had been understood and forgiven. Since it came, I have been reading it with excitement, each night, always before going to sleep, and sometimes waking sleepless in the middle of the night (my favorite hour for reading the *I Ching* at random), or at dawn. I have not been able to refrain from reading passages out loud to my husband (at decent hours only!), especially those passages on differentiation and the conflict between quality and equality. He was arrested and said: "Mark that, I want to read it again. I have never heard it as well expressed. This is a truth very few people see, and almost no women." (I could not share your other writings with him. He could not hear them. Perhaps they were too directed to women, or the inner life.) This is a new dimension in your writing, as well as, perhaps, a new dimension in us.

Then, unable to leave it behind, I took your book to town, to a gathering of late middle-aged women who have been meeting for ten years or so, to read and discuss philosophical, religious, and psychological books (Jung, Zimmer, Joseph Campbell, Tillich, Buber, Teilhard de Chardin, Suzuki, Benoit, etc., as well as your book and articles). I read aloud that wonderful passage on page 39—starting "Personal immortality may not matter at all" and going on to "our whole duty may be to clarify and increase what we are, to make our consciousness a finer quality." And then I read the passage on page 120 starting "There is a word I have never found," which goes on to "the sacred identity within us" to protect which is "our chief aim." They were all silent at the end, the silence not only of affirmation but of confirmation. This is what we all, facing the last twenty years of our lives, feel to be true. You have confirmed it in expressing the almost inexpressible.

Tomorrow I have to write a note to one of our group, the oldest, about eighty, who must have a serious operation. What can I say that will have any relevance? I found it in your notebook, the passage on the equal-ended cross surrounded by a circle (page 45). "Does Life, or God, what is the difference, build us with accepted experience, stab by stab of accepted understanding? As though each joy or sorrow is God, or life, saying, 'You See?' and we are needed, not forced, to say truly, 'I see.' " Coming from you, it will be a hand to hold in the dark.

Do not reply to this mammoth letter. It would be much too tiring. You must know that your book is like a long rich letter that friends feel like answering. I may perhaps write you again, now I have broken the ice-jam. Letters can be put aside for a quiet moment or a dull one. As we used to say of nondescript birthday presents, at least it's "something to open."

I am writing another book, too, slowly and heavily, with many interruptions and much discouragement. However, reading your book has given me new heart to go on. One must always write the truth, Dr. Johnson says somewhere, "It saves mankind from despair." This you have done.

Darien, Conn.
November 11th, 1968
Dear Leonard Bernstein,

I felt badly that we could not go backstage at the end of the magnificent concert Friday night that I went to with Evie Ames—to at least shake your hand. I would not have been able to say anything of what I felt, I am afraid.

The evening of Mahler songs, Dietrich Fischer-Dieskau's voice and your playing was a deeply moving experience. I have never witnessed before such a perfect meeting of poetry, music and artistic performance. The result was an extraordinary sense of distillation—as if down to one flower, one person, one experience—a very personal and private experience in the midst of that great hall and that crowd of people. One was alone with the most profound feelings in life: joy, beauty, love, separation, sorrow. And yet, of course, as with all creative acts, the private experience was resolved, accepted, transfigured in the perfection of the art.

This is something I could not thank you for with a handshake—or very well even with a note, but I had to try to say some of it.

Gratefully,

Anne Lindbergh

En route NY → Seattle

January 25th, 1969

Dear Lucia and Alan [Valentine],

We flew to Cape Kennedy before Christmas for three days to watch the launching of the *Apollo 8*. Very thrilling.

And then took a long slow exhausting milk run of a flight from Orlando, Florida, to Missoula, Montana. I had a martini at Butte (I wished it had been one of Alan's!) which got me through the last four stops. We landed in snow and it snowed all the time we were there. Despite snow and cold it was a warm happy family visit. Charles, Land, and Richard went out (in 38 degrees below weather) morning and evening to throw out hay for the cattle, Charles looking like Admiral Byrd at the North Pole in his arctic parka and pants. But I stayed inside, washed dishes and read to children—eventually, of course, catching their flu. On to Seattle, I by this time quite hoarse ("Don't mind me—it's just my voice," you say gasping), and eventually back to Darien where I spent a week recovering.

Since then (Charles went right off again to Europe), I have been working very hard trying to put down my mixed emotions about the *Apollo 8* launching and flight, working from nine to five with half hours out to run around the house to clear my head before lunch and supper. Probably this will never appear in print but be saved (and read?) by my great-grandchildren, who will think going to the moon very routine. I wonder? The moon, to quote the understatements by the astronauts, "does not seem to be a very inviting place to live or work." Perhaps, as an engineer at Cape Kennedy voiced his fears to us, the moon may turn out in importance and interest to be rather like the poles. In any case, I wrote steadily for two weeks, and thought and read a great deal in the process. I thought of Henry Adams standing in front of the dynamo in Paris at the turn of the century, and also of Lorenz's* last chapter in *Aggression* where he says space exploration does offer, to a superb degree, the moral equivalent for war (or words to that effect), and that must be why it has aroused such excitement in the world. People unconsciously sense this helps to keep us at peace.

I have not thanked you for your delicious scrambled proverbs of Laura Stevens. She was my roommate at Smith for one year so I know what a joy her perception and humor are to live with. Her proverbs reminded me of one of Ansy's which delights me often, which I pass on to you for the same collection: "I'll burn that bridge when I come to it"!

Much love to you both—

Anne

Kipahulu
Hana, Maui, Hawaii
February 1st, 1969
D.D.

I have been here since Monday when I arrived late evening by small plane from Honolulu. There was a cable here from CAL telling me he would arrive *Saturday* from the Philippines—six days after me! Anyway, it takes me about that time to catch up with sleep and the change in climate. I am down in the little guest cottage by myself, next to the beach. It is peaceful and comfortable, and up to yesterday there was no one at the "big" house up the hill but Mrs. Pryor, whom I like very much. Yesterday Sam Pryor and two guests flew in.†

It has, however, rained every day since I arrived—torrents of tropical rain. The sea roars all night and the trade winds shake the house. I go up

---

*Konrad Lorenz (1903–1989) was an Austrian zoologist, ethologist, and ornithologist. A pioneer in the study of animal behavior, he was a co-winner of the Nobel Prize in Physiology and Medicine in 1973.

†Sam Pryor, a retired Pan American executive and conservationist, and his wife, Mary, sold five acres from their extensive Maui property to the Lindberghs in 1968. A small house the Lindberghs called Argonauta (after a shell featured in *Gift from the Sea*) was built there in 1969.

and down to the big house for lunch and supper in a four-wheel-drive Jeep—in a raincoat, hat and sneakers. But I feel damp all the time. Not cold, though, just damp. It was like this the week we were here *last* year too, but I thought it was freak weather. Now I'm not so sure. I read an article in the paper about the return to "our usual wet weather winter climate"!! No wonder everything grows like tropical Yucatan!

The sun comes out occasionally, for perhaps an hour a day off and on, and I rush out to sit in it. I have not yet seen our property, waiting for CAL to show it to me. It *is* very beautiful. Honolulu is just like a suburb of L.A.—skyscrapers on a beach and everyone floating around in muumuus at the airport with "Aloha" chanting from the loudspeakers wherever you go. But Maui—this end of it anyway—is a wild beautiful untouched island. The coasts are rocky and dramatic with waves pounding on the black sands and spray dashing up on the cliffs (not exactly my kind of swimming but just CAL's cup of tea!). The green mountainous volcanic slopes fall down into the sea abruptly (a little like the Virgins but *not* such good weather). There are all the beautiful flowering plants and trees one saw in Nassau, Mexico and Africa: poinsettia, bougainvillea, hibiscus—but no hummingbirds.

The nearest shopping area is three quarters of an hour away over a rough stony road with blind curves negotiable by Jeep. There, there is a quite charming hotel, four or five small stores, a post office, and one big general store which sells everything from steaks and papaya to aloha shirts and Japanese sake cups. (I liked this store—lots of fun.)

It has been restful and I begin to sleep better, though sometimes when the rain and winds howl and that surf roars like last night I get scared and wonder if this little house won't cave in to the sea or get washed out by mud slides. Last night I got up with a flashlight (no electricity except for a generator-run system that keeps breaking down) to look out and see whether the waterfall wasn't coming in the back door—it sounded like that!

Today I am waiting for word from CAL as to when his plane gets into Honolulu and what plane he can catch from there to Maui so I can go meet him at the little airport at Hana. (The logistics seem to me about as difficult and the weather not as reliable as Treasure Island in Nassau—remember?) What a romantic C. is! Imagine buying a vacation home without even trying out the climate and locale for one season! However, I suppose we can always get rid of this property if it turns out to be more trouble than it's worth. At the moment, I recommend your coming to visit me in Switzerland. (That can be rainy, too, but I have a fireplace and a furnace and electric light.)

I don't think we'll be here long, as the Pryors are leaving in four or five days for a trip to Australia and I can't see our staying on much after that—though they have kindly offered us this guest cottage for as long as we want. I'm really rather anxious to get back and get to work again—

Love from a rather damp

Lotus Eater

Scott's Cove
Darien, Conn.
February 23rd, 1969
Dear Mrs. Marcos,*

I apologize for this late reply to your beautiful gift which my husband brought me from the Philippines.† We have both been working on an article for *Life* magazine on the *Apollo 8* launching (which we witnessed) and its setting in Florida, which is in a wildlife refuge. It was, in a way, an article for wildlife conservation, which you know my husband cares deeply about. The magazine had to have the article by Monday of this last week and we spent every moment of every day these last weeks at a desk, rewriting, correcting and checking details, to get it done on time.

I am just now able to get to my desk to write a personal letter. I was most touched by the message on your card, that my book *Gift from the Sea* had meant so much to you. This pleased me more than I can say, especially because of all my husband had told me about you and your family after his visit to the Philippines.

The beautiful old Chinese celadon bottle is a precious treasure. I have never seen anything like it except in museums. Its lovely shape, its muted milky-green color, and the many-toned texture of the glaze suggest to me the eternal mystery and beauty of the sea. I have taken it out to the quiet little cabin, away from the house, where I go to think or write when I am home. I have there only the things I really treasure and that bring peace and beauty. Perhaps your bottle is really too rare and precious a piece to be there, but it seemed to me to be the right place for it.

---

*Imelda Marcos (1929–) was the wife of then president of the Philippines Ferdinand Marcos, who was eventually deposed in a coup in 1986, after years of martial law.
†CAL made repeated visits to the Philippines during the 1960s, as part of his efforts to promote the preservation of indigenous species (including human tribal groups) threatened by technological development.

I shall always look at it with pleasure and gratitude to you and remember your kind words about my book.

My husband enjoyed so much his time in the Philippines and meeting you and President Marcos. He was happy about his visit and the interest shown there in preserving the beauty of your country. He wants very much to go back again and to bring me, too, sometime. I will look forward to this pleasure and to meeting you and your husband.

In the meantime, my warm thanks for your message and the beautiful gift.

Very sincerely yours,
Anne Lindbergh

Darien
Sunday, November 9th, 1969
Dear Ruth [Oliff],

I have the impression that I said nothing very clearly or to the point last night in our lengthy telephone conversation in the early hours of the morning. In the first place, of course, I was startled out of a sound sleep by the ring of the telephone and reached for the phone in a dazed sense of shock. A call like that, coming in the middle of the night, means sudden death or tragedy. I've never had a call like that that wasn't bringing me news like that, so I steeled myself for word of Charles's crash, a child's sudden death, etc. It was hard to talk normally after that preparation.

I realize how desperate you must feel to call like that. I was myself aware of how little I could do to help, and how appalling it was that you had no one nearer than the thousands of miles that separate us to talk to.

If I had the choice of a heart transplant (a *very* different thing than the valve operation) and death in a normal gradual weakening, I think I would choose the natural way. But the operation they are proposing for you, if I understand you, is not in the very experimental stage of heart transplants. It has been made hundreds of times.

Once you have made the decision, you should try to accept it and feel yourself in God's—or Nature's—or Fate's hands. It would be easier if you had a traditional religion to support you. I know how you feel about the usual orthodox religious comforts one is given. They aren't strong enough to support one. If one could only pray. I have thought a great deal about petitionary prayer. At one time I rejected all prayers of intercession as crutches, but now I think what I was rejecting was the *form*—the semantics, the too small form, or frame, of prayers. The validity of prayers has been attested to through the ages, but it has been delineated in too small terms and language.

Perhaps, I now feel, prayer opens the heart and connects us with some stream of compassion that feeds us and the world. It may not be answered literally, but I begin to feel it *connects* us to a life current. There are other ways of being connected with the life current: being with people you love, seeing the beauty of a flying bird or a flaming tree, or hearing music—feeling a sudden overwhelming gratitude for beauty and kindness or communication. One says thanks, and one's heart is suddenly infused again with the life current. Something is "answered."

I think there are also other ways to be calmed, strengthened, or more connected to the beneficent forces in the universe. The Eastern religions have taught their believers certain techniques. (Not so different from the Christian, except in language and form.) They preach quiet solitude, self-communion, and a kind of withdrawing from the battle of I-I-I. If you can stop the squirrel cage of the mind from going round and round, you can hear something else besides your own fears and worries. Even if you stop it by some artificial means, like sitting still and concentrating on your breathing. (I have tried it and it is calming.) You can count the breaths to stop yourself from thinking. ("One, two, three" as you breathe in, "one, two, three" as you breathe out.) Just that little recess from the squirrel cage helps, if you can do it two or three times a day. The few times I have felt close to death—once in a hospital—I have practiced this kind of breathing and quieting of the mind and it helps.

When I was afraid in an airplane, I used to make a kind of summing up: "No, I don't want to die. I would like to live longer for X, for Y, for Z, but I have lived a good life. I have done what I could. If we are here for some purpose (and I think we are), perhaps my purpose is over. I will accept that." And then some calm came to me.

We do not know what happens after death. To use a humble symbol, the electricity is still there even when the bulb is turned off. What happens to this force, this spirit that inhabits us? We don't know, but through the ages different religions have believed in some permanence of the spirit. The Buddhists believe in one kind of return. The Hindus believe in reincarnation, which I find more acceptable than the too literal Christian or Mohammedan heavens. I don't know, but I have really thought a great deal about death and believe—as the Hindus, the Buddhists, and many Christians, as well as a great delver into the subconscious like Jung—that the last third of life should be a preparation for death, or for freeing of the spirit. Protestants seem to me singularly negative in preparing one for the next step, whereas the Eastern religions pay a great deal of attention to this period of letting go. (Huxley, of course, was influenced by them also.)

I must let this go—I didn't mean it to get so long and philosophical. I don't think this is the moment for you to work out your philosophy of life and death. Just try to live from day to day as much as possible and experiment a little on techniques to still the squirrel cage of your fears and your mind. You might find you could get connected to the current of life. Many people love you and want to help you. Let them. Don't argue with their words. Accept their love and their help.

Much love, Ruth, and many thoughts (I do better on paper than over the telephone).

Anne

*Chalet Planorbe**
July 10th, 1970
Dear Helen [Wolff],

I am here, back in Switzerland, and begin to feel rooted again in this beautiful landscape after three happy days with Ansy and her husband and child in Paris. The weather, after a cold start, is now hot July weather, and I do hope you are having the same sort of weather in Chilmark.

The first week was not easy. CAL was here (met me, which was nice), but could only stay two nights and a day before going back to the U.S. and then on to the Philippines. He is very anxious for me to get through with the reading of my wartime diaries, which I won't do in the mornings but only in the afternoons. Even so, it is rather upsetting to read them and absorbs one in another time. It is too *personal.*

Sometime, we must talk very fully and frankly about this project[†] which I feel, as you do, should be made a secondary one. I'm not really against it but the timing I think is touchy. I don't think this is a problem you have to write back about—when we meet we can talk about it. In the meantime, I intend to concentrate on the middle-aged book.

It is always a little hard to settle down to this quiet life after a rather hectic spring, and this summer I am without my little dog, who got lost

*French for the snaillike Moon Shell.
†The publication of AML's letters and diaries.

a week or so before I left home (when visiting Reeve in Vermont) and hasn't been heard from since. It is absurd to let it bother one so much, but I find it very different living alone here with a dog and simply living alone. I miss him very much, especially here.

However, there are lots of birds and cats and the beautiful woods to walk in. . . . And one is fed by the country and the beauty all around. Also, of course, there are friends I can see. And you who live alone all the time, how do you do it? You do so magnificently.

I hope Chilmark is rewarding this year.

Much love to you—

Anne

Hawaii
January 21st, 1971
D.D.

It was so good to hear from you. I feel dropped out of the world. This is the most isolated place on earth: 35–45 minutes from the nearest village over a *very* bad road often washed out by the rains. It rained steadily the first week we were here—not only rain—driving storm, howling winds, and floods rushing down our slopes.

The house was not really finished and *no drainage* had been done around it at all, though CAL had warned both architect and contractor about it. Two inches of water, mud, and leaves came through our ground floor before we arrived and would have come again, after our arrival, had not CAL rushed out the first morning with a pail (our only implement) and dug out a channel and collected mud to make a dam in front of the back door. I patted up a mud dam while he dug trenches to channel the water around, not *through*, our house. Not only was there *no* drainage, but they had not made a rock bottom road before building the house, but just come in by Jeep over the slopes. Now the rainy season is here (and it is!), the slopes are a mass of rutted mud and washed-out gullies which actually channel the rain spillage of the mountain above us directly *into* our house! Also, of course, the roof leaks in spots (in the cloudbursts), and the ground floor tiles have been badly put in (spaces between the tiles not filled up so a grid effect results) which tends to collect dirt, sand, ants, and crumbs, impossible to sweep out.

Our first days were spent battling with the elements. C. borrowed a spade and dug trenches around the house to channel the by now three or four streams rushing downhill at us. I struggled with the wild inhabitants of our house who, to get out of the rain, no doubt, have sought shelter with us: ants, spiders, lizards, rats and mice. (I don't mind spiders and lizards but rats and mice give me nightmares and ants crawling over everything drive me batty.) However, we have set out poison and I spray everything and put all food in the icebox. The last thing I do at night is to spray under the bed and brush ants out of it before I climb in!

The car is now up on the "main" road and I slosh up to it in rubber boots and drive to the local store in Hana where, in a clutter of Japanese, Hawaiian and American goods, one can find all kinds of things including wine and vermouth—thank God!

CAL has now gone off for two weeks, making me furious at first. But I think it was really necessary and he didn't want to go. And, fortunately, the weather has now cleared. Yesterday, my first day alone, I washed all my underwear and hung it out on the balcony, burned the garbage and swept the floors (sweeping up an enormous dead rat under the sink!), put a load of damp dirty towels through the washer, washed my hair (perhaps like the song in *South Pacific*, washing "that man right out of my hair"!). And I feel much better.

Must run now, to town, with this—to do errands and some for my neighbor Mary Tay Pryor, who is an angel and a great help and comfort. It is going to take years to get this place in shape. A kind of equivalent to the Mexican *mañana* fever exists on this island. There are few (or no) good workmen or craftsmen or foremen or architects, and Honolulu is fifty miles away by small plane that doesn't come in bad weather.* You have to be right on the spot to see that things are done right, and my guess is we'll be here all of February *at least*.

I go to town every other day with lists of household necessities which I ferret out of the Japanese-Hawaiian general store. I couldn't buy a covered slop bucket, but *could* get a covered plastic diaper pail (pink!) which I'm using for garbage! However I rather enjoy that store. It's a real obstacle race to find anything, and everyone is so helpful and smiling, full of Hawaiians in bare feet and American hippies "like-wise," and a few elegant tourists from the expensively simple hotel, in shorts and sandals.

However, I am not as gloomy as I sound. On a beautiful day (and today and yesterday were really beautiful), it is as clear and sparkling as a perfect summer day in Switzerland. (I still prefer Switzerland!)

*Honolulu is actually 118 miles from Hana.

And who knows, I may turn Hawaiian after all. "If you can't lick 'em, join 'em."

Must run. Many thoughts, love—what fun it would be—will be?—when you visit us here, after we're organized!

A.

Conn.
Tuesday, April 27th, 1971
Dear C.,

I am not sure this will reach you but I'm sending it to Maui on the chance that you'll stop there on your way home from Hong Kong. Anyway, it will clarify me to write it out. I have been writing letters or talking to you in my mind ever since yesterday morning—was it?—when I talked to you on the telephone from Hong Kong.

It was certainly startling to have a call from Hong Kong, and even more startling to have you propose, saying it was "practically a presidential order," my going to the Philippines this May! (It *was* this May, wasn't it? You weren't by any chance talking about *next* May?) As you gathered, I feel it is next to impossible to go—certainly horribly difficult and inconvenient.

I would like to go with you to the Philippines sometime. I'd like to meet President and Mrs. Marcos, and Manuel Elizalde,* especially. Also, simply from what you've told me about it, I'd like to see the native tribes too, and I know that is an experience that can't wait too long (either from their point of view—or mine. The older I get, the harder it may be to do physically). I am so—this is the most important—touched that you *want* me to come, that you want to show me a new part of the world and to open up to me, as you have many times before, a totally new experience. I am grateful for this, deep down underneath, even though I object, complain, hold back, etc. So you see, I'd be coming for *you*—not on a "presidential order." (It's not *my* president, anyway.)

But really, it isn't easy—it isn't fair—to change your plans overnight. You don't tell me ahead of time what your plans are: where you are going and how long you'll be away, when you'll be back, etc. I don't mind actually; I know that's the way you live and must live. But I can't, on the

---

*A Philippine government official who claimed to have discovered an isolated tribe that lived Stone Age lives in the Philippine rain forest. After President Marcos was deposed in 1986, groups of anthropologists, journalists, and linguists met with the tribesmen, some validating Elizalde's claim, others insisting why it was a hoax.

other hand, sit around and wait for you and make no plans. I must go ahead and lead my life on the basis that you aren't there or that you are leading your own life unpredictably as far as I am concerned. So I make my plans.

I now have plans for May. These plans vary in importance, but they are not to be tossed over by a telephone call, even from Hong Kong—or a presidential order! I have planned to go over the first clean draft of Volume I of my Diaries and Letters and to write a first draft of the introduction to this before I take off to Europe. I have written Ansy I would come over whenever she wanted me, to be there around the time of her baby's birth. Julien may take off soon after the birth and she may be counting on me. Reeve is also starting a baby (due in November), is feeling somewhat unsteady and I would like to be around if possible, to see her again, give her advice, talk to her, etc.

I have told the Monastery of Regina Laudis* that I would come again to their seminar—May 30th through June 3rd. I have told DWM and his wife† that I would like to have them for the night of June 13th. (He will be looking for letters and pictures in his files the next week.) I have, of course, also written Smith and Amherst about pictures (as well as Con and DWM), saying we might come up.

I should see Marboch the end of May or early June for the pre-summer dental work. (I waited too long, he said, the last time.) Krissie is—or may be—coming east to look at colleges. She will go by herself to Northampton and possibly others, but I would like to see her en route.

Some of these plans could, of course, be changed. But it does jam up the spring or summer. I don't do things well when I'm under pressure and I don't travel well across time zones. I wish I did. It takes me at least a week to recover from a trip to the West Coast or Europe. Worse for Hawaii or the Philippines. Rushing things doesn't work for me. I can't appreciate anything after a long trip.

I have another proposal: can't we go to the Philippines next January? (From Hawaii.) The trip would then be broken—both going to the Philippines and returning to Hawaii—not as long as a trip.

The fall is not good because Reeve really wants me in Peacham in November for her baby's birth. (Richard wants me too!) We might

---

*A Benedictine abbey in Bethlehem, Connecticut, where AML and CAL sometimes went for retreats.
†Dwight Morrow Jr. had married Nancy Lofton in November 1970.

spend Christmas with them in Vermont and then go to the Philippines, via Maui, in January. I also think it would be nice if Reeve and Richard and the baby came to Maui in February? I think they'd both like to, if Richard could do some photography out there. And it would be good for her.

Reeve is very happy to be having a baby, so this is really a wonderful piece of news. (I should have told you on the telephone but I was too startled.)

I will give this to Mrs. Swanson to mail and I hope you get it and will be thinking about it—positive suggestions while flying home. (You see, I'm not *all* negative!)

It is very beautiful here now. The trees are all in tiny buds, the forsythia blazing yellow, and daffodils coming up on our slopes. One can eat out on the terrace and the birds are singing early in the morning. The dogwood and the fruit trees are still to bloom—just showing buds. Oh, why go to the Philippines the most beautiful month of the year in Connecticut?! Think about it!

XO XO

A.

Darien

Saturday, June 12th, 1971

Dearest Ansy—

Yesterday after calling you in the hospital (I hope it was not horribly inconvenient. I did not realize there was no phone in your room and there was so much difficulty in getting you: fragments of conversation from operators—French and U.S.A.—and nurses kept leaking through; the U.S. transatlantic operator could not speak French, and the nurse who answered in the hospital had no English, and I felt that my call was really stirring up a hornets' nest) and hearing your voice, I felt very much better. The telegram was somewhat garbled so your news about the three-and-a-half-hour labor was the first I heard of that.

I then rushed into New York for an emergency dentist's appointment, and came back to find your long and magnificent letter written on the day your Constance was born! It is a marvelous description both of the baby and the labor. I am staggered by your strength and your total awareness and your articulateness. (Perhaps someday this should find its way into a book. I am going to have it copied so Reeve can read it. I wish *I* had read it before I had a baby! Though that seems a bit topsy-turvy.) I'm glad you had a good midwife and assistant. They sound strong and helpful, though the hospital does sound a bit off-hand (but I guess they're not about the important moments).

Your description of the last hour and a half is superb. I can remember that feeling too, "as if I were tumbling down an endless precipice in an avalanche," and "It was stronger than I was, and I only *just* got through it with my breathing," and "It was almost unbearable, but not painful—just too strong for me." (I know just what you mean—I felt I was the whole earth giving birth.)

I am glad you can look at your baby through the glass of the little nursery. It is such a joy to keep looking at them because one really can't believe it and has to realize it freshly each time. It is really such a *present* each time they bring the baby in! I'm sorry about the after-pains. I can remember them. You don't get them with the first baby.

I called Reeve last night, but she was out when I called, and we had to go out for supper. I left the news with Richard. She called me back this morning and I could give her the news in your letter. She was so excited and it was fun to share it. She likes it that Constance is Tuesday's child (Reeve was too). Now, what were you? ("Fair of Face?") I can look it up. Your father is very happy too, and full of admiration for your courage and gaiety (he read the letter), and keeps saying: "Think of Ansy with a little daughter!"

Do rest, and don't get up too early. The labor was *not* easy. You have given birth to a world and you are bound to have a reaction. And it will take some time to get back to your usual strength. The day you go home is the worst, even though it's a joy. Even joy is exhausting. Be careful, darling.

XOXOXOXO
Mother

Planorbe
Saturday, July 10th, 1971
Dear Helen [Wolff],

Your letter of July 6th (on the jacket designs* and containing the November 15th, 1921, letter to ERM† about wanting to go to Vassar)

---

*For AML's first volume of letters and diaries, *Bring Me a Unicorn: Diaries and Letters, 1922–1928* (New York: Harcourt Brace Jovanovich, 1972).
†AML's elder sister, Elisabeth Reeve Morrow.

has just come. It is unfortunately Saturday, and the Swiss post offices close at noon (now past).

However I will write you immediately and mail it in Lausanne tonight (I am going in to go to a ballet with Monica.* Monica will know if there is—or where there is—a Sunday pick-up, and also how much to put on for special delivery in New York. You remember all her letters are always sent express!)

Now, to get to question (1) The Jacket. I have no objection to a photograph of me, of the period the volume covers, on the cover. I'd like to see the photographs, of course. I think it's rather a good idea, as it is self-explanatory. I am trying to think of what else would be better—the homes we lived in? No, rather dull. I think snapshots, family, pictures, group or action pictures would be better than the posed studio portrait kind of thing. But this we can all mull over. (Charles writes that he has found *thousands* of new photographs.) Anyway, for now, in principle, I am not opposed to this suggestion.

Now, on the new letter, which I remember very well. I think you have a good point, it does show a sense of independence trying to assert itself. And the letter comes into a period (Chapin School) where we have very little material and cut a lot out. The main problem I see is where to put this letter. It is dated November 1921, before the opening letter to Grandma Cutter from Scotland. The Scotland letter sounds much younger and is a far better entrance to the volume, I think, introducing everyone in the family, as you once remarked. I think the best place is after the Sunday, September 17th, 1922, diary insert. Elisabeth is at college and I am writing from New York (or Englewood). I don't think it should go after the 1923 letter to ECM because it makes too abrupt a volte-face with the succeeding letter to ECM from Smith College freshman year (September 23, 1924). Could you omit the date of the Vassar letter entirely?

As for the cuts, I have cut more heavily than you, as I think it is quite long and rather repetitious. I am returning the photostatted letter. I think my cuts are quite clear on the text itself. The only thing I suggest putting back in is the P.S. because I think it ends the letter better. It sounds less like a wail (an impossible wish). The P.S. is stronger and shows I was, sometimes, strong with E. Actually, in the end, of course, I did give in—chiefly, as I remember, because E. wrote me back rather

*Monica Stirling (1916–), British novelist and biographer, and a good friend of AML's.

a sermon about how selfish I was being ("When you think of all that Mother has done for you, you could do this little thing to make her happy"!) and I backed down. I never could resist a "moral" argument.

Please don't ever say anything about "forgiving" you for a "business letter." You are doing all this to make my book a better one, and I can only be grateful for such continued and painstaking concern about it. Charles says in his letter to me: "Helen Wolff is a wonderful woman: extraordinary ability, tact, skill, and consideration." I feel the same way. What you are doing certainly seems "beyond the call of duty." This is all for now—much love—

Anne

Planorbe
September 5th, 1971
Dear Betty,*

Your letter of late June was forwarded to me here by boat mail (six weeks) and when I recovered it, I was deep in last details of a manuscript due to be published next spring of *Diaries and Letters*. (The kind of thing one finds oneself occupied with at the end of one's life—going over old records, cutting, destroying and deciding what may be worth publishing.) I was much moved by your letter and wanted to answer it right away—though you generously and thoughtfully said not to—and here I am, three months later, trying to set down some of my thoughts about it.

I think my strongest feeling was that of wanting to argue with you about your statement that "sometimes you think" that "the gods have decided" to balance your "happy, varied and adventurous life" so far with "a stretch of the opposite."

I simply cannot believe that suffering and joy are meted out that way by fate or the gods. In any case, it seems to me you have had your share of suffering even before these last anguishing months, with your arthritis, your trouble with your eyes, your sister's harrowing death, etc. I don't think one earns or deserves suffering—or even that "suffering teaches." If suffering taught, all the world would be wise.

I *do* believe suffering, like joy, can open certain doors—if one is ready to walk through them or open one's eyes and see what is there. Joy does this very easily. It seems to me the heart is opened by joy, and then perhaps one is better able to accept pain. And I am glad for all of the

---

*Betty van Dusen, wife of Pitney van Dusen, theological writer, professor, and president of Union Theological Seminary.

joy that you and Pitney have had, for I think it does help one to see life whole. And suffering certainly opens certain doors that joy cannot open, inasmuch as it brings some understanding, or opportunity for understanding. I can, with difficulty, see some use for it, but not as rewards and punishments. (I know you said this perhaps lightly, and it is what we all feel at times—I often—but I think it is Puritan and unhelpful.)

If you have learned to live from day to day, you have learned what the saints and holy men have always told us was the only way to live. But we don't listen, and find it impossible to do, and never learn. I think of Amey who, approaching ninety, had a very serious operation for cancer, and who said when convalescing from the operation, "For the first time in my life I am learning to live from day to day."

You and Pitney both have given the world of your time a great deal: books, thoughts, inspiration, comfort, gaiety, love of beauty and poetry. But perhaps the example of courage, acceptance, and the ability of living from day to day is one of the most important gifts you could give to your children and those friends who know you—just what you are giving now.

I get back in another month and will go on working on the letters and diaries (second volume).* This will go on, I suppose, until I die. There are often lovely things in them about Elisabeth—and also you and Pitney.

Much love and many thoughts to you both,
Anne

November 30th, 1971
Dear Ansy,

Here it is, November 30th. Reeve is two days late—and maybe two weeks late, who knows?—and very restless. However, when I called her night before last, she said they were glad the baby didn't come on Thanksgiving day as they couldn't possibly have gotten out. (The roads are plowed in Vermont, even driveways, but not immediately.) There was a real blizzard. Reeve said she had decided, if they got caught, to ski down to the neighbors (about a mile) on her cross-country skis, stopping for pains. They are on a main road and can always get out with a Jeep or tractor. I was somewhat aghast. "Don't you have a toboggan?" I asked. "Richard could pull you."

"Oh, *Mother*," Reeve protested, "that would be *much* more danger-

---

Hour of Gold, Hour of Lead: Diaries and Letters, 1929–1932 (New York: Harcourt Brace Jovanovich, 1973).

ous." And I had memories of those poor skiers with broken legs, being pulled down the mountain by the ski-patrol boys!

It seems, though, that they *could* call the State Police, who would come in a ski-mobile (if their telephone is not cut by a storm). The vision of Reeve in the middle of the night, with a flashlight, skiing down to the next farm for her first baby is something awesome. It must be the Scandinavian blood.

We have had a great deal of rain here (snow on Thanksgiving), which is snow in Vermont. But today the weather is clearing and supposed to be clear for the next few days. I hope the baby chooses a clear night.

The White House called to get hold of your father because Admiral (Jerry) Land had died.* He was ninety-two and a marvelous man all his life: gay, warm, and witty—as well as a great head of the Merchant Marine. He was not ill long and had been to a football game the week before. He had a stroke, and everyone was relieved he did not live to be paralyzed. He did not apparently suffer. Your father will miss him, though; it is a last link with his mother. And he and Jerry used to tease each other. I again said I could not go to the service—though in this case I would like to pay my respects to such a gallant man.

I'm afraid I won't get into town again to shop and have no presents for anyone, including your two enchanting children—though I might get to Burch Books.

XOXOXO
Mother

Vermont
December 1971
Dearest Ansy,

Reeve came home yesterday from the hospital (called the "Bright Look" hospital! Rather nice small brick building like a New England hotel). Richard and I went to get her with the carrying basket. The baby[†] looks rather like Richard with Reeve's nose. Lots of dark hair (which may not last, of course), a turned-up nose, eyes wide apart (like Reeve), rather a wide mouth like Richard's, dimple in the chin—ditto. The shape of the head and the general coloring of the skin are like Richard, a ruddy look—not pale like Reeve.

---

*Vice Admiral Emory Scott ("Jerry") Land (1879–1971) was a first cousin of CAL's mother. He was a highly decorated naval architect, specializing in submarine construction.
†Elizabeth Lindbergh Brown.

The baby is quite calm and happy, nurses well, and sleeps content-edly—"looks" around quite alertly when awake, cries heartily for her meals right on the dot. I think she won't be too difficult a baby.

Still lots of snow all around the house, which is just as well as it's warmer in the house. There is really no heat upstairs except what comes up through registers from the floor below, but Reeve has a heater in her room and I have one in mine. I think the bedroom can be kept quite warm. But it's the kitchen where one lives, cooks, eats and sits. It opens into a sort of utility entrance room to the back door, where the washer, dryer, freezer are—and everybody's snow boots, coats, etc. hanging on hooks.

There *is* a living room (*and* a front door), but it's still full of cartons of unopened books, records, old furniture left by the former owner, saw-dust, planks, etc. This room opens onto the front veranda (now banked with snow), has a fireplace and a big bay window. It will be quite nice when they clean it out and fix it up, as it gets the sun most of the day. (The kitchen gets none and faces northeast.) I can do the cooking (such as it is), washing, shopping, and cleaning up. Reeve does everything for the baby and has her right next to her bed. She has Richard change and burp her! I keep thinking of your saying, "*Any way* you can get a diaper on a baby is all right."

I must stop now—Heavens! It's after one and I must get lunch for everyone, and go to Peacham and mail letters, etc. Reeve says she misses you *terribly*. If only she could see you and talk to you. "There's no one else like her—no one." Richard was quite impressed by your mushroom pictures.

Much love darling—
Love—love—
Mother

Peacham, Vermont
December 14th, 1971
Dear Monica [Stirling],

I have had this letter addressed for weeks, but it has been a crowded period. Helen came out for the weekend with the first draft of Vol-ume II of my *Diaries and Letters*—and wanted me to get onto it so we could have a new typewriter draft before I go to Maui. Helen—poor woman—worked on it all summer to get it in first shape—not to hurry me, but to give me more time to think about it. It is very hard to go over from many points of view and I won't know *what* I really want to publish—or feel it's right to publish—until I start writing the introduction. I won't know what I *think* until I start to write about it, and this will take real solitude and uninterrupted concentration, not to be had until Maui, I fear. (Late January?)

Helen seemed in surprisingly good form for not having had any vacation really this summer. Of course, she works much too hard and, I guess, has to, for her peace of mind as well as the outer pressures of publishing. We walked a little and fed my wild ducks in the cove, but mostly it was just going over the material.

At one point, going out to feed the ducks, I lent her a "hot pink" raincoat of mine and, looking at her, I was struck with how nice it was on her: "That's a lovely color on you," I said. And she answered (a little apologetically): "I guess it's a part of my widowhood that I don't wear bright colors." (However, at supper that night she put on a Thai silk blouse, a lovely muted Chinese-red color, that Kurt had given her.) I tell you this only to give you a picture of what she carries all the time without saying anything about it. It is this pall of loss which, I feel, makes her work herself to death. I do not know what any of us can do about it.

I have been very busy. Not with the baby—Reeve does everything for her—but doing all those things that make a house go: shopping, cooking, washing up, doing the baby clothes (in a washer and dryer), and feeding family as well as the cats, dogs, and birds at the window. After I have cleared up the breakfast dishes, I take the scraps and a can of cat food and some milk out to the big red barn where the cats live. This means putting on socks and snow boots and parka and scarf, as there is snow on the ground and it is sometimes *very* cold (20 degrees below zero the other morning). *Five* cats come prancing out over the snow to meet me! My favorite is a black cat: very furry and elegant with green eyes. She is the mother of one tigerish kitten. There is another big gray mother with two gray tigery kittens (same father?). Except at feeding time, they are all very wild. There is also a cart-horse (a Belgian) in the barn, but Richard feeds him. He is very sweet, enormous, and furry.

After two weeks I am quite used to my routine, although in the snow and cold all ordinary chores take on a kind of challenge (can I get up the slippery hill to the general store? Or through the snow to the mailbox?)

This is not a well-organized letter, written in bits and patches, and it will not get to you before Christmas as I hoped. Although I am desperately busy and active here, it is a happy life in this beautiful snowy country, and in a family that is happy with the new baby. I enjoy my work and though I drop into bed every night dead tired, it is satisfying to be needed and helpful—and it is very positive to be with the young who are gay and warm and compassionate and hopeful. Life in Vermont is not so unlike life in Switzerland and I feel less "homesick." I think of you often as I walk out to meet the prancing dancing cats with my basket of scraps. (I will be back soon in Darien—after Xmas.) DO give my *amitiés* to Nesta* and Mme Christen† (whom I bless for the exercises that I do each morning and evening, which keep me going).

Much love to you from Anne

Bainbridge Island [Puget Sound]
Monday, January 10th, 1972
Darling Reeve,

We are safely here. Dick‡ met us at the airport and took us straight to the hospital. He was very cheerful and said how much better Jon and Barbara looked—and were—but it was still a shock to see Barbara (first) and Wendy in wheelchairs in the visiting hall. (A friend of Barbara's had brought all the boys in to see their father and mother for the first time—a relief to all of them.)

Barbara is thin and drawn and pale and looks as if she were in pain, but she isn't in much. Her neck is stiff as a board and she looks like that. She has been under great strain and worry about Jon. But nothing is wrong with her seriously—the broken ribs will heal, and the tension lessen in the stiff back. Wendy, also in a wheelchair, looked pretty; the scar will hardly show when healed. Her arm is also cut and bandaged.

We then went in, one by one, to see Jon, still in the intensive care room. He was sitting up and, except for a bandaged chin, looked very natural. He talked and understood and responded to all I said, hesitating only once or twice over names (as I do all the time with *no* concussion!). He was terribly happy to see us (I almost wept at that), all the defenses down. And I just held his good hand (the other arm is broken), and told him how happy I was to be there. We also saw the doctor, who again remarked on his rapid improvement and said the slowness of remembering names would disappear completely. He will have to be perhaps

*Nesta Obermeier, a British expatriate and friend, daughter of Sir Francis Younghusband (1863–1942), British army officer and explorer whom the Lindberghs met on early flying trips.
†Eliette Christen, a Swiss physiotherapist.
‡Dick Robbins, brother of Barbara Robbins Lindbergh.

two weeks more in the hospital, but today they have moved him out of intensive care (where all the crash victims are put and are moaning and groaning), into a room near Barbara. She can go in and see him whenever she wants.

They are taking more tests today to be sure there are no clots in the brain. He will have to take medication for a year or two and will not be able to drive for a while, but all this is normal recovery for a bruise on the brain. He is now reading and rather bored and likes visitors. His broken arm and kneecap do bother him a bit but he is not in pain. He can't move much but they don't want to set them (i.e., give him a deep anesthetic) until they are sure the anesthetic will not threaten the healing process of the brain.

He asked me about you and the baby. (I told him how worried you were about him and how I had been reporting his progress to you.)

Krissie has been carrying on here like a pioneer woman. She was the only one who can remember anything about the accident. They were hit by a car without lights, on the wrong side of the road, driven by a man without a license who was drunk and who hid in the woods afterwards! Krissie was on the side of the car that was hit; the door flew open and she climbed out and pulled her mother and Wendy out. She could not extricate Jon, who was caught in the crushed car; she thinks they had to use an axe. She went with them in an ambulance to the clinic and then to the hospital (Jon and Barbara were both knocked out completely), then back to the house and carried on with the children and has been doing it ever since! A neighbor came in for the first days, but Krissie has organized all the driving, planning, etc., and is now, I hope, going to bring us in it.

I am obviously very much needed here, though how I wish I were as experienced a cook as *you* are! What I need is a manual on feeding an army! Do send me any *easy* recipes you have, including the applesauce meatballs that I left behind (if you have any time—which you won't—it *isn't* important). I must now get to the washer and dryer. This afternoon Krissie takes me to Winslow to learn the shopping technique. Jon would love a letter, I think.

Argonauta
Sunday, March 12th, 1972
Darling Reeve,

Your long letter, written in the snowstorm while Richard was at the town meeting, is here on the desk and I've just read it over again. You are probably now over the mood but I have to answer it anyhow. I ached when I read it (about wanting to write and feeling you never would) and smiled, too.

I wish you could read the diaries I am now working on, where I say the same things, harshly, to myself. "You say you want to write but what have you ever done to show for it?" etc. I was then expecting my second baby and was very gloomy and self-castigating about everything. ("What have I ever done but take—take—take all my life—never given back," etc.) But I *was* carrying a baby and that is not a good time to write; you are putting everything creative into a child. The same is true of you now. You should not be trying to write *now*—at least, not anything structured like a novel or a short story. There is, as you say, not enough time (for a sustained effort) and too much time (for self-criticism). For heaven's sake, don't make this a test period. You are nursing a baby, which takes a lot of energy and is a time of wordless communication. And you are recovering from the nine months of pregnancy—and now the change back to "normal life" which isn't quite normal yet. You say when you try to write you get "plunged into gloom, resent the baby, and dislike" yourself, all indications that you are tired and haven't enough extra energy. You are driving yourself at the wrong moment.

I *do* think you will write. I feel quite sure of it—but in what way or when I wouldn't know. I think you *will* write because you are incredibly perceptive about people and relationships and life situations, because you have a feeling for words and images and a drive to express yourself. And also a strong sense of cadence in a phrase.

You say you can't find your own voice. It is true what Richard says, that people always start by imitating. But I think there are other ways of "finding your own voice" than by imitating—and hating every word you put down. (Yes, I often feel like that, and words are clod-heavy blocks of wood, not a writer's tools at all.) You say you "have a hard time identifying 'yourself' in the crowd of other people's writings." All this adds up to the same thing: not hearing your own voice. I think you should try to find it.

My first suggestion is to stop reading! Or at least, to stop reading the kind of things you think you'd like to write. This makes you compare yourself all the time and makes it harder to hear your own voice. Read something different: poetry or anthropology or education or something quite unrelated, just for fun. (Poetry might be good because if you read it a lot, you might start writing in that form, which doesn't take such a sustained effort. You could jot down things—ideas, images, even as you nursed.)

Then start writing. Just a little—scraps—every day, a diary or a record of the baby, or anything trivial—but *of the day*, of *where you are now*. This is not to produce anything. It is just practice in being aware and will show you how much you observe, see, feel, and can articulate. Like your record of teaching, which you did when you were tired, but which has your voice in it. Don't try to make it a continuous record—just jottings down, scraps, observations: the birds, the cats, the snow, Molly, and people. I think if you do it steadily but not obsessively, you will find you enjoy it and you will eventually "find your own voice." It might not even be a notebook—just a folder with scraps of ideas in it. It's the daily putting down of observations that helps you to feel where you are. It's going against the grain to try to be where you're not. (Does this make any sense? It is a little like Krishnamurti saying you must be aware of all the outer things first: the tree, the sky, the cat, someone's face.)

There is a lot more to say but now I must go water those 115 cuttings (I planted ten more after your father left) before it gets dark. As I put on my old sneakers and take the trowel and hose and especially as I squish the muddy water with my wet sneakers, I see Mrs. Woodbridge in her old shorts, hair over her eyes, and hear Mr. W. saying pontifically, "My little girl has never been so happy as puttering around this place!"

Have finished the watering, almost, by dark. Some of the hibiscus cuttings have tiny sprouts, after ten days. Your father has been away ten days and will probably be away ten more. (Did he tell you?) He is flying from Mexico straight to the Philippines for an emergency—on the Monkey-Eating Eagle and the tribal situation. I am very disappointed, as I expected him back today. However, I don't feel as desperate as I did last year. (No floods, no mud, no rats—so far.) I have lots of work to do and am working hard at the introduction to Volume II (quite difficult, but it interests me).

Despite the lovely weather and beauty of the sea and sky, if I'm going to live alone, I'd rather be in Darien or Switzerland where I could telephone you or Ansy or Scott, and occasionally see you and your child—children! However, this year it's probably just as well I'm away from home with the pressure from the first volume and quite a lot of work to get through before June.

Speaking of writing—who is a writer? When does one qualify? Virginia Woolf, Elizabeth Bowen, Eudora Welty, Flannery O'Connor,

Jean Stafford? None of whom, as far as I know, had children. A woman writer is, to quote a nineteenth century writer, "rowing against wind and tide."* We cannot—or only with the greatest difficulty—produce a great "body of work." Why—as John Barkham, a reviewer I once met [asks about me]—"as an eager and talented writer [has] she published so relatively little in 40 years of marriage? After a promising start with those first books on flying, she tapered off into long silences broken by an infrequent volume of verse or prose." He is, of course, right and it still bothers me: the books I didn't write. In fact, I don't consider myself "a writer" but a woman who sometimes wrote.

And it isn't just being a woman. It is some other deeper conflict between art and life. Yeats wrote a number of remarkable poems on the conflict between "perfection of the work or of the life," which tortured him also. But he was a real poet and writer, and that side won out. With me, I think "perfection of the life"—the "why" or the "whether" of life—haunted me more. (Or one might say the religious point of view interested me more, or the understanding of life—psychological or religious—and I wrote less because of this obsession.)

So how much one writes, or in what form one writes, or how soon one writes isn't the most important thing. One has to live one's life and follow one's thrust, whatever it is. One reason I think you'll write is that you're married to Richard and he is an artist (one of the few genuine ones I've ever met). And he respects and recognizes the creative process and he will back you in your creative efforts. (I think Julien does the same for Anne.)

It is now time for the climb into bed, to read one of those sleep-producing paperbacks. It is a fairly peaceful life although isolated. I am rested, sleep, and look better than I did a month ago. I am working hard, which is satisfying and which I probably wouldn't be doing at home (you have to be quite bored and lonely to work this hard).

The land is somewhat lifeless here (no animals except mongooses and rats), but the sea is very alive and I see great whales (or their spouts and tails) quite often. The marvelous thing about whales is their rhythm—great, slow, and ponderous, like the Pacific: easy rolls and flips

---

*Harriet Beecher Stowe's metaphor, in a letter to her sister, for the effort it took to write novels while caring for a husband and seven children: "I have been called off at least a dozen times . . . to nurse the baby, then into the kitchen to make a chowder for dinner, and now I am at it again, for nothing but deadly determination enables me ever to write: it is rowing against wind and tide. . . ."

as if they were playing and not in a hurry, like elephants in Africa. They are totally in tune with the element they inhabit.

Must go to bed—much love, darling. Don't agonize over the writing—I'm sure you'll work out your life right.

XO XO
Mother

Argonauta
Monday, April 3rd, 1972
Dearest Ansy,

I must say, Father has really done it this time! "Lindbergh and the anthropologists have been living in isolation with the 24 surviving short, dark-skinned Tasadays for about two weeks." "The world's only surviving cave-men . . . on the side of a steep mountain deep in the southern Philippine rain forest," etc. Yesterday morning (listening to the news after the Jon L.'s all left for home after their week's vacation), I was startled to hear about their helicopter having broken down and their running short of supplies. I listened all morning but heard nothing more. In the evening, my neighbors brought me a Sunday paper saying the expedition had radioed for help and that an Air Force helicopter was going to rescue them, equipped with winches to pull team members up to the helicopter. No news this morning.

I don't know anyone better equipped to survive in the jungle than your father. He probably will *enjoy* eating the cave-men's food (if there is any left over) of "roots, palm pith, flowers and jungle vegetation." But how about those other forty-four anthropologists? Can they digest it?

And the thought of a helicopter pulling up the forty-eight members of the expedition, through a dense tropical forest with trees 45 to 150 feet high gives me nightmares. I hope there will be some news today. Sam Pryor (of Pan American), who is my neighbor, was going to try to get some information through Pan Am in Honolulu. I wish the Jon L.'s had not gone; we could talk about it. They had really a very good week, although incredibly strenuous. They tumbled out of their rented ranch wagon late Sunday evening, looking pale and wilted after a five-to-six-hour plane ride, then a short plane hop to Kahului, on the other end of this island, and then a three-hour drive down this tortuous cliff road, mostly by night. I had swept, made beds, prepared hamburgers and salad and flitted all the windows and doors for ants. They were too tired to eat, but drank gallons of milk and went to bed. Barbara had bought a mountain of food for the whole week (better stores in Kahului). And we had to rearrange the icebox to get the most perishable packed inside.

I had not put up the tent, so the two little boys slept on cots up in the two-bed guest room, with Krissie and Wendy in the twin beds. And Lars and Leif slept on air mattresses on the living room floor (like the chalet), and Barbara and Jon in the double bedroom downstairs.

It was midnight Seattle time before they got to sleep, but everyone was up at six the next morning, with pancakes at the counter (cooked by Krissie), before they all disappeared into the landscape—Lars and Leif to explore caves in the cliff and to the beach to watch for whales and porpoise, Krissie and Wendy—in short shorts and long long mermaid hair—to the Pryors' guest cottage to find the Pryor grandchildren, also here for vacation (one of them is a very attractive boy about Krissie's age, with whom she has corresponded; I suspect collusion on their vacation). Only Morgan and Erik were left roughhousing around the terrace. Jon got up late and looked rested, and we all went swimming in the Pryors' waterfall-pool at 12:30.

Since then, the days have flown and merged into one another so I can't remember. The tent was put up and various people slept in it. Barbara and Krissie did most of the cooking. I shopped (for sleeping bags, fishing rods, hooks and bait, more knives and forks, sun helmets, yogurt, dry cereal, and gallons and gallons of milk). But Barbara also seemed to have time to make jars of guava jelly and jam! (Picked from wild guava trees in the back of our house.)

She also helped me put up curtains and plant flowers. Jon led us all on a long hike up a canyon to a very high waterfall. (He walks with a slight stiffness but can take long walks and has quite a lot of flexibility.) We swam every day (very good for Jon). The little boys had snorkels and loved it. We hardly saw Krissie and Wendy at all; they were always off with the Pryor boys, who had brought their motorcycles! Leif spent most of his time fishing (I am still finding moldy bits of octopus bait in my icebox). Lars collected what he thought were Hawaiian stone grinders and bowls (granite stones which I will keep as door stops since Barbara refused to pack them and lug them home). (How "we gather as we travel—bits of moss and dirty gravel.")* And yesterday morning early,

*From the poem "Robinson Crusoe's Story," by Charles E. Carryl, in *Modern American Poetry: An Introduction*, edited by Louis Untermeyer (New York: Harcourt, Brace and Howe, 1919).

they all left with sunburned noses and wet bathing suits in plastic bags. Barbara took two jars of guava jelly and the rest are on my shelves.

I spent the rest of the day gloomily defrosting the icebox and throwing out Leif's bait—in between listening for news on the radio. I've also discovered there's a mongoose hiding in the house, under the icebox or the washer-dryer. (There were so many doors left open all week and mongooses love to come in and look around for food.) I keep finding his spore, which is long and narrow, just like everything else about a mongoose: long tail, nose, etc. In fact, you might say a mongoose was all nose—or all tail—whichever way you look at it. I have now put half an old hamburger on a paper plate *outside* the cracked living room door, hoping to lure him *out*. But perhaps it will only lure other mongooses *in*?

Much love to everyone. Must now start to eat my way through the leftover food in the icebox. I love hearing about all Charles Feydy's marvelous games and conventions—constructions. I wish I could see Constance sit down, letting go backwards—an act of faith—a crucial part.

XOXOXOXO
Mother

Scott's Cove
November 21st, 1972
Dearest Ansy—

I meant to write you on or after Reeve's weekend home (two weeks ago). She arrived with Elizabeth, Richard, Molly, and two kittens she had got from a Tibetan retreat near Barnet. (She has named them "Dalai" and "Lama" after the Dalai Lama!) Also, a young poet* I met at the Benedictine seminar and his wife arrived for Saturday evening, and your father unexpectedly turned up Saturday night. Full house!

It rained off and on all weekend. Richard went to town all Saturday and practiced on his flute all Sunday, while Reeve and I walked (in the rain) with the baby carriage and the dogs and the poet and his wife.

Reeve and I snatched your manuscript† out of your father's mail. I read it first, straight through again, with just as much excitement. The end is *much* better, I think, a great improvement. Reeve then read it straight through. She said she couldn't criticize it at all, she was so inter-

---

*Stephen Mitchell (1943–), American poet and translator.
†The manuscript for *Osprey Island*, a children's book by Anne Lindbergh Feydy that would be published by Houghton Mifflin in 1974.

ested. Lastly (because he came home after we'd read it) your father read it and I know he has sent you a long letter about it. Chiefly, he thought (in criticism) that it was rather slow at the start, though once you got into it, it was very, very good. He thought the end could be tightened. I'm not sure; I was satisfied with the end. I am not sure the beginning isn't a little slow—perhaps I gave you a wrong steer by suggesting you put in more Paris background (that could all be easily cut down).

Thanksgiving a.m.: very cold but bright and sunny
Krissie and her roommate, Rebecca (Kellogg from Concord, Mass.), arrived yesterday afternoon in blue jeans and pigtails, with knapsacks on their backs. They drove down in Rebecca's car. Rebecca is blond and Krissie is dark but they are both quite tall and look alike—like over-grown little girls. (Krissie is now called "Kristina" by her college mates. The telephone has been ringing for "Kristina.") I gather they are planning on seeing *all* their classmates who live around N.Y. during these three days. We went out and fed the ducks and geese from "nut island" in the coppery sunset, then they sat on the sofa and played duets on their recorders while I cooked supper. At the *last* moment, I learned that Rebecca is a vegetarian, so threw in a frozen cheese soufflé. (Maybe we can make that marvelous mushroom pie you sent me the recipe for. Krissie loves to cook.)

We asked them about Middlebury—very interesting but *very* hard, also bad food—this is true of all colleges. Your father asked them whether they studied problems of natural selection and the genetic pool and they looked baffled but listened attentively. Kristina likes her writing classes, especially poetry, and she and Rebecca are taking a religion-philosophy class they like. And they have bought a secondhand upright piano with no back, which they have squeezed in their tiny room, and both play.

I have been buried in 1,100 pages of new, uncut, unsorted, and unpunctuated manuscript (Volume III)*—very dull, painstaking work. And your father is sorting out his mail for the past six months. It is all spread out over the living room tables, chairs, and sofas. His "study" has turned into a storeroom and it is so full of bins of mail, boxes of books, magazines, files, etc. that he no longer works there. He will be around a while now, since he is working a lot [with] old records, letters, etc. for

---

Locked Rooms and Open Doors: Diaries and Letters, 1933–1935 (New York: Harcourt Brace Jovanovich, 1974).

two books that are being written about his father and grandfather. He commutes back and forth to New York or the Yale Library. We plan to go to Reeve's for Christmas, but probably won't get to Maui until February.

I'm afraid I won't do anything for Christmas because I am so chained to my desk on this infuriating detail work. It isn't "writing" at all. It is criticism, and seeing how bad it is. It is also like doing endless puzzles—fitting things into holes. However, it makes your father happy and he is encouraging, "Oh, *don't* cut that—it's interesting!" (Helen doesn't always agree!)

It has been a rather funny fall: the wettest November on record. And it seems to me so many friends are ill or dying (I have just reached that age when that class above me is dropping out) or have some chronic disease or a curtailed life. Aunt Edith is still going strong, but Dr. A. has lost the sight of one eye. Alan Valentine is almost deaf. Uncle Dwight had a clot that (temporarily) paralyzed his arm. Corliss* was in the hospital with phlebitis and Ellie Lamont just died of a stroke. (I saw *all* of the old guard—North Haven etc.—at her funeral service.) These are not accidents but the natural cycle of life. One has to accept it and be sympathetic, but it is nice to sprinkle one's acquaintances with the young, so that you don't see only the aging. Reeve and Richard and Elizabeth, Kristina and Rebecca and others. (I miss you and J. and Charles and Constance—but your letters are wonderful—and don't try to write too often—your own work is more important.)

Aunt Margot is ageless and has a beautiful big tent-like red coat that brings cheer whenever she sails into a room! I bought (this rainy month) a rosy-wine-colored velveteen raincoat, because I think one wants to put on something rosy on the rainy days. I also bought a long black and white plaid wool skirt and a pair of black and white plaid slacks, which I'm wearing today. Your father remarked at breakfast, "I don't *particularly* like those trousers." Ah me! I thought they were smart. (The way he said "*particularly*" made me realize that he "particularly" *dis*liked them.)

Kristina and Rebecca are reading your *Osprey Island* in front of the fire in the living room. I must get to my stint of manuscript pages—

XOXOXOXO

Mother

---

*Corliss Lamont (1902–1995), philanthropist and supporter of varied socialist and civil liberties causes. A onetime suitor of AML, he was a lifelong admirer.

January 21st, 1973

Dear Kristina,

It was lovely to get your letter to us and to hear so much about your Christmas in Maui. I am sorry about your flu, but perhaps I should be grateful since it gave you time to write us!

I was interested that you said you felt "very whole" during this vacation. I think feeling "whole" is very close to "holiness" and usually, when one feels that way, one is what in religious terms was called "in grace."

I don't think you ought to let the Arthurian legends and the "Quest for the Holy Grail" depress you. Let their beauty uplift you but don't try to *copy* them. They are evocative myths that need to be interpreted, not imitated. I think your instincts about "earthly things" are very sound. They *do* "go hand in hand with the spiritual" and one cannot cut them apart (as the Puritans sometimes did).

Your letter sent me back to an old prayer of St. Augustine that I've always liked, though it is stated in old-fashioned language, and which I think expresses it very well: "O Lord our God, under the shadow of Thy wings let us hope. Thou wilt support us, both when little, even to gray hairs. When our strength is of Thee, it is strength; but when our own, it is feebleness. We return unto Thee, O Lord, that from their weariness our souls may rise toward Thee, *leaning on the things which Thou hast created, and passing on to Thy-self, who hast wonderfully made them*, for with Thee is refreshment and true strength."

Then I have been reading Teilhard de Chardin*—a Jesuit who was considered a rebel and his works were not allowed by the church to be published until after his death, about the time you were born. He felt passionately that matter was spiritual and wrote a great deal on this subject, including a *Hymn of the Universe* in which I found recently another quotation I liked: "What would become of our souls, Lord, if they lacked the bread of earthly reality to nourish them, the wine of created beauty to intoxicate them, the discipline of human struggle to make them strong? What puny powers and bloodless hearts your creatures would bring to you were they to cut themselves off *prematurely* from the Providential setting in which you have placed them!"

Both these writers were *within* the body of the church and spoke in

---

*Pierre Teilhard de Chardin (1881–1955) was a Jesuit priest, paleontologist, geologist, and philosopher whose writings on theology and evolution brought him into conflict with the Catholic church, and whose teachings continue to influence writers, artists, and philosophers.

its language but you can also read someone like the philosopher Alfred North Whitehead, who had a much broader view. He was also a mathematician and a scientist and quite modern in his views—but a very spiritual man. He is quoted as defining God as "the creative force in the universe" and goes on to say: "God is *in* the world, or nowhere, creating continually in us and around us. This creative principle is everywhere, in animate and so-called inanimate matter, in the ether, water, earth, human hearts. But this creation is a continuing process, and the process is itself the actuality, since no sooner do you arrive than you start on a fresh journey. Insofar as man partakes of this creative process does he partake of the divine, of God, and that participation is his immortality, reducing the question of whether his individuality survives death of the body to the estate of an irrelevancy. His true destiny as co-creator in the universe is his dignity and his grandeur."

This letter is now so long that you will need another day in bed to read it! Sometime when you have a lot of time I will send you one of Teilhard de Chardin's books. His letters are wonderful because many of them are written to so-called "non-believers." He excluded no one, and his language in the letters is very direct and sympathetic. ("The world must have a God, but our concept of God must be extended as the dimensions of our world are extended.") His beliefs did not separate him from the world or people and he could write.

"May the Lord only preserve in me a passionate taste for the world, and a great gentleness; and may He help me pressure to the end in the fullness of humanity."

I am sure you will find your own way to journey toward your own "holy grail" and sitting in a tree in the woods is a good way to start. I used to sit on stumps and think things out—and writing it out is very very clarifying. It even helps to write only one's worries and fears and problems. Brought out to the light of day, the nightmares seem to wither to controllable proportions.

I'm glad you find it not so hard to talk in class. The more you do it, the less frightening it will be, and the clearer your thoughts will get. Although perhaps for you, as for me, thoughts are always clearer when one writes them out.

I hope this term is proving to be more expansive and freer—and more fun. I hope, when we get back from Maui—in April?—you and Rebecca will come for another weekend. We expect to leave here for Seattle and then Maui the end of the first week in February or the beginning of the second week. (Probably it will be the second week.)

Much love to you and my love to Rebecca. Thank her for her Christmas card, and congratulations on being eighteen!!

Granny-mouse

Argonauta
March 5th, 1973
D.D.

I was very glad to get your note on Mary—I was sure the operation would be hard on you as well as on her. I am grateful that there are no complications and some improvement, although "slow and reluctant." (I have puzzled over that last word—is the patient "reluctant" to get well, or is the hip "reluctant"? It is a good word, though—you always make a good and precise and delicate choice of words.)

You were *very* good to write me about CAL. I really thought he looked rather badly and had so little energy it was frightening. His friends here and elsewhere were rather shocked to see him so thin. I hope he will see the doctor here—a very nice and, I think, competent man—once a week. C. seemed to think they didn't have the equipment to take blood tests at this little hospital, but I'm not sure. In any case, he can make a twenty-minute flight to a big hospital at the other end of the island quite easily—go down in the morning and come back in the afternoon. (It is a three-hour drive on a very bumpy and winding tortuous road.)

I have finished a first draft of an introduction to Volume III but I'm not satisfied yet with it, or with the volume. The material is not as good in this volume—not as dramatic but also not as fully written or as universal. So I'm trying to explain more in the introduction, to try to make the experience more universal—otherwise it's not worth publishing. It was a neurotic period and that's harder to make universal, though goodness knows there are enough nuts around! (Only they don't recognize themselves as such.)

I am sitting up in bed writing. The ants are not too bad this year but the cockroaches terrify me—they scuttle so—and are so huge and evil looking. I spray them but they take so long to die it's awful and I can't sleep afterwards. Also there are lots of rats. I don't *see* them, just *hear* them at night and find their droppings everywhere: on the counters, under the bed, etc. They seem to eat everything—soap, curtains, plastic covers to the cookie jars, shoes, etc.—everything but poison. At night I am scared and read late and take a pill—but in the daytime I don't mind.

The weather has been beautiful but I'm not out too much. I work all morning at my table and then do light housekeeping midday or shop for groceries, which is an all-day expedition. But evenings—from four till six—are lovely. The wind, which blows ceaselessly all day, quiets down and I go out and weed our bushes or try to transplant something. The nicest hour is sunset—about 6:15—when I sit in my Sears Roebuck chaise longue on the terrace and have a drink and watch the sea and don't feel I have to do anything. I wish you were here for that!

Much love and thank you,

A.

Argonauta
March 6th, 1973, evening in bed
Dearest Margot,

It is terrible not to have written and it is ridiculous how little time there is to write—far less than at home. I work all morning on the introduction to Volume III, and the afternoons are taken up in doing the wash or sweeping out the dead ants or shopping in the general store. The maintenance of a house in the tropics with failing generators and intermittent water supply and *no* cleaning woman available is very time consuming. But still, these are purely physical problems and not like the nervous and emotional ones that attack one at home. The weather has been beautiful and though I am not outside much because of the logistics above, Con and I did swim twice and that was delicious.

It was very harmonious having them here and they were most good-natured and long-suffering guests: no electricity, lights (except kerosene), and two major water failures (no plumbing facilities!). Aubrey ate quantities of papaya and Con was so helpful with the cooking and washing up. We were quite busy, however, and I was grateful that she stayed two extra days after the two men left. We really could relax and pad around the house in our bedroom slippers and wrappers and eat minimal meals and talk a great deal—which was a great joy.

This is a rather odd unreal place, I think, but perhaps not as unreal as most resorts because our life is still so primitive, if sometimes difficult. It is very beautiful and is worth it at the end of the day when one can sit and have a drink and watch the sea, which is—at last in the evening—quiet and not roaring and pounding as it is with the trade winds the rest of the day.

Charles just loves it: loves the waves, the constant wind, the kerosene lamps, the generator that won't behave, the sudden rain squalls, etc. He likes battling with the elements and feeling he is in the wilderness. He is back in New York now for a meeting. I hope he returns soon, as he planned. He really needs the change and the rest this year, having lost pounds this winter with the equivalent of the Mexican "*tourista*" and a bad cold and cough on top of it. I think it's under control now, though it is a shock to everyone to see him so thin suddenly.

I am fine and beginning to settle into this life (after three weeks! It takes almost that long) but I do miss my "community" of sisters—especially *you*! I have very nice, kind and considerate neighbors, but no one really to talk to. But, of course, one works, and the beauty outside helps, and at night I find the tape recorder a great joy since it runs on batteries and I can have music. More than at home where one is always reading *every word* of the *New York Times* or filing mail or something. Here, because there is so little to do (except homework), no telephone and not much mail, one listens to waves, birds, wind—and music, if one wants.

It has been quite moving reading Volume III in the clear copy. There is much about you. I met you that winter and it was such a help. I always left you feeling exhilarated and freer. There were so few people to talk to then, and one had so little insight. It was a great discovery in my life and a great help that hard winter to know you. And when I read the descriptions of our talks I glow and think: Yes—it *was* like that—and it still *is*! I feel very lucky to have known you for so much of my life and hope you *take care* of yourself so we have some years left to go on talking!

Darien, Conn.
May 31st, 1973
Dear Stephen [Mitchell],

I am appalled by the time that has flown by since I received your letter of April. Actually it was also long in reaching me—forwarded to Maui—when I unexpectedly came home briefly to see Reeve, who fell off her horse and was quite seriously hurt (now all right) with a fractured skull, broken collarbone and concussion.

We have had a very odd and interrupted winter and fall. My husband, who has never been ill in his life, has not really been well since November: an obscure virus which, when finally gotten under control, left him very thin and rather down, followed by a prolonged attack of shingles, a real Job-like affliction (not serious but painful and *infuriating* to an active man). We stayed longer in Maui to help him recuperate, and came back to a spring that has telescoped into pressure-filled weeks (mostly finishing the manuscripts for publication—Volume III—extremely difficult and dull and painstaking work). I *hope* to finish, almost, this week.

All this explanation is only to tell you that I have been hoping to find a week—or a day—when I would be free to see you. . . . However, you may now be embarked on other plans, work or trips and the time for conversation may be past. . . .

In any case, I wanted to let you know that I was very happy to get your note and to hear that your experiment was successful and that you are "full of joy." Even if this joy at its most intense does not usually go on at that pitch, it is a great vision and liberation to have had it and the truth of it will remain at the core of your life and not be devalued by temporary eclipses.

With my love and thoughts and hopes for another meeting. Reeve and I spoke of you this last weekend when I went up to see her. She is writing again and spoke with gratitude of some of the things you had said to her—

Anne

June 8th, 1973
Dearest Ansy,

Your father came back from Paris very happy and full of enthusiasm for you, Julien, Charles and Constance. He had a wonderful visit and said he stayed on an extra day to help correct your book *Osprey Island*! I hope it was not too rigorous? I find it a great help and he is very perceptive in cutting out "deadwood" or "fat" as well as picking out the repetitions (the "very"s, "nice"s, "wonderful"s, etc.) in a manuscript. But I also find it exhausting and often discouraging. One loses the wood for the trees. One loses one's vision of the whole, or interrupts the life-rhythm by concentrating on the details. He is helpful but not always right—and he really does not insist but only suggests—so follow your own instincts once you've seen the corrections.

I have just had an intensive week of it. It seems to me I have been doing it all winter and spring. First my own corrections on the typescript, then CAL's corrections, then going over it together, then with Helen Wolff. Then a copy-editor went over it with a fine-toothed comb. Then I went over *his* corrections. Then CAL went over those. Then both of us together. Then Helen and I, etc. etc., ad infinitum. I am by now so thoroughly sick of the ego of the adolescent and young married AML I can hardly stand to publish it. It is not a very good book, most of it jotted down in shorthand and full of tumultuous ups and downs. Still, it is done now—except for the galleys, sometime in July. I only

hope Helen, who devours work, won't have the first copy of Volume IV*
ready for my perusal just after the galleys are done. I would like to get
onto something else.

Your father is a lot better—and even gained weight on his trip
abroad—What did you feed him? Love to everyone and two kisses for
Constance—

Mother

En route Kennedy → *Missoula*
June 8th, 1973
Dear Dwight [Morrow],

I was so pleased at your letter and that you liked Iris Origo's anthology.† It has given me a great deal of pleasure and I find it wonderful
to read at night before I go to sleep. One is taken up to another level
of eternal verities, and small troubles and distractions and worries are
left behind. I have found the same pleasure and nourishment from an
anthology *you* gave me (Elizabeth Goudge's *Book of Comfort*) which is
usually in the bookcase next to my bed.

You need not have written me but it was good to get your letter and
I was delighted that we both liked the same book—as well as having the
same traditions.

Speaking of traditions, I heard—partly humorous in a letter from
Nancy, and something from Margot—that you were somewhat interested in trying meditation for your health. As a non-Zen meditator—at
times—I thought I would tell of my experience with it. I have *not* gone
to any of the meditation groups, partly because I have no time but more
because I feel their approach (the young leaders), as I have heard about
it, seems somewhat superficial. I'm afraid that the bringing of a sum of
money, a flower, and a fruit, and being given "a mantra" to say while
meditating is too foreign to me; I could not do it naturally. I have met
and talked to various proponents of meditations—Zen, Buddhist, Indian,
etc.—and even been given instruction and read some books on it. And
I do find that setting aside two periods in the day for sitting quietly and
concentrating on my breathing does center me down and relieves the
pressure. I think of it not as "transcending" or becoming a Buddhist, but

---

The Flower and the Nettle: Diaries and Letters, 1936–1939, was published by Harcourt Brace
Jovanovich in 1976.
†*The Vagabond Path* (New York: Scribner, 1972). Dame Margaret Iris Origo (1902–1988) was
an Anglo-Irish biographer and memoirist who spent most of her life in Italy.

more as a quieting down routine that prepares me for prayer or work. In other words, it gets rid of the tensions and frees me—also rests me—to do more.

The first person who taught me was an old Buddhist scholar (a woman) who told me to breathe quietly and count my breaths in order to still the mind. She also suggested that I say silently with the incoming breath "coming to be" and with the outgoing breath "ceasing to be," which is a good quiet rhythm and does still one's thoughts. Another Zen follower told me that the rhythm of breathing should be: (incoming) one, two, three; (outgoing) one, two, three, four, five, six. (I find it hard to get to six!)

But rather than count breaths, which is meaningless and monotonous, or say a mantra which is foreign to me, I have found if I say inwardly something from my own Christian tradition, it is more natural and more helpful. So I hit on "Gloria in Excelsis Deo," which happens to have the three-six rhythm: incoming breath, "Gloria"; outgoing breath, "in Excelsis Deo."

I hope this doesn't all sound too ridiculous to you. I certainly find that the routine of "meditation" (if this is what I'm doing) *does* quiet me down when I'm agitated and the Transcendental Meditation organization has a good deal of well-authenticated scientific evidence that it brings down blood pressure, etc. Of course, it should not be effortful. You must find your own natural rhythm and try to just let it come easily, keeping your attention on it *without trying too hard*. (We Morrows were all taught to *try hard*—fine in certain stages and realms of life but not good when one reaches the sixties, or needs to let down and relax.) So one shouldn't strain to take deep breaths or meet someone else's rhythm of breathing. Just watch one's own gentle rhythm of breathing and sink into it. I also like to sit outside where the beauty of trees, seagulls, and the sounds of the birds all seem to flow through me and the "Gloria in Excelsis Deo" seems a part of the praise going up all around me.

So much for that. I have heard from Con that you probably cannot go to Maine because the doctors are trying out new drugs on you and want to see how they work. I am terribly sorry because I know how much Maine always meant to me and how much it means to you. But perhaps it is too soon after your time in the hospital to travel and try a new place and be separated from your doctors. (I am grateful they are so conscientious and careful.) These things sometimes take a while to get under control. It took months before the doctors got Charles's virus under control and by then he had lost a lot of weight and gone down in his blood count, which I feel was a cause of his catching shingles. He is now *much* better and the outward signs of shingles have disappeared though he still has the chest pains from time to time. However, it is disappearing and he is now gaining back weight, thank goodness.

We are on our way to the ranch in Montana for a ten-day visit with Land. We had planned to stop on our way back from Maui but our time in Maui was prolonged—to let Charles recuperate, for one thing—so we couldn't stop in the early spring.

I will telephone you when I get back, before I go to Switzerland (in early July). I do hope all goes well for you and Nancy. All your children seem to be getting on fine. I hope to see Connie when I get back. Much love to you and Nancy.

Anne

[Switzerland]
July 22nd, 1973
Dearest Con,

Your letter—the last letter from North Haven—came yesterday. How you managed to write it these last days and in the midst of a houseful of guests, children, and bad weather, is a miracle! I was *very* grateful for it, particularly, of course, because you gave first reactions to the reading of the introduction and the inserts from Volume III, which I knew would be painful and difficult and I had worried about.

As for your objection to the term "anachronism" [to refer] to Next Day Hill, I do think you are, in a way, right. My reaction certainly was—and is—subjective. I was not happy in that house in that period and was also influenced by CAL's discomfort. But I agree with you that I give the wrong impression and I think it will be easy to modify. I do think Next Day Hill was an anachronism, as all those big houses were: the Lamonts, the Davisons, the Guggenheims, the Pratts, etc. All soon to become museums, institutes, embassies, schools, etc. But my phrase suggests an empty form clanking on mechanically and uselessly, and that *is* the wrong impression. I will change it. I am grateful to you for bringing it up.

I am glad this year's July has been easier than last year's. This fact alone also cheered me. Charles has now been here a week and though I think he was very happy to come and to find it "just as he left it last year" (flowerpots on the balcony and larks singing in the mornings, cow bells clanging at night, cats coming to the balcony each evening, and fires for supper), it is very different from other summers and chiefly because he is not yet really well. He says he is "much better" and perhaps he is, but he still holds his arm stiff against his chest and does not want to do much. We have not walked—even down to the *laiterie* for the milk.

This slow recovery (he has had struggles since late February) has really totally changed the pattern of our lives. He has been better in adjusting to it than I. He has found much constructive work to do in a sedentary life and he carries on all the essential contacts (Pan Am meetings, etc.). But there isn't any extra. The trips away (to the Philippines, Africa, etc.) that gave him so much freedom and stimulus and adventure, and which are so creative for him, will not be possible in the near future—if ever (I don't know, of course). This virtually isolates me from the people I used to see when he went off—people he wasn't particularly interested in. And, at the moment, to see people *with him here* would be an extra burden to him (as well as to me).

Since I now have more energy than he, I find myself running twice as fast. Partly to spare him—trying to take more of the lifting, carrying, standing, running, etc. Partly because all that energy is bottled up in me—and that isolation, so that I tend to tear off to shop, do errands, see people I don't care too much about, dig in the garden, take walks, as an escape, I suppose. I'm not sure this is helpful for him—or constructive, even for me.

What I have to face is a new and different unbalance in our relationship and in our life. And I must somehow learn how to right it—not to make it *perfect* but to make it at least workable, so that I am not either exhausted, or so frustrated that I lose my temper over minor and unrelated details, or so depressed because of the apparent monotony or sense of imprisonment that I draw into my shell and give up.

Of course, it isn't really this desperate—only difficult. Good weather would help, and ever since he arrived it has been, in your wonderful phrase, "dungeon weather": damp, cold and rainy. So no breakfasts on the balcony, no casual sitting in the sun.

He is going to a meeting tomorrow and I am having the two weavers for supper. (But since I never know when he is going off, this is always a hit-or-miss last-minute thing.) I sound very gloomy and I'm not, really. I'm analyzing (one is gloomy *before* one sees well enough to analyze). Too bad we can't have a good "bathroom talk." Perhaps in Maine? So much love and thank you—

Anne

Friday, July 27th, 1973

Dearest Margot,

Your letter of July 21st has just arrived, brought to me—along with bills, packages, etc.—by the little postman knocking at the chalet door. It took a week to get here and I am writing right back.

From Dana's brief note I had no idea how serious John's accident was, how much pain it involved and how long it would take him to recuperate. I don't know that I can say anything very helpful but I have been thinking about you a great deal—as if I knew you were undergoing a great strain—writing letters to you in my mind when I couldn't sleep.

I have thought about you, Con and myself because I think we are all facing—or have faced or *will* face—somewhat the same situation. I have only been able to look at it lately, having let down, in the three weeks I've been here, from the compulsive (and real) activity and anxiety of this year. Also C. has gone off for a few days, to Frankfurt for IUCN,* which is very good for him and will stimulate and refresh him. He has missed his trips away. That gives me a chance to see to the bottom of my malaise of these past months without being pulled off center by my feelings toward him—or vice versa.

It is a great help to be able to get to the bottom of it (or *near* the bottom!). Better still would be to talk to you about it, but since that's out of the question, I will try to write. I think the first thing one must do is to face the fact that you and I and Con are approaching a period when our husbands are beginning, at least from time to time, to suffer those "diminishments" that Père Teilhard† talks about, accidents or illness, diminishments of strength, power, activities, that inevitably come to most people with aging. Unless one is a saint (and Père Teilhard was a kind of saint), it is difficult to accept the forces of diminishment "as a means of uniting oneself with God." In any case, he was speaking in his beautiful prayers (in *The Divine Milieu*) chiefly of himself. It is hard to accept the diminishments of others. (Pain and accidents are also in a somewhat different class. One feels they are unwarranted and *must* be abbreviated. Often they can be. Healing can take place, whereas aging is incurable.)

It is probably better that diminishments come earlier (if one has, as is usually the case, married someone older than oneself) to the husband, because women are more intuitively and naturally mothers and healers.

*See note on p. 237.
†See note on p. 273.

But this is only the most obvious aspect of the matter; there are so many complicated elements in being constantly "mother" or "healer" to a grown man. It is actually a total reversal in one's relationship. And then, since one does not find in oneself always the appropriate emotions, one immediately feels great guilt at being unable to alleviate the pain, cure the illness, or even be constantly compassionate. Worse than the lacks are those odd alien and inexpressible emotions of impatience, rebellion, frustration and a kind of totally irrational *excess of energy* called forth by what? I can only guess a kind of animal reaction against illness itself? I think this is what ECM felt and I am not sure it was entirely unhealthy. It made her hope and fight. An outlet for the frustration? An impatience at the passivity of one's role? A last fling of activity before the diminishments set in on oneself? Perhaps all of these. So you, if you feel these emotions, are not abnormal. I am not sure that there is not an element of healthy resistance in some of these emotions. They can engender hope, action, and a way out—if one can channel them correctly.

The worst and most destructive element is the guilt, and it is this one has to attack first. It is not your fault that you are well and he is ill, that you are strong while he is weak, etc. And there's only a limited amount you can do and you can do it better if you are free of guilt and remorse. I think one has to realize that the ill person is "given" by nature a kind of acceptance of the weakness that makes it easier for him to bear or at least to tolerate his illness and his passivity. You, watching with your full powers, are not given any anodyne and feel, in sympathy, the full extent of the blows he is suffering. Hence more anguish and guilt.

And, to come back to the reversal of relationship, remember, it has taken us years to adjust ourselves (I feel I have barely, if ever, gotten there) to a certain marital relationship based on equality of strength, or even a somewhat or sometimes daughter-father relationship where we look *up to the man* for strength and steadiness, comfort, etc. Now, suddenly, we lose our "father" again—or our strong companion—and are given, instead, another child! (I exaggerate, but you see the elements better that way.) To adapt to and understand deeply this change is a major undertaking. Don't be too hard on yourself if the course is not smooth; you are "rowing against wind and tide."

I also perceive—which one might have guessed—that the reversal of this core relationship has many ramifications in all one's other relationships. One is cut off, one is isolated, one is alone. It is almost impossible to maintain other relationships outside of the core one at this juncture, and one *needs others*—to live, to breathe, to grow, and to bring some kind of new life and air into the central relationship.

I know you know far more than I about the peace and strength and insight to be found in meditation—so I don't write about that.

Much much love to you, dear Margot, and love to John (I wish him well).

Anne

Switzerland
August 13th [1973]
Dear C.,

I have hoped you would turn up every day for two weeks and now I hope you *won't* come until after I get back from my weekend with Scott in Strasbourg (expect to be back Monday night or Tuesday midday). I may be reached Monday c/o Dr. Stahl (Dana's friend whom he is visiting in a nearby town. Tel 08-9259).

I hope you will not disappear again before I get back! Please water the flowers and feed the birds and the black and white cat who comes every night between eight and nine for scraps—quite tame—see you soon!

Love—

A.

December 3rd, 1973
Dearest Ansy,

Your father has just come back from Europe with his word, from having talked to you, of M. Feydy's death "from a clot." As a result of the operation, I assume. Terrible as the shock is for everybody, the finality does not have the horror of the possibilities for suffering—for everybody—of your last letter's news (just after the operation, when no one had been told but the children what the operation revealed).

This will be no comfort for the grief of Mme Feydy, but at least she will not have to watch her husband suffer for months and waste away, and have to keep up a pretense that he is getting better. I am afraid you are all due for a long, hard, gloomy winter but the children will help you to get through it. And perhaps you and Hélène can help each other.

I will, of course, write Mme Feydy, but it always seems to me people write too soon—when everything is in confusion and there is so much to be done—and it is all you can do to keep going. When the letters keep pouring in so glibly, one sometimes feels outsiders accept too quickly and easily the death of someone who was so close to you that you can't yet believe they are dead.

I have just found a small female dog—housebroken—for Aunt Edith*—and I hope she will accept the reality of it (she likes the *idea*!). Sometimes people don't really want to be helped. They prefer to go on feeling miserable (she is very lonely). And you must just *let* them, and not make them conform to *your* idea of happiness ("Don't you want to sit with your feet up, dear?")!

I am letting Mrs. Saunders take this out to mail with the two envelopes for Charles and Constance—Will write again—

XO

Mother

Argonauta, Maui
February 10th, 1974
Dear Stephen [Mitchell],

I am appalled at the way time has gone by since you were in Switzerland last summer and I said I would write you about the Hermann Hesse book you gave me. It is true I have been carrying around your letters: the nice one from the Rhône Valley mountains with the charming poem to the little son of your host and hostess; and the one—with book—that met me when I got back; and the Dogen[†] essay on the realization of truth for months now, intending to answer them and carrying on a kind of mental dialogue with you.

I like the Dogen very much. I had read it before, but it was good to read again, especially at this period of life when so many of my older friends are dying or about to die. One tries to understand it, and accept it without shock or feeling that it is an accident, or an end, or something final. I like particularly the paragraph about firewood turning to ash: "firewood is at the stage of firewood—ash is at the stage of ash," etc., and "Life is a period of itself; death is a period of itself. They are like winter and spring. We do not call winter the future spring, nor spring the future summer."

I am glad things are going well for you and am sure you will find what you are looking for "inside."

I also thought of you when I visited Regina Laudis again in November, taking a friend of mine, a Swiss sister of a Protestant community

*Edith Cutter Yates, Elizabeth Cutter Morrow's younger sister.
[†]Dōgen Zenji (1200–1253), Japanese Zen Buddhist teacher.

near Neufchâtel, to see it. Her community is a good deal freer than Regina Laudis; I thought they might not want her to talk freely to their community. However she did talk to the whole community (through the grill—which shocked her) who were terribly interested. Mother Jerome in particular found her sympathetic.

This same sister, Soeur Yvonne, also came with me to our reading discussion and meditation group and met a member of the San Francisco Zen Center, Yvonne Rand (now an ordained—what? monk?), a very interesting and free and enlightened young woman I like very much. She also was impressed with the Swiss "Soeur Yvonne." ("What she *is*—is impressive," she said.) Odd, how all these lives converge.

As for my outer life: my husband came home at the end of the summer quite ill with some virulent bug which we now think may have been a form of typhoid. I couldn't get a doctor to come to the chalet and was about to bundle him up and take him by Volkswagen to a hospital, when he decided to doctor himself with some antibiotics he had been given on a Pan American flight when he had paratyphoid! Even so, it took him a month to get well.

Yvonne Rand told us that Suzuki Roshi used to say that we (Americans) moved around too much. I certainly feel that way myself. My husband seems to find roots in movement and perhaps that is more in accord with life. I would like to be *more* rooted in some land. Not Hawaii, which seems to me a rootless, touristy place. New England or Switzerland could hold my roots better.

I seem to be fine and it is good to be quiet and alone for a while. This is certainly a long and wandering letter. I must go out now and try to swim or walk the black beach, before the sun goes down.

I hope the poetry in you is just running underground and will fountain again before long—with my love and thoughts and apologies!

Anne

[In the winter of 1974, Charles Lindbergh's health deteriorated rapidly. In June of that year, he was admitted to the Harkness Pavilion at Columbia-Presbyterian Medical Center, and his children were told that he had been diagnosed with lymphatic cancer two years earlier. He had forbidden his wife to tell anyone, including family members, about his diagnosis and treatments.

In late July, Charles and Anne were informed that nothing further could be done for him, and that he had only weeks to live. Charles told his wife that he wished to spend his last days in Maui. Against the advice of most of his doctors, who feared their patient would die en route, Anne called upon her family

and friends. With the support of Jon, Land, Scott, Dana Atchley, Dr. Mil-
ton Howell* and John Hanchett† of Maui, Sam Pryor, and United Airlines,
Charles was taken to Maui, where he lived out his remaining days in the com-
pany of his wife and three sons in the Pechins' guest house on the Hana coast,
not far from Dr. Howell's clinic. Ansy and Reeve stayed in touch by telephone.

Charles Lindbergh died early in the morning on August 26, 1974, with
Anne and Land at his bedside.]

Tellina,‡ Darien, Connecticut
September 22nd, 1974
with Spirit of St. L§
Dear Mr. and Mrs. Pechin,

You must be back in Hana now, looking at that beautiful coastline
that is now engraved in my mind from our week there. I wish there
were some way of my telling you what your generosity in letting us use
your guest cottage meant to my husband, to the boys, and to me, and to
every member of my family—even those who were not there, who have
shared with us (by letter or in talk) the experience of that week before
my husband died.

To my husband, it meant carrying out his last wish: "to go home to
Maui." To us—my sons and I—who were privileged to share it with him,
it meant a chance for an intimacy in his life, his thoughts, his feelings,
that we never could have had if he had been in a hospital.

I hope you do not feel that the beautiful guest cottage is marked with
tragedy because of the experience. Of course it is a deep sadness to lose
a husband—or a father—but for him it was a kind of triumph. He was
so happy and at peace to be there, to hear the waves and the birds and
to have his family about him. For us it will always be one of the richest
and deepest experiences of our lives. And I feel this kind of blessing will
go down through the families of all our children into the lives of our
grandchildren, who will be stronger to face life and death because of it!
I am grateful to all of Hana and Kipahulu—all of Maui, in a sense—for
the outpouring of love and help and sympathy that surrounded us there.
But the core of it seems to me expressed in that beautiful little cottage
and your great kindness in letting us use it.

---

*Dr. Milton M. Howell, a physician based in Hana, Maui, who had treated CAL for several
years, and who took charge of his care in the last few days of his life.
†Manager of the Hana Ranch, who helped with the logistics of CAL's burial.
‡Another in the series of shell names the Lindberghs gave to their various homes.
§AML enclosed a copy of *The Spirit of St. Louis.*

I am now back in a world very different from Hana—in the rush and pressure of many duties and demands and the complications of "settling an estate" and finding a new life alone—but I hope when things are in somewhat better order, I can find something from our life together—Charles's and my life—that can go to your life there, as a more personal and tangible expression of our gratitude.

I think our first meeting was on the David Grays' porch in Kipahulu. I will look forward to meeting you again when I return to Maui, this winter sometime, I hope. With my warmest wishes for you and deep gratitude—

Anne Lindbergh

P.S. I want to add a practical note. I have worried about the bills that we could not find out about before we left Hana. My son Land, before we left, called the telephone company and asked if we could obtain the telephone bills for your cottage from August 18th through August 29th. They were very nice but said it was all computerized and they could not pull them out. (The telephone bill will be astronomical!) There will be other bills, too—electric—water?—cleaning? We did speak to Dr. Howell and to John Hanchett about trying to get these— if possible *before* you arrived home—so you would not be met and faced with a sheaf of unknown bills. However, no bills have up to now reached me. I feel these must be straightened out. In fact, my husband kept insisting that we should pay you rent for the cottage and I would happily do so. I feel much in your debt for your letting us be there. Do let me know what we owe you.

Tellina, Darien, Connecticut
November 11th, 1974
Dear Bill [Jovanovich],

I wanted to send you just a line to thank you for coming out to see me in Darien last week, and to tell you how much it meant to me. It wasn't just the relief of feeling we saw eye to eye on the technical aspects of Charles's papers, or even your kindness in taking those requests off my shoulders.*

It was more, I think, simply the release of meeting you again—instead of the public image of Charles or the public consequences of death and

---

Autobiography of Values, a memoir by CAL based on a manuscript he had been working on at the time of his death, was published by Harcourt Brace Jovanovich in 1978. It was edited by Bill Jovanovich and Judith Ann Schiff, of the Yale University Library.

loss, [to share] the private image, and so clearly. Many devoted friends of Charles saw only one side of him, but you, I think, perhaps more than any "friend" of the past decade, saw the many-faceted personality (and he perhaps also saw a many-faceted person in you). It may be because of this, among other things, that he felt very close to you and had such confidence in you. These things are—for me—easier to write than to say, hence this note.

I am looking forward to lunch on the 22nd and, though it is a totally unnecessary luxury for me to be picked up by George and taken to town and back, I accept with gratitude—this time! If it turns out that he is needed in the afternoon—or morning—I can easily take a train either way. And, of course, you know that if you find yourself unexpectedly pressed that week, you could always postpone our appointment.

Gratefully,

Anne

As you know, I had a good weekend with Helen and think I can start to do some cutting on my manuscript shortly.

First Year After Death

[From an unfinished manuscript on widowhood]

One is so disoriented, one tries to make a map of grief. But one cannot make a map. Grief is not a place, as C. S. Lewis says, it is a process. I am just at the beginning. It is a journey—a long journey, unmarked and roadless—but other people's signposts can help.

In the numbness of first grief, nature protects you; the amputated limb does not hurt at first. But everything that one passes through numbly or automatically must be, at some point, relived actively, eyes open, aware, vulnerable. What one goes through under anesthesia, one must suffer painfully and fully later, in some way: in dreams, in images—waking up startled at night to hear in memory the labored breath, to see the emaciated body, to hear the hammer blows of the nails being pounded into the lid of the coffin. (Terrible sound. I realize in my dreams now that he is dead—but somehow not yet buried. I am stopped at that moment.)

The first reaction, the morning he died, was one of gratitude to God that he had been taken—that he was no longer imprisoned in the suffering body, that he did not have to be moved to the hospital to be separated from his family by an oxygen tent and deeper painkillers. This was the first image to work through and one I have not entirely lost.

I have not yet reached the real man I was married to for forty-four years. When I do, I will feel more pain—more sense of loss, vacuum, loneliness—but perhaps a greater sense of him, of who he really was, of his presence now. It is one month since the death. I still cannot see him. I do not dream about him, but wake heavily and painfully, coming up from great depths as if from drowning, dimly aware I am still at a burial service.

Last night I dreamed of someone I *hoped* was him, an approximation. I rushed to give him the embraces, the arms around him, I could not give to a dying man that last week. But the image was not him. It is still too soon to see him. It would be too painful.

In intense grief, one sees the world as even more beautiful than before although—or perhaps *because*—seen through tears. But I think the tears are irrelevant. One sees the world as unbearably beautiful because one sees through love. I remember it looked like this when I was young and "in love." It is love that illumines the world—not grief.

There are so many faces to grief: numbness, apathy, loneliness, panic, anger, resentment. A sense of dust and ashes over everything, except the world of nature, which is still beautiful. But the *world*—the worldly world—the emptiness of it. People still touch you, but ideas and things, and even books, hardly at all.

Going over the records of the past five years, I think how little he was with me, how much away! The living, of course, always have regrets. Have the dead no regrets? No sense of time wasted?

One moves slowly backwards in time, from the last days to the days before the last, to the days which, for what it was worth (one learns it was not worth much), he felt a little better or ate a little more. Back even to the days when we had some hope—the days when he came back from the hospital—only to go downhill again when he tried to work, when he had to rest three times going upstairs, when he watched me exercise and said, "I couldn't *begin* to do that." Back to the days of discouragement, of realizing he was losing more strength each day. The days of hope are hard to remember and the days of slow realization of growing weakness, harder.

Will I ever get back to the well man—the well memories?

Yes. The rush of time is hurrying him away. I should not be so busy, but everything pushes one on relentlessly.

The sense of numbness alternates with the sense of sharp grief or

292 · *Anne Morrow Lindbergh*

realization—unbearable, but it brings with it a sense of closeness. "Blessed are they that mourn." Yes, because it is so difficult to mourn. Those that mourn "shall be healed." But so little of the time *can* one mourn. One has had an amputation and one is numb most of the time. One goes on living automatically, out of habit. One is even astonished at what one can do, as in early convalescence from a bad operation. ("See, I can wash my face. I can hold a spoon.") "Look, I can go to the bank. I can drive to Vermont and back. I can meet and talk to people."

Numbness is hard to bear because it is separation. Mourning is hard to bear because it is pain, but along with pain comes closeness. "Blessed are they that mourn"—who have that closeness.

Disorientation is constant. One is a wavering compass needle. True North has been taken away. Not only direction has gone, but the resistance that allowed one to move in space. It is as if one had been pushing against "something" and the "something" had been taken away; one is put off one's balance. One staggers forward. Marriage is, of course, a kind of play of forces: a dance, a give and take. Without the countering force, one is left unsteady, hardly able to stand or move. There is a form of boxing—Japanese? Chinese?—that illustrates this. Jujitsu? One is left shadow boxing—that is it.

One is unsteady all the time, off balance. But one knows one must learn over again, from the beginning, how to walk, speak, act alone. I don't doubt that I *will* learn, but it will take time. There are things that help: meditation, being out of doors, working in the earth with growing things, *some* reading (very few things are right: some poetry, some spiritual reading, Teilhard de Chardin), *some* people, the ones I can be real with.

There are also intolerable things: the worldly world, shops, gossip, worldly people, the unfeeling hurry of city streets, catalogues of clothes, gifts, the mountains of unread mail, and much of the machinery one has to go through in the settling of an estate.

One is burdened with more things than one can possibly do, and with half the strength. This is terribly distracting when one wants, most of all, to be focused. Everything that keeps one from focusing is negative and almost everything one is pressed to do keeps one from focusing. I spend hours trying to find letters, records, files, deeds, stock certificates, without much success. This adds to one's feeling of disorientation; one flounders in a sea of paperwork, arid and senseless, very separative.

I went up to Reeve's a week ago. It was a great help to be in Vermont.

There was sharp grief at first, being there without him, but closeness, and being indispensable, in a practical down-to-earth way to a daughter, and finding a place, even if temporary, in a warm loving family. And the beauty of walks in the woods, the beauty of autumn—sharp as grief, close as grief—was very healing. I find the wild calls of the geese at twilight also bring me this sense of sharp pain and closeness.

This is "mourning": these glimpses of pain, grief, loss, plus something else—a closeness or an eternal quality that is sustaining. This is healing.

Now, back at home, on the whole I live fairly steadily and automatically but slowed up by constant weariness; one functions by rote. Most of the time I feel his death is impossible to believe; it is either totally impossible or, in flashes, absolutely intolerable.

Children and grandchildren help. Kristina is coming this weekend, I hope. I love hearing about the children. How enchanting to picture Charles, saying "Little Pig, little Pig won't you let me come in?"

The funniest condolence phrase I've yet struck came in a very nice letter from a lawyer. His letter was human throughout, but when he came to express sympathy or cheer, he lapsed into the language most familiar to him: "It would be an error to extrapolate from the present as a proxy for the balance of the future."!! Hmmm?!?

"So few people help," I wrote last week, and it has been proved again. I went to New York just for the afternoon. I stopped at a bookshop to get something to read, and then at the bakery for Italian bread. "You have not been here for so long. You have been away?" "Yes, I have been away." Out into the street quickly.

"The World" is alien, even my own dear group of New York friends. It was nice to see them at book group, and the silent meditation was good though quivery, not deep. I felt all the antennae. And afterwards, listening to the talk—politics, books, money raising, etc.—I felt again, I inhabit another world. I don't belong here. I felt silent and out of step. I should not have come.

It was akin to the feeling when one has just had a baby and goes out for the first time. One is weak and feels far too vulnerable, except in the tiny circle of the baby's cradle, as if one had had a layer of skin peeled off. One is raw to touch. "Where someone lays a finger, it leaves a bruise."

I must stay in my own small circle, my own quiet country world, where I can follow the tiny round of habitual duties: feed the birds, mulch the bushes, weed, clip the vines. Everything outside helps, but the desk is mountain high in other arid duties I must get through. There are promises to keep, obligations. I always was bad at this. Now I must learn, but it is a new worldly challenge, and one has so little stamina to attack such a burden.

I am back further now, past the grave, into the period of illness, of last summer when he came home and lost strength day by day. I dreamt he was trying to walk on crutches. No, no—I efface that dream. I turn away. I can't bear it. But it is always veiled, heavily cloaked: I can't see his face and am only dimly aware it is him.

I wake heavily, unrelieved. Once I woke and found humming in my head an old popular tune from about the time we were married: "I'll get *by* as long as *I* have *you*." I can only guess what the dreams are, although sometimes there is a clear one. I dream I am at a party and see someone I think is Charles—his back. I rush toward him and try to throw my arms around him. But the man turns, and it is not Charles but someone else, a caricature of him. I cannot see the real man; perhaps it would destroy me at this point.

This weekend I thought I would try to have a friend, a dear friend, to walk with and have supper with; holiday weekends are so long. But though there were good moments, I found, again, we were in different worlds. She was inhabiting the "real world" of public events, politics, books, etc.—being positive, cheerful, practical—and I was bogged down in some other world far away, like a woman bearing a child or getting up for the first time after: weak, vulnerable, oversensitive, vague and inefficient, disoriented, slow.

Perhaps one *is* "bearing a child": the new relationship with death or with the dead person. And one wants to be working only at that; everything else seems irrelevant. No, not my relationship to my own children. That is real. Anything I can do for them or their children is real and constructive and goes "with the grain," not against it. It gives me focus and orientation.

Other people, however, I can only see sparingly, in little touches, not continuously. Perhaps one could see those who have gone through almost the same thing, but our experiences are so different, even in death, loss, and grief.

Over the weekend I came, for the first time since his death, to my little writing house. It is such an intimate place and full of his care for me. (He kept the stove full of kerosene, put up the blinds last spring, filled the cans, etc.) Also full of my writing self, my alone self. Because I had a guest in the house, I realized, I must come out and be alone even to write a letter, away from the impingement of even a dear friend. After putting down the rugs, filling the stove, and sitting at my desk to write a letter, I realized I must do this each day, even for a short time. It will help me focus.

And after the growing of this child—a new relationship with the dead—will come the growing of the new child that is me without him. I am sure, if I live long enough, this will come. I must and will learn to function alone. A new person will be born. But one has to start at the very beginning: learn to walk again, alone; learn to see, alone; learn to act, to take action, and to live alone.

In the meantime, one must learn to function in a world—several worlds—that are unfamiliar and unreal.

In this sense I have to *be him*, or carry on his role, which I am unaccustomed to and very unskilled at. And it *must* be done now, when I am running on half steam: inefficient, tired, distracted. It is difficult to find oneself when one is carrying on another's role.

At the end of the afternoon I try to do something outside: clip shrubs and vines, transplant begonias to the house, water or spread peat moss in the evergreens. This is steadying and I feel more centered, rooted in nature and its cycles, but not really closer to him. That comes only in rare sharp flashes in the evening: hearing the wild geese cry as they come into the cove, or looking out at the stars on a clear night. These are sharp stabs of grief, but bring closeness also. They are a luxury, a few seconds out of the day. Most of the hours are spent completely numb, plodding automatically, unfeeling, as if carrying a heavy unseen weight—a blind, dumb, nameless weight of sorrow which makes everything slow, heavy, wearying.

Yesterday, it poured sheets and waves and long drips of rain all day. It was dark and unrelenting. I was glad for my shrubs and trees that needed it, but it was a hard day to go ahead in, to be constructive. Two people came from the Yale Library to talk to me about his papers and the provisions of the will and its consequences. They were very kind and I think it was clarifying to them and to me. But after they left I was at loose ends, unable to concentrate, as I am much of the time, my powers of focus used up by *one* effort, by a few hours in the morning usually. If I can work outside in the afternoon I am somewhat relieved, as by sleep, but yesterday it was impossible because of the rain.

Last night I could not sleep until early morning, in this state of—what? Not grief. I was distracted and miserable, both physically and nervously. Unable to rest, I took sleeping pills. I read Chekhov's letters like a drug, and finally got up and exercised, falling into a heavy unrefreshing sleep in the early morning hours. Perhaps all the nervous tension resulted from the lack of my daily letting down in outdoor work; I must try to keep to a schedule with some outdoor tasks each day.

But this morning I woke to a beautiful fresh rain-washed world. Many leaves have fallen but the rest are golden. I could sit on my overturned rowboat and praise God for the beauty around me, for the cycle of life, and feel part of it again.

Almost two months since his death. I hate time rushing him away. And I am still numb, except in flashes. I get along adequately, if automatically. I sleep, most of the time, a little better and don't need as much help from sedatives. Of course, I usually wake at least once at night and sit up and read for an hour or so. But there is some gain.

I think I am further away from the actual trauma of the last days: the death itself, the emaciated body. But I am still in his illness. The terrible period of disappointed hopes when he came back from the hospital and then each day got weaker and could do less, although he tried so hard to do something: work at clearing up his office when he could only get up the stairs carrying books and letters in a basket, because he had to hold onto the banisters with one hand, pulling himself up.

I mind that I did not give him more sympathy, more extravagant expression of love. But we were both hanging on to our self-control, to our hopes. Pity or too much sympathy would have broken us down, would have been a betrayal. But I mind.

I am glad for the week in Maui; it also had such sharing. There was no veil between us because he knew he was dying. We could talk to him whenever he wanted. We were terribly driven the first week, all of us. He wanted to arrange every detail of his burial and had us taking notes and running here and there, thinking only about the grave, the coffin, the stone marker, the service. (This was a relief, because it was in another world than the material.)

After it was reasonably in order—the grave all done, the stone planned, the coffin, its lining, his clothes, covering, etc. settled—he felt relieved. I am glad I then broke through and spoke about death and what he could tell us. I said that it would help us because we would have to face it—I, first of all.

He said, "I don't feel I'm 'facing' anything. And it's not what you think. I know I have been near death at least three times this week. It's not terrible. It's very easy and natural. I don't think it's the end. I think I'll go on, in a more generalized way, perhaps. And I may not be so far away, either."

I am glad I told him that I had been praying for him, and for me, sitting in the little white church while Land and Jon worked on the grave. Although, at my telling, his face contorted with emotion, trying not to cry.

And this after he had been cross at me. He *was* cross, naturally. He was so fragile, so weak, on such an edge all the time, and his rest and sleep were so important. And I was so overanxious and overfussy. When I came into the room and saw him with a bare shoulder or back and the wind blowing on him (with pneumonia), I would put the sheet over him. I had to do *something*, I felt. And he would bark out, "Put it back the way it was! You *must* understand. I need to rest. I am not being unreasonable . . ."

But, of course, he let out his frustration on me, not the nurse. That is natural. Who else could he let out his terrible frustration on? Only someone he was as sure of as me.

It was terrible to have him cross, as if his character, or our relationship, had changed. I could hardly bear it. But later he would say—yes, this time, choking with tears—"I feel so awful to have hurt you." And I could hold his hand and, to his saying he was sorry, say obliquely what I couldn't say directly: "You don't have to say 'I'm sorry.' I feel the way Scott did when he was a little boy, with his great eyes looking at me solemnly, saying 'You don't have to say "I'm sorry" to me, Mother. You don't ever have to say "I'm sorry." I love you so much, you don't have to say "I'm sorry." ' "

I could give Charles that. Perhaps because I had sat in the little church that day and prayed that I might be more gentle and less anxious, and that I would be given a chance, another night, twenty-four hours more, to show my gentleness and love. And it was given. And the understanding of his frustration was given, by remembering how babies always count on their mothers to understand and forgive their tantrums. Only with their mothers do they trust enough to let off steam. And the memory of my child's wonderful answer to me was given to me to give back to C. I am grateful for that.

It has suddenly gotten very cold, unseasonably so. I have been doing all the year-end jobs, the out-of-doors ones. They are the easiest to do, even the ones we did together: draining the hoses, putting them away, potting the begonias for indoors, taking the geraniums (what are left) inside, digging in the bedraggled chrysanthemums in pots by the door. There is a kind of companionship doing these jobs, even alone, that is so different from the desk work—which I avoid as long as possible and only do with the greatest difficulty.

However, when I had to go down into the "bomb shelter"* to turn off the garden water line, armed with his written instructions, I was shaken. His instructions were so precise, so detailed, but also—which I'd forgotten—so humorous! They have that kind of slightly sarcastic tone, poking fun at the dumb woman plumber—like his instructions on the pressure cooker: "Note: If the above directions have been carried out exactly all will be hunky-dory. But it is possible that if the two emergency switches at the head of the stairs are observed with thoughtfulness, certain disturbing questions will arise . . ." etc. He was having such fun writing those instructions!

Humor is the hardest thing to remember, but if you leave it out of the picture all reality is gone. It is the vital ingredient.

The other night as I was cooking my supper, I looked out of my dark kitchen window that has the bird-feeding tray attached to it. There was a funny animal hunched up there, obviously eating. What was it? Not a squirrel: too fat and pale-colored. Not a cat: too small and a long hairless tail. A rat? No, not with that long-haired sandy gray coat. Then I saw its little pointed long-nosed face, white with pink at the tip of the nose, two small black ears like crumpled pansy petals, and pink again, at the tips. "Obviously a possum!" It didn't seem to mind me at all. Looking right at me through the partly shaded lighted window, it went on eating with its little black-fingered hands.

I watched fascinated and delighted and felt how pleased he would have been. What was it eating? I went downstairs to read in the encyclopedia. It said possums are marsupial, carrying their young in pouches, and that the newborn possum after "maturition" crawls "without help from its mother" into her pouch where a nipple immediately swells with milk and the lucky baby settles down until it can feed itself. (This possum had no baby—no pouch.) Possums eat, the encyclopedia said, small

---

*When building Tellina in 1962, CAL researched and designed a bomb shelter for it, equipped to withstand even a tidal wave, in the event of a "megatonnage underwater burst" along the coastline. He felt it was practical to build a bomb shelter in a nuclear age. AML stored cases of Pedro Domecq sherry in it, which was also practical.

insects, eggs, fruit, berries, etc. Nothing like that was on my shelf, only wormy crackers and melba toast which I'd cleared out of the cupboard. It has come now two or three nights in succession and evidently enjoys melba toast—or worms!

I find things C. S. Lewis wrote in *A Grief Observed* very apt. "No one ever told me that grief felt so like fear." I am also reading a new edition of Chekhov's letters which came out last year. It is wonderful: lively, and astonishingly current in a way. But he was such a modern man: humane, witty, anti-clerical, anti-political, pro-feminist, anti-prudery, pro-sexual freedom, etc. A down-to-earth doctor, a witty and compassionate observer of people and situations, and always an artist, astute and critical of himself and others. He was so real, so honest, perceptive, and so in touch with life and suffering. It is *so* difficult to find anything to read that is quite right, something that is not escape, that is related to life and death, but that does not offer false or esoteric comfort. Teilhard de Chardin's letters would be the best; there are several other collections of his letters that I cannot seem to get, besides the three I have.

Last night for the first time I slept through the night without a sleeping pill, though I did take a mild sedative and had to read quite late. And this morning I woke to a beautiful mild fall day. I went out and sat on the old overturned boat and looked up at the sky above the crooked pine: so alive it was, with gently twirling leaves, with flocks of birds going south, with white comet-tails from distant planes, with soaring gulls motionless above far trees, with wisps of cloud substance, the early makings of a cloud.

Meditating on the boat bottom, I felt a great sense of oneness with the earth and the earth cycles, and a sense of closeness to him also and gratitude for his life and his love and all the things he had given me and that we shared. Particularly this morning, I felt gratitude for the sky. ("You will have the sky!" as Mother said to me when I first told her I was engaged to marry, so long ago.) Yes, I have had the sky, and have it still, and feel an almost greater sense of it than before. I understand more his love of it and feel one with him in that.

I know these moments of joy, of release, are due to many things. Partly that I am stronger after two months. I sleep more, I don't wake as often with those terrible nightmares or the less terrible but still sharp pains of indigestion knotting my stomach—nervous indigestion, of course, but still painful. Partly I am stronger, partly one is better on a beautiful day.

It has been a beautiful fall and I have been nourished by all I have done around the place. I find a kind of satisfaction in doing the clearing-up jobs we used to do together. Strange, you'd think I'd miss him more here. Gathering sticks in a wheelbarrow to stack for kindling, empty-ing the hoses, turning off the garden water: it is as if we were still doing them together, as if he were going on in me.

I feel, in a not at all spiritualistic way, that he is "at my side" when I'm working like this. I cannot explain it rationally, but it is nourishing and comforting. Perhaps I feel grateful for all he had taught me to do, all the practical things. As Reeve said, "He prepared us so well for his death." I don't really feel this at the desk though. There I feel painfully alone and inadequate. I feel I am wading through molasses, I do it so inefficiently and slowly. Perhaps I feel his impatience here, even disapproval, at the way I am doing it.

Yesterday was such a beautiful day that I worked all afternoon out-side (some desk work in the morning and evening—that was all), raking and hoeing up the bad patches in the lawn and reseeding and putting peat moss around. And planting bulbs. All that outside work must have helped to give me such a good night's sleep.

It is not that I live "happily." It is not happiness. There is mostly unhappiness. One plods along heavily, carrying that constant burden of loss, of emptiness, of unexpressed grief. (If I could only cry more! But I am dry-eyed—a dry-eyed ache most of the time.) It is worst at night, especially at suppertime.

But there are moments of joy, like this morning on the boat, or last night at sunset, going down to feed the swan family. (How big the two gray cygnets have grown. They survived the summer. He didn't.)

Autumn, I think, is a good time to meet grief and loss. The tide is going out. One is in harmony with the dying and receding of nature, because one is in this part of the cycle oneself. But it is comforting also because one works in the expectation of new life to come. One works for the continu-ation of life. It is like working with children. I think it would—it will—be harder to meet the spring, when everything is bursting with blossoms and growth and fecundity: the time of love and mating and nesting.

No mail and no papers came since it was Veterans Day. Last year we were in Birmingham. It made him happy to be honored by all the [armed] services. He was already ill, but I am glad he was able to do it. I had dreaded it (the open car parade!) but it was moving and fun to do it, once more with him, a last repetition of that early aviation life, and early married life too.

Mother B. (abbess of Regina Laudis Monastery) called. It was so good to hear her voice and though we spoke very little, really, a word or two, I felt connected again with some deeper level I always feel at the monastery. And when I put the phone down I could cry: blessed healing tears. The dry-eyed parched aridity was broken for a few minutes. I went back to the desk and read—or reread—Jon's letter to me that ends with the lines from a poem by St. Colombo: "Oh, my love, my God, may Thy blood flow in my heart. Who but Thee can give me tears?"

I don't know that I understand it completely, or at all. I only know that it strikes an inner chord and releases me. The need for tears is great.

I go to sleep about midnight and wake almost an hour later, shaken by a deep and troubling dream. This time I uncover it before it disappears: he is in bed and I am trying to get him something he wanted to eat. How happy I was when I could find a soup, a zwieback, a stewed fruit that he liked! But the dream—or waking up from it—was not happy. I suppose it is the waking up, the remembering, that is so terribly painful, unbelievable and shattering all over again.

We have been having an unusually warm, mild week. Most of the brilliant leaves are off the trees, though the maples are still golden and the oaks a deep russet. No wind, still, warm as spring. One by one the leaves fall, spiraling gently to the ground. Sometimes I think they're birds fluttering down. Sometimes they come in a rush and a rattle like rain. It is good weather to be languidly out of doors, raking or digging in bulbs.

Kristina is here this weekend. She is very sympathetic and easy. I am interested in her life and like to talk to her. She is sensitive, aware, articulate, with a lovely sense of humor and no pose, direct, something always of country about her, woods, fields, winds and water. She has moods, but there is an air blowing through the moods.

A wet fall Sunday. Kristina and I had a good walk yesterday in the mild damp golden afternoon. ("Season of mists and mellow fruitfulness"*— this year we have had a European fall.) Then I dug in twelve more tulips at the front of the house, bordering the bushes, before tea and some talk about her life and her family, and supper on the sofa. She is very easy and companionable.

I had a much better sleep, right through from about midnight to 5:30, and then back off for another hour's nap after some reading in bed. I

---

*The first line of the poem "To Autumn," by John Keats.

woke shortly after eight from a very vivid dream, not cloaked this time, but clear as a cry in its symbolism.

I was in a warehouse, or perhaps my own house in a state of moving. Desks, papers, letters, and old magazines were dustily piled everywhere in confusion. I suddenly realized that I had lost my wedding ring. I got down on the floor to try and find it with my hands, feeling on the bare wood; it must be nearby because I had heard it click falling. Nancy came by, because we were to go somewhere together. I rushed up to her and said, "Nancy, the most dreadful thing has happened." But to her expression of sympathy, I said, "Well, not *so* terrible, but hard. I've lost my wedding ring."

"Oh," she said, firmly and practically, "we'll find it," and set about looking among the piles of dusty papers. "I know what wedding rings mean to one's family." But as she looked among the papers, I knew she couldn't find it there. "It can't be there," I said, "in the papers, because I heard it click as it fell."

I woke up then with some relief to find I still had my wedding ring, and it was another loss.

So very strange how the unconscious cloaks its messages so that they are acceptable. Freud said dreams are the guardians of sleep. This dream was the clearest I've had, well enough masked that I could remember it. But why Nancy? (Her husband is ill with cancer too.) The stacks of dusty papers in confusion are clearly what I am living in now. No, I won't refind my marriage among them. And perhaps they are hiding the "ring" from me—keeping me from finding it.

One keeps looking. Dana got me his wallet from the safe-deposit vaults in the hospital. I had been dreading the trip to the hospital for it, the first time since his death, and dreading opening the sealed envelope too. Yet, still, hoping to find something of him in it, something undiscovered, some secret messages.

When I finally opened it at home, there was nothing significant: a poor passport picture, a little money, some addresses, his driver's license, a folded sheet of blue paper with some numbers on it—his [Pan Am airline] pass numbers and Social Security number, the safe combination. I felt numbly disappointed. He is not here either.

January 7th, 1980
Dearest Scott:

I tried to call you yesterday, Sunday, at about 2:30 my time, which I assumed was 8:30 your time. The bell rang and rang and I imagined I had called too late and you were in the big room watching television. I shall try again today.

Nothing in particular to say, only I feel it has been a long time since I heard anything, and I feel out of touch. This is my fault more than yours since I have not written and there are always so many duty letters to get through that any personal ones get pushed aside.

I feel I have been racing ever since I got back from Switzerland. Reeve and I made two trips out west this last fall, one to Minnesota for a Historical Society meeting. This was combined with a Lindbergh Fund* meeting, a first one in Minnesota, which we have been working toward for several years. Reeve, Jim Newton, Jim Lloyd, and Land, in particular, have been pushing to get the fund down off its New York "charity ball" basis, onto a more solid and less spectacular but more practical level, based in Minnesota; they are very down-to-earth and sympathetic to your father's point of view of a *balance* between technology and conservation.

At one of the meetings I had to make a speech and answer questions (some interesting—some not). And there was a discussion in which Land and Reeve took part. When Land was asked, "What does it feel like to be a son of a famous person?" he answered, "I have no basis of comparison. I've only had one childhood!")

I really want to know how you are, and how Alika is, and if you have had any answers to the letters you sent out last summer, and what the visit was like from the editor of *International Wildlife* magazine. (Was that the magazine that was sending someone to interview you?) I want to know how the monkeys are, and if you have done any more writing on your thesis. (Don't feel guilty about it. Theses take forever and you are doing so much outside work.) I cannot say that I have done any writing since this summer. There are still bits and patches of extra writing that turn up in connection with the last volume.† It all seems very far in the past, with the appalling series of crises we are into at this moment in Iran and Afghanistan. Actually the Iranian crisis and Carter's handling of it has brought about quite a resurgence of patriotism in this country as well as upgrading Carter's popularity.

---

*A foundation established on the fiftieth anniversary of CAL's New York–to–Paris flight, whose mission is to promote the Lindberghs' philosophy of balance between technological innovation and the preservation of nature. Its name has since been changed to The Charles A. and Anne Morrow Lindbergh Foundation.
†*War Within and Without: Diaries and Letters, 1939–1944* (New York: Harcourt Brace Jovanovich, 1980).

The oil crisis has cut down some on the driving (prices have gone up a lot for gas), and big cars are out, which is fine, but they say we may have a "crunch" in the spring or summer and long lines at the gas stations again. Now you can get gas, but it is rising in price all the time, and stations close early.

One of the reasons I wanted to telephone you was to tell you that Erin is on her way to Morocco on an exchange-student plan for about six weeks or more. She will write or call you. She is a charming, open, natural girl, with outdoor habits (she herded cows on the ranch), and also quite a bit of talent drawing.

I still remember and have kept the letter you wrote me when you and Alika managed to get a day or two at the beach last spring. That letter had so much joy and beauty in it. You should get that more often. It does revive one. Much love—I will try to call again early—

Mother

[Summer 1980]
Dear Lucia [Valentine],

You are now back in daily life which is much harder.* One cannot keep the high moments. And though physical care and quiet and routine help one to "go on," they are dusty fare: what is the use of routine when the center of it has dropped out? The vacuum must be filled, but not perhaps immediately.

I don't really believe widowhood is as negative as I sound, or as people say. The first stages are hideous, but slowly the ill image (of the person one has lost) dims, and the vivid image of the realer person in the midst of life comes back with greater vividness than one could believe. One does then understand one's partner, one's marriage, one's life, one's mistakes, their mistakes, etc., without remorse or pain and with a new sense of freedom or release. But not, I think, if one rushes things or gets too tired. ("Widows always get sick," my dentist warned me. "Pay attention to anything that goes wrong—don't neglect it"—good advice.)

I asked two widows much older than myself (in their eighties and I in my seventies) to give me some advice. One of them, elegant, intellectual and artistic, said, "I'll tell you what it's like. It's HELL," practically stamping her foot! The other, squarish, midwestern, feet on-the-ground, said contemplatively, "When I was first widowed (she was widowed twice), I was told never to drink alone . . . I think it was very *bad* advice!"

*Alan Valentine died in 1980.

I laughed and have remembered it often. How else can one get through that worst hour between five and seven in the evening? After supper one can climb into bed with the day's mail to reread—or better still—a good book.

Much love and many thoughts,

Anne

Musical Chairs

[SPEECH DELIVERED AT THE COSMOPOLITAN CLUB, FEBRUARY 23RD, 1981]

When I was asked to make this talk, I said I could only speak on something I was working at myself. My first idea for a title was "Tasks at the End of Life," since that is what I am working at now.

"Tasks at the End of Life" sounded too negative and, as I started to write, I thought of the game musical chairs, which seems to describe life in its different stages and at my particular stage. (If you are not there yet—you will be!) What you will hear is not so much a lecture as some unfinished exploration I am sharing with you.

Musical chairs is a game we used to play at children's parties. When I was a child, it was not called musical chairs, but "Going to Jerusalem." Some of you may remember those rather stiff children's parties, well regulated by adults. All the chairs in the house were stretched out in a long line, alternating backs and fronts. There was one less chair than the number of players. The children marched around the long line to "Onward Christian Soldiers" or "Here We Go Marching to Georgia," drummed out on the upright piano by an old aunt. The aunt would suddenly lift her hands from the keys and the music stopped; at this point every child scrambled for a chair. Since there were not enough chairs for everyone, obviously someone was left standing when the music started again and had to withdraw from the game.

I was not very fond of this game, as I was usually dropped out early. Of course, there were a few moments of fun when one accidentally sat down on half a chair or on someone's lap. But that was against the rules, and you were always thrown out along with the extra chair.

Going to Jerusalem was a game of attrition. At the end everyone was left out except one sole survivor who had grabbed the last chair. The game, I suspect, had moralistic connotations. The title certainly came from the Bible, where the line is "Going *up* to Jerusalem." The phrase refers, I am told, not only to a geographical journey but to a kind of pilgrim's progress through life, the journey of the soul toward heaven. This concept was certainly part of my childhood, handed down by grandmothers: life was a journey toward heaven. Life as a journey has remained with me, but heaven is dimmer. I see life as a journey toward insight.

But what is insight? Not knowledge, which is an accumulation of learning. Not wisdom, exactly, which is a distillation of years of experience. Certainly not serenity or acceptance. The definition I found was the following: "Insight implies depth of discernment coupled with understanding and sympathy." Insight, then, is not simply for oneself; it should radiate to those around you. A further illustration adds, "The ecstasy of imaginative vision, the sudden insight into the nature of things." Quite as difficult to reach as heaven!

If the game is any indication, the journey is neither straight nor easy. It is full of stops and starts, stumbles and jerks, and sudden confused standstills. My talk is perhaps an exploration of insight and how it develops. Insight comes, I believe, with age, but does it come automatically, at the end of the journey, or does it come as we are marching along? Glimpses of insight seem to come *not* when we are moving ahead in the procession, but in the jerks and stops. When we pause and have to look around, there are, as T. S. Eliot says, "hints and guesses."* There are "hints followed by guesses" in the choices we make at each new start, the paths followed and those discarded. But of course we have to keep on marching or we would never get to Jerusalem!

You cannot press the image too far, but there seem to be periods in life when we are progressing confidently. (You say to yourself, *"Now* I have the secret, *now* I know.") All at once the music stops and you drop out of the procession—at least *that* procession. The pattern changes; you are left standing alone. The game becomes Still Pond, No More Moving.† It is always a surprise and a readjustment. I think both men and women experience these abrupt changes, but they are perhaps more obvious in women's lives. Men, and women who follow one career, seem to be on an escalator mounting steadily to the top floor. But career or no career, most lives have intermissions along the way. At each halt there

---

*From the last stanza of "The Dry Salvages" (the third of the *Four Quartets*):

   . . . *These are only hints and guesses,*
   Hints followed by guesses; and the rest
   Is prayer, observance, discipline, thought and action.
   The hint half guessed, the gift half understood, is Incarnation.
†Still Pond, No More Moving is another game from AML's childhood.

is a moment of hesitation, even of panic, then a re-evaluation. At each new start, there are new glimpses of insight and other tasks and rewards.

Reviewing my life lately—since I am at one of the later stages—I have been totting up the ledger. What do I mind at this stage of life, what do I enjoy? What are the limitations and what are the enrichments?

I live alone at the moment, a state I am not accustomed to. My childhood was spent in a close, cheerful family life of four children and attentive parents. My older sister and I, from earliest memory, shared a room. We had two painted white beds divided by a chintz screen covered with trellises of blue roses. The screen was supposed to keep us from playing together at night, but we found we could talk through the blue roses. In college, I had roommates with whom one discussed everything: professors, courses, books, poetry, food (potatoes and Brussels sprouts), dieting (one was always too fat), men, and love. Endlessly love—was it real or wasn't it? We quoted Katherine Mansfield, who wrote how hard it was to tell the difference between real love and false. Much more difficult, she said, than telling the difference between toadstools and mushrooms. It took a terrible lot of toadstools, she admitted, before one found a genuine mushroom.

The year after college, I found a "genuine mushroom." I married and leapt into a totally new pattern. Early married life, since I married an aviator, was spent accompanying my husband in an open cockpit plane on his survey flights, laying out air routes for mail and passengers across the country. Later trips took us over Canada and Alaska, "North to the Orient." Another flight crossed Greenland and Iceland and circled the North Atlantic. The "Lone Eagle" was no longer alone. Neither was I, not for a moment. I was much too busy operating the radio, navigating, co-piloting, refueling, holding the funnel as my husband poured in the gasoline. I was absorbed in the day-to-day routine, packing up, moving on.

We stopped long enough to have a child. The next stage—a normal enough role, but new to me—was the bearing and bringing up of children: making a home, many homes (we moved nineteen times, I once counted, before settling in Connecticut). The house was never tidy. The children had every known childhood ailment. Someone was always in bed with a cold, or two were fighting in the bathtub. There were unexpected crises: goldfish in the toilet bowl and snakes under the radiator. Being wife, mother, housekeeper and sometimes writer (for in those days we had help), I was never alone and I longed to be. I wrote a book about the need to be alone, to find one's core. Who was I really, aside from wife and mother? Who had I been before I gathered this menagerie around me? Who would I be when they dispersed to the winds?

And suddenly they were gone. Almost overnight, it happened. The children left for school and college and then marriage. My husband was still traveling much of the time, a role I had abandoned when the children arrived. I faced my first experience of being alone, a state I had looked forward to but when it arrived, it was difficult to use. The music I was marching to had stopped. I had a husband; I had work, a vocation of writing. So much silence and solitude spread out in pools around me, diluting my drive to write. It was too great a change, too solitary.

I had my first taste of loneliness. I discovered then that the pain of loneliness is not actually in being alone, nor is it simply the withdrawal of a companion. It is the sudden loss of a role, an occupation. The rug—or rather, the chair—has been pulled out from under you. After being the indispensable co-pilot and the indispensable mother, I was no longer needed at all. To feel no longer needed robs one of a sense of value. Much of loneliness is the illusion of lost value. Actually we are needed always, all our lives if we have children or grandchildren or pupils or friends, but we are needed only *intermittently*. It is not a steady occupation you can depend on.

At such times you take stock. You pick up the pieces and try to fit them together. I found mine fitted into a new pattern. I did some flying with my husband. Not to open up air routes again—that need was over, and he also had been through changes. He was now concerned with the environment and the threat to its beauty, its wildlife, its resources. We went to watch whales in Baja California, wild animals in the reservations of Africa, and eagles in Montana. Life was well balanced between solitude and sharing. I had quiet periods in which to write, and travels sharing a pursuit of my husband's, equally vital to me. It was a good period.

Then the music stopped again, and I was a widow. Widowhood is the essence of being alone, not sometimes, but always. I could talk for an hour about widowhood, but I won't, because you're not all widows or widowers. But some of you may live alone, and by middle age, most people have had losses. This is universal as we go marching on. I am going to speak about some of the losses in this period and ways to meet them.

When the music stops, one looks around. There are certain facts to be faced. There are signposts approaching "the Third Age,"* announc-

*The period of "middle adulthood" described by social scientist Erik Erikson as between the ages of forty and sixty-five.

ing limits. First of all, I mind the closed door, the threat of the dead-line. There is less time, less strength, in certain ways, less scope: these are concrete and measurable losses. But the deadline threat is not new. One has met it before in life: Sunday evenings with the homework not yet done, cramming for examinations at college, packing for a journey, or finishing a book. It was described by the seventeenth century poet Andrew Marvell:

But at my back I always hear
Time's winged chariot hurrying near.

But this deadline is the end of life. How to meet that pressure? Well, not by hurrying. There is only a certain amount of time, and you have to come to terms with it as you do with space in packing for a journey or moving to a smaller house. (What to save? What to throw out?) What are the priorities?

Some of the priorities are duties: what you *have* to do. ("Tasks at the End of Life.") There is inevitably some tidying up, finishing off the loose ends of your life or work. If you have lost a husband or wife, you have the task of trying to finish their projects. There is a certain satisfaction in putting things in order, but not much joy. You have all done it: redrafting the will, going over papers, photographs, posses-sions. Some tasks to be done meticulously, a few sentimentally, tied up in ribbons. But most clearing up is giving or throwing away. Furniture too big for a diminished household is easy to get rid of. Passing on family chairs and tables to another generation is the happiest solution. Your own home is freer and less burdened, and the children's houses are cluttered and gayer.

But one cannot spend the rest of life in tidying up. Time is limited and must not be wasted at this stage. What is waste? I made a list of my own wasteful activities. I'm sure everyone's list is different, and it changes in different periods of one's life. My present list starts with *getting tired.* I find being tired is a terrible waste. I was brought up not to accept "being tired." At Miss Chapin's School we sang a hymn that started out:

Awake my soul, stretch every nerve,
And press with vigor on!—

That was fine for the eighth grade—not for the Third Age. You'd be exhausted by noon. Besides, getting tired, I find, leads to *more* waste, like reading the back pages of the newspaper just from inertia, or flipping through mail-order catalogues to fill the hour before supper.

Perfectionism is another waste on my list. It's all right to be perfectionist in your special area, what you care most about: your skill, your art, your scholarship, even an important letter. But perfectionism in household tasks is a waste. I don't try to scrub all the black off the pots and pans, and I don't see dust any more.

Clutter is a waste on my list. A good example is what comes in the mail: letters, requests, advertisements, appeals. My husband had a rule: deal with each piece of mail, each paper, only once. Excellent, if you can make an immediate decision. Since he threw 80 percent of his mail unopened into a large barrel, that worked for him. And I have a daughter who took after him. She has two cartons, one marked "love" and the other marked "money"; she finds almost everything fits into one of these two categories. But I have a great deal of mail that is neither love nor money. When I don't know where to file it, I put it into an envelope marked "conscience." Clutter is impossible; it blocks out vision.

There are many other wastes on my list. Down at the very end is a big waste that underlies many of the others, a hidden leak in the bottom of the barrel. This is *trying to live by other people's standards.* I remember an old aunt saying to me, of cocktail parties, I think, "I no longer put things in my stomach to please other people." Should one put things in one's mind to please other people? Read books to please other people? Or go to parties to please other people? By the time one reaches a certain age, one should be able, as Marianne Moore said, "to have the courage of one's peculiarities."

I have been talking about the tasks, the losses and the wastes in the Third Age, the limitations of growing older. These are what are noticed first—what everyone complains about. But there are also enrichments and enlargements, overlooked, particularly in the modern Western world. We need to be reminded that in other cultures and at other times, the Third Age was not regarded as a diminishment. In simpler communities and earlier times, in Europe and even in America, older citizens had an honored place and special functions, as the advisors and arbiters in times of trouble. We still keep this tradition in our Supreme Court. The ancient Chinese revered the old and in the traditional Hindu concept, the man and the woman in late middle age handed over their tasks and burdens to their children and retired from worldly life and its problems. This Third Age was called "retreat to the forest." But this retreat, according to Hindu tradition, was not pictured as a closed door, a limitation. Life was not over but beginning with a new purpose: to be free to search for the meaning of life—some kind of parallel, perhaps, to insight.

The ancient Hindu concept seems too rigid for the modern Westerner. Unlike them, we have no customs or rites to guide us through our transitions. We have to explore and find paths for ourselves.

Here I might start on my list of non-waste activities. There is still work open to us, work perhaps now with fewer distractions, work one enjoys or work one has followed all one's life: a career that can continue, even if retired, at least from the sidelines, an abiding interest that one follows, even in old age. I have always remembered Bernard Baruch saying in his eighties, "I'm just as good as ever—for two hours of the day." I consider that a splendid statement. It does imply choice. If you have two good hours, or four or five, in the morning perhaps, you must use these hours for the most important work. Less important business or pleasure can wait for the afternoon. My choice is to write in the mornings and, when I can, spend afternoons outside.

For me, a non-waste activity is the outer world of nature, which means far more to me now than when I was young. The outer world doesn't have to mean safaris to Africa or living in the wilderness. In my life, it is in small outdoor jobs like pruning bushes, planting bulbs, or bird watching. There are mornings when the only thing that gets me out of bed is simply that I must put out suet and seed for three woodpeckers, two nuthatches, and a flock of chickadees. It is not compassion or ornithology; it is making a connection with a realm of life outside my own. Feeding the birds is a rite that unites me to the web of life around me. I lose myself. I feel part of the pattern of the seasons. Nature can be cruel, but the cycle is reassuring—the sense of unlimited life going on. To merge with the cycle is nourishing in a very basic sense.

In the same way, I look at the stars at night. I find the circle of navigating stars by which we used to fly. I repeat their names, like an incantation: "Capella, Castor, Pollux, Procyon, Sirius . . ." And from a much earlier stage in my life, I remember the psalm I learned as a child: "The heavens declare the glory of God, and the firmament showeth His handiwork." Looking at the stars, one is extended to another dimension.

On the human plane also, surprisingly, other dimensions open up. The definition of insight, you remember, included understanding and sympathy. If one has married and had children, there are grandchildren.

Free of cares and guilt, one can watch these familiar strangers. They carry reverberations of the past (one recognizes a father's humor or a husband's inventiveness). In the other direction, they are periscopes into the future. Through them one sees glimpses of what the future may hold. You extend your life backwards and forwards. And whether they are *your* grandchildren or someone else's, your pupils, or younger co-workers, you will find them very receptive to your attention and, especially, to your praise. You demand less from them than you did from your own children. And you have learned to listen.

Listening is a key to friendship, and friendship with all ages becomes more enriching as one marches along. Your contemporaries have weathered their trials and so have you; you have more in common with them than you once thought. Communication becomes easier. It leaps ahead more swiftly, skipping the preliminary steps. One is less shy; one has dropped the mask and some of the pride. And you know that time is short. As in the old Housman poem, you feel like saying:

> *Take my hand quick and tell me,*
> *What have you in your heart.*
> . . . .
> *Ere to the wind's twelve quarters*
> *I take my endless way.**

I am not overlooking the losses. There are losses that cannot be replaced: of friends, of family, of husband or wife. One must, and should, grieve. But I don't believe grief is impoverishing or a waste. Neither do I think grief is simply to be endured. It is a live emotion, like joy, love, or anger, and, like all strong emotions, it can enlarge life. Unlike depression—which is not a live emotion but a withdrawal, an ebb tide—grief is a full tide. It sweeps away irrelevancies and distractions. Petty emotions are lost in its path. Even regrets and remorse are washed out to sea. One is left closer to the mysteries at the center of life.

Yeats knew this when he wrote the last lines of this poem, "Dialogue of Self and Soul":

> *When such as I cast out remorse*
> *So great a sweetness flows into the breast*

---

*From XXXII, "From far, from eve and morning," in *A Shropshire Lad*, by A. E. Housman (1859–1936).

We must laugh and we must sing,
We are blest by everything,
Everything we look upon is blest.

Yeats was, I think, describing insight and one way of reaching it.

T. S. Eliot, in *Four Quartets*, defines other approaches to insight when he speaks of "moments of illumination." There are such moments when one seems to break out of the boundaries of the ordinary world. One recognizes them as moments of beauty, stillness or wonder: listening to a Bach fugue or to a thrush's song on a spring evening, a moment of meditation on a still morning, or sitting in a chapel alone, or wordless communication with an old friend. These are the moments of "absolute unmixed attention" that Simone Weil describes. They are cracks into timelessness or, in old-fashioned terms, glimpses of eternity. I think one can cultivate the cracks. We are more open to them when we are out of the procession. (When we were young, we were pressing ahead to the next chair.)

At such moments, the losses and the limitations, the tasks and the gains of the second half of life are forgotten. One is reconciled even to the hardest losses. One feels close to the people one has lost. Not that one has brought them back to one's side, but one feels no longer separate from them, or from anything of importance. Separateness itself—standing alone as a child or feeling abandoned in age—has melted, evaporated like a mist. And here at the end I can only quote Eliot from his poem "Dry Salvages":

The moments of happiness—not the sense of well-being,
Fruition, fulfillment, security or affection,
Or even a very good dinner, but the sudden illumination—
We had the experience but missed the meaning,
And approach to the meaning restores the experience
In a different form, beyond any meaning
We can assign to happiness . . .

Tellina, Darien
October 24th, 1981
Dear Vicki and Stephen [Mitchell],

Your letter folded into the little box with the precious quartz crystal was waiting for me in Connecticut when I got back from Switzerland not long ago. I felt badly it had been waiting so long, but perhaps I found it at the right moment. It is always hard to come back from Switzerland, where there is more time and peace, and the mountains. (I miss all three in Darien.)

The crystal is very beautiful and makes me think of mountains. (Perhaps childhood memories of crystal mountains in fairy tales, up which the knight had to climb to find the treasure or free the princess.) But this crystal seemed beneficent, and not an ordeal to be met; it pleased me very much that you should have chosen it for me. I find there is an inner mountain slope caught—or reflected—inside. (Did you notice this?) I don't know much about crystals but feel very open to this one and its tradition. So I often leave it under my pillow or in my pocket when I walk in the fields here, and I am sure I "will get to know it." I am very grateful to both of you.

I don't know where I am going to die, Stephen, so I can't forewarn you. (*Not*, I hope, in Maui or Darien.) I don't feel like dying yet; I have one more book I hope to write. But I do think often about death—chiefly in the sense of "Time's winged chariot drawing near."

October has been very beautiful here. I think autumn is my favorite season and I feel in tune with it. It was good to see you both and I hope I can again before long—Darien is nice in the spring—and the chalet is a quiet place to walk and talk.

I hope all is well with both of you and send my love and grateful thoughts.

Anne

Saturday, January 16th, 1982 [DIARY]

It is hard to start a new year—half a month late. I find it appalling that I have done no writing on a new book—only notes—and not many of them since coming back from Switzerland. Of course, it has been busy, but where has it gone to? There have been emergencies. Richard's back problem. Reeve and he were here in my house when I came home.

I feel that the children are all going through crises: Land and the giving up of the ranch; Jon and Barbara (who has not been well), who are beginning to plan to move to a smaller house; Ansy and Jerzy* in Washington, distressed by the Polish crisis, and she by the anniversary

---

*Following a divorce from Julien Feydy in 1975, Ansy moved from Paris to Washington, D.C., and married the Polish-born composer, conductor, and pianist Jerzy Sapieyevski. They had one son, Marek.

of her melanoma operation last year; Reeve in suspense (and badly over-worked) with Richard's pain and depression in his long convalescence from the back operation; Scott and Alika pinched for money.

There seem to be so many minor, or major, emergencies. "Just living" takes so much time and strength. This is age, I realize, although I have been well. I get so tired.

I am slowly finding things to make my life (technically) more effi-cient: a new snow-plower, a new mechanic at a nearer gas station (due to Elsie's* neighborly suggestion) for my car, taking the train to New York (not easier—but possible). But there must be other psychological reasons for my avoiding working on that book. I do *anything* rather than face it. Why?

Sunday, January 17th [1982]

Perhaps I avoid working on a book on age because I have not solved the problem myself. ("It is insoluble," Mina says.) Perhaps insoluble, but still visible, analyzable, even describable.

One lives in the midst of other people's crises. Con telephones me that Aubrey is in the hospital again. He fell, and they still do not know if it was another (small) stroke or only an increase of his diabetes (the blood sugar has increased tremendously). This can be treated but it is more complicated and more perilous. And I do not see any way out for her. It can only get worse: more of an invalid's life for Aubrey, more anxiety for Con, more isolation and diminishment of life.

This morning I wake feeling better. It is bright and very cold. I put out grain and fat for the birds. Berwick† rushes out and then back in again. I call Reeve and find out that Richard is back on "total bed rest" again. She is steady and hopeful and says he is having two medical vis-its a week and they are trying to find out what "sets him back." He is, of course, depressed and thinks there is something wrong that "they" haven't yet found out. This is not a downhill picture: Richard will get better; it is only long and slow and incredibly hard to decipher. *Why* does he regress? Was it the trip to New York? Or climbing the stairs (once) on his return?

---

*Elsie Wheeler and her husband, "Link," bought the large house in Darien from the Lind-berghs when they moved into the smaller house they had built.
†AML's cairn terrier.

Sunday, January 31st [1982]

Some kind of thaw has set in. A gray day, overcast and drippy, still slippery underfoot. I got out yesterday, backing all the way, and went to have my hair done prior to my evening's engagement of supper with friends in New Canaan and a show of old movies (silent) afterwards in a big barn hall, with a musician who creates musical accompaniment to silent movies.

I have been dreading this evening all week. *Why* did I get caught? Because one can't refuse everything if one is a widow. Supper is small-ish with very nice people. Then we go on to the barn where we see silent movies and hear the musician (I almost wrote "magician"—for he seemed like one), miraculously fitting music to the films' mood and meaning. It is good entertainment (old films of Chaplin, John Barry-more, Lillian Gish, etc.). But the evening was very long (and rather cold in the barn) and ended up rainy.

It was somewhat spoiled for me by realizing that the whole affair was a benefit performance to raise money for the New Canaan Art Center. I felt as if I were "on show," to benefit the performance. And why not? I might add—somebody to get more people interested in the cause. All money raising has an element of this publicity courting.

My problem was that I wasn't very interested in the cause. It was good entertainment, but not exactly art—or not an art I am very open to or knowledgeable about. I find in today's magazine section of the *N.Y. Times* a definition of art by Pasternak which satisfies me: "Contemporary trends of thought imagine that art is like a fountain, whereas it is a sponge. They have decided that art should push forth whereas it should absorb and become saturated. They think it can be broken down into methods of depiction, whereas it is composed of organs of perception. The proper task of art is to be always an observer *to gaze more purely than others do*, more receptively and faithfully. . . ."

Perhaps the composer was following this tenet. The people who watched were merely being social, and being entertained. My friend introduced me to everyone—out of kindness I am sure, but it made me feel "on show" too. And before the evening was up, I felt recognized more than I enjoy, and obliged to be smiling all the time. It was a "smi-ley" evening and I came into my dark and silent house with relief, feeling I had eaten too much and smiled too much. And it will no doubt lead to other contacts I don't particularly want. Why did I go? One has to take some chances—if one lives alone.

Les Monts-de-Corsier
July 14th, 1982 [DIARY]

I have been in the chalet ten days—arriving on July 3rd with Berwick. The plane was so full that they put me in first class, which was very comfortable with lots of room for Berwick so I didn't have to hold him on my lap.

I found the chalet had been opened by M. Parker,* and the light and water turned on, but *filthy*—inside and out: deserted and dusty, rugs rolled up, dead flies, paint flaking off, everything damp and mildewed downstairs. And outside, the shed enlarged to take in the new oil tank—quite a neat job. But my yard overgrown with long grass, weeds and briars, and strewn with the workmen's broken wine bottles, tools, lumber, bits of plaster and broken tiles, even odds and ends of clothing. I start immediately to clean up.

First a trip to Châtel† in the new car which I have trouble with (gear shift, while I have been driving an automatic) and am very nervous about—to do some shopping. The landscape looks the same, green and hazy toward the mountains and lake. Everyone is out in the fields, cutting or raking the hay. I go to the big co-op on the edge of town, as it is the easiest, and buy enough for two or three days for Berwick and me. It is Saturday and things shut early.

Sunday I go to Nesta's for lunch, a disastrous day. I was too tired. I had trouble with the car (my own mistakes in shifting) and got it stuck on the hill leading up to Nesta from Lausanne (after picking up Monica). Nesta's "François" went down to rescue me. I climbed the hill carrying Monica's radio, my own bag, and leading Berwick. It was hot, exhausting and humiliating.

Nesta had the exiled Princess Olga (of Yugoslavia) and the exiled Queen of Romania and her lady-in-waiting. I was hot and tired, and royalty bother me. I don't know when to curtsey and when to address them as "Your Highness" and when as "Ma'am." I felt very shy (about eighteen) and very upset about damaging the car (probably burnt out the clutch). François got it uphill, finally, but then the battery was dead. I had to be driven home, humiliated and upset.

Monday was a perfectly beautiful day. I had breakfast on the balcony

---

*The Swiss handyman and plumber who cared for the chalet.
†Châtel-St.-Denis, the district capital of Veveyse, a few miles north of the chalet and the nearest town of any size for groceries, etc.

and looked across at the lake and the Dents du Midi, remembering how Scott had trimmed the tops of my trees last fall to give me this beautiful view. And then there was my "guardian angel" tree at the corner of the balcony looking down at me. I felt better.

I telephoned Scott, and M. Paschoud at the garage who said he would go to Nesta's and get the car. I called Mme. Lavanchy, a cleaning lady I had written to: yes, she would come Tuesday afternoon to clean, but then she was going on her vacation—for *three weeks!* I felt cross but there was nothing to do about it. It was nice to talk to Scott, who sounded very relaxed and glad to hear me. He says he is going to Brazil on an exploratory trip to talk to the primatology center there. I am delighted.

I sweep every day and find something new: the radio in the big armoire, the bird seed (I hang up the feeder). My lavender bushes are blooming; they survived. I cut the grass from around them. I pull down the chaise longues from the attic to sit on the balcony in the evening.

Little House
Friday, January 7th, 1983 [DIARY]

A week into the New Year. I have not written since I came home from Switzerland. It was the same last year. I go for walks every afternoon with Berwick and this keeps me sane. Desk work in the mornings. There are family problems—Land has not yet sold the ranch although there was a firm bid which fell through; it is very hard on him. He has done all the hard work on a family-owned ranch. Barbara and Jon are separating. I knew this last spring, but I hoped it would not come off, or would not cause so much anguish.

I go down to Anne's for Thanksgiving. It is a beautiful weekend and we walk with the children and have a quiet Thanksgiving lunch. Her book has come out and has had some very good reviews. It is charming and gay and well done.

Reeve comes for her last visit before the baby. We stop and have supper with Krissie and Bob (I bring a casserole and wine).

Aunt Edith died peacefully in her sleep. I am glad for her. She was so tired and sad and had so little to live for. She was afraid of dying; I'm glad it was so easy. I went to the service in the Englewood cemetery. I had not been there since Mother's death.

We stood around the grave site, just a little round hole for the can of ashes. I had never been to a service where there wasn't a grave and a coffin. It seemed very artificial. I looked at the tops of the trees and felt grateful Aunt Edith had escaped. We said the Cutter family psalm (121st). I don't know that I believe in graves that have to be cared for and visited. I don't object to cremation, but shouldn't the ashes be scattered to the winds? It seems like a contradiction to burn a body and then bury it in a can.

We went back to the house for a brunch. The dining room (neglected for so many years when I went to see Aunt Edith in bed) was polished and clean, and the beautiful table glowing with candles, silver, plates of sandwiches, and cakes and wine. All the treasures Aunt Edith loved—china, glass, silver—were out on display as if for a wedding or some splendid party (and she used to love parties). So much of it was suggestive of ECM and Next Day Hill (which she had learned and copied from her older sister)—antique furniture, Mexican silver, old plates, and a "groaning board" of food. I felt odd—partly that it was so nostalgic and partly that I was the oldest person there (probably).

When I left, I knew I would never see the house again and that my ties with Englewood were now completely broken. With Aunt Edith's death following the deaths of Dana and Mary Atchley* last spring and the departure of Connie Chilton and Ann McGavin from the Elisabeth Morrow School, I felt there was no reason to go back to Englewood. I am not too sad about it, but an era is closed.

I miss Dana terribly and was glad I had seen him in the last months of his life even though he could hardly speak (our eyes and our hands spoke). But I was grateful he did not have to live any longer. And all summer, and even now, I think about him every day with gratitude and sometimes with humor too, remembering his warm affection and his perceptive and humorous and *practical* advice as a doctor. In a sense, his death returned him to me—as he was in his good years. What a gift to have known him!

Christmas at Reeve's: quiet and warm and loving with the children, and Richard well and walking around without pain. Reeve and I fed the animals (I protesting). She is so active and I worry for her, but she enjoys throwing hay down for her horses and sheep in the big dark dusty barn. (She is the little mother to us all.) I go back in another month to take over when she is in the hospital. I am somewhat apprehensive. I am not the person I was eight years ago when her last child was born (Susan-

*Dana Atchley died in June 1982 at the age of eighty-nine, having practiced medicine until he was eighty-five. Mary Atchley died in May of that year.

nah). How quickly one grows old in the seventies! I feel the change each year now. Especially getting up in the morning, stiff and slow. But by the time I've exercised, had my bath and breakfast, I feel vigorous again. Nevertheless, only the mornings are really good—at least, for thinking, writing and any difficult job or decision or action. I can shop in the afternoons, or write checks, or see people, sometimes, though I often fall asleep after lunch—or *want* to. And after my nap, I never quite get back to morning vigor. But I walk with Berwick and am invigorated by that, and the beauty of bare trees against a late red sky and then tea.

So much of my life goes into sorting the mail: answering letters or worrying about them; requests—saying *NO*—politely; throwing away begging letters, appeals, advertisements; clearing up clutter, which keeps accumulating—newspapers, magazines. A lot of it is still the trailing glory of CAL: people who are writing books about him, or want to interview me about his, or our, lives, or people who met him once and want an autograph or some book signed or some comment verified. It takes time, it adds clutter and it deadens one to real life—one's own life. Has one not a right to one's own life?

I have also become a kind of matriarch. Children, grandchildren, cousins, friends who knew me once. This is my life and I want to be open to them—but is it my life?

Little House
A gray and cold Monday, January 10th, 1983 [DIARY]
I am afraid of any new writing. It does not come easily. I have tried sporadically to write about age, widowhood, living alone. There are many thoughts written down, but they will not come together in a form. They are not a book. A notebook perhaps? What am I afraid of? Afraid of failing? Afraid of facing the end of my writing—a period of aridity without writing? But I am not totally arid; when I am moved to writing a letter to a widow or talking to a troubled woman or man, living alone, I can give out something I still have to give. There is a spring there, still flowing—but only for people. I cannot do it in the abstract, in solitude.

Once, of course, I had people: a husband, a family of children. They fed my need for people. Now I live alone; I need people and am stimulated by them. Once I needed solitude to write; now there is too much solitude. I fill it with duties, anything to fill up the vacuum.

What do I enjoy in my day? I am appalled at my list: putting out seed for the birds, or suet, and watching them peck at it; walking with my dog and looking at the bare trees against the sky; I like seeing or talking to my children on the telephone, but that doesn't happen every day; getting into a warm bed at night with a good book; listening to a good concert on the radio. I don't particularly like eating or cooking though. I love my tea at five after the walk, and my cheese and wine before supper. Of course, I like seeing people when I can. Going out to someone's house for tea or supper always stimulates me—or having a friend or friends come to me.

There is not too much of this, except chatting on the telephone, but there is more than there was in my first years of widowhood. It is really a rather bleak life, devoid of people. Once a week I go into New York and see people—the reading group—but I am exhausted driving back in the traffic (especially in the winter's short days and bad weather), and usually exhausted the next day.

I am happy if I feel I have helped someone in a crisis in life (or even not a crisis) to see their lives more clearly. Sometimes I feel this after a talk with Elsie, my neighbor, or with Anne B., a younger friend, or one of my old secretaries (who become surrogate daughters)—a talk over tea, or walking. The Darien discussion group is a new opening and quite stimulating, though more psychological than the group in New York (which is older, and is made up of women struggling with the problems of age, illness and loss). These women in Darien are still looking for their "identity." (And Dr. Davidoff,* who directs them, is passionately devoted to helping women to that end—passionately and compassionately.) I feel I am beyond that age and desire.

I am happiest when I am helping others to live: the visit from Barbara after Christmas, with Morgan, her youngest. I do not know whether I *helped* or not: I listened and was impressed with what she had worked through after the blow of separation from Jon. I was there to understand and to admire and to love her. This is, again, the mother-daughter relationship; to do this occasionally is enough to live for.

Little House
Tuesday, March 22nd, 1983 [DIARY]
What happened to January? And February? On January 24th Reeve's baby, Jonathan Lindbergh Brown, was born. Richard called me that morning and I went up the next day. Rosemary drove me in her car,

---

*Dr. Ida Davidoff (1904–2001), friend of AML's and former professor of psychiatry and psychology at Albert Einstein College of Medicine, also a marital and family therapist in private practice in New Canaan.

staying overnight in her Vermont house and driving down the next day. I took boxes of food, and casseroles Mrs. Swan had cooked, and frozen and fresh vegetables, bread and fruit, so I would not have to shop or cook much. I was afraid of the driving in snow in Reeve's car. I was nervous about this grandmothering stint, wondering if I would be equal to it physically. I hadn't done it for eight years (Susannah's birth was eight years ago, the first winter after CAL's death). But I was stronger then, eight years younger. Would I be able to be on my feet that much—all day, as Reeve is in her daily life? But once I arrived in the Vermont house I felt like another person.

It was, of course, a very joyous period. The first son, and Reeve so safely through the experience—which had some possible dangers, for a late baby, and after her two difficult years, one following her own surprising "seizure" (due to scar tissue from the concussion seven years before) and the resulting drugs she had to take. And that year followed by Richard's broken back and operation and long and painful healing process. Those were two painful years and hard on them both, but they survived and with the new baby, life had straightened out. Reeve seemed so well and took the birth in a relaxed way. Richard could now walk and is out of pain, though still must be very careful. The baby was perfect in health and looks: a calm and comfortable baby, and sturdy.

I have written a sketchbook piece about this baby's homecoming, but it does not describe my sense of renewal from the ten days in that happy family. I felt I was back in the river of life again. I was needed. I was used.

Lizzy and Susannah were eager to help, to hold the baby, to rock him. I trembled somewhat to see him in Susannah's arms like a big doll. But Reeve was not nervous and she taught them carefully and brought them into the special circle around a new baby and mother. They must not be left out.

It was a privilege to hold the baby and carry him upstairs. Once I was worried when I heard Susannah fall at the top of the stairs and break into sobs. But before I could get to her, Lizzie was there next to her, on her knees, the baby safely in her arms, *not* crying.

"Don't cry, Susannah, the baby is all right. *He* isn't crying. *See?* He's all right." I thought this was extraordinary of an older sister, to comfort rather than to capitalize on her younger sister's fault: instead of using the incident to build up her own role in taking care of the baby, she was being mother to Susannah as well as the baby. Lizzie was, of course, very careful and gentle with the baby—and very proud and happy to be trusted.

The days went swiftly and happily and I lived on many levels, remembering my own babies and my mother or Miss Waddington at my side. I thought too of CAL. What was there of him in this child? And of my first baby. There was something very familiar about this child but whom he resembled I couldn't pin down.

It was hard to leave. I share so much with Reeve, but I knew I must leave the family to its own private circle.

March 24th [1983] [DIARY]

February went into great sadness in our reading group, with two of our members' husbands dying of cancer at almost the same time. It is our age, I realize. Death is not really an accident any more. It is all around us. It always was, only we didn't realize it. Now one is faced with it every day. Death from old age is not really a tragedy, but death from cancer does always seem a horror. There is—or seems to be—more and more of it, an epidemic almost, like the Black Death in the Middle Ages.

It is, or may be, easier for Margot, who is so convinced of life after death or some kind of reincarnation. I am—or remain most of the time—open to the possibility of some kind of survival of the spirit, but it is very vague and abstract. It is simply an open question in my mind, like the end of Lewis Thomas's chapter on death.* What happens to the spirit? he asks, and follows with several rather inconclusive suppositions (or more questions), then states, "Nature doesn't waste anything." That is all we know.

The services, however, were a great help and very beautiful.

I want to be cremated, but not buried in a can like Aunt Edith—scattered to the winds, in a loved place, under a tree. And I want my service to be traditional and abstract, not personal. *No eulogies.* Music (mostly Bach) and psalms, prayers and hymns (if anyone can sing). CAL's service, reduced to a simpler form, would do. All this I have written out in my prayer book. And I want to die at home, and not to have my illness, if mortal, prolonged by life-sustaining machinery. Pain should be relieved as much as possible, even if it shortens life. After this period of death and ashes, we have to go on living.

Corliss came out for lunch. I keep trying to see him as he was—is—a very old friend, but it is so unsatisfactory. Is this age, or illness, or my

---

*From *The Lives of a Cell: Notes of a Biology Watcher,* by Lewis Thomas (New York: Viking, 1974).

lack of anything in common with him any more? Perhaps in this case it is age and illness: he had a very serious illness over Christmas and was in the hospital for a heart operation. (They put a pig's valve in his heart!) He said he feels much better, but I felt everything was an effort for him.

But it was not that exactly, but a kind of disconnectedness in our conversation. He seems very much there at one moment, discussing an editorial in the *Times* that day, and then not there at all when I talk to him about his work and his writing. There is very little *personal* talk or contact. Perhaps it is too painful for him. He is lonely, he says, so the only thing to do is work. If Helen had lived, would he have been like this? I felt very sad when he left, as if he were in full retreat.

There it is again. Mortality, so close to the surface—behind every face, every mask. One knows that under the thin crust of daily life lie the dark chasms: mortality, tragedy, separation, change. For the old, to sicken and die is not tragedy but normal life, but one would like them to die at home, in peace, without suffering or panic. When the young die, or even those in full life, it is accidental, a shock, an abnormality. At times like this, one crashes through the thin crust of daily life and faces the eternal sadness. . . .

Old photographs fall out. One of my mother, young, younger than I now am, with my first baby in her arms, holding up a twig for him to see. And then another, a close-up of the baby staring at me from that calm brow and wondering face. The great wise questioning eyes—so beautiful. I fall again into the pit of "the lost"—that tragic event. Why did it happen? Where did he go? Why?

Why to all the tragedies one reads about every day in the newspapers? The Holocaust, the tortures of civil wars, of El Salvador. ("They don't waste bullets on the children"—just pick them up by the feet and dash their heads against the walls.) The slow cruelty of Communist prisons. The swift and careless cruelty of the atom bomb. We seem doomed. Religion has always said so but we have not believed it. We refuse to look beyond the show of daily life. An accidental detail can trip the spring and the trap-door opens beneath us—we fall into the abyss.

And yet sometimes, as at last Sunday's concert, the opposite can happen: one rises above the daily movie. One reaches another level, one floats above, released by the oboe concerto of Telemann. This too is life.

Chalet Planorbe
July 21st, 1983 [DIARY]

June went to doctors, and dentist's checkups. Then Ansy, Jerzy, and Marek came through en route to Maine for Con's seventieth birthday reunion celebration. Margot and I flew up to Portland and then took a driver and cab to Rockland, stopping for provisions on the way. We are a large group farmed out in different houses.

The ferry at Rockland is just the same. We load our groceries into a friendly car going over. Ellen Hallowell (Pratt) is on the same ferry—quite unchanged, vigorous and open and warm, now a widow. She spends every summer on the island.

It is cool on the ferry and I watch the landmarks of the ride to North Haven: the Edward Hopper lighthouse, the "monument" buoys, the small green humps of the White Islands in the distance, and then narrowing into the thoroughfare, with the fields sloping down to the water and the old-fashioned summer houses overlooking the harbor.

The dock is full of people waving. Rhidian is there to meet us and we transfer groceries into a ranch wagon and drive off past Waterman's store (the main street is now one way) and up the hill, around past the church, and down the dusty road to Pulpit Harbor. It is all full of memories and the next three days are more so.

The weather is very beautiful, hot by day and cool at night. I felt I was walking in a dream. I had forgotten how beautiful the place was: fields green, with tall grasses and daisies; dark pines against the sea; and the Camden Hills across the bay, with those green humps of islands strung out between us and the mainland. We had breakfast in our own houses and then wandered about meeting our children or grandchildren: Ansy strolling along casually, Charles* in blue jeans with a staff of driftwood he carries with him. Why? Is it a joke? Or a protection? Or a companion? We take a long hot walk in the woods toward the Cabots' place where he talks to me about his computer projects, of which I understand very little but listen and ask questions because I am so fond of him.

The children are rehearsing a play (*Annie*) they are giving on the terrace of the Thatcher house. Children's voices echo through the pine trees. Many of the cousins have not met before and pair up: Marek with Rhys Morgan, Anne and Wendy Fulenwider with Constance Pendleton, who runs the play.

---

*Ansy's son, Charles Feydy.

What is extraordinary about this weekend are the different layers people are living on. Grandmothers and grandfathers are living half the time in the past, in happy memories, observing the young as the older generation once observed us. Fathers and mothers are busy, but delighting in the freedom of informal living and being relatively free of burdens, since children entertain each other. For the children, it is wild discovery of each other, of this new and yet familiar and safe-of-rules world. They are living totally in the present.

Yes, the beauty of the place helps one to live in the present. The song of the white-throated sparrow is hauntingly everywhere, or the sight of a white schooner rounding the bluff.

And Charles? In what world is he living? Not in the children's world—nor in the adults'. In his own world of the mind, I think. I wish he had a companion.

There was one big dinner of neighbors, toasts, and speeches in the old dining room and playroom of the main house (rather too much for Aubrey, who left early), and the uproarious night of the play, *Annie*, performed by all the grandchildren on the terrace of the old house. Images: Annie, the waif who found good fortune, Wendy F.; Marek, Annie's dog, on all fours; Lizzie B. as FDR with cigarette holder in jaw, pointed skyward; Susannah in high-heeled shoes, swinging hips as a sophisticated lady; and Connie P. as the brash, hard-hearted orphan asylum matron.

For me, the happiness was marred by the absence of Reeve, caught in Vermont with her baby home from the hospital in Hanover, but still terribly upset by his ordeal the week before: a virus infection, a high blood count, and various diagnoses of his reactions and complications. . . . Even after three weeks, he is unable to sleep and cries fitfully, although Reeve's latest letter says he begins to sleep a little more at night. . . . Reeve and Richard are worn out. Fortunately their own pediatrician is encouraging and sees no sign of neurological disorder. I telephoned every morning from North Haven but although Reeve was calm, I had the uneasy feeling it was a terrible ordeal, as it was.

Back to Connecticut for the last five days of packing, shopping, dentist's appointments and seeing people, the most important being Mina, who is, one *must* assume, dying; she has a blocked artery that nothing can be done about. She is very weak and stays in her bed, and looks ravaged. She is not in pain, only increasing bodily weakness. I go to see her, as I have several times this spring—as she evidently wants to see me. Driving up, I try to think of what I can bring her and what I can say. She does not want sympathy; she wants understanding. And she wants to express herself, to analyze, to be aware of what she is going through. For despite the physical frailty, she is mentally and psychologically super-sensitive and alive. I was astonished and somewhat disturbed to have her talk so much, since she needs oxygen regularly when she feels overcome with weakness.

I began to understand, however, that she wanted to explore, be aware of, and express what she was going through. She must explore the process of dying as she has always explored and expressed the process of living. I can listen, and I do, with the greatest interest and sympathy and admiration. I can also confirm her feelings, her stages in the process of dying with Charles's experience, which she is eager to hear and finds reassuring.

She was taken out in her wheelchair to look at the garden, which had always meant so much to her, and now she was "beyond that." She only wanted to get back in bed. I told her about Land pushing C., that last week in Maui, out to look at the waves dashing against the cliffs, a sight he loved most in Hawaii. But he by then was "beyond that" and only wanted to get back into his bed. Yet he wanted to talk to us about the process of dying. He said it was easy to die—he had been very close to it that past week, he said, it wasn't anything "to face." Mina was very interested and kept describing some of her sensations: to look at the bouquet of flowers on her bureau, and to want to change *one* flower (she who always made such exquisite flower arrangements), and to realize she did not have the strength to cross the room to the bureau. (I could identify with her in this and understood it.)

It was a strange afternoon—to be talking and listening to someone on the verge of death but so passionately alive in spirit and mind, so hyper-sensitive and so stimulated, as if she were eager to talk, eager to explain, eager to share. A strange kind of "high" in the face of death. She must have been exhausted afterwards, I realized, but I could not deny her my attention, or deny her the outpouring of impressions. She did not want to let me go, and said it did her "a world of good." I thought of the letter we received about Mme Carrel's death and her last week, which had been evidently unusually alive and vigorous, described in this letter as "*le bien de la mort*"*—a sudden flowering of life that you sometimes see in an old apple tree with a fountain of young shoots exploding from its trunk.

I was rather shaken myself, driving home, realizing I would probably

---

*Could be translated from the French as either "the good death," "the well-being of death," or "the goodness of death."

never see her again. Realizing that an almost fifty-nine-year friendship and conversation was ended, I realized too that I was losing a mother figure—not a physical mother but an artistic one.

Sunday, July 31st, 1983 [DIARY]

I have been in the chalet a month now, with Barbara, who has just left. It has been a very pleasant month. Barbara and I live very harmoniously side by side. We are alike in some ways: oversensitive and overconscientious. She is a lot more practical than I am, and I am at this point in my life a little more relaxed. She is working her way through the pain, shock, and rejection of a divorce* and the facing and finding of a new independent life. I feel she has made great strides since Christmas and is over much of the (quite natural) bitterness and beginning to enjoy her new strength. We have talked a great deal, perhaps too much, but it has interested me.

Facing divorce and facing widowhood have certain superficial similarities but basically they are totally different. Widowhood sustains more of a wound but it is easier to live with the pain, which is two parts love. In divorce there is almost no love, which is torture, hell. On the other hand, if one can get through the bitterness of divorce—throw it away, put it behind one—there is another world to walk into. There is the adventure of finding a new self, a new interest, and a new life. For the widow this is more difficult, especially the older widow. One does not want to throw away the past. There is much one wants to hang on to, to carry on, to finish. There is so much baggage to go on carrying on this journey, while the divorced can throw away a lot of accumulations, happily and triumphantly. And then, with a widow, there is the sense of there being less strength, less time, and less energy to start a new life.

How is one to live? This is what I meant to do in a book but cannot achieve—or get to. Is it distractions? Or the general lowering of my life-force in aging? Or the lessening of pride and ambition? The lessening of vanity? A kind of humility? Why write another preachy book? Why not give directly to people? This is perhaps just laziness—or weariness—or fear of failure. I must face this, this summer, and give up gracefully if it is really my age and my failing energy and slowing of mind as well as of body, so I forget words and have to search and scratch for the right word.

*Barbara and Jon Lindbergh divorced in 1983.

I do not have the psychological energy to focus for hours on pulling my files and files of notes on old age and widowhood into some acceptable form. There is so much of value there that I hate to lose it. It should be given, but in what form? Perhaps it is impossible to make a book of it, even a book of scraps and pieces. To make it into a book I would have to give up much that I have found of "a new life" after widowhood.

Chalet
August 10th, 1983 [DIARY]
It has been a week since I received the first full and long letter from Reeve on Jonathan's condition. After three terrible weeks at home—when he cried day and night but the quality of the crying differed, first screaming and writhing, then just a colicky baby's crying, then continual fussing, as "natural as breathing"—the family pediatrician advised his going back to the hospital. It gave Reeve and Richard some quiet time to sleep, and it gave the baby five days of hospital care and feeding. He had been losing weight and "not thriving," due partly to his mother's breast-feeding having diminished.

He returned after five days, much quieter and eating and sleeping better. However, they made more tests and said that they now think he had encephalitis; the last "CAT scan" showed some signs of brain damage. They said there was no way of predicting what that will mean in terms of his development. . . .

Reeve has been obviously in agony, envisioning anything from "minimal impairment" to a "total disaster." Their own family pediatrician does not think this last image is realistic and does not expect such a serious outcome. But Reeve, of course, is shattered by the month of no sleep and constant anxiety, and now the total uncertainty. And she is constantly on the watch for the worst symptoms.

She does report that Jonathan now seems "cheerful for the most part, happy to be home." He responds to his family: his father and mother and the girls. Richard feels he is alert and trying to communicate, responsive at an increasing rate. Richard seems to everyone strong and supportive, but Reeve is obviously on the edge of panic, in spite of her courageous, honest letter. I could hardly bear to read it.

After reading it several times I decided to call Ansy, *not* Reeve, to find out how things were. Ansy and family are now in Darien and I was able to get her. She gave me quite a good picture and said Connie F. had taken Reeve to Dr. Rosen in Pennsylvania, to help her panic and also to find out more about brain damage. I also found out that Heidi was there and Mr. and Mrs. Brown were living next door to stand by if Richard or Reeve needed to leave. All this is helpful and may ease the situation but not appease the anxiety.

It has been hard for me to do anything since but think about Reeve. I know what she is going through and identify with her so much. Perhaps Rosen can reassure her, let her express her fears, let her cry, all of which is hard to do as a mother in the midst of a family.

I telephoned her the day after she got back from Rosen. Her voice was so lifeless I hardly recognized it and, better than anything else, it told me what she had been going through. It was, of course, heartbreaking and I longed to say something hopeful to dispel that graven discouragement, but I realized that she has to stay on the lowest level to remain steady. They have to take the gloomiest estimate, out of fear that hope will let them down again. She cannot stand any more seesawing from hope to despair. "We live from day to day."

Hope is cheap for the outsider who does not suffer the consequences of being let down. I am not exactly an outsider. In fact, I am possibly overreacting because this situation is a horrible repetition of my own tragedy so long ago. What I did not realize was that my tragedy is haunting *her*. Perhaps Rosen can help here. Perhaps she has always identified too much with me?

I decided not to call her again until things were on a steadier level. I went out that night and looked at the stars and tried to pray. In my heart I begged Charles to help her through this—I, who have no strong belief in immortality! Still, prayer helps—and perhaps the focus prayer brings.

I do have a strong feeling that her worst fears are unjustified, brought on by her exhaustion and encouraged by the careless and unjustified predictions and prognoses of a lot of experts who, I suspect, only want to ensure that they are not blamed in the future for a false diagnosis. Also, there is no doubt that she identifies with the old tragedy that happened to me and her father. How terribly the ghosts of an earlier history haunt the present! Must the scars of one generation go on and on?

Darien
Friday, December 2nd [1983]
Another month gone by. All the time since my return has flown—with nothing written. It has been a difficult fall, chiefly because of my worry about Reeve, who is still depressed and "living from day to day."

I made a trip down to Gardenville to see Dr. Rosen and find out what he thinks about her. Both he and Hazel were warm and welcoming. He has mellowed a good deal and retired from much of his practice. He has white hair and a limp from his old accident, but he can still play eighteen holes of golf and is as perceptive and strong in his mind and life-force as ever. He is very hopeful about the baby's recovery.

After the visit to Rosen—a hearty and optimistic atmosphere—I went up to visit Reeve in Vermont, where I stayed for almost a week, seeing the picture through her eyes and living in a rather pessimistic atmosphere. This baby is perfectly beautiful: a big healthy child of nine months with the motor ability of a four-month-old baby. He cannot turn over or sit up by himself. He does not try to crawl. His motor ability is being worked on by physiotherapy three times a week, as well as every day at home. In a week I saw some improvement.

He is *not* a sick or passive baby. He responds to one's talking, cuddling, smiling, or playing—done chiefly by the college girl whom Reeve has had for a month, who is remarkably sweet and gay and open with him. His two sisters are also marvelous with him. They adore him and rush to pick him up, play with him and talk to him. And he responds, trying to make sounds like theirs. They are the most spontaneous members of the household and are, I think, the most healthy influence on Jonathan.

Reeve and Richard are tender and careful with the baby, but it is all tinged with sadness or stiffened with apprehension. Reeve told me she felt she had "lost" her baby and had a "changeling" in its place. She looks for, and finds, of course, the worst signs.

Richard is just rather stiff and dutiful with the baby, so different from the way he treated him before the illness, with joy and gaiety. The St. Johnsbury pediatrician, who has had him from the beginning and knows the two girls also, said to Reeve, "I do not know how it will end but I do not see total disaster." But she cannot believe him, or does not dare to.

I don't feel the baby is a "changeling." He seems to me the same baby but caught in a net, struggling to get free, struggling to talk, to sit up straighter, to respond to his sisters, to hold a spoon. Certainly he is behind, but not "astray"—just trying to catch up. However, except for the girls, it is a very gloomy atmosphere. I rack my brains to think of ways out for the parents: a visit to Darien, a trip to Florida, Christmas in Darien (it would be too gloomy in Vermont). Everything is compared to last winter's hope and joy. I understand the sadness and the long gray vista they envision ahead. But I cannot really believe in that scenario.

After the week in Vermont, the family (without the baby, left in Vermont with Beth) did come down to Darien for a weekend and it was quite a happy time. Jon and Karen* turned up for one night with them. It was a full house and I packed a bag and moved down into CAL's office and slept in the single bed I had in Next Day Hill before I married. I can remember sleeping in that bed when C. and I were engaged and he was a guest for the weekend. One morning when he left early, he came into my bedroom to kiss me—still asleep in bed—before leaving silently for town. (Long Island? Some trip?) How good and chaste we were!

Fort Myers Beach, Florida
February 15th–28th, 1984 [DIARY]

My last day in a two-week visit to Fort Myers Beach to be with Reeve, Richard, the two girls and Jonathan. I meant to work every day and have not even written in my diary. *Why not?* The whole fall and winter have gone like this—into what? An obsession, natural enough, in a mother and a grandmother, over Jonathan and Reeve's exhaustion and despair. I arrived exhausted from too much desk work, as usual.

This winter I have not really been ill (one week of a bad cold) but I have felt so much older and get tired so quickly. The day in town exhausts me. My arthritic hip wakes me every night, though the pain is controllable with aspirin and exercise by day. Mrs. Swanson comes regularly and faithfully, but she also cannot really help me enough. Shopping for groceries exhausts me. My life is not well organized. I must somehow make some changes. Get new people? More help? Or move to Washington to a better climate and a more comfortable condominium? It *has* been a long, cold, and disagreeable winter and I have minded it more than usual: the weight of worry over Reeve and the baby and her despair also affects me. I can do so little to help.

Here in Florida I have at least been able to see and feel what she is carrying. I understand her problems living in suspense. She has bloomed in the sunshine and with the ease of living and the support given her by wonderful Mrs. Ruggles, a staunch tough Vermonter helper, and the moral and affectionate support given her by Jim and Ellie.

I have also rested. I had a return of the Meunière's dizziness when I arrived, so that I had to go to bed and rest a great deal, but Jim's medi-

---

*Jon had married Karen Wylie Pryor, a writer and biologist specializing in behavior and learning.

cation and much sleep and some walking on the beach have restored me somewhat. I find Florida—at least this kind of boardwalk beach living—rather boring. I am in a separate cottage two doors down from Reeve and Richard. We meet for walks and supper, and Jim and Ellie enliven our talks and our evenings. They have poured strength and confidence into Reeve and she looks much better and seems more hopeful about Jonathan's progress, which continues, but very slowly.

He is such a beautiful child. One's heart aches for the struggles he makes to gain control over his body—still recovering from his disease—and his struggle to communicate with people. He is a very alert and responsive baby and longs to break through his restrictions. I think of Cyril Connolly's saying, "In every fat man, there is a thin man wildly gesticulating to be let out." There is a strong, well, vigorous and rebellious child inside of Jonathan's stricken body, struggling to get out. I feel he must succeed! He has made progress: he is freer with his arms and can direct his hands better—in the last day or so knocking over a small box (of sunburn cream!) we put within his reach, looking triumphant afterwards, and smiling at our shouts of praise.

Aside from the times with the children or the evenings with the Newtons, there have been walks down the beach. The middle of the day is too hot and too bright and full of people: either pacing up and down two by two, like passengers on an ocean liner; or joggers tearing by, relentlessly athletic; or groups of picnickers spread out on the sand; or bicyclers pumping their way, sometimes in tandem; or children digging up and building sand castles; or women sunning on bright towels or in lounge chairs. I feel the lack of privacy. The beach becomes a boardwalk and everyone has a group, or a husband. I feel very husbandless here.

But evening and morning it is bare and beautiful. Only the squadrons of gulls sitting alert but motionless, all facing the wind, and tiny sandpipers sweeping the rim of the waves, with their tiny runs. The sunsets are beautiful, and the sea and skies expand, and the people disappear for their drinks and supper.

Little House
March 30th, 1984
Dearest Scott:

When I write that address on the envelope I feel: this is hopeless. This *can't* be right. This letter will be dropped into the Amazon delta and never get to him.

I have a letter from Alika, from which I gather that it was very discouraging for you when you got back to Brazil and found things in a mess, or not well cared for. Only one man, who could hardly be called a caretaker. But I also gather that the work goes on and that you are still planning on coming to the U.S. at some point for "new equipment."

I have been having some of my diaries and notes copied and came across the wonderful letter you sent me after your father's death, about the most frustrating thing in life being the unfinishedness of things. (You said it better.) This must be truer in Brazil than anywhere else. It set me thinking about my life since then; I did not always follow your wise advice: I tried to "finish up" many things about and around your father's life. But I have endured, and become myself again, or perhaps just a *different* self, who finds life "tenable" and even happy much of the time. Too long to go into fully here.

I have talked to Reeve this morning. She is helping Jim with the book he is putting together of his taped memories of CAL, Edison, Ford, Firestone, and Carrel.

The baby is improving: he is more active and more responsive to sounds—his name being called and his parents' voices and the children. He enjoys playing games ("Peek-a-Boo") and laughs with them. He holds his head up better and reaches for things better. He cannot yet turn over but he tries to move around more. I am hoping Reeve and the baby will come to Switzerland this summer so that Mme Christen (a wonderful physiotherapist) can work on Jonathan.

Much love to you, Scott, and I hope we see you before long. We all miss you—especially,

Your Mother

Little House, Darien
April 2nd, 1985 [DIARY]

I am determined to spend some part of the day in the Little House: meditating, sitting on the bench outside, or inside writing something in my diary—perhaps just the day's events. It is beginning to be spring, but gusty, cloudy, and cold. The miniature reticulata iris have been a staunch little row—bright blue flames on the south side of the house, where it is sheltered, for almost a month, breaking through the dead leaves before anything else. The miniature yellow iris next. And now the daffodils begin, one or two here and there. The forsythia is not yet out, but almost. There are a few robins, and on a sunny morning I hear the cardinals, "Cheer, cheer, cheer," high and triumphant. We have had some warm days when one hears a great chattering down in the cove, the geese and ducks proclaiming spring.

It has been a long winter, beginning with Jonathan's death on January 8th, found dead in his crib that morning, with no cry, no illness, and no warning. I have not recovered from that tragic blow, coming after months of hope and progress in his motor ability sparked by my bringing Mme Christen over from Switzerland to treat him with her creative and intuitive therapy. He improved greatly after each session, one here last spring, one in Switzerland last summer, and the third just after Christmas, again here. For Reeve, it was a second death, the first being when he was so ill with encephalitis and [she was] told that there was evidence of brain damage and he would always have difficulties—a retarded or handicapped child. "Why did it have to happen *twice?*" she cried.

I will remember until my death her shriek—a long piercing cry echoing through the house that morning when she went down and found him. And then her screams, "My baby is dead! My baby is dead!" Mme C. and I rushed downstairs. And there he was, turned over, lifeless and estranged, I felt, not the baby we knew. So swiftly does death change a body. The eyes were closed; he died in his sleep. I could only say, "He's gone. He is not there at all." Feeling so overwhelmingly that the child, the spirit, had gone, leaving a shell that bore no resemblance to the child we knew. Only the golden hair was his, was alive, was real to touch: smooth, silky gold.

The rest of the morning was a nightmare: the house filled with strangers, the secretaries, the police, the coroner, the ambulance corps—all so gruesomely reminiscent of my baby's kidnapping. So long ago! I could only say to her, "The horror goes—the pain remains—but the horror will go."

I do not know how that day passed. Mme C. washed and dressed the baby. I did not see him taken away, but before he was taken, I said I wanted to sit in the room with him and with Reeve, and say a prayer. I remembered how much I minded having CAL's body rushed out before I could do this. I could only kiss his temple and go out, because he himself had wanted to be taken swiftly from his bed to his grave before the press could know of it and be there.

Reeve was well controlled and talked to the undertaker and arranged to have him sent to Vermont. She talked to Richard and to her minister and arranged for a service in the Peacham church. We called off a lunch in town for Mme C. to meet some editors. People came to the door (kind neighbors) with soups and casseroles. We called Jim in Florida and Dr. R. and Krissie in N.Y. (Reeve called.)

Jim flew up for the night, Krissie came out, and Richard came down from Vermont. We had supper before the fire. That was all quiet and strangely comforting. Ansy came up the next day and we all drove up for the service.

Little House
April 5th, 1985 [DIARY]

Good Friday: a beautiful soft day, sunny and springlike. Hard to associate what "Good Friday" was named for, Christ on the cross. But one can give thanks on such a day: "Praise God from whom all blessings flow." I sit on the little blue bench outside my writing house and try to meditate. "Gloria in Excelsis Deo," with the birds interweaving their songs and cries with my breath.

I pick up Louisa* and we drive out to the country swiftly, beating the traffic, eating sandwiches she has fixed ahead of time. We pick up Berwick from Mrs. Swanson, then home and unpack the car. She has brought all kinds of food—apples, brioche, croissants and wine—several bags and books, etc.

We take naps. I feel very tired. After, a brief walk to the Delafield Island causeway, watching the mockingbirds fluttering over us and touching the soft furry buds of the shadblow, not quite in flower, and looking at lowering skies over the marshy flat.

At night, Susan Hoguet† runs in with a quiche she has made for us (very delicious). We sit and eat in front of the fire and I talk about the death of Jonathan. She also talks to me about how I shall manage my old age. She is quite practical and kind and knows me well. She thinks it will kill me to move to Washington. She is going to a retirement home; I couldn't bear to. We are all in the same boat.

I feel, in fact, very old and tired—just this winter. One grows old in jerks. I did not feel old last summer—tired often, but not old—when

---

*Louisa Munroe Harris, a friend of AML's since childhood.
†Susan Hoguet, author-illustrator of children's books, among them (as illustrator) *Next Time Take Care*, text by Anne Spencer Lindbergh (New York: Harcourt Brace Jovanovich, 1988), and *The Tidy Lady*, text by Anne Spencer Lindbergh (New York: Harcourt Brace Jovanovich, 1989). A good friend of Ansy's, as well as a close friend and companion of AML's.

I had Reeve and the children and Jonathan and Richard in my chalet, because I felt useful and because there seemed to be a future to look forward to. Jonathan took the future with him. Of course, there is still the present. There is Kristina and Bob's baby, Anna, a great joy. Anything I can do for them is a joy. Bob's catastrophic accident last summer body-surfing, which led to a broken back and paralysis for the rest of his life in a wheelchair, has been another tragedy this year.

Wednesday, April 24th [1985] [DIARY]

Back home again after two weeks in Florida with Reeve and her family and Land, flying in for a business conference on problems of the ranch (our inability to sell it) and Maui. He has been struggling over both for over three years, alone much of the time and doing only maintenance work: no animals, no help, and really no incentive to go on. This is the common lot today of the farmers and ranchers and part of the nationwide recession. All the loan companies in Montana are closed and many farms and ranches are going through bankruptcy. It is not his fault, but he blames himself for not getting out of it fast enough. He sold the cows at the right moment, but he should have, he says, sold the ranch at the same time.

We are all in the same condominium on the beach at Fort Myers (one of Jim's). Land and I are in the same apartment, and Reeve and the two girls and Richard two floors below us. We meet for meals and walks on the beach.

Switzerland
Saturday, July 27th [1985] [DIARY]

The first weeks have been busy with *very* hot weather—very un-Swiss-like—and many people. The heat, rather than the people (all friends), tires me—and just getting the chalet running again. It is an awkward house to run easily, awkwardly planned, with the main living on the second floor. One is climbing up and down stairs all day. It was not built for older people. But we were not old when we built it. In active middle age, we wanted solitude (isolation, really), quiet country life, far from people and towns. Now this is, or can be, isolation, loneliness, inaccessibility, and a certain amount of discomfort. My friends do come see me. . . .

Susan W., Faith's daughter, arrived a week ago to "help" me. She has been a year in Grenoble and speaks French very well. She is a warm, open, fresh-faced, healthy girl, very eager to help—with tact and efficiency and energy. I say "girl" because, though she is (or will be) a senior in college next year, she seems younger. She has really helped me, washing dishes and laundry, carrying groceries, shopping, taking Berwick for walks, and even cutting down the overgrown bushy bank behind the kitchen windows and digging a hole to transplant my big lavender bush.

Con is struggling with the long ordeal of a dying husband. I feel so for her. I keep thinking of C. and our similar time with him. One cannot help going over it in one's memory, reliving it. It was easier for me; the children gave so much support. And it was not as drawn out, and C. was so courageous and wise and patient. He was himself till the end. Much of it was not easy—for him or for us—but we managed. People must be allowed to *die in their own way*, I realize more and more.

And their "ways" are so different. C. on the whole was far-seeing and patient, accepting of his death and planning openly for it. Aubrey seems to be "fighting" all the way; he is a fighter, so that is his way. But I feel he is fighting the "Battle of Britain" in this last fight and Con has to fight with him, which is sapping every bit of her strength and spirit. She is almost numb after so many years: no spark left of that intuitive creativity, no time, no rest, and no let-up. Margot, too, is working with a husband who is, I fear, retreating from life—gently, slowly and almost unconsciously. This may be *his* way, quite different from Aubrey's and very different from Margot's (who is also a fighter and is trying, and has tried for years, to fight for him, for his health and his physical flexibility).

But one has to let them choose their own avenues of retreat. Is there not a moment when one should accept one's retreat? To say, Death is not so terrible. I have reached the point in my life when I am ready to let go—to ease out of life? I remember Amey in old age telling me, "It's so hard to know when to hang on and when to let go." I didn't appreciate what she meant then, but I do now. She taught me the little I know about age.

Eglantine is looking forward, almost, to life after death. Margot believes, less tangibly, in reincarnation, and Yvonne, of course, is steeped in the Christian faith, in resurrection or "living in Christ." As for me, I believe, in my own vague way, that something "goes on," but I do not define it. Spirit, surely, is not wasted. Does it merge into the "great unconscious" or does it remain only—only? Is this not enough?—in the minds and hearts of others? CAL certainly believed something "went on," and I do sometimes feel close to that "something."

It is harder with the death of a child. What remains of little Jonathan? One cannot bear that spark snuffed out. Or my first baby? Mme Christen, whom I have just seen, spoke of Jonathan as a little angel. It would be nice to believe in angels, and sometimes I almost do. Now I must stop.

At least this writing in my diary lets me tap down to a deeper, quieter level. It is worthwhile, even if not a book—the last book. I must go to lunch preparation—just picnicky. But first, I must rescue, with a glass and a piece of paper, a brown and gold butterfly with a black eye on each wing, escaped from the lavender bush and beating its wings against my window pane . . .

I was successful! He is free.

Darien
January 2nd, 1986
Darling Reeve:

I will be thinking about you this long and difficult week. I will not try and call you, but I am here if you want to call me. I am enclosing excerpts from *The Sacred Pipe* (Black Elk's account of the seven rites of the Oglala Sioux, recorded by Joseph Epes Brown) which Susie sent and wrote me about.

I know we fret that anniversaries mark *distance*, that time is bearing those we love and have lost further away. But perhaps we have too linear a sense of time. Time is perhaps, as the old Mexicans felt, not a river running away, but an ocean around us in which we are steeped. Time, in the article about the Navajo craftswoman, "surrounds her, as do her dwelling place, her family, her clan, her tribe, her habitat, her dances, her rituals."

Anyway, my love is around you!

Acknowledgments

This book was written over the course of forty years by Anne Morrow Lindbergh, who never thought it was a book at all. Yet years later,
after her death, members of her family saw this material and thought it
should be published in some form. The gathering and editing of Anne
Morrow Lindbergh's diaries and letters from 1947 to 1986—and one or
two pieces of her other writings—took place, sadly, without the author's
skillful editorial assistance. But the project was completed nonetheless,
through the hard work, patience, determination, and perseverance of a
great many people, all of whom deserve thanks.

First of all, "The Team": Land Lindbergh, Reeve Lindbergh, Kristina Lindbergh, and Carol Hyman. We worked together not for four
decades but for four years, whether at the Yale archives, in Vermont,
over the telephone, or by e-mail: reading, selecting, editing, arguing,
often laughing, and sometimes close to crying our way through the
material as we steadily labored to get the job done. We did it, dear team.
God bless us, everyone!

We thank our families, too, whose support and forbearance made
the work possible. Janet McMillan kindly and patiently sent Land to
Vermont and Connecticut whenever his fellow team members needed
him. Patton Hyman offered us his valuable wisdom, some delightful and
delicious dinners, and his legal expertise. Andrew Hyman transcribed
literally hundreds of pages of handwritten letters and gave us the benefit
of his very perceptive and often refreshing thoughts. Nat Tripp and Bob
Conte put up with many hours of intense conversation among the team
members, and Nat also treated the whole crew to night after night of his
superb cooking when we got together in Vermont.

From the beginning, the project had the support of the Lindbergh
Literary LLC, composed of Anne Morrow Lindbergh's literary heirs:
Jon M. Lindbergh, Land M. Lindbergh, Scott M. Lindbergh, Reeve
Lindbergh, Constance Feydy Hoffman, and Marek Sapieyevski. We
are grateful for their trust and for their faith that someday something

positive would emerge from our efforts. Constance Feydy Hoffman also typed out quantities of wonderful letters written to her mother, Anne Spencer Lindbergh, by her grandmother, Anne Morrow Lindbergh. Several of these are included here. Thank you, Connie! Thanks to Barbara Robbins and to Susie Miller for sharing family photographs of people and places AML loved.

Thanks to our Morrow and Morgan cousins and to our beloved aunt, Margot Wilkie, for their interest and assistance along the way. Thanks to the Valentine family—Garrison, Laurie, and Sarah Valentine—for providing letters from Anne Morrow Lindbergh to both of their parents and for sharing family photographs of Alan and Lucia Valentine.

It would have been impossible to create this book without the assistance and encouragement of Judith A. Schiff, William Massa, and the archivists and staff at the Sterling Memorial Library at Yale University. Thanks so much to you all.

Thanks to Jennie Dunham and the Dunham Literary Agency, for good work on our behalf.

Finally, we are grateful to our editor, Altie Karper, and to everyone at Pantheon/Random House for believing in Anne Morrow Lindbergh once again, and always.

Index